RELIGIONS OF THE WORLD

RELIGIONS OF THE WORLD

AN INTRODUCTION TO CULTURE AND MEANING

Lawrence E. Sullivan, General Editor

Fortress Press / Minneapolis

RELIGIONS OF THE WORLD
An Introduction to Culture and Meaning

Published in collaboration with Jaca Book, Milan, Italy. The following chapters were published originally as part of *Religions of Humanity* series, by Olivier Clément, Julien Ries, and Lawrence E. Sullivan: Chapters 2–3, 6, and 8–14. International Copyright © 2000, 2007, by Editoriale Jaca Book spa, Milano, Italia. All rights reserved.

Cover image: Holi, The Festival of Colors, India © Poras Chaudhary / The Image Bank / Getty Images
Cover design: Laurie Ingram
Book design: PerfecType, Nashville, TN

Library of Congress Cataloging-in-Publication Data is available
ISBN 978-0-8006-9879-9

The paper used in this publication meets the minimum requirements of American National Standard for Information Sciences—Permanence of Paper for Printed Library Materials, ANSI Z329.48-1984.

Manufactured in the U.S.A.

18   17   16   15   14   13   1   2   3   4   5   6   7   8   9   10

For Lesley, cuore del mio cuore

BRIEF CONTENTS

CONTENTS

Chapter 1—Indigenous Religious Traditions—Robin M. Wright   31

Chapter 2—Hinduism—Julien Ries   61

Chapter 3—Buddhism—Julien Ries   79

Chapter 4—Jainism—Andrea R. Jain   95

Chapter 5—Sikhism—Nikky-Guninder Kaur Singh and Todd Curcuru   109

Chapter 6—Daoism—Lawrence E. Sullivan   129

Chapter 7—Confucianism—Yong Huang   143

Chapter 8—Shinto—Lawrence E. Sullivan   159

Chapter 9—Judaism—Lawrence E. Sullivan   177

Chapter 10—Early Christian Foundations—Julien Ries   199

Chapter 11—Roman Catholicism—Julien Ries   217

Chapter 12—Orthodox Christianity—Olivier Clément   235

Chapter 13—Protestant Christianity—Lawrence E. Sullivan   249

Chapter 14—Islam—Julien Ries   265

Chapter 15—Zoroastrianism—Anthony Cerulli   283

Chapter 16—New Religious Movements—Marie W. Dallam   305

CONTRIBUTORS

Anthony Cerulli is assistant professor of religious studies and Asian studies at Hobart and William Smith Colleges and a fellow at the Institut d'études avancées de Paris, specializing in the history of South Asia.

Olivier Clément (d. 2009) was a French Eastern Orthodox theologian who taught at St. Sergius Orthodox Theological Institute in Paris.

Todd Curcuru is a 2012 religious studies and mathematical sciences graduate of Colby College.

Marie W. Dallam is professor of religion in the Honors College at the University of Oklahoma, specializing in new religious movements.

Yong Huang is professor of philosophy at Kutztown University, has served as president of the Association of Chinese Philosophers in America, and is general and founding editor of *Dao: A Journal of Comparative Philosophy*.

Andrea R. Jain is assistant professor of religious studies at Indiana University-Purdue University Indianapolis. Andrea's current research projects include a book on the intersections of modern yoga and consumer culture, studies on Christian and Hindu protests against the popularization of yoga, and studies on modern yoga gurus.

Julien Ries is a Belgian religious historian at Louvain University who was elevated to cardinal in the Roman Catholic Church in 2012. Much of his work is in the area of religious anthropology, and he is an honorary member of the International Association for the History of Religions.

Nikky-Guninder Kaur Singh is Crawford Family Professor of Religion and chair of the department of religious studies at Colby College. She has published extensively in the area of Sikh studies.

Lawrence E. Sullivan, general editor of this volume, is president and CEO of The Fetzer Institute in Kalamazoo, Michigan. He also holds appointments as professor of anthropology and theology at the University of Notre Dame. From 1990 to 2004, he directed the Center for the Study of World Religions at Harvard Divinity School and is a lifetime fellow of the American Academy of Arts and Sciences, past president of the American Academy of Religion, and a former deputy secretary-general of the International Association for the History of Religions.

Robin M. Wright is associate professor of religion, affliate professor of anthropology, and affiliate professor of the Center for Latin American Studies at the University of Florida.

PREFACE

Lawrence E. Sullivan

A story is told about Giotto, who revolutionized medieval art and prepared it for the Renaissance. Pope Boniface VIII tried to entice him to compete for an art commission, but the master was too busy to submit studies for the contest. When the pope sent his personal messenger, he found the artist in a fury of artistic labor and pleaded with him to gather some works that would demonstrate his skill. Giotto impetuously plunged his brush into crimson and, with a single continuous stroke, scribed freehand a perfect circle. Pressing the gesture drawing into the messenger's hands, Giotto told him to show the pope, declaring that Boniface would recognize its value. At a glance, Boniface perceived that Giotto surpassed all other painters of his time and awarded him the commission.

Through a series of gesture drawings scribed by experts, this volume draws portraits of the major religious traditions of the world.

Our hearts run toward approachability: helping students immediately recognize the essential features of a religion. We strive for the directness of Giotto: each chapter draws a religion in bold strokes and in different lights: in the perspective of history, individual personal life, communal existence, the literary life of Scriptures and commentary, the arts, and the observation of outsiders. With these portraits and gesture drawings, readers will quickly recognize the distinctive features of their neighbors, the religious faces of the world; and readers will be equipped to become more familiar with them in the future, via the suggested readings.

The book is designed to meet the needs of readers from quite different preparations and backgrounds regarding the study of religion. Some students may know a religion well, but perhaps it is only the one they grew up in. Others may have no previous exposure at all to religious practice and belief. Other students and teachers, exposed to multiple faiths to varying degrees, fall at various points across the spectrum between these outer poles. Any of these starting points is a good place to begin with this introduction.

My teaching has been dedicated to students across the range of these situations, from teaching three years at a state university, the University of Missouri at Columbia, to nineteen years at private universities, the University of Chicago and Harvard University, where I directed the Harvard Center for the Study of World Religions from 1990–2004, and eight years at a religious university, the University of Notre Dame. Students in all these different schools come in motley shapes and sizes, religiously speaking: varying stages of preparation, with motivations that range from affection or disaffection for their familial religion, to ardent passion as religious seekers, to studied cynicism, to general ignorance or cold indifference.

Nothing is better for learning than this hearty, jousting mixture of motives and experiences. No matter where a student is coming from, he or she brings a distinct value and perspective to discussions about religion, which often continue in corridors, dorms, and dining halls after leaving the classroom. Socrates, the great Greek thinker, educator, and war veteran, mentor to the philosopher Plato and the warrior Xenophon, carried on his discussions about religious topics not only in the academic hall but also in the marketplace, the dining room, and the steps of the public square. To get thoughts rolling, he had to stir up a variety of positions and prompt new questions by acting like a gadfly.

Our current cultural moment accomplishes this for us, stirring things up for us willy-nilly. Religious studies classrooms in North America today are likely to have students not only from families with faith backgrounds in many different religions but also those unfamiliar with the faiths of their ancestors; students who are both motivated believers and those who do not adhere to any faith; and people of native heritage from this continent or elsewhere. These differences of viewpoint, experience, and background create a cultural opportunity characteristic of our times and lead to lively, instructive engagements about religion. This volume has been created for just this fascinating teaching and learning situation.

Structure of This Book

Each chapter of this book offers different entry points to the religion in question. No single approach wears out its welcome. A map locates each tradition in space. A summary history charts its development over time. Brief vignettes describe key practices and interpret major beliefs. Excerpts from significant Scriptures and texts give a feel for the tradition in its own words. In addition, each author, possessing special knowledge of the tradition, highlights the half dozen ideas and actions that best reveal the features of the religion. Besides providing different entry points for different readers and teachers, the flexibility of this format makes allowance for the different characters of the traditions in question.

The book begins with traditional religions among indigenous peoples. The United Nations estimates that some 250–350 million people today identify themselves according to their indigenous heritage.[1] Although this initial chapter recognizes the significance of religious traditions among native peoples of the world, it can do no more than point to their richness and mention some key points that are often the focus of religious attention in these communities. Close examination of all the particular tribal and ethnic religions, which have been a principal focus of my professional life, would be deeply rewarding but would also fill an encyclopedia of its own. This first chapter outlines the importance of religion among all aspects of indigenous life and prepares readers to face the many neighbors in today's world whose religious experience is intimated here.

A first set of four chapters deals with religions arising over the centuries throughout South Asia: Hinduism, Buddhism, Jainism, and Sikhism. The separate accounts of distinct traditions, provided in separate chapters, nevertheless reflect their fascinating interactions over the centuries.

A second set of chapters introduces three religious traditions arising in eastern Asia: Daoism, Confucianism, and Shinto. Like the religions of southern Asia, the religions of eastern Asia have crisscrossed one another's paths many times over the centuries, deeply affecting one another's thoughts and deeds. Through missionary teaching, intellectual curiosity, spiritual quest, territorial expansion of political realms, and immigration, all the religions of Asia have made their way across the globe in ways explained in each chapter. We place these religions toward the outset of the volume because of the helpful thought process that is set in motion, in conjunction with a book intended for use in Western schools, when one takes the familiar concept of "religion" and applies it to less familiar concepts and practices.

There follows a set of three religions that all mark their descent from the same person, Abraham, who is described in the Hebrew Bible and in the Qur'an as the "father of many" and who lived during the early second millennium BCE. Abraham's covenant with God established a monotheism that continues to this day in the three traditions that recognize Abraham as their ancestor in faith: Judaism, Christianity, and Islam. In the Hebrew Bible and in Jewish tradition ever since, Abraham descended from Shem, the son of Noah, the survivor of the great world flood. Muslims hold that Muhammed the Prophet descended from Abraham through Ishmael, Abraham's son. Christians hold that Jesus the Savior descended from Abraham through Isaac, another son of Abraham. These three traditions are sometimes called "the Abrahamic religions," but the label invites questioning and precision.[2]

Given the long history of Christian influence on most countries and cultures where this volume will be used, and given as well the sharp, centuries-long differences among the several large branches of Christianity in those places, Roman Catholicism, Eastern Orthodoxy, and Protestantism receive individual attention apart from Christian origins. Christians of one stripe or another, as well as non-Christians alike, can thus learn something new about their ubiquitous Christian neighbors and the impact of Christianity on culture.

The penultimate chapter presents Zoroastrianism, whose founding is attributed to Zarathustra, a prophet living in Iran some six centuries before the current era, whose teachings are gathered in texts called the *Gāthās* and *Avesta*, and whose followers today number in the hundreds of thousands. Immigration and persecution have spread Zoroastrians across the globe, though some twenty-five thousand still live in Iran and another seventy-thousand in India.

Last, a final chapter deals with a prominent feature of our modern culture: the birth of new religious movements that spring from all the traditions mentioned in the preceding chapters as well as from other sources and independent roots in contemporary times. Though any one movement may be small in numbers, these religious movements often capture headlines and our imaginations far beyond their scale because of their dramatic responses to traditional teachings and present-day realities.

Acknowledgments

Colleagues generously assisted in preparing this volume. Ross Miller of Fortress Press brought initiative, clarity, and positive support at every stage. In particular, Julien Ries of Louvain University in Belgium, together with Sante Bagnoli and Pepe Bolognese of Jaca Book in Milan, Italy, helped develop the multidisciplinary approach through a previous international publication where several chapters of the present volume were first published. I am grateful to Rob Lehman and my fellow trustees of the Fetzer Institute for their encouragement of my continued teaching and writing while discharging my office as president and CEO. Peggy Quinn wrangled the materials and coordinated exchanges with the authors and publisher. Wendy Karrick managed the calendar required to complete the project. My wife, Lesley Antonelli Sullivan, as always, has generously given wise counsel and guidance throughout the work. My children, Mariangela, Lawrence, Carolyn, Lesley Grace, and Catherine, span the age range of the readership intended for this volume. Their ongoing engagements with the issues featured in this volume have sharpened my approach.

My faculty colleagues and students at Missouri, Chicago, Harvard, and Notre Dame have helped foster in me a genuine love of learning and teaching about religion, with all its knotty entanglements, through their willingness to disclose the transformative impact that the study of religion makes in their lives. Those of us who teach and study the religious lives of others owe them not only our critical attention but also a debt of thanks for the privilege to weigh, understand, and make decisions about the truths they seek to embody in their lives. No matter what those judgments may be, our lives as individuals and communities resonate more sonorously with what they evoke in our awareness.

◆ **NOTES**

1. See Ken S. Coates, *A Global History of Indigenous Peoples: Struggle and Survival* (New York: Palgrave Macmillan, 2004), 12; Marisol de la Cadena and Orin Starn, eds. *Indigenous Experience Today* (Oxford: Berg; New York: Wenner-Gren Foundation for Anthropological Research, 2007); and John H. Bodley, *Victims of Progress*, 5th ed (Plymouth, England: AltaMira, 2008), 2.

2. See Jon D. Levenson, "The Idea of Abrahamic Religions: A Qualified Dissent," *Jewish Review of Books* 1 (spring 2010); and Levenson, *Abraham between Torah and Gospel* (Milwaukee: Marquette University Press, 2011).

Facing Our Neighbors: Introducing Religions of the World

Lawrence E. Sullivan

Wondrous Signs

Religion deals with all the things that appear to us—whether those things are mundane, like water, fire, and birth, or mysterious, like life before this universe or life after our death; and religion wonders about the signs of those appearances.

Religion propels human inquiry into restless motion by posing questions basic to being human. When Bono, of the rock group U2, delivered the homily at the National Prayer Breakfast at the White House on February 2, 2006, he emphasized how religion provokes lifelong inquiry. "The reason for this gathering is that all of us here—Muslims, Jews, Christians—all are searching our souls for how to better serve our family, our community, our nation, our God. I know I am. Searching, I mean."[1]

Fig. Intro. 1   Bono, lead singer of the rock group U2.

The religious traditions in this volume illustrate the long search for answers to such fundamental questions as the following: What is the meaning of the signs that appear to us in the world? Such signs may be natural objects untouched by humans, like the sky, which is a

Fig. Intro. 2   The temple of Heaven, Beijing, China.

creative supernatural being according to many religions, from ancient China and ancient Egypt to the contemporary Barasana people living in the Northwest Amazon basin in South America.

Or, signs that give rise to religious wonder may be cultural objects, the work of human hands, like the bread of the Christian Eucharist. Christians have wondered and debated: Is this only bread, or is it the sign of the real presence of the body, blood, and soul of Jesus Christ, a fully divine being?

Religion questions appearances and inquires about things and their signs: What is the true nature of the realities seen in these signs? Whether one wonders about the origins of the universe or the communication of the Ten Commandments, what claims do these things and their significance place on us, our thinking, and our moral life together? In

contemplating such religious questions at the Prayer Breakfast, Bono stands beside Moses on Mount Sinai, both of them wondering what real-world commitments flow from their religious experiences and convictions. In Bono's

Fig. Intro. 3   The goddess, Nut, is represented with outstretched wings on this Egyptian coffin, circa 500–25 BCE.

Fig. Intro. 4 Eucharistic bread used in Christian liturgies.

appearances, we are led to ask: What role does religion play in shaping the distinctiveness of our human species? After all, such wondering is a uniquely human capacity that distinguishes human beings from other things. Whether one looks through the eyes of faith, or history, or sciences like psychology, economics, anthropology, sociology, or natural history (including evolutionary biology and ecology), the central question is: *How does religion instigate and sustain the kind of thinking, feeling, and acting that define human nature and that mark human culture so deeply in every part of the world?* The introduction of the social sciences into colleges and universities just over a century ago—relatively recent, given that the first universities were founded over a thousand years ago!—was justified in significant part by their ability to address this central religious question.

case, he wonders "about God, who He is or if He exists," and concludes, "If there is a God . . . He is with the vulnerable and the poor. . . in the cries heard under the rubble of war . . . in scorched places." In the same way, Moses also felt that his lofty religious experiences obliged him to lead his people toward liberation in very concrete ways.

To ponder searing questions, religions gather the appearances of significant realities in this world. In the life of the Buddha, for example, one finds signs like unusual birth, a chance chariot ride, the suffering of old age and hunger, a putrefying corpse, and a house afire. The life of Moses presents other signs: burning bush, slavery, Ten Commandments, trumpet blast from a cloud, cries of the poor, ravages of war, and forces of nature. Religious traditions arrange these signs systematically—in myths, rites, creeds, teachings, laws, prayers, sacred histories, or moral codes—in order to experience and reflect on them critically and in order to respond to them deliberately through worship, thought, and social action.

When we view religion as a source of wonder about the things that appear in the world and when we understand that it raises basic questions about the significance of those

Fig. Intro. 5 Illustration depicting Moses on Mount Sinai.

Fig. Intro. 6 Bronze statue of the Buddha, Kamakura, Japan.

Religious Wonder and Disciplined Learning

Readers of this volume will observe religion from different points of view: the curiosity of scholars, the open heart of seekers, the skepticism of cynics, the protectiveness of converts, the detachment of spectators, the spiritual regret of those who have lost faith, and the love of neighbors who still have theirs.

The study of religion helped give rise to new disciplines of study and ultimately proved worthy of inclusion in the academy. In the modern research academy, religion is central to the groundwork of founding figures in these new disciplines. A brief sample of groundbreaking studies of religion, all of which established new fields of research, makes the point:

- in psychology, Sigmund Freud (*Moses and Monotheism*, *The Future of an Illusion*, *Totem and Taboo*) and Carl Jung (*Psychology and Religion*);
- in sociology, Emile Durkheim (*Elementary Forms of the Religious Life*) and Max

Weber (*The Protestant Ethic and the Spirit of Capitalism*);

- in anthropology, Edward Burnett Tylor (*Primitive Culture*) and Bronislaw Malinowksi (*Magic, Science, and Religion*).

In political economy, Karl Marx published *The Holy Family* (1844), breaking with his mentor, the theologian and Scripture scholar Bruno Bauer. Also in political economy, Adam Smith published *The Theory of Moral Sentiments* in 1759 as a first step in his career, reconceiving the predominant religious thinking of his day. In that work, Smith reevaluated love and benevolence; relocated conscience from the private sanctuary, where the individual speaks alone with God, to the public forum of social relationships; and offered an alternative explanation of the social bond based not on the altruistic love cultivated in religion but on the psychological desire to enlist feelings of sympathy and approval for the self from impartial outside observers. God administers the universe as a system beyond human concern. The economy and human happiness, however, fall to human governance. So fundamental to Smith was his rewrite of religion, he revised *The Theory of Moral Sentiments* five times, completing the sixth and last edition shortly before his death, in 1790.

Religion, Violence, Peace

Your inquiry about religion may begin with the dramatic experiences of violence connected with religious groups. The search for scientific knowledge of religion continues in today's quest to probe the link between religion and violence. Violence associated with religion has drawn dramatic attention in recent years. Consider three examples. On November 18, 1978, 918 people died in "Jonestown" in Guyana when the followers of a North American religious leader named Jim Jones led his followers to commit murder—the victims included a visiting US Congressman—and mass suicide. A poisoning with sarin nerve gas in the Tokyo subway in 1995 by a religious group known as Aum Shinri Kyo was the most damaging terrorist attack in the modern history of Japan. And on September 11, 2001, terrorists acting in the name of Islam hijacked planes and crashed them into the World Trade Center in New York, the Pentagon in Washington, and a field in western Pennsylvania, sending thousands to their deaths.[2]

Religion is by no means only associated with causes of violence. On the contrary, religion has proven to be a powerful inspiration to quell violence. Thich Nhat Hanh, a Vietnamese Buddhist leader who is a forty-second-generation monk in his Zen lineage, fearlessly led other Buddhists, in the midst of ferocious war-torn circumstances of the Vietnam War during the 1960s, to reconstruct destroyed villages, establish schools, and build medical centers. Exiled from Vietnam in 1973, Hanh moved to France. Through a change of mindfulness that he calls "Engaged Buddhism," his principles and practices today lead individuals and communities out of a violence-generating mindset.[3]

More recently, Dharma Master Hsin Tao of Ling Jo Buddhist Monastery in Taiwan, an orphan forced to become a child soldier at age nine, was called to a religious awakening by Guan Yin—"She who hears the cries of the world"—the bodhisattva of compassion. After years of meditation in isolation, he created the Museum of World Religions in Taipei, which opened in 2005, to display the love that arises in the world's religions. In Japan, an international group of religious leaders from various traditions, all committed to one another to overcome

violence, awards the annual Niwano Peace Prize. In this they are similar to, and collaborate with, the World Conference for Religions of Peace (WCRP), a multi-religious coalition that has worked in armed conflicts to mitigate violence in Sri Lanka, Iraq, Sierra Leone, Liberia, Indonesia, Eritrea, and Ethiopia.

Christian leaders and groups also draw from their religious faith to work for peace and extinguish fires of violence, in society as well as in the heart. Such Christians take their cue from Jesus' Sermon on the Mount: "Blessed are the peacemakers, for they shall be called the children of God" (Matt. 5:9 King James 2000 Bible). When Dr. Martin Luther King Jr. received the Nobel Prize for Peace, he delivered a lecture explaining that his philosophy of non-violent love and service is rooted in the First Epistle of Saint John: "Let us love one another: for love is of God; and every one that loveth is born of God, and knoweth God. . . . If we love one another, God dwelleth in us, and his love is perfected in us" (1 John 4:7, 12 KJV).

The Community of Saint Egidio, an international group of lay Catholics based in Rome,

Fig. Intro. 8 Thich Nhat Hahn, 2006.

Fig. Intro. 9   A statue of Guan Yin, Mount Putuo, China.

religion is a net healer of violent division through its disciplined cultivation of shared religious values, such as love and forgiveness. These opposed positions are argued in a variety of publications.[4] Daniel Philpott contends that instead of making blanket generalizations about all religion as a whole, one should undertake nuanced, granular studies and comparisons of specific religious traditions, with particular histories, in focused places and times. Recently, Philpott interviewed leaders in northern Uganda who are healing their war-torn communities by extending forgiveness toward those who perpetrated unspeakable violence on them during attacks by the Lord's Resistance Army, led by Joseph Kony. For these Ugandans in the Gulu area, the power of forgiveness to heal and transform their future is rooted in their religious faith.[5]

concentrates on ending violence and working for peace as a function of their Christian calling to serve the poor, observing that war is the greatest cause of poverty in today's world. Among other violent conflicts they have worked to resolve, Saint Egidio brokered an end to the fourteen-year civil war in Mozambique. Mennonites, a small but effective Protestant Christian group, have particularly dedicated themselves to work for nonviolent solutions to conflict in the most violent situations in our world, including Nepal, Somalia, Colombia, and in the post-conflict zones of Northern Ireland and Nicaragua, to consolidate the peace in these countries.

Intense focus on religion is leading to new approaches among political scientists, who hotly debate whether religion is a net cause of violence in the world, because it inflames deeply held differences; or whether, on the contrary,

Religion, Sciences, and the University

During the years I directed the Harvard University Center for the Study of World Religions, from 1990 to 2004, John Huchra from the Smithsonian Astronomic Observatory and the biologist Stephen Jay Gould helped break new ground for religion and science in programs titled "The Age and Fate of the Universe" and "Science and the Spiritual Quest," for example. Leading neurobiologists also investigate how prayer and contemplation may reshape the brain, mind, and behavior.[6]

Religion has also become a generative focus for the budding science of ecology. Religion and spirituality have gained increasing attention at international gatherings on the environment such as the United Nations Environmental Program in Rio de Janeiro, in 1992,

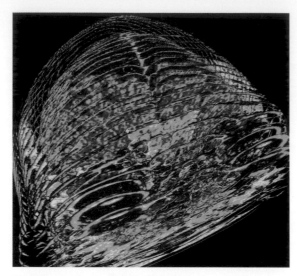

Fig. Intro. 10 Image of a brain scan.

and its successor, Rio 2012. The Earth Charter process included a Task Force on Religion and Spirituality, with repercussions in academic settings like Yale University's Forum on Religion and Ecology, anchored in the School of Forestry. Harvard University Press published a nine-volume series on Religions of the World and Ecology from 1997 to 2003 under the general editorship of Mary Evelyn Tucker and John Grim, who coordinate the Yale Forum. They concluded that, since religious evaluations of the world and the human role in it affect the earth in substantial ways, the new ecological sciences should be intent on understanding religion. In their *Journey of the Universe*, a film and book combination, Brian Swimme, an evolutionary philosopher, and Mary Evelyn Tucker, a historian of religions, reweave scientific discoveries in astronomy, geology, and biology with insights from the world's religions. Religious pilgrimage is one of the largest reasons for human travel on the planet. Religious leaders from around the globe met in Assisi, Italy, to form the Green Pilgrimage Network, which

is dedicated to lowering the environmental impact of the 150 million spiritual pilgrimages undertaken each year.

Religion thus remains a fertile source and great test of the explanatory power of scientific ways of thinking in the university. Think for a moment of these "new" sciences as extensions of the long religious quest: new ways of wondering about the things that appear in the world and the meaning of the signs in which they appear. Using terms and ideas valued in our day—whether the multiple dimensions of quantum physics, the eons of evolutionary time, or functional MRIs of the brain—these disciplines deepen the long search that springs from the heart of religion itself, opening new ways to wonder about things, their appearances, and their meanings.

Since its origins, which straddle the end of the first millennium, the university has been involved with religious inquiry into all the things that appear to us, from the mundane to the mysterious. Whether one dates the university to the founding of Al-Azhar, an Islamic educational institution started in Egypt in 970, or to the first universities in Europe, such as Bologna in 1088, Paris in 1150, and Oxford before 1167, or to the cathedral schools in the early Middle Ages, religious inquiry has remained a constant fire in the belly for universities, in complicated and interesting ways.

The social and natural sciences, with critical views of religion at their roots, extend the wondering of religion into our current day. This suggestion may startle Daniel C. Dennett and Richard Dawkins, but why not view these sciences as intimately related to religious inquiry? Dennett, a cognitive scientist and philosopher, energetically forwards a rational disenchantment of religion in his *Breaking the Spell: Religion as a Natural Phenomenon*, and he argues for more scientific study of religion in the future. In him, religion and science are joined at the hip. Dawkins, the biologist and gifted science writer, after several popular works critical of religion, has written the best-selling *The God Delusion* to denounce belief in a personal god as a false belief. Dawkins treats belief in God as one treats any scientific hypothesis. At first glance, Dennett's and Dawkins's views seem to hurl themselves at religion from the outside, which is how they present themselves. On more thoughtful inspection, however, their strong views may sound a lot like criticisms long found within the heart of religions themselves. In their zeal, they are not alone. Though Dennett and Dawkins call for more scientific study of religion, scientists themselves zealously debate how a university should handle religion. The evolutionary psychologist Steven Pinker, for example, successfully led a faculty effort to ban the study of religion from the undergraduate requirements at Harvard, a school originally founded for religious purposes.[7]

In his *Exploring Reality: The Intertwining of Science and Religion*, John Polkinghorne, an English theoretical physicist and an Anglican priest, sees affinity between religion and the sciences, contending that religion and science are close cousins, bound together as family members of the same truth-seeking lineage.[8] Francis S. Collins, the physical chemist and medical geneticist who directed the Human Genome Project, declared in his book written after he succeeded in spelling out the human genome, *The Language of God: A Scientist Presents Evidence for Belief*,[9] that the evolutionary creative process is a source of awe and wonder and that scientific breakthroughs on the frontiers of genomics have awakened and confirmed his religious awareness of an almighty God, not limited in space or time, who created the entire universe.

The historian of religion and science Ioan Couliano has made an interesting case concerning the interrelationship of religion, physics, magic, and mathematics in *Out of This World: Otherworldly Journeys from Gilgamesh to Albert Einstein*.[10] Couliano argued that great leaps forward in both science and religion stem from remarkably similar ecstatic experiences. Ecstasy—"seeing the world from some n + 1 dimension"—dramatically shifts one's perceptions of the world, whether the ecstatic person is a religious mystic or an innovative physicist or mathematician.

Some proponents of science criticize religion by asserting that it is, for instance, driven by the will to power and authority over others; or by a false consciousness of economic relationships; or by disguised feelings of guilt for atrocious deeds. Ironically, however, these criticisms thereby expand the audience of those who attend to and wonder about religious questions well beyond the restricted confines of practicing believers. Think of Dennett and Dawkins. Through scientific, studious approaches to religion, sociologists or textual scholars or neuro biologists who are nonbelievers and secularists focus ardently on Buddhist meditation, Hindu chant, Christian art, and holy Scriptures. Does science allow us the freedom to hold religion close, as humans have always done, but while keeping it at a "safe remove," the way a test tube lets a virologist handle a dangerous virus, or an asbestos glove allows a technician to hold a molten object without getting burned? Hold that thought. The new disciplines studying religion, from linguistics and depth psychology to neurobiology, have brought increased attention to religion. Perhaps this is one reason why Steven Pinker prefers not to include religion among required subjects of study at his university.

Studies of religion rearrange the signs and meanings already apparent in the world's religious traditions for their own purposes in order to understand religion better. For their part, religious communities frequently remain open to scientific studies about them and make use of these scientific reassignments of meaning, often by including scholarly studies of their communities in their ongoing education about their own religious life. The anthropologist Linda Schele recounted to me that she offered instruction to Maya Indian religious leaders in Central America in reading the spoken language encoded in Maya glyphs, a skill lost over the centuries. Maya elders enfolded her scientific deciphering into the communities' own religious self-knowledge.[11]

The same reciprocal process is at work for Christians and Jews who use text-historical criticism to enlarge Christian and Jewish understanding of their own Scriptures. Such scientific studies, far from dismantling religion from the outside, have become a nearly mandatory part of the education of ministers and rabbis.

In addition to the myths, rituals, creeds, arts, and meditative practices treasured by believers in the traditions, scientific researchers are thus adding to the interpretive fabric of traditions by weaving their own recombinations of those same signs and meanings. They recombine the signs of sacrifice, initiation, body painting, ecstatic poetry, ritual dance, altar construction, and festival processions, for instance, into theories about the origins of religions, histories of certain rites, economic or psychological explanations of religious community, and sociological or neurobiological accounts of religious experience. In other words, both the practitioners and the scientists who study them are linking those religious signs to the underlying meanings revealed in the new scientific images being brought to light in their fields (e.g., eons-long scenarios of adaptation and survival in evolutionary biology, the "fight or flight" functions of the amygdala in neurobiology, the "fission or fusion" mechanisms of kinship and social organization in cultural anthropology, or the deictic structures of prophetic oracles brought to light in linguistics). This is arguably the same process of religious wondering that has gone on for millennia.

Doubt, Disenchantment, and Critical Experience of Religion

As practitioners of both science and religion wonder about the same signs, some scholars risk underestimating the critical capacity of religion and claim mostly for themselves and their new sciences the critical function that is a defining hallmark of human existence everywhere, a critical capacity long vibrant within religion itself. Two quick examples dispel the notion that fundamental criticism and systemic doubt come at religion only from the outside

Fig. Intro. 11 Example of a Maya glyph, circa 600–900 CE.

and in the modern period. First, just before the Buddha's enlightenment, Mara, the lord of death, tempts him with exterminating doubt, evil, and death.[12] Second, Mother Teresa of Calcutta journaled her lifelong anguish in her spiritual diary: "haunted by religious doubt," "the terrible pain of loss . . . of God not being God, of God not really existing," "such convicting emptiness." The critical experiences of the Buddha and Mother Teresa, two paradigmatic religious figures, reveal how the religious life, intensely lived, calls the meaning of religious life itself into question.[13]

Are sacred things just delusions, mere fabrications? Is religion itself manufactured? Such questions lie at the heart of religion, which is, after all, a reflexive mode of being: wondering deeply about the trustworthiness of our own capacity to wonder; and wondering about the reality of those realities that apparently lie beneath the outward signs reflected in the images of the religious imagination. That is why systematic doubt, equal at least in force and scope to the criticism and doubt coming from the sciences, abounds in religious traditions around the world, from the "dark nights of the soul" described by St. John of the Cross, as well as many other accomplished Christian saints, to the mind-shattering koans of Zen Buddhism. "Without thinking of good or evil, show me your original face before your mother and father were born." This koan comes from the *Wumenguan*, a collection of forty-eight koans gathered by Wumen, a Chinese Zen monk of the thirteenth century, who comments that this koan can transform your whole body into an inquiry, a "Great Doubt," as if you had swallowed a red-hot iron ball that you cannot vomit out.[14]

Disillusionment is deliberately induced during religious initiations to provoke the

Fig. Intro. 12   A Zen Buddhist monk.

critical experience of symbolic death so central to the process of maturation, often imagined to be like the death of a seed in agricultural societies, or the sacrificial death of an animal that nourishes the life of all in nomadic and hunting communities. From this critical deathlike experience, the initiate and the community are reborn to new states of life, growth, and understanding.[15] The disenchantment, disillusionment, and doubt that occur in the heart of religion may in fact be the best context to evaluate recent critical methods and theories for the study of religion.[16]

To repeat, the focus question is: *How does religion instigate and sustain the kind of thinking, feeling, and acting that define human nature and that mark human culture so deeply in every part of the world?* Each chapter in this volume

Fig. Intro. 13 Indian diksha initiation ceremony, 2008.

addresses that central question by using all the perspectives available to the modern study of religion: history, social sciences, objective description, art, and textual study, as well as views from within the belief system in question.

"Religion" and Making Introductions

It is important to point out that the word *religion*, as used in this introduction, especially in its opening sections, is a concept; it is a way of talking in order to learn. Specific cultures and communities may not use or have the word *religion* at all. They may instead speak of a "path," "way," "practice," "faith," "observance," "creed," "tradition," or any one of many other non-English terms.

That people in a given place and time do not use the term *religion* and do not speak of "religion" in this conceptual way should not deter us from using such general terms of analysis in a proper way. On the contrary, using

our imagination to distil general concepts from varieties of religious experience is a great gift. It is what humans do. As long as we remain cognizant that we are using conceptual language, we will avoid mistaking our own generalizations for particular cultural expressions. As in any disciplined inquiry to gain knowledge, the technical terms of religious studies allow us to transform understanding by moving back and forth between expressions initially unknown to us, on the one hand, and our own individual cultural experience, on the other.

The ready availability of intimate knowledge regarding the most deeply held cultural beliefs of our neighbors' throughout the global community has become a distinguishing hallmark of our times. Entering most university libraries today, students have at their fingertips—through archaeology, anthropology, sociology, linguistics, and new schools of history arising from colonial and postcolonial studies—ideas and practices little known and little available to their great-grandparents. The fact that many of us do not yet initiate ourselves in this way does not change that fact. The material circumstances are there. All that is needed is a shift in awareness. This volume may be a trigger of that shift in awareness for you.

The terminology developed in religious studies (e.g., *myth*, *ritual*, *sacred*, *initiation*, *soul*, *supernatural being*) gives us a handle on this situation of religion in the world. These terms are heuristic, meaning they are tools for discovery through exploration. We use them to find out what is there, for gathering things and inspecting them, but they should be held lightly in hand as our understanding progresses. Every community embodies particular experiences, beliefs, and practices, and has its own ways of describing and evaluating them. These are the religious neighbors whose lives are portrayed in each chapter of this book.

This is a book of first introductions, a starting place for religious believers and nonbelievers alike to understand one another better as neighbors on this planet. Each chapter portrays the face of the religion in question by sketching its profile in different poses. These "gesture drawings" depict the religion in vignettes that best reveal its character. Each chapter outlines about ten thumbnail studies in the form of historical narratives, geographic maps, key rituals, major events, central beliefs, textual excerpts, select bibliographies, and glossaries of important terms.

The mix of vignettes and approaches is weighted differently in each chapter in order to accommodate the distinct character, and outline the particular features and history, of the tradition in question. This allows attention to fall on distinctive issues of special interest and concern, such as the changing roles of women in diverse religious communities today.[17] Sakena Yacoobi of Afghanistan is a striking example of such change. Motivated, strengthened, and sustained by the Muslim understandings of love, as cultivated in Sufi practice and the recitations of such mystical poets as Rumi and Hafiz, Yacoobi founded the Afghan Institute for Learning (AIL) in 1995. In the crucible of war and in the face of policies designed to restrict female education, Yacoobi organized at the grassroots level to bring education and health care to girls and women in rural as well as urban settings. Her fellow female teachers suffered to provide these services. During the Taliban regime, her organization supported eighty underground home schools for thousands of girls. Today, through forty-two program sites, AIL reaches 350,000 women and employs 400 Afghans, 70 percent of whom are women.[18]

The First Binding: Signs to Meaning

The word *religion* derives from the Latin word *religare*, "to bind together." At least two kinds of special binding occur in religions. The first kind of binding fuses signs and their meaning: in religion, the meaning of religious matters is linked to realities other than their everyday appearances. This first kind of binding makes it clear that the signs of ordinary appearances, like fire, are in fact symbols bound to a fuller, more extraordinary meaning, rooted in an altogether different kind of being. For example, in Zoroastrianism, fire is the symbol of the seven Holy Immortals and is the purest and most noble sign of the mind of Ahura Mazda, who created them, and all things, before the beginning of time.

This first kind of binding also links religious items to one another in complex arrangements and associations. A small Hindu temple in Delhi or a Shinto shrine in a residential neighborhood of Tokyo, for instance, are holy offerings are presented and consumed. Religion relates these diverse but significant things by linking the signs of their appearances to their deeper shared meaning: the life and times of the god or goddess. Thus in this first kind of binding—binding a sign to its deeper meaning—religion also "binds together" diverse things into more integrated wholes by linking them all to their shared underlying meaning. Ultimately, religious awareness of the deeper meaning of the outward signs that appear in the world may reveal an interconnected and meaningful cosmos at its largest reach in space and time.

Religions wonder about their own power to bind: by linking things and signs together through their deeper meaning, is religion distorting reality or distilling it into a crystal-clear vision of truth? This question occurs at the heart of various religious traditions, as the reader will discover in the chapters within.

The Imaginal World, Religious Ambivalence, and Hidden Relationships

Since religion is clearly a powerful exercise of the creative imagination, religious traditions internally debate whether religion has sufficient faith in its own imagination to bend the world to its meanings and purposes. Or should religion instead rein in or even reject the fervid imagination through iconoclasm and self-denying disciplines that hold the imagination in check?

Religion wonders deeply about such questions. It includes both the impulse to affirm and the impulse to deny the religious imagination of meaning. Belief and doubt are both

not because of the architectural shape of the material of stone or wood from which they are constructed but because they are linked with a god or goddess.

By fostering awareness of the deeper meaning that underlies surface signs, religions discover significant connections among very diverse things, such as a temple or shrine building, a divine being, a holy name, a divine action performed in ancient times, and a morning ceremony in which chants are sung, cleansing waters are poured, ritual clothing is worn, and food

Fig. Intro. 14   The Hie Shrine, a Shinto shrine in Toyko, Japan.

aspects of religious wonder. Across the world, religious authorities, such as high priests and sacred kings, have vied with the mystics, prophets, and reformers in their own communities who sought to call their views and actions into question. Religion has long recognized the fundamental ambivalence of signs and the innate ambivalence of realities that the most important signs designate. Divine beings, for instance, are often described as deeply ambivalent: fascinating enough to draw one to them with love and devotion but terrifying enough to provoke fear and trembling. In the Bhagavad Gita, an important Hindu Scripture of terrible beauty, the fierce warrior Arjuna beholds the loving divinity Krishna in his cosmic form on the plains of a world-ending battle. The vision of Krishna, center of loving devotion, "devouring all the world on every side," reduces the fierce warrior to terror, pleading for mercy.

Religious traditions have noted that even the syllables in a word can be recombined to reveal utterly new meanings, sometimes directly opposed to one another. The Yaka people of southwestern Congo think of the recombinant process of language as weaving. They heal infertile women by partly unraveling them and then reweaving them over a nine-month ritual period, rearranging the syllables in the names of their afflictions. *Loka*, for example,

Fig. Intro. 15 Depiction of Krishna and his charioteer, Arjuna, in battle of Kurukshetra.

signals a "binding" that unhealthily entangles life. *Kola*, on the other hand, means "health," the state where the same life flows through unobstructed, as signaled by the rearranged syllables.[20]

Complex relations of outward signs like sacred letters, syllables, and words reveal the hidden relationships among all the underlying realities that those sounds can signify in the sacred wordplay of traditions. Even the sounds may be recombined to reveal hidden affinities throughout the world, like some universe-wide game of Scrabble.[21] Relationships among all things can be revealed through contemplation of their recombinant signs just as the four letters of the genetic code (A, G, C, and T) unveil unseen bonds among all life forms in the biomass of planet earth. Practices like Kabbalah reveal new meanings and hidden links until the underlying wholeness of reality and the fundamental unity of all things in the world are revealed.

The Second Binding: Appearance to Awareness

Through the ongoing contention between belief and doubt, meaning and question, affirmation and discipline, religious life attends to a second kind of binding: the binding of reality to a human awareness that is creative, reflective, and self-conscious. The truth is so obvious that it often escapes our attention: the human imagination is the only place in the universe where reality appears in a way that makes it the subject of interpretive reflection and knowledge.

Reflection and interpretation are labors of the imagination. The moon and other things that appear in the world do not fit in the human eyeball, as Aristotle pointed out long ago. Rather, we "see" the moon, as the poet Hafiz did also, through signs and images that arise in the human imagination. Our imagination forms an image of the moon after signs of its light make an impression on the retina of our eye and often after the light passes through a telescope, an invention of the human imagination that first casts its own image of the moon for our better viewing.

Human imagination is constantly processing signs—and signs of signs, in the case of scientific telescopes and digital files. These signs are fused with human awareness in ways that generate the images that allow us to reflect on their deeper meaning, whether in scientific studies of the lunar surface, the meteorological and agricultural reports about the harvest moon, the exquisite emotional lunar poems by the seventeenth-century Japanese poet Basho, or the Romantic melodies, such as Debussy's *Claire de lune*, that evoke strong emotions associated with memories of friends and times long gone, and so on.

Religion cultivates critical awareness of this basic situation, an awareness that there exists a conspiracy between things and the human imagination, to their mutual benefit: an awareness that the meaning of things is revealed when, and only when, they appear in the imagination. Consequently, the imagination must be watched carefully, for it can hallow reality with religious meaning or desecrate it to the point of meaninglessness. Religion brings home the responsibility that humans bear for the religious imagination, within them but affecting the critical understanding of the world and all the things that appear there, including the human role in it.

By calling all things and the meaning of their signs into question, religion furnishes human beings with a critical experience of the

Fig. Intro. 16   Memorial to a famous haiku by Basho, Tokyo, Japan.

world.[22] In fact, religion calls into question this unique situation: that among all things in the universe our human awareness bears unique responsibility for the imagination that reflects on the world and discloses its meaning. This experience generates critical questions and choices.

Mind as Mirror: Imagining a Universe, Viewpoint, and Place to Stand

Many religious traditions, from classical Greek piety and medieval Christian mysticism to various schools of Buddhist meditation, describe disciplined cultivation of human sense perception and special awareness as "polishing the mirror of the mind," so that images of reality can appear more accurately and their meanings be apprehended more clearly.[23] The ancient Greeks eyed the murky "mirror of Medusa." Instead of displaying the outer world, the mirror reveals the invisible, cryptic one. The gods appear there, for example; the mirror dulls their splendor so humans can look on them without expiring. But mortals pass before it unseen. Warriors, however, prepare their minds for war by gazing at their own faces through the lowered visors of their helmets, catching glimpses in this mirror on the wall of the glory (*hebe*) within them, which will shine forth during the upcoming battle and reveal their immortal fate.[24]

Over centuries, Christians also reflected on the mind as mirror of the world and questioned the trustworthiness of the imagination. Do the mind and imagination turn the world to fiction? Should we believe or should we doubt the picture that the mind presents? Saint Paul states, "Now we see but a poor reflection as in a mirror"

Fig. Intro. 17 Tang dynasty bronze mirror with design of clouds and dragons, circa eighth century CE.

(1 Cor. 13:11 NIV). The Christian theme of the mirror-mind is developed further in Saint Augustine's *Confessions*, in Saint Bonaventure's *Journey of the Mind to God*, where he places the mind's mirroring capacity on the bottom rung of Jacob's meditative ladder, and in the *Paradiso* (Paradise) of Dante, which abounds with mirrors that signal his own transformation as his imaginative mind takes in more of reality during his passage from this world to other worlds.[25]

These ancient Christian writers foreshadow the modern crisis of the subject. They worry that the self may be a broken mirror that poorly reflects reality, just as the scientists Dennett, Dawkins, and Pinker worry about the distortions of religious thinking. In the case of the early Christian writers, however, they worry not only about the distortions of religious thought but also about the imperfect human reflections that form the basis of all forms of knowledge. Each Christian writer mentioned above proposes solutions for corrective vision.[26]

Today, mirror images of ourselves and of our world multiply exponentially through our technologies of image capture and distribution. "Real" events, from weddings to bungee jumps, appear to lack the full impact and significance we yearn for in popular culture unless they can also be photographed and seen in other settings to bear testimony to the event. The "soul" was once imagined in the form of a shadow or reflection in a pool or mirror. Today the technological capacity of our minds to mirror the world invites more questioning than ever,[27] questions about signs and meanings that for so long have been at the heart of religious inquiry.[28]

Today, camera phones and IMAX cameras mirror our every living moment and thought. YouTube, Facebook, and multiplex movie theaters place mirror images of every possible thing, both "real" and fictive, into every imaginable human space, from the rooms of our homes, to restaurants, planes, trains, and automobiles. Scientific imagery is being captured from every level of the universe, from electron microscopy of nickel molecules, to MRIs of the brain while listening to music, from sonar and temperature pictures of the deepest trenches of the oceans, to ultraviolet and infrared probes of the outermost rim of the universe billions of light years away. Images of every aspect of our world, from the macro- to the nano- scale, are being gathered for our reflection through the creative instruments, like the Hubble and Chandra telescopes, that extend the capacities of our own imagination.

What do we make of it all? With knowledge of the world so much at stake, it is no surprise that our powers of reflection and imagination are being called ever more into question. We must know: Through our imagery and imagination, are we truly reflecting the world we live in? Is the tiny seed of the self—an infinitesimal speck on the ocean of time and being—capable of all that? Is that believable? After all, the moon still does not fit in our eye. Or are we living increasingly in a wallpaper world, like the character Truman Burbank, portrayed by Jim Carrey in the movie *The Truman Show*, a digital-thin surface world papered only with virtual images of our own making? More deeply, how would we know the answer to this question? That is, where would we stand in the universe to see all this more clearly?[29] Short of human beings removing themselves from their place in the world and seeing all reality from some wholly other, divine Archimedean point of view, one may fairly ask what is the experience from some "n + 1 dimension" of our universe, which would help us see how accurate our mirroring of things might be, an experience that some religions (and scientists) might describe as an ecstatic moment of clarity?[30]

When humans irrepressibly wonder about things, appearances, and their meanings, we often seek to know whether there is such an outermost limit, an imaginable observation post that can serve as a check on our potential subjective distortions. Is there such a referent point exterior to ourselves, some ultimate meaning that is self-evident? Questions like these have been and remain fundamentally religious questions. Each of the traditions sketched in this volume has addressed questions of this sort, in the distinctive terms of their cultures, times, and developmental histories. Understanding their questions and answers takes some doing, but it is a worthwhile exercise.

The effort to understand those religions enlarges one's admiration for the human capacity for inquiry and enriches what it means to be a human being in the world. Is the puny religious drama of humankind equal to the grandeur of the cosmic stage set by the Big Bang of the universe and the long evolution of life? This was the question that the famous physicist Richard Feynman put to the novelist Herman Wouk. Feynman thought the answer was clearly, "No!"[31] Wouk, a playwright who knows a good drama when he sees one, pleads his case for the universe-altering power of Job's religious questioning of God.[32] Wouk counters Feynman by pointing out that *only* humans can or care to ask such a question, calling God and the universe to accounts and thereby bringing to light the critical purpose of the religious life. Where else in this vast universe is there a creature that raises such a question about the whole thing? The religious question is a turning point in the entire cosmic drama, because of its exponential difference from all other questions in the universe. Like a Big Bang of its own, the religious question stirs all other inquiries into motion and infuses a new kind of force into the universe, this time an imaginal and reflective power that affects all things, transforming them forever.

In the second binding, in other words, religion self-consciously links the images of reality to the "imagination," a word that literally refers to the mirror condition of human reflection in which "images are born." *Religion, especially during processes of initiation, cultivates the awareness that it is in the religious imagination that the world appears in a meaningful way.* This awareness imposes on human beings a sense of creative responsibility for the world and the people and things that appear in it. Such responsibility is instilled in the young Navajo woman, for example, during her Kinaalda, a four-day ceremony that transforms her from a child to a woman. Seated on a sacred sand painting at the center of the Hogan, the ceremonial hut that is a microcosm of the world, her body is refashioned, molded like corn pollen or clay in

the image of Changing Woman, the primordial being for whom the ceremony was first performed during the time that the Holy People emerged from below the earth. Changing Woman and the Holy People formed the world as it is known today by placing things around them—mountains and landmarks—with the ritual intention and attention being cultivated in the young woman during the Kinaalda. She models her awareness and her responsibility for life in the world on that of Changing Woman.[33]

The religious person is encouraged to remain mindful that humans are symbolic beings. We reflect realities beyond ourselves: in language, science, art, dream, and mathematics, but especially in religion. Words, theorems, visual art, numbers, the constants of physics, and religious ideas and practices point beyond us for their meaning, whether we are calling our mother's name as toddlers, naming the Washington Monument or a lost object no longer visible, describing the speed of light in a logarithm, or reminding a friend about Buzz Lightyear. Only in human beings does the meaning of such things in the world arise in the form of signs, symbols, and images that reflect back on the world's things in the forms of calculus, Japanese, love songs, and other forms of understanding.

The religious imagination is the outermost expression of this human capacity to point beyond ourselves, whether one accepts the idea with enthusiasm or not. Religion constantly generates fundamental choices about the nature of reality and the role humans play in it. For instance, only through the religious imagination of human beings does the entire world itself become hallowed, no matter what one makes of that benediction. Religion binds things to utterly different kinds of being than those appearing in its signs. Moses' burning bush (Exod. 3:1-21) becomes a sign of the all-powerful God whose name is unspeakable. Is this a delusion or a delight? Through religious wonder, the beings and worlds that appear as signs in the religious imagination are called into question and are thereby critically experienced and understood.

Realities of the First Order

Religions often point to events that happen "in the beginning," such as creation, and therefore concern themselves with primordial realities in that chronological sense. Reference to "first things" indicates, however, that the religious meaning of signs is primordial in another sense as well: the signs point ultimately to realities that are the first of their kind, first in their quality of being: "those beings than which nothing more primary may be conceived." Their meaning is ultimate. Primordiality seems deeply rooted in the human imagination as it relates to the world, for it appears not only in religion but also in science and other domains of knowledge. In many religions found in this volume, the ultimate meaning of signs is located in the beginnings of time, when the gods and superhuman heroes were fully present, visible, and active. Temples mark the space where these supernaturals once performed their prodigious acts, especially their momentous acts of transformation or disappearance, which also mark time with a dramatic break-point to which humans constantly return to evaluate their own existence in time. Those first beings created the world or reshaped it after destruction and then withdrew from full view, rendering what is primordial relatively invisible but highly meaningful. All subsequent things that appear in the world point back to those first things, which

are now ironically less apparent, though their meaning is all the more basic. In other words, signs point to primordial realities for their ultimate meaning, something religions ceaselessly inquire about.

This was the sense Mircea Eliade, a leading historian of religions, intended when he used the term *archaic* the way he did, drawing on Greek philosophical notions of the *arche* as a "primary structure" of thought but also of ontology, a fundament in the order of being, as being appears in the imagination, and not merely a "first beginning" in chronological time.[34] The primacy of things that are first of their kind in the order of being makes them the ultimate meaning for all the subsequent appearances and signs that represent them, whether in order of time or rank order of being. All other things that subsequently appear in the universe become their signatures, marks of their identity, and surrogates, pointing back toward them for their originative meaning.

Of course, the historical language of many religious traditions, rooted in hunting, nomadic herding, early agriculture, pre–Iron Age technologies, and the like, makes it a chore to see this strategy for what it is, though the effort is worthwhile. The exotic terms, unfamiliar to us, have their own charm but require some historical and cultural study to understand as a stratagem: to anchor knowledge and meaning in primordial appearances, putting first things first.

Interestingly enough, here affinities between religion and science may help. Our contemporary sciences may help us understand this strategy of the imagination—the search for primordial conditions—since the sciences seem to continue the archaic tradition of extending new knowledge and of anchoring the ultimate meaning of ongoing manifestations and signs in the universe by pointing to their most primordial foundations, whether in the sense of chronological time or of first-order in quality of being. The application to evolutionary biology is obvious enough.

Searching for primordial realities is also one way of thinking of the important scientific projects being carried out by CERN (the European Organization for Nuclear Research), including the Large Hadron Super Collider, the largest and highest-energy particle accelerator ever built, some 570 feet beneath the mountains of the French-Swiss border near Geneva. Constructing it involved over 10,000 scientists and engineers from more than one hundred countries. Recently brought back online after a shutdown for safety checks after it opened in 2009, the CERN Hadron Collider represents the billions of dollars going toward exciting research that, if it succeeds, will back up the clock of our knowledge about the origins of the universe by some 1^{-42} nanoseconds of time. Those primordial moments and the primordial conditions of energy and bosons during them are thought to be the most revealing sources about the laws of nature and the fundamental questions about the physics of energy in our world.

A similar preoccupation with primordiality drives the NASA COBE (Cosmic Background Explorer) satellite project directed by the Nobel Prize–winning astrophysicist George Smoot at the University of California-Berkeley. Using the Explorer 66 satellite to record and measure cosmic microwave background radiation (CMB), Smoot and his team peer back into time, capturing pictures of the background radiation first set in motion by the Big Bang at the birth of the universe. Their work demonstrates that the universe burst forth from a single point of infinite density, radiating background energy that still fills the entire universe with microwaves.

Fig. Intro. 18 Experiment on solenoid of Large Hadron Super Collider in Geneva, Switzerland.

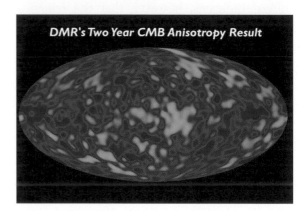

Fig. Intro. 19 Following the removal of dust and gases and charging particles in the Milky Way Galaxy, the cosmic microwave background (CMB) anisotropy is visible.

Smoot and his team have been capturing images of that energy, like someone tracking down the light still traveling from a camera flash 14 billion years ago. He created a map, a picture of energy set in motion when the universe began, showing temperature fluctuations that are the seeds of present-day galaxies. With new technology, scientists stare toward the origins of time. Our hope is that the tain-like mystery of deepest, darkest space, like the opaque black backing of a mirror, will reflect back to us the primordial story of our universe and its preconditions. Not unlike the visored Greek warrior facing the Mirror of Medusa, a glimpse of nearly invisible primordial space-time may reveal something of ultimate significance about our ultimate fate as well.[35]

Given the much longer history of religion, in comparison to the recent history of new sciences, we may be allowed to wonder whether the strategic search for primordial realities, which seems so innate to the imagination and to human knowing, owes its origin, development, and continued existence to religious experience, religious wondering, and religious inquiry over the long history of our species.

History, Experience, Culture

Recent introductions to the study of religion tend to come in three flavors, placing a primary emphasis either on experience, history, or culture. This introduction combines all three approaches.

History offers a general framework to guide us; and the study of religion offers keys to understanding history. Take, for example, the history of the city, which so defines human life on the planet today. For ten thousand years, humanity has moved in ever greater numbers toward the city, even at the cost of trading the longstanding family home in the placid countryside or small village for a squalid dwelling in the poorest, most violent quarters of Bukavu, Delhi, Rio de Janeiro, Mexico City, Jakarta, or Los Angeles. The cultural geographer Paul Wheatley demonstrated that the increasing urbanity of human life on our planet began with a religious attraction.

He has closely studied what he called urbanogenesis—the birth of cities[36]—and he concludes that, based on the archaeological and cultural evidence from the ten oldest cities

in ten separate settings of the globe, the city itself—the very idea of the city as a mode of human existence—is religious in origin. That is, when one peels back the onion of archaeological time to look at their earliest footprints in space, these cities were not the outcome of new technologies, economies, or architectures. Religious sanctuaries did not follow the settlement of people in thick urban clusters. Rather, their essential forms, cast into the ground of these sites and fixed in stone, preceded any such dense settlements. At their root, cities prove to be ancient sacred centers of pilgrimage to which people traveled temporarily for religious reasons and then returned home. Like the ancient structures underlying Beijing in China, Benin in West Africa, Tenochtitlan in Mexico, and Mohenjo-daro in Pakistan, these early seeds of what became cities had what Wheatley demonstrated were cosmo-magical structures designed to attract, through religious practices, beneficent forces and to repel malignant ones. The primary function of cities was to align human life with the most significant forces, cosmic and sacred, by placing humans at the center of the world and all powers, including those that transcend it. Centering of this sort is as much an act of awareness, predicated on and cultivated by religious acts and disciplines, as an act of geographic siting.

The present volume examines the distinctive histories of the separate religious traditions featured in each chapter. The table of contents arranges the communities treated into an outline of traditions, each one of which has its distinct history. Each individual tradition receives its own treatment. This framework emphasizes the importance of what the great scholar of Islam Marshall Hodgson called "the primacy of the dated and the placed."[37] The volume uses history as a peg to fix our focus on what is believed and

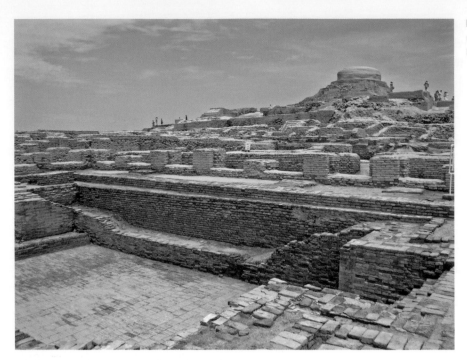

Fig. Intro. 20 Ancient ruins at Mohenjo-daro, Pakistan.

practiced in specific spaces and times. Founders of the particular religions and their specific reformers, principal events, and writings are all set in their historical context. The development of ideas and communities is traced over time.

Nevertheless, experience must also be a key feature. That is because chronology alone is not a sufficient account of history, especially religious history. The British philosopher C. P. Snow once accused writers who confused history with chronology as merely placing "one damn thing after another." History must also mean "evaluating the quality of our existence in time." That is why it is necessary to somehow come to grips with the quality of religious experience, on an individual as well as communal scale. The vignettes in each chapter convey the quality of the religious experience in that tradition, as do the art, the occasional personal testimonies, and the descriptions, from time to time, of religious moments and events as experienced from within the life of practitioners.

It is also important for readers to bring their own experience to the process of understanding. The fact that we are dealing, at every step, with signs, symbolic orders, and the conditions of the human imagination frees us from settling for exclusively economic, social, or historical explanations of the religions of others. For one thing, religions cannot be exhaustively accounted for by descriptions of their geography, ecology, language, material conditions, or even historical events. It is true that every set of religious symbols, from myths to creeds and rituals, relates to the political, social, and economic life of the community from which it springs. But the historicity of religious experiences cannot absolve us from the responsibility of questioning more generally the nature and meaning of existing in time, if we want to fully understand the humanity manifest in particular historical situations.

Hindu, Jain, and Buddhist thinkers mentioned in this book, for example, do not limit their claims to specific people in specific places and times. They reflect on the general human condition and on cosmic existence more broadly. To understand them, we too must reflect on human nature at its widest reach and deeply probe the nature of our own experience. In the course of thinking about the ninth-century Japanese Buddhist thinker Kukai and his vision of the ten worlds (or the religious ideas of the Navajo, the Barasana, the Inca, or the Yaka), we must come to grips with what we ourselves think about the world and the mind-body practices that affect our views. Where do our experiences of the world and Kukai's intersect in ways that ground our understanding of his ideas and practices? The study of religion, then, like all exercises in the humanities, is an invitation not only to accumulate more historical data in a detached way but also to plumb more deeply one's own views about important realities and evaluate one's own experience of existence in time.

This is the central meaning of culture: to creatively engage the resources that we inherit in each generation. Those resources include language, art, specific material and economic conditions and the skills to work with them, as well as patterns of thought and value. At a certain point, usually associated with adolescence, cultural actors in every society and in each new generation assume their own responsibility for cultural production and reproduction. Communities generally set aside some time for reflecting about culture, an intense period but also one open for learning. Thus free from full economic responsibilities, the ascendant generation can make its transition into their mature cultural role, whether through initiation in traditional villages or through apprenticeship in trades or labor associations in cash economies, or through other technical and educational preparations, such as the college education suited to

Fig. Intro. 21 Statue of Kukai (774–835, CE), Japanese monk, founder of the Shingon ("True Word") school of Buddhism.

knowledge workers. During this time of transition, the upcoming generation is furnished with know-how and information about the world. But whether it is the Okiek women of Kenya or the young men of the Greek polis, the culture also contrives to stage for them a set of critical experiences as well as a mode of critical reflection on those experiences that can transform their awareness of themselves and their world.[38] This transformation of awareness develops sensitivity to the uniquely symbolic nature of human life as well as to the range of expressions, meanings, responsibilities, and self-disciplining skills required to handle such awareness well. Within the pluralistic global community that young adults enter today, it makes sense that knowledge of the religions—recognition of the profiles, motives, and meanings important to our religious neighbors in the global community—play a part in that changing awareness.

I wish to extend my thanks to the authors who joined me and contributed chapters to this volume. We have taken pleasure in the thinking and the writing that went into the preparation of the text as well as in the teaching about religion that readied us for the task. We offer the volume to you, kind readers, with excitement and hope. We invite you, students and instructors alike, to meet the religious neighbors we introduce in it. We hope you will enjoy and benefit from your acquaintance with these longstanding and remarkable ways of life as much as we enjoy knowing about them in our own professional lives. And we hope as well that your deepening knowledge of these neighbors and their religions will make a positive difference in your lives and in the life of the world you share with one another.

◆ NOTES

1. See the transcript of Bono's remarks at the National Prayer Breakfast, February 2, 2006 at http://www.usatoday.com/news/washington/2006-02-02-bono-transcript_x.htm.

2. See also the case of the Branch Davidians in Lawrence E. Sullivan, " 'No Longer the Messiah': U.S. Federal Law Enforcement Views of Religion in Connection with the 1993 Siege of Mount Carmel near Waco, Texas," *Numen* 43, no. 2 (1996): 213–34.

3. See Thich Nhat Hanh, *True Love: A Practice for Awakening the Heart* (Boston: Shambhala, 1997); and also the interview with Thich Nhat Hanh in *The Power of Forgiveness*, a documentary film by Martin Doblmeier, at http://www.thepowerofforgiveness.com/index.html.

4. See especially Mark Lilla, "The Politics of God," *New York Times Magazine*, August 19, 2007; William T. Cavanaugh, "Does Religion Cause Violence?" *Harvard Divinity Bulletin* 35, nos. 2–3 (Spring/ Summer 2007): 22–35; and Mark Juergensmeyer, *Terror in the Mind of God: The Global Rise of Religious Violence*, 3rd ed. (Berkeley: University of California Press, 2003). For a summary of where the religion question stands in political science, see Daniel Philpott, Monica Duffy Toft, and Timothy Samuel Shah, *God's Century: Resurgent Religion and Global Politics* (New York: W.W. Norton, 2011).

5. See the video *Uganda: The Challenge of Forgiveness* at http://vimeo.com/40450751.

6. See James H. Austin, *Zen and the Brain: Toward an Understanding of Meditation and Consciousness* (Cambridge, MA: MIT Press, 1999); Richard J. Davidson and A. Lutz, and J. P. Dunne, "Meditation and the Neuroscience of Consciousness: An Introduction," in *Cambridge Handbook of Consciousness*, ed. P. Zelazo, M. Moscovitch, and E. Thompson (New York: Cambridge University Press, 2007); and R. J. Davidson, "The Neurobiology of Compassion," *Wisdom and Compassion in Psychotherapy: Deepening Mindfulness in Clinical Practice at the University Of Wisconsin*, ed. in C. K. Germer and R. D. Siegel (New York: Guilford, 2012).

7. Lisa Miller, "Harvard's Crisis of Faith," *Newsweek*, February 11, 2010. For a sharp-headed and sharply-worded examination of the recent debates over religion and science in the university, see Terry Eagleton, *Reason, Faith, and Revolution: Reflections on the God Debate*. These

are the "Dwight Harrington Terry Foundation Lectures on Religion in the Light of Science and Philosophy" that Eagleton delivered at Yale University in 2008.

8. John Polkinghorne, *Exploring Reality: The Intertwining of Science and Religion* (New Haven: Yale University Press, 2006).

9. Francis Collins, *The Language of God: A Scientist Presents Evidence for Belief* (New York: Free Press, 2006),

10. Ioan Couliano, *Out of This World: Otherworldly Journeys from Gilgamesh to Albert Einstein* (Boston: Shambhala, 1991)

11. Her breakthroughs, made in collaboration with scholars like David Kelley, Peter Matthews, David Stuart, and others, used linguistics, ethno-astronomy, archaeology, semiotics, anthropology, and art decipherment. See "Breaking the Maya Code," a transcript of a filmed interview with Peter Mathews, at www.nightfirefilms.org.

12. Ananda W. P. Guruge, *The Buddha's Encounters with Mara* (Essex, UK: Wisdom Books, 1998).

13. Mother Teresa, *Come Be My Light: The Private Writings of the Saint of Calcutta*, ed. Brian Kolodiejchuk (New York: Doubleday, 2009); David Van Biema, "Mother Teresa's Crisis of Faith," *Time* August, 23, 2007.

14. See case 23 of the *Wumenguan* in Sumiko Kudo, trans., *The Gateless Barrier: Zen Comments on the Mumonkan. Zenkei Shibayama (1894-1974)* (Boston: Shambhala, 1974); Thomas Kasulis, "Ch'an Spirituality," in *Buddhist Spirituality*, ed. Takeuchi Yoshinori (Delhi: Motilal Banarsidass, 2003); and Victor Sogen Hori, *Zen Sand: The Book of Capping Phrases for Koan Practice*, Nanzan Library of Asian Religion and Culture (Honolulu: University of Hawaii Press, 2003).

15. Sam Gill, "Disenchantment," *Parabola* 1:3 (1976): 6–13.

16. Theories, for example, by Russell McCutcheon, Donald Wiebe, Luther Martin, Armin Geertz, Michael Pye, Daniel Dubuisson, Thomas Lawson, and, standing somewhat apart from these, my admired teacher Jonathan Z. Smith.

17. Rita Gross, *Feminism and Religion: An Introduction* (Boston: Beacon, 1996); Nancy Auer Falk, *Unspoken Worlds: Women's Religious Lives* (Independence, KY: Wadsworth, 2000).

18. See Greg Mortenson, "Sakena Yacoobi," *The Atlantic*, November, 2010, http://www.theatlantic.com/magazine/archive/2010/11/sakena-yacoobi/8275/; and Rahim Kanani, "Dr. Sakena Yacoobi: A Case Study in Leadership, Courage, and Conviction," *Forbes*, September, 9, 2011, http://www.forbes.com/sites/rahimkanani/2011/09/19/dr-sakena-yacoobi-a-case-study-in-leadership-courage-and-conviction/.

19. Hafiz poem about the moon, found in *Love Poems from God: 12 Sacred Voices from the East and West*. Translated by Daniel Ladinsky. London: Penguin Compass, 2002, page 175. Used by permission of Daniel Ladinsky.

20. René Devisch, *Weaving the Threads of Life: The Khita Gyn-eco-logical Healing Cult among the Yaka* (Chicago: University of Chicago Press, 1993).

21. Jewish mystical systems of recombination and wordplay, for example, have caught on and become better understood through such studies as Moshe Idel, *Kabbalah: New Perspectives* (New Haven: Yale University Press, 1990). See also Moshe Idel, *Le Porte della Giustizia* (Rome: Adelphi, 2001). In fact, practices of mystical wordplay and recombination are found the world over, as among the Kari'na tribe of

Venezuela (Marc de Civrieux, *Religión y Magia Kari'na* [Caracas: Universidad Catolica 'Andres Bello,' Instituto de Investigaciones Históricas, 1974]).

22. The word *critical* derives from the Greek word *kritein*, meaning "to choose, to decide."

23. Alex Wayman analyzed how the mind is polished in Buddhism, from India through Southeast Asia, Tibet, and especially in China (Alex Wayman, "The Mirror as a Pan-Buddhist Metaphor-Simile," in *Buddhist Insight: Essays by Alex Wayman*, ed. George R. Elder (Delhi: Motilal Banarsidass, 1984), 129–52); Wayman, "The Mirror-like Knowledge in Mahayana Buddhist Literature," *Asiatische Studien* 25 (1971): 353–63. Wayman's work follows the important lead of Paul Demieville, "Le Miroir spiritual," *Sinológica* 1 (1947): 112–37. Emiko Ohnuki-Tierney used the image of the mirror to examine the frontiers of critical thinking in Japanese history (*The Monkey as Mirror: Symbolic Transformations in Japanese History and Ritual* [Princeton: Princeton University Press, 1989]).

24. Jean-Pierre Vernant, "The Mirror of Medusa," in *Mortals and Immortals: Collected Essays* (Princeton: Princeton University Press, 1991), 141–50. Edward Peter Nolan takes a broader look at the mirror-as-mind in classical thinking from antiquity to the beginnings of the Renaissance in *Now through a Glass Darkly: Specular Images of Being and Knowing from Virgil to Chaucer* (Ann Arbor: University of Michigan Press, 1991).

25. Dante ascends from the lowest to the highest otherworld throughout his Easter transition from death to eternal life. Mirrors are featured in canto 2 (the trinity of mirrors is introduced), canto 13 (God's goodness is mirrored in the nine angelic orders), canto 21 (Beatrice instructs Dante how to turn his eyes into revelatory mirrors of inward vision and awareness), canto 29 (Beatrice praises God for creating so many mirrors of himself in the heavens), canto 30 (features the reflecting mirror of the great River of Light), canto 33 (Dante becomes enraptured in vision as he peers into the laser-like trinity of self-reflecting circles, a symbol of divine self-knowledge).

26. Tom A. Tharn, "The Medieval Christian in 'Mirror-Mode': A Brief Sketch of the Mirror as Sacred Tool from Paul's '*In aenigmate*' to Dante's *Paradiso*," *Dulia et Latria Journal* 1 (2008): 33–45.

27. See the important works by Charles Taylor, *Sources of the Self: The Making of the Modern Identity* (Cambridge, MA: Harvard University press, 1992); and his following analysis, *A Secular Age* (Cambridge MA: Belknap Press of Harvard University Press, 2007).

28. In *The Tain of the Mirror: Derrida and the Philosophy of Reflection* (Cambridge, MA: Harvard University Press, 1986), Rodolphe Gasché uses the image of a mirror to discuss the contemporary need for the critical disciplines to reflect on our world and our place in it, in a condition of ubiquitous imagery. "Tain" refers to the sheet of blackened tin on the backside of a mirror, which enables it to reflect images. The inherent formlessness and opacity of the tain, so evocative of mystery and limitless enigma, allows anything to be reflected in it. On that analogy, the capacity of our minds to act as mirrors presents special difficulties today. For the reasons that Gasché analyzes, our mind-mirrors require extra polishing today, through criticism, of the rough assumptions and obscure preconditions of our human capacity for reflection. (In the same vein, see Edward Peter Nolan, "Mirrors in Modern Theory and Cultural History," the appendix in his *Now through a Glass Darkly*.)

29. Questions of this sort seem to be the takeoff points for Robert Sokolowski, *The God of Faith and Reason: Foundations of Christian Theology* (Washington, DC: Catholic University of America Press, 1995); but also for the scientist Michael Shermer, "The Really Hard Science," *Scientific American*, September 16, 2007, who advocates not striving for an omniscient observer-point outside all systems but instead an "integrative science" that blends all possible points of view, a panoptic.

30. Ioan Couliano, *Out of This World* (Boston: Shambhala, 1991); Mircea Eliade, *Shamanism: Archaic Techniques of Ecstasy* (Princeton: Princeton University press, 2004).

31. Feynman spelled out his views on religion in his book *The Meaning of It All: Thoughts of a Citizen Scientist* (New York: Perseus, 1999); see also Richard P. Feynman, "The Relation of Science and Religion: Some Fresh Observations on an Old Problem," talk given at the Caltech YMCA Lunch Forum on May 2, 1956, available at http://calteches.library.caltech.edu/49/2/Religion.htm.

32. In *The Language God Talks: On Science and Religion* (Boston: Little, Brown, 2010), Wouk dramatically restages Job's argument with God, placing it into the last lecture given by the fictive character Aaron Jastrow, a doomed inmate of the Auschwitz death camp. Through Jastrow's words, Job, the quintessential man of long-suffering faith, exercises once again the quintessential right to wonder, a right that the religious person ironically earns through his faithfulness.

33. Lawrence E. Sullivan, *The Religious Spirit of the Navajo* (Philadelphia: Chelsea House, 2001); please see the extensive analysis and interpretations of initiation rites among South American native religions in Lawrence E. Sullivan, *Icanchu's Drum: An Orientation to Meaning in South American Religions* (New York: Macmillan, 1988), 303–85.

34. See Mircea Eliade, *Patterns in Comparative Religions* (Omaha: Bison, 1996).

35. George Smoot and Keay Davidson, *Wrinkles in Time* (New York: William Morrow & Company, 1994).

36. Paul Wheatley, *The Pivot of the Four Quarters: A Preliminary Inquiry into the Origins and Character of the Ancient Chinese City* (Edinburgh: Edinburgh University Press, 1971).

37. Marshall Hodgson, *The Venture of Islam*, 3 vols. (Chicago: University of Chicago Press, 1977).

38. See the extraordinary book by Corinne Kratz, *Affecting Performance: Meaning, Movement, and Experience in Okiek Women's Initiation* (Tucson: Wheatmark, 2010); and Werner Jaeger, *Paideia: The Ideals of Greek Culture*, 3 vols. (Oxford: Oxford University Press, 198).

CHAPTER 1

Indigenous Religious Traditions

Robin M. Wright

Introduction

The category "indigenous religions" of the world merits an encyclopedia all its own. For, as many tribal peoples as there are in the world today, each has its own set of beliefs and rites that relate humans and all other living beings to the ultimate sources of life. Insofar as possible, this chapter will present a "tip-of-the-iceberg" sort of perspective on the common concerns expressed in these traditions. I prefer to use the terms *indigenous religious traditions* and not *indigenous religions* because the term *religion* by itself has a colonial connotation for many indigenous peoples, which reflects their historical relations with Christianity, Russian

Orthodoxy, and other so-called world religions that were complicit with colonialist expansion and its repression of the "other peoples" (indigenous), their rites and beliefs. For centuries, colonial societies have denied that indigenous peoples had "religions" at all; as the great photographer of Native North American cultures Edward S. Curtis stated, "There seems to be a broadly prevalent idea that the Indians lacked a religion. . . . Rather than being without a religion, every act of his life was according to divine prompting."

The difficulties in discussing "indigenous religious traditions" also lie in the fact that,

Fig. 1.1 Kwakwaka'wakw (Kwakiutl) potlatch with dancers and singers in photo by E. S. Curtiss.

unlike the "world religions," which have a center of faith, a body of orthodox doctrine (with a multitude of local traditions), a relatively unified politics, a meta-narrative, and a corpus of theological texts to which both scholars and laypeople can refer, indigenous religious traditions can only be characterized by diversity recognizing that each "people" (or "tribe" or "nation") has a unique vision of how the universe came into being, is structured, shapes peoples' behaviors in life, and can undergo periods of total collapse followed by regeneration. Those visions are communicated and transmitted mainly through oral narratives or performative remembering of primordial acts in collective ceremonies. No single set of features can be applied to the creator deities of indigenous peoples, nor do indigenous peoples necessarily understand the "function" of "creating" in the same way as non-indigenous peoples, since each indigenous culture has elaborated its own

system of meanings regarding what they believe to be the ultimate reality.

Similarly, while scholars can find relative agreement in meaning among the followers of a single "world religion" for notions such as "soul," the "afterlife," "the person"—with indigenous religious traditions, there is such a diversity of perspectives that, although it is possible to speak in general terms about some aspects of these notions, there are nevertheless wide variations in the ways each of them is understood. Indigenous religious traditions, in short, are characterized by *heterodoxy* in contrast with the orthodoxy of the world religions. There is no set of unique features characterizing all indigenous religious worldviews. For the purpose of understanding some of their similarities and differences with the so-called world religions, we will explore the beliefs and practices in a variety of indigenous traditions, but without making any claims to universalities.

Some Common Elements in Indigenous Religious Traditions

On the most general level, native traditions share one or more of the following features in their worldviews, or *orientations to ultimate reality*: (1) They attribute enormous importance to ancestral lands, sacred geography, and local sacred sites, which are seen as portals to the primordial past through which people can receive the original life-force of their own deities or ancestors. (2) Access to sacred knowledge is gained by those who have undergone the trials and privations of initiation or are apprentices to the religious specialists. (3) Great value is invested in kinship obligations (consanguineal and affinal) and their fulfillment, which are considered to be the arena of harmony and conflict, as well as key features in native peoples' orientations to ultimate reality. (4) The sacred traditions are transmitted principally by oral and performative means, through narratives about prior worlds, when communications between humans and other-than-human beings (animals, spirits, deities) were normal (5) They emphasize demonstrations of generosity, giving thanks to the creators for the gift of life and abundance, showing humility and rejection of displays of individual power and arrogance, seeking to abide by the "ways" of the ancestors, and being respectful to animals or other nonhuman beings. (6) They recognize the sacred powers of the spirits and deities and their material embodiment and emplacement in this world. These powers can be overwhelming—dangerously mixed blessings that impart to humanity special knowledge—or they can be focused in benevolent, caring, strong leadership that guides humans through their life crises. (7) They share responsibility in ensuring the continuity of the order established in primordial times, through the ritual means bestowed on humans in the primordial past.

Indigenous peoples have traditionally sought to forge their ways of life in consonance with all other forms of life in their natural surroundings. This has profound consequences for understanding their spiritualities. Firstly, all of life is conceived in terms of innumerable short- and long-term cycles, from the short cycles of flowering plants and the alternation of day and night to the longer cycles of human life, the life of social units, to the longest cycle of all: the cosmos, which—like human life—is born, grows old, transforms to the spirit world, and regenerates in a new cycle. Concepts of human life cycles are thus modeled on other life cycles of the world around them and the larger cosmos in which their world is situated. From the time children begin to become aware of the ways of the world, they are taught to be morally responsible for respecting and maintaining these cycles.

The extent to which indigenous religious traditions have developed calendric modes of time passage, the cycles sometimes can be extraordinarily long—for example, the Maya and Aztec of Central America are celebrated for having developed "long count calendars" that last tens of thousands of years, starting from the calculated date of creation to a foreseen "end-time," followed by the regeneration of life. It is remarkable how indigenous cultures the world over celebrate cosmos-generating rituals with such calendric precision that the religious specialists guard and transmit the times of long-cycle transitions over many generations (e.g., the new fire ceremony of the Aztecs, celebrated every fifty-two years; or the Sigi ceremony among the Dogon of Mali, which are celebrated in cycles of sixty years).

Fig. 1.2 Dogon masks, Mali, Africa.

Dogon mask dance. They are actors in a cosmic theater, aiming to re-create the creation of the world, of men, of vegetable and animal species, and of the stars. What is happening is that this period of danger and disorder that has been brought about by death is now brought to an end by the evocation of the fundamental moments in the genesis of the universe. The audience, enthusiastic but solemn, watches with great attention the development of the different stages in the ritual.

Secondly, humans are one among many kinds of animate beings who share in life-forces, or "souls," and whose "ways of life" or "cultures" are believed to be very similar. The belief that all beings possess one or more "souls"

is called *animism*. All beings in nature are animate, exercise intention (hunting, making shelters, performing rituals); however, the bodies of nonhuman beings (birds, fish, trees, stones) differ from humans and amongst themselves. Consequently, their perceptions of, and perspectives on, the life around them, their relations to other kinds of beings, and their senses of time and space vary. While many indigenous peoples believe that distinct kinds of beings may share similar cultural patterns, the perceptions of these "other peoples'" own worlds—which are biologically, historically, and culturally situated—in turn shape the ways they understand and relate to each other. So, according to the stories, a human may see a vulture (of the "vulture people," considered to be a potentially treacherous tribe) eating grubs from a rotten log on the ground, but from the vulture's point of view, it is actually catching live fish from a pool of water. The vulture, from its perspective, sees as living food what humans see as rot; the rot of the vulture in turn can ruin the corporeal beauty of human beings, making what was once beautiful become ugly with an abominable stench.

Shamans are prime examples of what it means to have a multi-perspectival point of view of the "worlds" that constitute the cosmos since they have been schooled in the mastery of the knowledge and powers of the "other peoples" in order to communicate with them. When a shaman's soul transforms into a jaguar, to the outside observer, it may look like he is "snuffing" or drinking a psychoactive, but from the shaman-jaguar's point of view, he is actually "drinking the blood of a deity," that is, incorporating its life-force, which enables the shaman's soul to transform into an other kind of being, a jaguar spirit, and fly into the other world of the deities.

Thirdly, indigenous peoples' worldviews are in general highly transformational, that is, one type of being may transform into another (animal into human or human to spirit, and vice versa). In primordial times, these transformations occurred very frequently because the "boundaries" of time, space, self, and other were as yet porous and indistinguishable. Today, primarily religious specialists (shamans, especially) are adept at soul transformation, while normal human beings' souls are believed to undergo transformation mainly during moments of ritually defined life passage. Only in certain contexts can nonhuman, spirit beings actually transform into humans; the vast majority of the other spirit beings retain their unique, visible, material form (as plants or animals), covering their invisible (except to shamans) forms or selves. If an exchange occurs between beings of different worlds, a transformation occurs in

Fig. 1.3 Nineteenth-century face mask from an island in the Torres Strait, Australia.

the item being exchanged. Thus external, material forms, or "bodies," cover spiritual forms. Furthermore, external bodily forms are often adorned and painted, indicating some vital quality of their inner selves.

Such religious acts as worshiping a deity, finding a lost soul, changing from one to another form of life, and intermixing of divine and human worlds are not only perfectly possible in these traditions but are also much desired. A person cannot become fully human with an adult identity, for example, until he or she has been introduced face-to-face with the sacred "other peoples" in initiatory experiences. This may have been the foundation for the monumental cave paintings found at Lascaux, for example, places where initiates were presented to the full power of the sacred "other" hidden within the depths of the earth.

Sacred narratives often explain differences between the perspectives of native and non-native peoples to be the result of separations that occurred at the end of the primordial age. At that time, non-native peoples were given certain kinds of knowledge and native peoples were instructed to live in the knowledge of their ancestors, which new generations of adults should reproduce.

Fourthly, natural forms of symmetry and asymmetry figure prominently in native representations of life—from the weaving of tapestries with designs that recall both natural and historical forms to the building of houses modeled on the structure of the cosmos. Social relations are also ideally based on symmetry—as, for example, in reciprocal trade relations in marriage—although asymmetric forms such as social inequalities emerge from differential access to and ownership of sacred power.

Societies with peoples not considered to be fully human by other societies (generally

Fig. 1.4 Shipibo bowl from Peru, on permanent display at the University of British Columbia's Museum of Anthropology, Vancouver, Canada.

actions of primordial beings and deities who made or transformed the features of this world, and left them for humans to care for and minister to their creations. Stated another way, the primordial beings left evidence of their presence in the marvelous forms of creation of this world (for example, Devil's Tower in the Black Hills, considered to be a sacred place for many native peoples of the Plains). Each of these creations has its own sacred time and space; humans are entrusted with the responsibility of caring for, preserving, and respecting what the primordial beings had made. The deities left material representations of their bodies in the earth, along with sacred symbols for humans to use in ceremonies in order to remember and renew their connections with the divinities.

One of the great dilemmas in native thought is how a world in which there is constant change developed from a primordial condition of infinite space and unchanging time. How can a way of life be perpetuated for all times despite constant changes that threaten order with chaos? How can human life, with all its limitations, transcend the trials of death and decay? The most important way is re-membering primordial acts and events through rituals that prominently feature sacred symbols associated with the bodies of the deities. The sacred is in some way always and everywhere present in contemporary life as long as humans—especially the knowledgeable elders, priests, holy people, or shamans—continue to guard, keep, and minister to the sacred in this world. The major world religions, by contrast, require loyalty to hierarchical structures, centralization of religious authority, and constant renewal of the historical founders' original acts enshrined for all to worship, where spiritual governance has become hegemonic in its power.

based on cosmology and creation narratives, but also captives of war) have often been used in exchange relations or to labor for their "superiors." Captives of war, for example, were sometimes incorporated into the societies of their captors as domestic servants or laborers. This inequality does not necessarily imply the kind of chattel slavery as understood by the West. Although hierarchical relations of dominance and submission have certainly been documented in many historical indigenous societies of the world, the relations of master or owner can rather refer to relations of symbiosis, complementarity, authority, and obedience on the model of parental relations to children, or owners to their domesticated pets.

Fifthly, indigenous peoples believe all life to have come into existence through the

Fig. 1.5 Aboriginal Art of the Dreamtime, Carnarval Gorge, Australia.

Sixthly, native religious thought can be profoundly dualistic. All of existence can be divided into a series of interlocking, complementary oppositions, producing a whole (similar to the principles of yin and yang in Chinese Taoism). Life and death, female and male, harmony and disharmony, self and other produce dynamics that play themselves out on the stage of life in history, as they do in any culture. In non-christianized, indigenous religious traditions, however, notions of "good" and "evil" are not understood in terms of a struggle from which there will finally emerge a victor; rather, the "enemy other" is actually seen as necessary for the existence of collective self-identity. Sorcery, while discouraged and feared, is as much a part of tribal spiritual life as the harmonious joy of celebrating and dancing with one's own kin and allies from other tribes. Further, sorcery may be seen as a necessary societal mechanism for limiting the abuses of power or to redress perceived wrongs.

"We Are from the Forest, Earth, and Air": Universal Knowledge

The following speech was presented by a Barasana shaman, Tukanoan-speaking indigenous people from the Northwest Amazon in Colombia, to accompany the film "Traditional Knowledge of the Jaguar-Shamans of the Yuruparí Tradition." This tradition was officially included in 2011 by UNESCO in its "Representative List of the Intangible Cultural Heritage of Humanity."[1] Centuries ago, all of the indigenous cultures of the Northwest Amazon region and upper Orinoco had traditions similar to the one presented here. After several centuries of historical contact, the reduction in the indigenous populations due to diseases, enslavement, and rubber-gathering, along with Catholic and Protestant missionary repression of the tradition on the basis of a false association with the Christian devil, has meant that this tradition—which is based on a profound understanding of the sources of "vital energy" in the cosmos—remains alive only among a few communities. For that reason, the Barasana people sought to protect the traditions from disappearing altogether by seeking UNESCO recognition as a vital heritage. Similarly, their neighbors of the Arawak language family have gained international recognition for their jaguar-shamans' knowledge of Yuruparí.

As the following statement shows, the Yuruparí tradition speaks to issues of cultural continuity and spiritual links with the entire habitat, and is an embodied and emplaced spirituality (see figures 1.6–9 below):

"Traditional Knowledge of the Jaguar-Shamans of Yuruparí"

(spoken by Maximiliano Garcia, Makuna of the Northwest Amazon, Colombia; translation by the author)

We are from the forest, the earth, from the air itself;
We come from the Ancestral Anaconda,
Historically we have protected the environment. We are like Guardians, the Protectors of Nature. We are owners of universal knowledge!
We are from the Pira-paraná River,
Territory of the Jaguars of Yuruparí
Our ancestors travelled from the lower part of the Apaporis River,
Entering the Caquetá River, then crossing over the Apaporis River.
Going to the headwaters of the Apaporis River,
And entering the Pira-paraná until reaching its headwaters.
We are the many different ethnic groups living there with different languages.

Each group has its own way of taking care of the world.
Its own way of carrying out healing,
But we all share the same system for taking care of the world.
. . .
Knowledge is made up of physical and spiritual elements. There are elements that enable thought to continue,
Such as the yajé vine.
The Yuruparí plumage
And the Maloca [longhouse] which is a physical representation of the cosmos;
With each of its divisions symbolizing the most important sites of the territory
And is the center of knowledge for taking care of the territory,
According to the seasons of the ecological and cultural calendar.
There is also coca and tobacco,
Coca is a very valuable element for the continuity of knowledge;

Fig. 1.6 Yuruparí jaguar shamans.

Fig. 1.7   Dance of the Panpipes, northwest Amazon.

For the continuation of knowledge that enables learning.
Because coca is "thought,"
It is a means that enables us to understand things better.
That enables us to have an appropriate and healthy system of human behavior.
Tobacco is the very essence of life,
It is like the sensitivity that exists within a human body.
Which enables us to understand better, to accept things with wisdom.
Just as we have vital organs for the functioning of our bodies,
So the territory has its vital organs.
Its vital organs are the sacred sites
Found in rivers, hills, lakes, or stones.
In these places, there is knowledge.
There is wisdom,
There is understanding and power.

It is here that the system of organized thought
And self-governance are concentrated.
They are sites where energy flows and which gives life to the rest of nature.
Traditional knowledge is reflected in the daily activities of the women,
It is a knowledge they have acquired over millennia for preparing food.
For carrying out rituals, for caring for the family.
For health and for the transfer of this knowledge
Our knowledge is a holistic system
That is not concentrated only in the shaman.
Or in specific people.
. . .
We want to conserve this knowledge
Because it is our life.
It is the knowledge of the forest.

Fig. 1.8 Hipana, the sacred waterfalls that mark the place of origin of indigenous peoples of northwest Amazon.

And with this we want to guarantee life for
all people on this earth.
The continuity of the knowledge, of
"thought," the power to care for the
territory,
This is the model for living
That we have maintained for a long time.
It is the model left to us by our ancestors
And this is what we want to preserve.
It is a model that can help
With intercultural tools,
For solving the global environmental crisis.

Maintaining Life and Health through Ritual

The mythical and cosmological structures that
make up the traditional knowledge of the jaguar-shamans of Yuruparí represent the cultural
heritage of the many ethnic groups living along
the Pirá Paraná River in southeastern Colombia, in the department of Vaupés. According to
ancestral wisdom, the Pirá Paraná forms the
heart of a large area called the "territory of the
jaguars of Yuruparí," the "jaguars" being the jaguar-shamans, an elite group of highly trained
and knowledgeable specialists who guard the
ancient knowledge of the cosmos. They understand that the cosmos is a living being with
"sources" of energy, just as the human body has
its own "sources" of energy that make the life
force (blood) flow throughout the system. In
other words, the sacred sites contain vital spiritual energy that nurtures all living beings in the
world.

The jaguar-shamans follow a calendar of
ceremonial rituals, based on their sacred traditional knowledge, to draw the community
together, heal, prevent sickness, and revitalize

Fig. 1.9 Jaguar mortar, Chorrera culture, east coast of Ecuador (1500–300 BCE).

nature. The rituals feature songs and dances that constitute the healing process. The vital energy and traditional knowledge of the shamans are believed to be inherited from a powerful, mythical demiurge called "Yuruparí," which, among the Barasana, was an anaconda that lived as a person and is today embodied in very sacred trumpets that are made from a palm tree, which altogether make up the body parts of the Anaconda Ancestor. Each ethnic group conserves its own Yuruparí trumpets, which form the centerpiece in the most sacred *Hee Biki* (Grandfather Anaconda) ritual. During this ritual, traditional guidelines for maintaining the health of the people and the territory are transmitted to male children as a part of their passage into adulthood. The traditional knowledge concerning care of children, pregnant women, and food preparation is transmitted among women. In short, in the Northwest Amazon, indigenous peoples' heritages are embodied in the sacred instruments, which are the vehicle that enables the young initiates to grow and understand the world, and to live a healthy life. They were, in Tukanoan tradition,

created at sacred places, which are conceived of today as the vital organs of the founding ancestor of the tradition.

Among the Kogi peoples, a priestly society of the Sierra Nevada of northern Colombia, the *mama* priests likewise have a deep knowledge of the dynamics of nature in the universal sense, known as the "law of *Aluma*," or the "Great Mother." Changes in the environmental cycles due to global warming prompted Kogi priests in 1995 and 2012 to issue a "Warning to the Younger Brother" in the form of two BBC films, explaining how the ways of life of the white man "younger brothers" are bringing on the destruction of the planet. The priests' message urges that something be done immediately before the world is completely destroyed.

Fig. 1.10 Native Americans from southeastern Idaho, late nineteenth to early twentieth centuries.

Fig. 1.11   Early twentieth-century Catholic mission station in Nauru, Micronesia.

Contact, Displacement, Prophecy: Indigenous Religious Traditions over Time

After centuries of contact, few—if any—indigenous peoples can be said to be living the same religious traditions as their ancestors of four or five centuries ago. With regard to the importance of ancestral lands, historical change has been most dramatic in countries such as the United States, where the policy of forced removal from ancestral lands and relocation to government-designated reservations or boarding schools dramatically changed Native peoples' lifeways and religious traditions, forcing many of the elder religious specialists to seek alternative ways of guarding the traditions. Not all were successful, and these changes caused

irreparable harm to the indigenous peoples and their cultures.

Those non-indigenous societies, assuming a constantly expanding frontier and exhibiting an unrelenting drive to settle and develop supposedly "unoccupied" lands with "unlimited" resources, have paid little attention—until very recently—to the long-term future of environmental effects on the populations of humans and nonhumans whose predecessors have lived on those lands for thousands of years. With few exceptions, all of these factors have radically changed native peoples' relations to their ancestral homelands and consequently put in question the viability of maintaining their ceremonies and traditions. By far the greatest struggle that indigenous peoples throughout the world have confronted over centuries of contact with exogenous, invading societies has been the latter's drive to homogenize land and people, against the fundamental principles of cultural diversity that have defined native cultures for millennia. Nevertheless, in recent years, with the increasing recognition of indigenous peoples' cultural rights by international institutions, many native peoples have seen this moment as a welcome opportunity to establish protective guarantees for their cultures and religious traditions. By the same token, sometimes these so-called revitalization movements have been politically driven to acquire external funding, which is ultimately used to re-signify and update traditional culture.

Among indigenous societies in many regions of the world (especially the Americas,

Fig. 1.12 Wooden statues of nineteenth-century native savant, Kamiko, a Baniwa prophet.

Africa, and Melanesia), the phenomenon of "prophet movements" characterized early contact histories, in which visionaries and religious savants proclaimed the imminence of a new order, following a period of transition in which the invading societies would either be eliminated or be forced to assume a subordinate position. These prophesied utopian orders often celebrate the coming of a religious regime of "world transcendence," negating the reality of death as well as the military power of the outsiders.

Prophets have fulfilled numerous other functions. Prominent among these has been their leadership in rebellions against colonial oppression, utilizing ideologies grounded in mythological themes of world destruction and renewal. They initiate what in many cases eventually became historical traditions of religious resistance; their movements cannot with any justice be considered as passing reactions to domination. Their views of the coming end-times offer distinctly spiritual solutions of transformation that cannot be understood solely through social scientific "explanations" of such phenomena in political, economic, or military terms.

Features that have been common to prophet movements from early colonial times to the present day include political and economic displacement; the expectation of an imminent catastrophe and the reinstallation of a paradisiacal state; the awaiting of a salvific figure, who helps people out of the path of destruction from the whites; the total suspension of normal living routines; rejection or eager acceptance of foreign clothes, goods, or foods; ceaseless dancing and unbroken festival performances as signs of admission into the envisioned utopia; dreams and visions; miraculous abundance of food; the incarnation of gods in material or human form;

the prominence of celestial powers; the reversion of the transformed earth to native control; arduous restrictions on believers; and the transformation of the believers' bodies into healthy, invulnerable, or even immortal beings.

Historical prophet movements have often been marked by the ways in which native peoples have appropriated Christian symbols, practices, and representations of authority, often independently of any kind of missionary interference. Christian missionaries, for their part, have often been surprised by the manner in which native peoples have converted en masse to the religions they have introduced—sometimes with the same enthusiasm with which they have followed prophetic leaders. Conversion movements can be interpreted as solutions to two kinds of issues faced by native societies:

one, external, referring to the disorganizing and de-structuring effects of contacts with nonnative societies. Such disorganization frequently manifests itself as a rise in accusations of witchcraft and sorcery, demonstrating the unease and the threats to traditional ways of life by the advance of Western civilization and the transformations it brings. Conversion offers moral reform, which enables native peoples to control the witchcraft and regain their integrity vis-à-vis intruders. The other problem is internal, having to do with dilemmas inherent to cosmologies and inherited from primordial times; for example, the ontological status of affinal (in-law, "outsider," "other") groups and their perceived threat to the continuity of consanguineal or descent kin groups; the challenges of harnessing dangerous shamanic power for the

Fig. 1.13 Engraving of a nineteenth-century New England missionary preaching in a kukui grove in Hawaii.

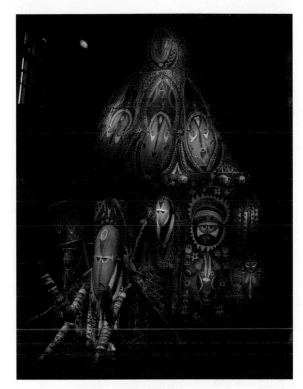

Fig. 1.14   Initiation ritual tableau in a ceremonial house in village of Apangai, Papua, New Guinea.

purposes of social reproduction; and so forth. Clearly, explanations may draw equally on both hypotheses.

Cosmogony: The Primordial Times of Creation

There is an enormous diversity in the scenarios of creation that indigenous peoples have elaborated. Sacred stories sometimes affirm the divine origin of the universe as an "intention," a self-germinating seed, floating in an infinite space of nothingness. The primordial state of being undergoes transformations, gradually or abruptly, over multiple epochs. Creation may unfold as the thought, dream, or intentions of divine being(s), who, after numerous episodes

of relating how they made the world ready for peoples (in the broadest sense of the term *people*), later withdraw from creation leaving future generations to take care of the new world. The divine beings are self-generated and self-generating principles that set the universe in motion. They hold within themselves the duality of being and becoming, manifesting themselves as specific phenomenal beings (the sun, moon, animals, etc.), although, in so doing, they do not lose their original nature of constant becoming or intentionality.

In other cases, creation occurs through the transformations initiated by primordial beings from some preexisting state or condition to a radically other state, which is then transmitted for all future generations. Countless narratives affirm the existence of other worlds that preexisted the current one; each is imperfect and suffers catastrophic destruction by flood, fire, other natural disasters, putrefaction, or petrifaction. From this destruction, a variety of symbols appear, which then serve as vehicles through which the order created can be reproduced and new worlds brought into being.

Thus, in the sacred text of the Quiche Maya, called *Popol Vuh* (Book of Counsel), the first humans were "mudmen" who had no possibility of sustaining life—they were simply dissolved. The second was a race of beings made of wood, which again did not satisfy the gods and was destroyed by a flood. A third, a race of humans was excessively vain and also did not satisfy the gods because the humans could see like the gods and tried to be like them. So the gods threw dust in their eyes and made them short-sighted; these first men and women were then made to praise and give thanks to the deities as well as to populate the earth.

Native peoples imagine the primordial times as epochs when all was possible,

Fig. 1.15 Map of indigenous religious traditions in the world.

GREENLAND
(to Denmark)

C A N A D A

PACIFIC

OCEAN

UNITED STATES
OF AMERICA

ATLANTIC

OCEAN

MEXICO

BELIZE

GUATEMALA   HONDURAS   VENEZUELA

NICARAGUA   GUYANA
                                 SURINAM
COSTA RICA   COLOMBIA   FRENCH GUIANA

PANAMA

ECUADOR

                              B R A Z I L

PERU

BOLIVIA

PARAGUAY

CHILE

ARGENTINA   URUGUAY

NEW
ZEALAND

0   1200 miles

0   1800 kms

N

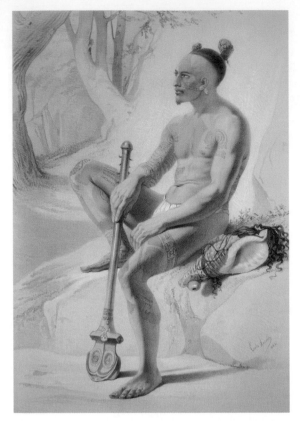

Fig. 1.16 Tattooed indigenous man from New Caledonia, Oceania, 1846.

this orderly transmission, the original order has been subject to all manner of disorganization, departure from the original norms, and senseless violence. Harmony versus disharmony, and predation versus reciprocal relations are the elements of eternal struggles in which humans seek to maintain not only order, beauty, and harmony but also the means for controlling abuses of power, in whatever form they take.

For many native peoples, creation is not a closed circle in which what happened in the primordial times will last for eternity, for often the stories leave the question unanswered of whether the creator ever really went away forever or still lives somewhere in the present world. Also, divine order may occasionally intervene in history when conditions call for it, through prophets whose messages, received from their deities, warn not only of coming dangers or offer a utopia where there will be no more sickness or suffering but also give counsel, preparing the souls of their followers to always remain watchful and faithful to the old ways.

Cosmology: Space, Time, and the Orderly Structures of the Universe

There are two main orientations of spatial structure: horizontal and vertical. Neither consists of continuous, straight-line arrangements of different worlds of spirit beings and deities. The complex constructions of indigenous cosmologies and the plethora of values associated with the different parts of the cosmos permit us to make only a few broad generalizations. Usually, native peoples think of each of the multiple worlds in the universe as relatively flat planes, circular and bounded by water. Some traditions

undifferentiated, simultaneous, when the forms of things had not become fixed. Either a single creator being or a group of creators lived in a perilous world in which humans, animals, and spirits warred among themselves, committed errors that would later become part of the human condition, sought to create order despite the perennial existence of anti-order that destroyed what was created, and so on.

Another phase in the history of creation introduced into the world the essential means for biological and cultural transmission—namely, sacred plants, sacred sounds and musical instruments, and sacred rituals, leaving these for all future generations. Although humanity was given the responsibility for maintaining represent islands of earth piled up on top of a primordial water animal such as the turtle, others as pieces of rock floating in endless space, yet connected with other worlds by various kinds of holes and tubes running through their centers. Horizontal structures include markers of the main directions (mountains, lakes), as well as one or more centers, comprising a sacred geography of important places situated around a center. The universe is a series of layers, which can be arranged either vertically or horizontally, which are different "worlds" in which different kinds of beings live.

The vertical structures of the universe vary widely in composition, from simple three-layer arrangements (upper world, middle world, underworld) to massive, multilayer compositions inhabited by a great variety of beings. There is a clear correlation between the multilayered-cosmos idea and the structures of spiritual power or knowledge in society, as well as, homologously, the arrangement of the vital points on a person's body (heart, umbilicus, crown), which connect the person with the spiritual sources of power and knowledge.

In general, the upper worlds are associated with the creative and life-renewing forces of light (the sun), lightness, and liquids (rain), with important places where soul transformation takes place, as well as dwellings of the ancestors, often featured as worlds of order, beauty, and happiness. They may be associated with the highest deities, the primordial beings who were responsible for all of creation and its imperfections.

The underworlds are associated with places of darkness, netherworlds of the bodily remains of the dead, animal souls, and monstrous, inverted beings who can cause sickness to humans. Or they consist of worlds where the progenitors of animals transform the souls of the dead into animals who return to earth and provide food for their descendants and family in times of need.

The middle world, the center of the universe, is the place where all life-forms as we know them, began, including human life. Tropical-forest peoples imagine the earthly plane as the concentric rings of a tree, considering the innermost circle of the earthly plane the most ancient, where the "true people" live while the outer rings represent different moments in time, associated with different places and "other peoples" they have experienced or become aware of; the outermost layer, the bark of the tree, is the border between one people's universe and another's. Different kinds of space and places of being in the horizontal layers are systematically related to one another through the narratives that delineate the extent of each people's "worlds."

Horizontal spaces highlight the center, or multiple centers, associated with a wide variety of images (cosmic trees, mountains, waterfalls, ladders, vines) symbolizing sources of energy in the cosmos. These form part of the larger conception of the universe-as body, consisting of multiple organs and energies that work together. The peripheries, or spaces on the outer margins, often express in inverted form (demonic spirits, enemy others, "outsiders") the key values of the center. These enemy others constantly seek ways of penetrating a people's universe to predate on its food supply or to realize some other form of exchange. A variety of intermediary elements, openings, and penetrations connect inner and outer realms in the same way that upper and lower realms are interrelated. In native South American cosmologies, the places where sacred beings first appeared often become models for innumerable spatial constructs.

Indigenous cosmologies illustrate a remarkable quality of flexibility in their construction.

Far from being fixed and static "things out there" or "models of how the universe is structured," cosmologies are better described in terms of their plasticity, their capacities to expand and contract, their permeability (that is, their "openness" to the external world). Mythic narratives of the creation often display this feature of expanding and contracting worlds to mark major moments of transition and growth from one state of being to another. The religious specialists are the "guardians," as well as the "artisans" of the cosmos, for they interpret events and occurrences in relation to possibilities of cosmic change.

The creation stories often provide a "cultural cartography" of the territorial conceptions of indigenous peoples. As one ethnographer notes, "Virtually every landmark in the forest or along the river has some significance in the myths of origin of one group or another." These symbolic conceptions of space have persisted despite substantial changes in social organization and economic and political life. They are integral to the cultural identity, health, and continuity of indigenous peoples. Along with indigenous environmental and land-use knowledge, these conceptions of identity are fundamental to the determination of land-tenure policies and the delineation of indigenous territories in modern peoples' attempts to have a positive effect upon the conservation of ecosystems. To incorporate indigenous environmental knowledge, land-use practices, and conceptions of sacred space into an indigenous territorial model entails combining detailed ethnographic, historical, and ecological knowledge. Linking these cultural conceptions with political, economic, and religious considerations provides an integrated approach to the conservation of ecosystems and is more in keeping with the land-extensive subsistence practices of indigenous societies.

Beings and Their Relationships

This section discusses the nature of humans and other-than-human beings who populate the world and with whom native peoples interact.

Interrelationality

What constitutes, for indigenous peoples, the self, the person, categories of person-in-time (ancestors and their descendants)? The person consists of several "souls," modes of consciousness, mental and physical faculties, intentionalities, sentiments, bodies, along with ongoing relatedness to different kinds of beings. The religious beliefs and practices of indigenous peoples are characterized by a conviction that spirit moves through all things, animate and inanimate, subjects and objects, and that the living are intimately connected with the souls of their deceased ancestors.

The universe is most definitely not a human-centered place to live but consists of multiple types of beings, each in its own spaces, each having distinct points of view, attributes, physical and spiritual characteristics. Each kind of being is related to most others through culturally defined types of relations—for example, predator/prey, ally/enemy, master/pet, owner/owned, parent/children, in-laws, and so on.

The elaborate structures of space and time that order the universe, coupled with the frequent beliefs in multiple souls and a rich symbolism of the human body, integrate humanity into the cosmic system through which life unfolds. Humans' relationships to the divine are often mediated by priests, shamans, diviners, religious artists, and other specialists. These interactions take the form of worship, prayers of thanksgiving, and supplication, sacrifice, mystical union with divinities, ritual combat with spirits, or the celebration of divinely instituted festivals, preferably as nearly as possible to the way they were done "in the beginning."

Bodies and Souls

L. Sullivan[2] has distinguished two systematic tendencies with regard to beliefs regarding the soul in South America but that may apply to other areas of the globe as well: (1) There is a physiological element, which affirms that the soul is situated in specific body parts, coterminous with the functioning of the bodily organs and defined by "animal" appetites (food, sex). Often, such souls extend to animals who are the doubles of their counterpart human soul-elements. (2) There is also an epistemological element, in which spiritual elements are associated with specific human faculties (thought, memory). Here, the human being is affirmed as a self-contained and autonomous being set apart from the object of its perceptions. These are broad categories that are not necessarily separable but rather manifest themselves in synaesthetically intertwined images of beauty and sensual delight, or fear of unknown powers.

In some cultures, the most important of the souls are linked in a network extending back to the primordial times; in others, the stronger attachment of the soul may be with ceremonial groups based on names, residence, or types of ritual performance.

Among the Guarani peoples of South America, there are two kinds of souls: one is linked to the animal appetites of the person, while the other—considered to be more important because it comes from the ancestors—is the "name-soul," which is bestowed on the child by a shaman shortly after the child's birth. The name-soul is the reincarnation of the ancestor into life; the name-soul is the sacred life-principle of the person. All throughout one's life, the person must struggle to maintain the strength of the spiritual name-soul over the physical appetites and desires or emotions of the animal soul. One does this by singing the "beautiful words" that come in inspiration from the ancestors.

Multiple souls gained throughout a lifetime constitute the person and his or her connections with other beings (e.g., companion spirits). Each of these souls leaves the body at the moment of death and returns to the place in the cosmos from which it originally came. Dream-souls and dream interpretation are particularly important in identifying the souls of other peoples, enemies, and sorcerers. Sonic imagery—in naming ceremonies, sacred music and song, drumming, sacred flutes and trumpets—is fundamental to the production of the

Fig. 1.17 Quoniambec, Tupinamba Chief, sixteenth century CE.

person. A rich symbolism of corporality is connected to the notion of the person. Through this symbolism, indigenous cultures express fundamental values defining spaces constitutive of human life.

Among the meanings attributed to the notion of "transformation" in indigenous belief and practice is that human bodies and "selves" are complex and socially constructed. Traditionally, this has been expressed through body ornaments, masks, "coverings" or clothing, mantles of jaguar pelts, bird feathers, bear robes, loincloths, body painting, tattooing, and hairstyles. These kinds of "clothing," adornments, and alterations are often understood both as ways of "domesticating" an animal interior, essential to the socialization of cultural beings, while highlighting a specific cognitive, spiritual quality or power that the person has gained through life passages. These external manifestations mediate between the interior self, society, and the cosmos. In rites of passage (birth, initiation, and death), persons acquire cognitive and emotional qualities, which constitute them as persons.

The body is also the locus of moral issues that are fundamental to becoming fully human. In many cultures, control over body orifices—by fasting, for example—is the mark of a fully cultural human being, while transgressions of boundaries between beings that ought to be maintained separate provoke catastrophic transformations; this is perhaps the most important knowledge that initiates acquire when they are exposed for the first time to the sacred.

A beautifully decorated body is one that is fully ornamented, with earrings, beadwork, kneebands, featherwork, elaborate hairstyles. Body painting or tattoos, representing a variety of metaphysical and moral properties, are etched in exquisitely symmetrical patterns, as

Fig. 1.18 Totem on an Indian (Tlingit) grave, Wrangell, Alaska.

among the Maori peoples of New Zealand or the Marquesas Islanders.

Being a member of a community implies consubstantiality, that is, the sharing of body fluids as in sexual relations, or spiritual connections to ancestors such as a collective umbilical cord–soul, or even a collective body-soul, common to members of the same social group, (nuclear or extended families, siblings, clans).

Body painting is intimately connected with notions of self and other and can thus be linked to historical contact—for example, a change in diet regime, or food taboos, or conversion to Christianity bring about fundamental changes in notions of corporality (often in a negative sense), sicknesses such as obesity, diabetes, caries, and a host of other irregularities.

Ancestors and descendants

The importance of bonds that tie the ancestors' deeds to their living human descendants are found throughout the indigenous world: in North America, there is the emphasis on the importance of a person's acts having repercussions for the "seventh generation." In South America, for the peoples of the Northwest Amazon, the deities created a world "for their descendants," a bond that ties the ancestors' deeds (whether these were errors or gifts) to living and future humans, who must abide by that order and are responsible for reproducing that order, until another "end-of-the-world." Similarly, the concept of a continuing relationship of mutual dependence between the living and their ancestors is central to Mapuche (Chile) religion and the moral order of their society. Among the Guarani Indians of the southern Cone of South America, cults to the bones of ancestral holy people (*karai*, "big men") have been well documented. In Africa, Siberia, and elsewhere, families maintain ancestral shrines with the assistance of local shamans. In Australia, as in Africa, Amazonia, and highland South America, the physical landscape is seen as a sacred geography, where portals to the sacred are found everywhere in the traces and marks left by the ancestors for their descendants to remember their deeds and as guides for the future.

Ritual life

Rituals are highlighted by feasts held at important moments of the agricultural cycle, or by the spectacular rites of passage for moments of birth, initiation, and death throughout the indigenous world. These renew the links of humanity with primordial creative powers. Ritual music, songs, and chants are the great symbols of religious culture, expressing change, social and cultural reproduction over time, and the very acts of creation.

Religious specialists

Shamans, priests, diviners, ceremonial dancers, sorcerers, artisans, and prophets are responsible for managing these interrelations, interpreting the realities of the external worlds of other peoples, spirits, enemies to people of their own society, coordinating ritual relations among spirits and humans, ensuring that the most fundamental principles of the universe are observed, acting as the guardians of morality, holding at bay possible attacks from spirit beings, determining whether the newly arrived Europeans were human, and so on. Religious specialists differ ontologically from "normal" beings of a species. (Animals and plants may have their shamans or medicine people too.)

Generally speaking, whereas the shamans derive their power from direct knowledge and experience of the deities and places of the cosmos, the priest's or holy person's power is based on the accurate recall of canonical and esoteric knowledge, which is essential for rites of passage—that is, for the reproduction of society, the renewal of the world, and the ontological categories that define the nature of being. While the shamans are relatively more egalitarian or "democratic" in their internal organization—that is, anyone can become a shaman who accepts the years of arduous training and perilous experiences—the priests come from a specific lineage or class chosen at birth and are trained throughout their lives. Priestly *functions*, it should be noted, such as chanting at passage rites, may also be exercised by the elderly men or women of the society without there being a recognized class of priests with political and religious functions.

Traditionally, priestly societies are organized into hierarchies and sacred societies, linked to the distinct functions priests may perform. While the shaman's influence and prestige depends on his or her performance and capacity to retain a local clientele, the priests' influence extends over large networks of communities who depend on them for their knowledge and power. At initiation rites, postbirth and postdeath rites, a new group of adults, or a natal family, or the integration of the deceased into the communities of ancestral souls, all imply shifts in the composition of the entire society to a new situation. In some societies such as in ancient Mongolia, priests could at the same time be shamans as well as diviners and political leaders. [3]

Eschatology

A final important dimension of religious life in indigenous traditions is eschatology, which refers to views of the end of times, whether that be the death of a specific individual or the demise of the cosmos itself. At the death of an individual, all of the components, spiritual and material, that have been bestowed on that person during his or her lifetime may become reintegrated into ongoing cosmic processes. The afterlife of an individual is imagined in a wide range of potential forms, sometimes as a process of alienation from the world of the living and enclosure in a separate existence without meaningful interactions, and other times as reincarnation in some other form, or an ongoing communication between the living and the dead. Eschatology also refers to the broader cosmic sense of the end-times as the "end of the world," the destruction and regeneration of the universe in general.

As we have seen above, indigenous traditions generally attribute enormous importance to the mystery and power of death as an integral part of human existence. For many cultures, the condition of mortality implies a transitory, ephemeral life, one of constant metamorphoses. Sacred stories often explain that death entered the world in the context of a trial—the failure to pass a test or to undergo an ordeal, making a fatal choice, or giving an inopportune signal. The rituals associated with death are among the most elaborate of all processes of passage, occupying a critical theme in all native traditions. These involve processes of administering the passage of the deceased between existence in this world and incorporation into the other, processes of healing the sentiments of kin whom the deceased have left behind.

Anthropophagy, for example, was once a practice among various peoples of lowland South America, of Papua New Guinea and other areas of the world. It generally took two forms: the consumption of the flesh remains or the ashes of a cremated kinsperson or the consumption of the flesh of the enemy killed in war. The first practice has been shown to be more related to assuaging the intense suffering, or "consuming grief,"[4] at the moment of loss of close kin.

Among the hill-dwelling indigenous peoples of the northern Philippines, the practice of taking heads was not only a demonstration of a young man's becoming a warrior, but it was also a way of casting away the burden of grief at the loss of kin because of feuds and raiding, and in that sense it can be considered a piacular rite.[5] For the Tupian-speaking peoples of the Atlantic coastal region of South America, the elaborate rituals related to warfare, taking captives, sacrificing the captives, and eating the flesh of one's enemy represented a critical transition that had as much to do with vengeance as they did with reproducing the social foundations of

Fig. 1.19 Inca cult figurine, located in the Enthnological Museum, Berlin, Germany.

time and memory. Shamanic vengeance and warfare were other means for retribution at the loss of kin and the grief death brings.

Spectacular solutions to the dilemma of what to do with the deceased of the noble classes in more complex indigenous societies can be seen in the mummification practices of the Inca. All efforts seemed to deny that death had taken the deceased royalty away; rather, the royal deceased continued to hold a privileged position socially, ritually, and politically in their society long after being placed in tombs, where specially designated persons gave them food and drink and cared for them. In societies such as those of the Xingu region of central Brazil, the *Kwarup* ceremony is regularly held as a pan-tribal occasion, lasting several weeks, explicitly

to "honor the dead," the most important chiefs and aristocracy of the tribes.

In the Americas and other areas of the globe, it is common to find the theme of immortality in myth as a condition that existed in the primordial world: at the moment of death, the person would be secluded for a period of time, at the end of which he or she would reemerge rejuvenated. This cycle of eternal return was interrupted by the error of a person, and so mortality was introduced into the world. Shamans and prophets, however, are believed to "never die" and continue to give counsel to their living kin at their burial places. In this, we see direct links between notions of immortality among native peoples of the highlands and lowlands of South America.

In numerous eschatologies, the entrance of the soul of the deceased into the other world is conditioned on his or her moral behavior and virtues in this life: those who kill, for example, do not succeed in completing the way of the dead souls, falling into an abyss or being attacked by swarms of bees (as among the Makiritare of the Orinoco region of South America). The notions different peoples have about life after death vary a great deal, from a completely other existence, an inverted image of this world, to the transformation of the

Fig. 1.20 Petroglyphs near the west bank of the Orinoco River at Caicara, Venezuela.

deceased into the gods after being devoured by them, or the transmigration of the souls of the deceased into species of game animal that may serve the living as food in times of need.

Eschatologies not only refer to the end-times but also to the possibility of a future regeneration, after the destruction of this world. The cosmogonies of many indigenous cultures throughout the world contain the seeds of regenerative hope, and therefore we should not consider the movements associated with them as the exclusive result of external pressures, as they many times have been, but rather as pondered and divinely guided solutions for dilemmas and processes internal to the native cosmogonies themselves. In all cases, prophets—emissaries of the deities—have acted as interpreters of the signs of the times, foreseeing the violent destruction as a necessary condition for the regeneration of the world.

Creating the World and the Day: A Baniwa Account from the Northwest Amazon

The following selection is the first episode of the creation story of the Baniwa Indians of the Northwest Amazon region in Brazil (taped in 1998, from the oldest living shaman then alive) and is followed by an interpretation of the story.

In the beginning there was only a little stone ball called *Hekwapi*
Nothing else around. A vast expanse of nothing around the little ball.
There was no land, no people, just the little ball of stone.
So the [Creator] "child of the Universe" looked for earth. He sent the great dove *Tsutsuwa* to find earth for him,

and put it all over the little ball. He made that stone ball become the earth.
The name of the "Universe child" was *Hekwapi ienipe*.
He made the Sun rise up then above the new earth, above the hole in the earth called *Hipana*, the navel of the Universe.
The Universe-child was all alone, so he went to look for people.
He went to the Universe-navel at *Hipana*, the navel of the sky.
He heard people coming out of the hole, singing their names as they came.
They came out one after another, and he sent each one to their piece of the earth.
Then he looked for night, he obtained night which was inside a little, tightly-sealed basket.
On receiving the basket of night, its spirit-owner instructed him to open it only when he reached home.
On his way back home, he marveled at its weight and opened the basket up just a little bit,
Then darkness burst out, covering the world with the first night,
and the sun fell out the western door.
The Universe-child waited for the sun to return,
He and the birds waited for it to return.
When they saw the sun entering the sky vault at the eastern door, the birds began to sing—
For it was the beginning of a new day.

The Universe child embodies the idea of self-generation. How did it come into being? There is no answer; it always was, along with the little stone ball, and the vast emptiness around it. In one sense, the Universe child means the universe *as* child, which throws a new light on the nature of the first being. The universe was not like any human being but rather was more like an "illuminated intention," the great spirit whose external body shape was the sun, which later underwent various bodily transformations over time. In other words, rather than imagining the creator deity as a "human-like person," it is better to think of a self-generated and generating principle that brings into the light of day the first generation of living beings and distributes them on parcels of land all over the earth, which was at that time still miniature.

There is a deep hole located at the place, called *Hipana*, considered to be the center of the universe, the connection to the other world through a spiritual pathway that only the shamans and dead souls can follow, the opening through which ancestral beings emerged from their prior, virtual existence into the first world. This opening is called the "Universe Umbilicus," the primal cord of birth, an idea that is commonly associated with religious traditions

grounded in the concept of descent, here in the male line, as the central axis that generates all life. That axis, according to the traditions, became embodied in the child of the sun deity, who introduced the first rites of initiation to humanity. Through the powerful sounds made by this being, the world opened up to its present size. These powerful sounds are engraved on the boulders of the sacred rapids, as an everlasting reminder of origin.

Indigenous religious traditions, as we have seen in this chapter, focus on many of the same issues and concerns that we see in all other religious traditions. The complementarity of opposites—for example, good and evil, dark and light, shaman and sorcerer—however, is not understood in the same senses as in Christianity or Zoroastrianism. Indigenous religious traditions characteristically embed their metaphysical questions in a language and art of the sacred that is embedded in the natural, material world in which they live. That is, religious

Fig. 1.21 Petroglyph of Capihuara, Cassiquiare Canal, Venezuela.

images and metaphysical questions are intertwined in such a way that the interpreter can understand these question through the symbolic attributes of material images. Indigenous religious traditions are notable for the ways in which they harmonize their life cycles with the rhythms, cycles, and forms in nature. All of nature is imbued with the power of the sacred, the divinities who once were living, whose lives and acts are remembered and celebrated at cosmically significant celestial moments in time (e.g., the annual appearance of certain constellations) and at geographical points of intersection between spirit and matter comprising a "map" of the world.

While many indigenous religious traditions exhibit a great concern for the end of long cycles of time, with its correlated fear of the return of a "long, dark night" in which many people die, the world in which humans live nevertheless holds a comforting promise that a new world will come into being if the old one is destroyed. A cycle, therefore, is not just an endpoint but rather is the beginning of another long cycle of time to come.

The prophecies in many indigenous religious traditions have served multiple functions: to warn non-indigenous societies of natural catastrophes due to cosmic imbalance from the destructiveness and greed of the "younger brother" (as the Kogi Indians of the Sierra Nevada in Colombia call the white man); or to maintain the importance of the ancestral traditions, for without these, the "enemy" culture will come to dominate, meaning the destruction of the indigenous world; and finally, to critique the disastrous relations between the indigenous peoples and the West, because although exogenous societies "conquered the Indians," in the end, the enemy outsiders did not "defeat them."

Fig. 1.22   Petroglyphs in South Mountain Park, Phoenix, Arizona.

◆ STUDY AND DISCUSSION QUESTIONS

1. In the religious tradition of the so-called Yuruparí, what are some of the key symbols and how do you think they represent key ideas of the tradition? How does native discourse about their religious tradition compare with an outsider's perspective on the same? Compare the Makuna version of the Yuruparí tradition (as seen in the film) with the Arawakan version of creation presented at the end of this text. What do they have in common? What are the key questions each tradition focuses on? Why do you think the Yuruparí tradition was declared a "nonmaterial patrimony of humanity"?

2. Discuss the importance of the following themes in indigenous religious traditions: symmetry and asymmetry, complementary opposites, reciprocity, anomalous beings, the circle and the cross, matter and spirit, conversion to Christianity, or other exogenous religions.

3. What are some of the issues indigenous peoples worldwide face with regard to the continuity of their religious traditions? How can humanitarian agencies assist indigenous peoples in continuing their traditions? In what ways have non-indigenous societies incorporated indigenous religious traditions into their religious practices? How has this appropriation of native religiosity been seen by native peoples themselves?

◆ KEY TERMS

Affinal relations
Animism
Apapaatai
Australian aboriginal dreamtime
Consanguineal kin
Cosmogony
Cosmology
Dogon Kanaga masks
Eschatology
Guarani theory of souls
Interrelationality
Perspectivism
Popol Vuh
Prophetism
Religious specialists
Sun dance
World Tree of Life
YAJÉ
Yuruparí tradition

◆ FOR FURTHER READING

Carrasco, David. *Religions of Mesoamerica: Cosmovision and Ceremonial Centers*. Prospect Heights, IL: Waveland, 1998.

Conklin, Beth. *Consuming Grief*. Austin: University of Texas, 2002.

DeLoria, Vine, Jr. *The World We Used to Live In*. Golden, CO: Fulcrum, 2006.

Olupona, Jacob, ed. *Beyond Primitivism*. New York: Routledge, 2007.

Pentikäinen, Juha, and Mihály Hoppál, eds. *Northern Religions and Shamanism*. Ethnologica uralica 3. Budapest: Akadémiai Kiadó, 1992.

Robbins, Joel. *Becoming Sinners: Christianity and Moral Torment in a Papua New Guinea Society*. Berkeley: University of California Press, 2004.

Rosaldo, Renato. *Ilongot Headhunting. A Study in Society and History 1883–1974*. Stanford: Stanford University Press, 1980.

Sullivan, L. E. *Icanchu's Drum: An Orientation to Meaning in South American Religions*. New York: Macmillan, 1988.

———. *The Religious Spirit of the Navajo.* Philadelphia: Chelsea House, 2002.

K. Turner. A Revival of Mongolian Shamanism. *Shamanism Annual*, issue 24, December 2011, 3–10.

Wambagu, Njeru, and John Padwick. "Globalization: A Perspective from the African Independent Churches." *Journal of African Instituted Church Theology* 11, no. 1 (September 2006).

Wright, Robin M. *Cosmos, Self and History in Baniwa Religion: For Those Unborn.* Austin: University of Texas Press, 1998.

———. *Mysteries of the Jaguar Shamans: Ancient Knowledge of the Baniwa Maliiri.* Omaha: University of Nebraska Press, forthcoming.

Wright, Robin M., and Neil L. Whitehead, eds. *In Darkness and Secrecy: The Anthropology of Assault Sorcery and Witchcraft in Amazonia.* Durham: Duke University Press, 2004.

◆ **SUGGESTED WEBSITES**

www.indiancountrytodaymedianetwork.com

http://www.creativespirits.info/aboriginalculture/spirituality/

http://scholar.harvard.edu/olupona/contact_owner

www.sacredland.org/in-the-light-of-reverence/

http://afrikaworld.net/afrel/

http://www.unesco.org/culture/ich/RL/00574

◆ **NOTES**

1. http://www.unesco.org/culture/ich/RL/00574
2. Sullivan, 1988, chap. 5
3. K. Turner, in *Shamanism Annual*, 2011.
4. Conklin, 2002.
5. Rosaldo, 1980.

CHAPTER 2

Hinduism

Julien Ries

Introduction

Hinduism is the religious belief shared by the great majority of people living in India. In order to understand Hinduism, one must start with the ideas and cultural concepts of the Aryans, the Indo-European invaders who penetrated the valleys of the Indus and Ganges Rivers two thousand years before the modern era. The name *Hinduism* itself derives from nineteenth-century Western (British) officials and Christian missionaries who so named "the" religious tradition based on their own assumptions and observations. In fact, given the diversity of Hindu gods, practices, and beliefs, it is more accurate to talk of "Hinduisms." It is also necessary to remember that the oral tradition (or Veda) of Hinduism has been transformed over the centuries as a result of contact with non-Vedic cultures rooted in India long before the arrival of the Aryan conquerors.

Hinduism is structured on a number of constants, which have been described by Indian studies. The essential ideas are:

- The Veda, an oral tradition that preceded written language, is the source of many fundamental notions that provide a structure for the religious and social thoughts over the centuries;

Fig. 2.1 Lingaraja temple in Bhubanesvar, India. This temple is dedicated to Shiva who is represented in the forms of the construction.

- A cosmic order (dharma) that includes the universe, humanity, and life and whose harmony precludes chaos;
- A cyclic concept of time that signifies a perpetual return;
- A system of castes that has to define the social fabric; and
- A concept of the stages of life and of the techniques by which the spirit is liberated (yoga), an idea perhaps inherited from pre-Vedic times.

Vedism ignored temples and images of divinity. Influenced by factors not yet fully determined, Hinduism at the start of the modern era underwent a profound change with a new concept of devotion, *bhakti*. Sacrifice gave way to offering (*puja*) and to prayer before statues and other representations of deities in the temples erected by the believers. Here, the faithful turn to the deity of their choice and bear witness to their love in a context of personal relationships.

This emphasis on offering and prayer explains the great popularity of the gods of the *bhakti*, like Vishnu and Krishna. The pietist movement, animated by the warmth of an intensely lived devotion, underwent various changes over the centuries. A number of sects developed from Hinduism, many of which continue to the present day. In the absence of a doctrinal authority, in an evolving religion that conserves and reveres its ancient teachings, one can today study the emergence and roles of numerous founders and reformers.

Modern Hinduism

India and Southeast Asia are home to 700 million Hindus, with millions of others living in various regions throughout the world. In India, Hindus make up 82 percent of the population. According to the precepts of the faith, one does not become a Hindu; rather,

TIMELINE
BCE

3300–1500	Emergence of Indus River Valley culture
2300–1200	Composition of the Rig-Veda
1600–1000	Aryan migration into India from northwest
ca. 1000	Aryan migration into the Gangetic Plains (northern and eastern India)
ca. 800–400	Composition of the principal Upanishads
ca. 200 BCE–200 CE	Composition of the Laws of Manu; and of the Bhagavad Gita

CE

300–1700	Composition of the Puranas
ca. 1200	Muslim entry into northern India
1757–1947	British rule in India
1863–1902	Lifespan of Vivekananda, Hindu sage and representative to the western countries
1869–1948	Lifespan of Mohandas (Mahatma) Gandhi, political activist
1947	Indian political independence and political/geographic partition

Fig. 2.2 Painting of cows being led back to their stables by mythic characters, conveying peace and well being. National Museum of Delhi, India.

Fig. 2.3 A Hindu prays in a temple dedicated to Shiva in Geyzing, western Sikkim, India.

one is born a Hindu. Hindu society continues to exist in the context of a rich cultural, social, and religious heritage that has existed for four millennia, as regulated by the eternal dharma (or order of the cosmos), in which humankind is integrated.

A rite of adoration, of offering, and a cult of deities, or *puja*, which replaced the Vedic sacrifices, is celebrated daily both in Hindu homes and temples. The number and variety of these temples is indeed impressive, with most in northern India dedicated to Shiva, most in the south to Vishnu, and to the various other deities according to different regions. Each displays an exuberant mythology and is adorned by great towers (*gopura*) at the four entrances. Everywhere one encounters small chapels, in the trees or beside walls, and miniature places of prayer can be found in city streets. India is the land of the sacred par excellence.

Each morning and evening, long lines of believers make their way to the temples to place flowers and other offerings before the statues of the deities. Pilgrimages wend their way toward the thousands of sanctuaries and holy places. During their festivals, a statue of the honored deity is carried on a huge cart, adorned with flowers and pulled by dozens of believers. Prayers, litanies, hymns, music, and cries of joy mark the solemnity.

Fig. 2.4 Ramakrishna. He may be considered as the refounder of contemporary Hinduism.

Fig. 2.5 Mohandas (Mahatma) Gandhi. Father of India's Independence and leading figure in modern Hinduism.

Everyone lives among the permanent signs of purification: water courses, lakes, and rivers are all considered sacred. At Benares at sunrise, the crowd immerses itself in the sacred waters of the Ganges, while on its banks the rite of cremation for the dead is marked by the casting of ashes into the river. In Hindu belief, the cow is the symbol of Mother Earth, the one who nourishes humankind, and is therefore considered sacred.

A disciple of Ramakrishna, Vivekananda (1862–1902) created the Hindu mission, a religious order of swamis, who serve as community leaders committed to teaching religious doctrine and to organizing displays of solidarity. Hinduism therefore has become a missionary movement with both religious and social aspects. Mohandas Gandhi (1869–1948) sought the total freedom of India from English rule by basing his actions on two principles: the embracing of truth (*satyagraha*) and

nonviolence (*ahisma*). Through his efforts, he rehabilitated the lower castes and obtained independence for India.

Pre-Vedic Religion

In 1922, the first evidence of a magnificent Bronze-Age civilization that flourished between 2500 and 1700 BCE was discovered, first in a valley of the Indus and later in Pakistan and in other places in India. To date, three hundred

Fig. 2.6 A Hindu prostrating himself on the path of the sacred river of Mahanadi during the Festival of the Sun in Uttar Pradesh, India.

Fig. 2.7   Festival of Khumba, held every twelve years at Harwar in Garhwal, India. A priest holds the holy fire as pilgrims bathe.

sites have been identified. This civilization is known as Pre-Vedic, Hindusian, or as Mohenjo-Daro and Harappa, after the names of its two major archaeological sites. The excavations of Mundigak and Mehrgarh have shown that this urban civilization was preceded by a Neolithic agricultural culture dating back to 7000 BCE. Scholars today have more than 3,500 inscriptions that they have not yet been able to decipher, even though there appears to have been much contact between India and Mesopotamia.

The religious documentation found in these sites is important and includes many figurines, many depicting female forms and hundreds of signs or personal seals. These latter were used to authenticate objects, to show ownership, and to place them under the protection of the deities.

Many of the seals show a crowned, three-faced, horned god seated on a throne like a yogin, with animals turned toward him. It is believed that this is a prototype of the god Shiva, lord of the animals and prince of yoga.

The many female figurines cause one to think of a great goddess. One seal, found at Mohenjo-Daro, shows her between two branches of an Indian *papal* tree, which today remains a symbol of maternity. She is crowned and is seen escorted by seven young women. It is the Mother Goddess, already represented in Mesopotamia in the tenth millennium, and is indicative of a matriarchal society orientated toward life.

Among the other details of the findings, particular reference should be made to the importance of animalist art, the familiarity of

Fig. 2.8 Steatite seals showing positive and negative forms of a unicorn and bull, both of which are mythic animals of Hindu traditions.

animals with the divine, the importance of the sacred tree, and the cemetery at Harappa with various grave goods testifying to a belief in an ultraterrestrial existence.

The Spread of Hinduism

In the second millennium BCE, peoples who are today called Indo-European came from the lands north of the Black Sea to the valleys of the Indus and of the Ganges Rivers and settled there permanently, introducing a new culture. These newcomers, who brought with them Vedic ideas, mixed with the local population, forming the nucleus of Hindu culture and religion. Hinduism expanded eastward from India, first to Sri Lanka and then to Southeast Asia all the way to Indonesia. In the eighth and ninth centuries CE, an important Hindu kingdom developed on the island of Java, where the remains of the great temple of Prambanan, the famous capital of the kingdom, can still be admired today.

Hinduism is present in India—the religions' cradle—where 827 million people (over 80 percent of the population) profess the faith. Other countries with substantial Hindu minorities include Bangladesh, Bhutan, Burma, French Guyana, Guyana, Indonesia, Malaysia, Mauritus, Pakistan, Seychelles, Sri Lanka, and South Africa. Other small groups are found in the United Kingdom and the Netherlands.

The Veda—Praise and Cult of the Gods

Toward 1900 BCE, some Aryans from central Asia and the Caucasus made their way into India, advancing slowly with their herds through the Indus and Ganges Valleys. They brought with them an oral and spiritual tradition, Veda, representing an eternal law, *sanatana dharma*. By the time this law was written down, in 1800 BCE, the Aryan travelers had occupied all of India. No archaeological remains of this period have as yet been discovered.

The Vedas are the most ancient Aryan religious texts of India and consist of four collections. The Rig Veda consists of 1,017 hymns in honor of the 33 deities, to whom the faithful offer praise, invitations to share in sacrifices, and prayers for protection, happiness, and salvation. The Sama Veda is a collection of melodies and chants used during the celebrations that reaffirm the faith. The Yajur Veda, intended for priests, is a record of the rituals, especially those concerning the seasonal sacrifices for agricultural work and for harvest. The Atharva Veda, the Veda of the magic formulas, consists of spells and elements of popular cults combined with later reflections.

As in Aryan society, the spiritual world is divided into three groups, according to

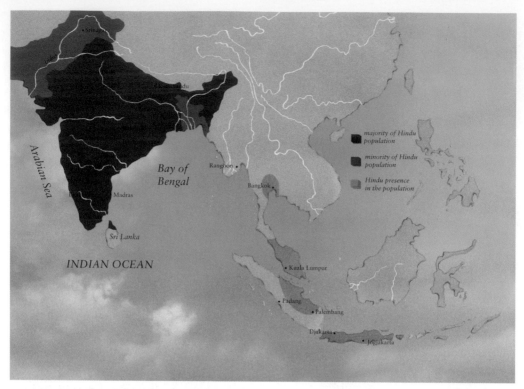

Fig. 2.9 Map of the spread of Hinduism in Asia.

function. The sovereign gods, Mitra-Varuna, are the gods of the sacred, of the cosmos, and of the universal rule (*rita*)—assuring maintenance of the cosmic order. Indra and his Maruts, representing the second group, are the gods of war and conquest and serve as the guardians against enemies. The third group includes the Ashvin, or Nasatya, young gods who are believed to travel throughout the heavens daily and who play an indispensable role in fertility. Agni is the god of fire, a divine power and messenger of the gods; two hundred Vedic hymns are dedicated to him. The soma, the finest offering that can be made to a deity, consists of drinking an intoxicating liquid made from a local plant, symbolizing life. The entire religion consists of cultic and utilitarian practices, with the gods in the service of men. Predominantly a patriarchal belief system, the Veda has few feminine deities.

The Brahmana: Salvation through Sacrifice

By around 800 BCE, the Aryans were organized into four basic social classes (*varna*). The *Brahmins*, the dominant class, have a monopoly on the Vedas, the sacred, and the cults. They are the priests who look after the relationships of the community with the sacred on behalf of the entire community. They look after the Vedas and take care to pass them to succeeding generations. The *Kshatriyas*, noblemen and warriors, rule over society. They have military power, and

Fig. 2.10 Indra, god of thunder and of rain.

Fig. 2.11 Varuna, god who created the universe, is venerated as the god of the waters.

they form groups, each one headed by a raja or monarch. The *Vaishyas*, farmers and craftsmen, produce society's wealth. They have the economic power since they are the cultivators and the breeders, which produce goods for trade. *The Shudras* (more recently called *Dalits*), who are non-Aryan servants, are excluded from the Vedic rituals. To each class is attributed a determined color, which is distinctive: the Brahmins are allotted the color white; the Kshatriya, red; the Vaishya, yellow if they are merchants, and blue if they are farmers; and the Shudra black.

Conscious of their own dignity, the Brahmins recorded the passages and commentaries of the Vedas, or Brahmana, texts that deal with rites of sacrifice. From a Vedic belief in the gods, they pass to the mysticism of sacrifice, which becomes a sort of clockwork movement regulating the progress of the universe.

During this time, Brahma-Prajapati emerged as a new god, Lord of all creatures, a primordial being whose word is a creative force (*vac*). He is time, the year, and the sacrifice, the all and the fullness. Tribute to Brahma-Prajapati occurs on the site of an excavated pit, where a high altar is built and on which the sacred fire, or Agni, is placed. The five courses of bricks placed here represent the five worlds, the five

Fig. 2.12 Shiva, supreme deity for certain Hindu followers.

Fig. 2.13 Brahma-Prajapati. Government Museum in Madras, India.

seasons, the five cardinal points. Atop a heap of wood is placed a lotus leaf, which symbolizes the earth; a golden lamina, which symbolizes immortality; and, finally, a statue of a man, representing Prajapati. Agni (the sacred fire) serves as the immolator. Such sacrifice through fire is believed to grant entrance to immortality, giving this ritual great importance.

Three fires are lit for every sacrifice: the *garhapatya*, the fire of the mother of the house who offers the sacrifice; the *ahavaniya*, the fire of the offerings, which carries the gifts to the gods; and the *dakshinagni*, the fire of the south, which stands guard over the ritual. Central to the consecration is the idea of faith, *shraddha*. By means of the sacrifice, humans are believed to be born a second time, with the third birth occurring with the fire of cremation.

The sacrifice became the basis of the three Aryan social classes since the ideology corresponded to the theology. The members of the three classes are called on to pass through four stages of life: first as disciples of a guru, then as masters of a house (*grihasthin*). Subsequently, they retire with their brides to become inhabitants of the forest (*vanaprasthin*). Finally, they extinguish every fire and renounce all worldly things, living as hermits (*samnyasin*).

The Upanishads

Derived from the words *Upa ni sad*, or "sitting beside," the Upanishads are sacred texts that emerged between 800 and 600 BCE, each having its own doctrine of initiation, as communicated by a guru. The Upanishads impart to the faithful secret knowledge about the nature of sacrifice, the divine, the cosmos, the nature of life and death, and the path of salvation by means of gnosis (higher knowledge).

may be realized through successive rebirths. Thus one's actions in this life are believed to determine his or her role in the next, making the concept of karma central to the idea of retribution. In accordance with this belief, transmigration (death and rebirth) will continue to occur until the karmic force is exhausted.

Upanishad Brahmanism emphasizes a double doctrine: first, Brahman-atman, or salvation via the search for identity through ecstatic experience; and second, karma-samsara, or the influence of one's acts on the chain of existence, on spiritual liberation, and on salvation. The atman makes humans immortal beings who reach Brahman through ecstatic experience. Because humans remain free to act, their future existence will depend on their choices, with every good action moving them toward salvation. Insofar as humans act in accordance with the dharma, they will change the world. Thus the Upanishads describe an ethic of moral responsibility. Ecstasy dissipates the power of the karma, thus obstructing transmigration and bringing about the conjunction of the atman with Brahman, finally bringing humans into the realm of the divine.

Yoga and Its Techniques of Salvation

The word *Yoga* is derived from *yug*, meaning "to tie" or "to unite." With origins that date back to pre-Vedic India, the term is used by all the forms of knowledge and religions of Vedas, as well as by Buddhism, to the present day. Yoga can only be learned through the help of a guru who can be *Ishvara*, the pure divine spirit, the ideal of the yogin and the *yogini*.

Yoga is based on the theory that humanity is composed of both matter (*prakriti*) and

Fig. 2.14 Agni, god of fire and one of the oldest Indian deities.

As new doctrines emerged, mention is made of Brahman, who, on a higher spiritual level, is the Absolute and is represented by a divine character, Brahma. Atman is the eternal and immortal principle that animates the individual, moving one toward spiritual growth and ultimately salvation. In the Upanishads, the atman is called on to liberate the individual spirit from the body, thus achieving the perfect identity with Brahman and so leading one to salvation, or moksha. Samsara (as opposed to moksha) is the passage from one existence to another. The karma is an invincible force that fuels a continuing cycle of rebirth, so that the fruits of one's actions unrealized in one lifetime

Fig. 2.15   View of the Undavalli Caves and the Ananta Padmanabha Swami Temple. Located near the Krishna River, India.

spirit (*puruhsa*). To detach one's spirit from the material, one needs a deep knowledge that can overcome all ignorance and a progressive practice of liberation.

The yogin must begin this journey of spiritual liberation by living in accordance with ten virtues: the respect for all living creatures (ahimsa); the respect for truth (*satya*); the respect for property (*asteya*); the respect for chastity (*brah-macarya*); a poor life; a morality of purity; strength of spirit; the absence of personal ambition; entrance into the cult of a divinity; and the thirst for knowledge.

The techniques consist of complex exercises, which are simultaneously physical, spiritual, and moral and which include the disciplines of breathing, concentration, and meditation.

Various methods for liberation have been proposed over the centuries: the karma-yoga, by means of free action without the expectation of recompense; the bhakti-yoga by means of adoration and mystic love; the hatha-yoga, very well known in the West, by means of physical exercise; the mantra-yoga by means of the chanting and prayer; and the jnana-yoga, by means of gnosis or a superior knowledge.

These various techniques seek to give the yogin a path of liberty by freeing him from the material concerns of daily life, from the empty waste of time, and from the dispersion of his spiritual powers. Through discipline and the rhythm of respiration, he will define his consciousness and his thoughts; concentration abolishes multiplicity and fragmentation, and unity is achieved. In this way, the yogin raises himself to a superior level and may experience spiritual liberation while still living in the material universe.

Bhakti—The Religion of Salvation

Around 500 BCE, devout Hindu began to place their trust in a personal god, a beloved deity able to return this love. Derived from the word *bhaj*, meaning "to share," this new form of devotion was called bhakti: it is a fervent and tender practice allowing the faithful to receive the love of the god whom he or she adores. Vedism did not make use of temples and statues, while Brahmanism offered sacrifices and puja. With the emergence of bhakti, many temples were constructed, and India became filled with sacred images. Women participated enthusiastically in this popular fervor because they wanted to see the face of their god and to offer him tribute (often in the form of flowers and fruit). Thus, by surpassing Vedism and Brahmanism, the Hindu religion assumed a new aspect, for the first time providing the believer (bhakta) with a loving God who loved him or her in return.

Vishnu became a supreme god, a Bhagavan, a gracious Lord who appears on earth every time the sacred order (dharma) is threatened. As the popular deity who safeguards the cosmos, Vishnu elicited great devotion, with many temples dedicated to him. The myths of his ten *avatara*—that is, incarnations, descents to earth—were staged, recounted, put to music, and celebrated, constituting the Vishnuite sacred liturgy. Among his forms, Vishnu became a fish to save the first man from the flood, a tortoise to give origin to the animals, and a man-lion to combat demons. It is believed that at the end of the world he will become Kalki, the white horse. Growing steadily in popularity and power, the rich mythology of Vishnu celebrated a god who was close to man and served as the custodian of the world, eventually becoming a hero to supplant the Brahmins, Rama, then Krishna, and finally Buddha.

Fig. 2.16 Yoga being practiced in Nepal.

Fig. 2.17   Vishnu Surya, who represents the Rising Sun.

Fig. 2.18   Shiva with three heads. The head in the middle represents the creative aspect of the god, that on the right is his protective aspect, while that on the left is his destructive aspect.

Another important bhakti god is Shiva, the lord of life and death, the creator, destroyer, and re-creator of the cosmos. (It should be noted that, unlike many Western religions, Hinduism supports the idea of cyclic time, in which birth and death, creation and re-creation are constantly recurring facets of existence.) In art, Shiva is depicted with three heads, representing his threefold role as the creator of the cosmos, its keeper, and its destroyer. He also has three eyes, the third centered on his forehead, representing the eye of knowledge. The cult of Shiva is a fertility cult that probably derives from Mohenjo-Daro and whose devotion centers on the adoration of the *lingua*, a cylindrical stone that serves as the symbol of both creation and fertility. Originally not as popular as Vishnu, Shiva has made great progress over the centuries, with the many Shivaite sects currently enjoying great popularity in India.

The Bhagavad Gita— "The Celestial Song"

The Bhagavad Gita (the Song of the Lord), analogous to the Bible in India and the best-known book of its religious literature, consists of a dialogue between the god Krishna and his faithful Arjuna. Inserted in the sixth book of the Mahabharata, one of the great sagas, it is considered as a sacred document, a sort of "Krishna's gospel," describing the third god of the bhakti who reveals himself as Bhagavan, the supreme Lord, and dictates the behavior expected of his faithful, the *bhakta Arjuna.*

The Gita unifies the previous doctrines and mystical teachings in a harmonious synthesis. It describes the first path of salvation, the karma-marga, the path of actions, but goes beyond it by teaching about the action done according to duty (dharma) without seeking recompense. It mentions the path of knowledge pre-announced in the Upanishads, jnana-marga, but transforms it and leads the believer to the Bhagavan, the supreme being superior to the Brahman. It proclaims the indispensability of the path of devotion and of love (bhakti-marga), which is the path of the abandonment of oneself to Bhagavan Krishna, a personal god. In this belief system, the individual may act freely, but always with reference to Krishna, who is the creator of the world and who will thus conclude his cycle.

The revelation of the Gita must be seen as part of the mythic vision of the epic poem, which presents a struggle and where humanity achieves salvation as a result of the obedience of the bhakta to the Bhagavan, through devotion to Krishna.

It is believed that the wheel of the samsara will finally stop for those who show their devotion to Krishna through their love and who entrust all their actions to their god. This will mark their escape from the cycle of rebirth, as a result of the psychological help of the Bhagavan who supports their efforts, removes the deceptive veil of illusion, and reveals himself to his believers, in accordance with the strict interpretation of Hinduism.

Fig. 2.19 Rupestral (carved in stone) temple at Ellora. The most famous is the Kailasa, or the paradise of Shiva.

Liberation through the Devotion to Krishna

Bhagavad Gita
The Lord says:

VI, 47. Whoever among all the yogin remains in me and, full of faith, adores me from the deepest of his soul will be deemed by me as having achieved the apex of the yogic union.

VIII, 5. Whoever, remembering me in his last moments, abandons his mortal body and leaves, will have access to my being; there is no doubt at all about this.

VIII, 7. Remember me at all times and fight, with your mind and your judgment oriented toward me. And you will come to me without any doubt.

XII, 6. Those who place all their actions in me, who have no other pleasure but me and who adore me and gather all their thoughts in me by means of an exclusive discipline, for them I will be the one who will immediately pluck them from the ocean of transmigration and of death.

The god Krishna, who had his origins in the region of Mathura, has assumed a very important role in Hinduism, owing to the Bhagavad Gita, which has strongly influenced Indian thinking for more than two millennia. The doctrine of the karma, stating the influence of one's acts on transmigration, and that of salvation, which is liberation from the rebirth cycle, have undergone deep changes.

The above extracts demonstrate the new orientation toward salvation. The relationship of love between the believer and Krishna during one's life realizes the ideals of yoga to the highest degree. This orientation will be a permanent invocation to Krishna during the life of the *bhakta*. At the moment of a devotee's death, it is believed that Krishna will terminate his or her rebirth cycle. These texts show the importance of the union between god and the individual (achieved through the bhakti) and provide a personal link between humanity and divinity.

◆ **STUDY AND DISCUSSION QUESTIONS**

1. Consider and discuss how the absence of doctrinal authority in Hinduism, and the fact that it is largely a polytheistic tradition, might affect individual beliefs and practices. Compare your ideas with reference to other traditions that do impose doctrinal authority (for example, Judaism and types of Christianity).

2. Using the description of yoga in this chapter, compare its practice and meaning for Hindus to the practice and meaning for non-Hindus who routinely practice yoga in modern industrial societies.

3. Study more about Hindu classes, or castes (*varna*), and assess their significance for Hindu society from a religious perspective.

◆ **KEY TERMS**

ahimsa

Aranyaka

atman

Bhagavad Gita

bhakti

Brahman

Brahmana

dharma

gopura

karma

Krishna

moksha

puja

purusha

risi

rita

samsara

satyagraha

shraddha

soma

swami or svami

Upanishads

varna

Veda

yoga

◆ **FOR FURTHER READING**

Basham, A. L. *The Origins and Development of Classical Hinduism*. Edited by Kenneth G. Zysk. New York: Oxford University Press, 1991.

Clooney, Francis X., SJ. *Hindu God, Christian God: How Reason Helps Break Down the Boundaries between Religions*. New York: Oxford University Press, 2010.

Doniger, Wendy. *The Rig-Veda: An Anthology*. London: Penguin, 1981.

Eck, Diana. *Banaras: City of Light*. New York: Columbia University Press, 1998.

———. *Darsan: Seeing the Divine*. New York: Columbia University Press, 1998.

Fairservis, Walter A., Jr. *The Roots of Ancient India*. 2nd ed. Chicago: University of Chicago Press, 1975.

Gandhi, Mohandas K. *An Autobiography: or The Story of My Experiments with Truth*. Translated by Mahadev Desai. Boston: Beacon, 1957.

Muesse, Mark W. *The Hindu Traditions: A Concise Introduction*. Minneapolis: Fortress Press, 2011.

Pintchman, Tracy. *The Rise of the Goddess in the Hindu Tradition.* Albany: State University of New York Press, 1994.

Rambachan, Anantanand. *The Hindu Vision.* New Delhi: Motilal Banarsidass, 1999.

Sarma, Deepak. *Hinduism: A Reader.* Malden, MA: Wiley-Blackwell, 2008.

Sharma, Arvind. *Classical Hindu Thought: An Introduction.* New Delhi: Oxford University Press, 2000.

The Bhagavad-Gita: The Song of God. Translated by Swami Prabhavananda and Christopher Isherwood. New York: Signet, 2002.

The Upanishads. Translated by Swami Prabhavananda and Frederick Manchester. New York: Signet, 2002.

CHAPTER 3

Buddhism

Julien Ries

Introduction

More than 2,500 years ago, after a long and difficult search, Siddhartha Gautama suddenly discovered the solution to the problem of human suffering that had tormented his soul. After a night spent in meditation beneath a *papal* tree, he achieved "the Awakening to Truth" (or "the Enlightenment") and thus obtained the supreme peace of the extinction of passions and the definitive liberation from suffering and from the cycle of rebirth.

Resuming his pilgrimages, the Buddha shared this wisdom with his fellow men and women, leading them on the path of liberation from suffering and beginning his role as guide and physician to humanity. This chapter explains the fundamental elements of Buddhist wisdom—from the Buddha's concept of humanity and of the human condition in the cosmos to the role of human action charged with a karmic power (relative to the law of cause and effect found in actions); the idea of nirvana; the noble path of awakening; and the three refuges: the Buddha, the law, and the community.

After 2,500 years, Buddhism continues to be the revered religion of much of humanity. Over the centuries, in its encounters with other cultures, Buddhism has undergone several changes, which has given it a historical

TIMELINE

BCE

ca. 563–483	Lifespan of Siddhartha Gautama (the Buddha)
272–236	Lifespan of Ashoka, Indian king who helped spread Buddhist values
ca. 250	Buddhism spreads throughout India
200	Mahayana Buddhism begins

CE

50	Buddhism spreads to China
ca. 100	Creation of the Lotus Sutra
ca. 300	Buddhism spreads throughout Southeast Asia
399	Buddhism enters into Korea
552	Buddhism is accepted into Japan from Korea
630	Buddhism spreads into Tibet
ca. 820	Tendai and Shingon Buddhism introduced in Japan (by Saicho and Kukai, respectively)
845	Persecution of Buddhists in China by Wu Tsang
ca. 1100–1500	Buddhism declines throughout India
1133–1212	Lifespan of Honen, founder of Pure Land sect of Buddhism in Japan
1173–1262	Lifespan of Shinran, founder of Jodo Shin in Japan
ca. 1200	Zen Buddhism emerges in Japan; practiced by Dogen (1200–1253)
1578	Establishment of the title "Dalai Lama" in Tibet
1956	International Buddhist Congress to encourage understanding of Buddhism globally

Fig. 3.1 Face of a reclining Buddha, Thailand. This monumental statue transmits a profound serenity.

complexity vital to our understanding of its various facets. At the beginning of the common era, a new Buddhism of devotion arose from contact with Hinduism. Over these two millennia, the disciples of the Buddha have organized themselves in a number of schools and approaches, in regard to both meditation and devotion. The last sections provide a few ideas about this vast movement.

Buddhism Today

In the sixth century BCE, in the valley of the Ganges River, Gautama the Buddha started preaching his message based on a faith in the

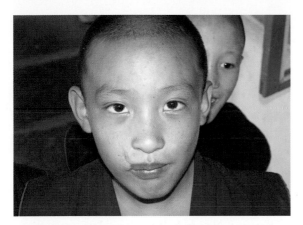

Fig. 3.2 A Tibetan refugee in India. The tragedy of the exile leads to the exercise of the fundamental attitude of Buddhism: compassion.

human being and on his ability to find peace and happiness through good actions. This wisdom was accepted in India, China, Ceylon (Sri Lanka), Tibet, and in all the countries of the Far East.

Europeans encountered Buddhism in the course of the nineteenth century as a result of colonization, but they did not find it easy to understand. Some European colonists opposed it in the name of their religion, while others welcomed it with a romantic enthusiasm.

Today the situation is very different, with modern Buddhism seen as a universal message. In 1956, on the 2,500th anniversary of the Buddha's birth, an international Buddhist congress tried to formulate precepts and indications favoring the expansion of the Buddhist message around the world, to start national and international associations, and to found a missionary Buddhist seminary in Bangalore in India. Since then Buddhist missionaries have been active all over the world.

Modern Buddhism is presented as an awakening, so that human behavior will lead to the truth—and thus to liberation from fear, anguish, and suffering—starting them on the path to happiness. Surrounded in their existence by the flux of events, humanity resembles a wheel, an evolving creature, a nucleus of sentiments and will, a flame that feeds itself, an existence that depends on all that has gone before. Awakened to his duties, humans must master themselves, establish the balance between themselves and

Fig. 3.3 Buddhist monks collecting alms in Laos.

the external world (other people and the environment), give direction to their sexuality with energy, and renounce the slavery of desire. The goal is to reach a state of peace (nirvana), which is a spiritual and physical balance characterized by goodwill and an attuning of oneself to others. Thus, for modern humanity, Buddhism offers itself as the path of awakening to duty and progress attained through continuous personal effort, in a state of inner peace and benevolent compassion in social life, with a spiritual outlook at the world but without religious preoccupation. Conscious of the precariousness of the human condition, the Buddhist looks for his awakening, liberation from suffering, and inner enlightenment.

The Spread of Buddhism

Ashoka (272–236 BCE), the third ruler of the Maurya dynasty, helped to spread Buddhism

throughout the Indian kingdom, which was then much greater in size than today. The dark red parts on the map (see fig. 3.4) show the areas where Buddhism is today the majority religion; the light red shows where it is a minority; while the small wheels show particular presences in Europe and America. According to recent data, in Tibet, Thailand, and Myanmar (Burma), more than 85 percent of the population practices Buddhism. In Cambodia, Laos, Bhutan, and Sri Lanka, the number ranges from 70 to 85 percent. Nearly half the population practices Buddhism in Japan, Mongolia, Taiwan, Vietnam, and Singapore. Minority Buddhist populations exist in South Korea, Hong Kong, and Malaysia.

Buddha the Founder

Around 563 BCE, Siddhartha Gautama was born to a prince of the noble clan of the Shakya

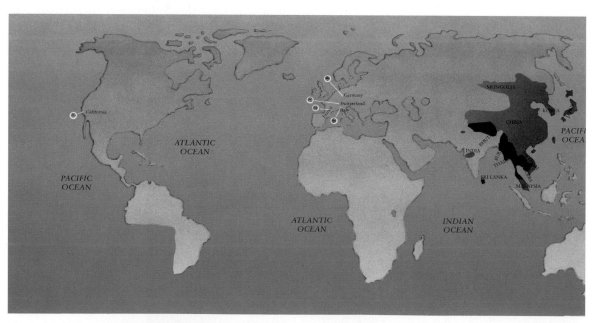

Fig. 3.4   Map showing the spread of Buddhism.

at Kapilvastu, north of Benares, India. By the age of twenty-nine, he was married and the father of a son, but his life was disturbed by the tragic nature of the human condition. During this time, Gautama was struck by four encounters, which had a profound effect on him. First, he met a decrepit old man, followed by a sick man bent over with pain, then a corpse carried to a traditional funeral pyre, and finally a serene and happy ascetic hermit. He started to wander in solitude, and one brightly moonlit night, as he sat looking eastward beneath a *papal* tree, he was suddenly enlightened and awakened to the truth. He thus became the Buddha, also known as the Awakened One, Shakyamuni, the Sage of the Shakya.

After this profound spiritual experience, he again began to wander and in the Park of the Gazelles at Benares met five ascetic young men, to whom he described the four noble truths he had discovered: (1) the truth about suffering: that indeed everything is suffering; (2) the truth about the origin of suffering, which is desire; (3) the truth about the surcease of suffering by suppressing desire; (4) the truth of the eightfold path leading to the end of suffering.

The first noble truth is something that the Buddha himself realized—that suffering, *duhkha*, is universal and can be found in birth, illness, old age, death, union with whatever one does not love, and separation from what one loves. Suffering is a state of agitation, unrest, conflict, and lack of harmony, but it does not impose itself as evidence.

The second truth teaches that the origin of suffering is desire, *trishna*, which is the thirst for passions, a longing either for being or nonbeing, which chains each human to the eternal cycle of rebirth. The source of suffering can be found in the human conception of life: an illusory attachment to the self and to material things as if they were permanent. This ignorance leads humanity to egoistical actions, from which he must purify himself through a number of rebirths.

The third truth, that of nirvana, leads to a state of repose, to the distancing of oneself from all things, to the extinction of desire, and to the cessation of all cravings. It opens the way to harmony and happiness. The attainment of nirvana involves several steps—beginning with the annulment of love, hate, and error in oneself, and ending with their extinction at the moment of death.

The fourth truth stipulates the eightfold path, the marga, which leads to nirvana. By following this path, one achieves morality

Fig. 3.5 Buddha depicted giving his first sermon in Sarnath, near Benares.

Fig. 3.6 Statue at rupestral (carved in rock) temple at Ajanta, India. This statue relates a moral story of a little boy who has nothing to offer, giving the Buddha a fistful of earth, and showing that the intention behind a deed is more important than its results.

fundamental aggregates (*skandha*), twelve bases, and twenty-two faculties of comprehension. Humans perform actions. Each action is willed, that is, first thought and then carried out by means of the creative physical, vocal, and mental activities, which can be either good or evil. Each action carries in itself the effect of retribution, which humans will inherit for their own happiness or sadness.

When the Buddha speaks of action, he uses the Hindu word *karma* as his keystone and emphasizes the inexorable link between actions and results. Each action produces the need for retribution, both in life and after death, since actions never perish even after millions of cosmic eras. The karma belongs strictly to the individual and is not transferable: it leaves its distinguishing mark on beings and is their property and their heritage. Because of the nonexistence of the self, the karma has its own efficiency. Therefore evil actions carry with them the necessity of rebirth in order to atone for them. The karma subjects the human being to the cycle of rebirth and of suffering

through the commandments, the concentration or mental discipline needed to maintain a state of alertness, and finally, wisdom (*prajna*), which is the result of teaching, reflection, and contemplation.

Humanity, Action, Rebirth, Nirvana

According to the Buddha, the human being is an accumulation of elements that are always in motion and that center on various experiences. Such experiences do not occur because of a self or a person, but constitute an ever-changing complex over time. These elements imply five

Fig. 3.7 The *cakra* (wheel) is the symbol of impermanence, teaching that one can never halt one's life and guarantee success, and that neither wealth nor honors can make life complete or stable.

Fig. 3.8 Reclining Buddha, Polonnaruva, Sri Lanka. Because of one's bad or imperfect actions, one has to undergo various rebirths to achieve nirvana, the end of suffering and rebirth. This reclining Buddha shows the achievement of nirvana.

(samsara). The collective force of actions (of the karma) creates, organizes, maintains, and conditions the entire universe, thus taking the place of god the creator, whom the Buddha never mentions.

Nirvana constitutes the end of suffering and rebirth, the reward of good actions. Being a state of freedom from the necessity of another rebirth, it resembles the extinguishing of a flame. It is the cessation of desire and as such can be reached in this life, as the Buddha did in the moment of his enlightenment. In short, it is the state of sanctity. The nirvana is, however, much more. It is light, joy, and fullness, perfect knowledge, unchangeable happiness, a perfect beatitude for the one who experiences it—that is, the one who frees oneself from the conditioning of existence by death. This aspect, stated in Buddhist texts as "the other bank, the island, the refuge, the retreat, the immortal, the wondrous state, the beatitude," remains a mystery.

The Buddhist Community and the Noble Path of Awakening

As the one who started the walk (marga) that leads to liberation, the Buddha wanted to give his followers the means to reach their destination. In order to lead them toward nirvana, he founded a community of mendicant religious (bhikshu), who, wearing the yellow garb of Indian monks, follow the ten fundamental rules set out in 250 precepts, a number that is doubled for nuns. Each infraction of the rules carries with it a specific sanction. The monk is expected to live in poverty and is forbidden eleven things: killing of living creatures, theft, incontinence, lying, fermented drinks, afternoon meals, dance, music and shows, floral wreaths and perfumes, sheets and luxury coverlets, and possession of gold and silver. Every fifteen days, the monk must publicly confess any disobedience of the rules.

The monks, who must undergo a two-year novitiate and be ordained by a chapter of ten senior monks, become candidates for sanctity (arhat). Chaste and poor, and expected to meditate on the human condition, each monk must beg for his daily meal every morning. The monastic institution does not have a spiritual leader or hierarchy. There are only prerogatives regarding precedence, calculated according to the date of ordination. At any time, the monk can give up his duties and return to the secular world.

The Buddha (also called Shakyamuni or "the Sage of the Shakya") completed his community known as samgha with a brotherhood of "laypersons" (*upasaka*), who were secondary but trustworthy members for whom generosity was the major reason for existence. It was the responsibility of these *upasaka* to build

monasteries and obtain food and means of sustenance for monks and nuns. Immersed in the preoccupation of daily life, the layperson finds refuge in the Three Jewels: the Buddha, the law (dharma), and the samgha, without hope of an immediate access to nirvana, but with the hope of better rebirths in the worlds of men and the gods. For laypeople, generosity toward the religious is the best means to gain merits.

At Ajanta, in the Indian region of Maharashtra, sixty miles northeast of Autangabad, there are thirty caves dug in the hard basalt rock, where a number of Buddhist monks settled in the second to first century BCE and in the third to sixth centuries CE. These painted caverns, originally meant to serve as shelter during the rainy seasons, offer a precious historic and archaeological record of the life of the samgha.

Fig. 3.9 Drums are a fundamental element for the rites and dances of Tibetan Buddhism, as these monks demonstrate at Kampagar, northern India.

Fig. 3.10 Vihara, a Buddhist two-storied rupestral (carved in rock) monastery at Ajanta, India.

From the Buddhism of the *Shravaka* to Mahayana

During the first five centuries, all the disciples of Shakyamuni remained faithful to his teachings. Known as *shravaka,* "listeners," they had collected three baskets (*pitaka*) of writings that date back to the Master himself: discipline (*vinaya*), the sermons (*sutra*), and the doctrine (*abhidharma*). The conversion of Emperor Ashoka (272-236 BCE) and his missionary zeal gave the decisive impulse for the spread of Buddhism throughout India and in Ceylon from 250 BCE. These are the centuries of *Hinayana* (or Small Vehicle)—a Buddhism essentially for monks—which saw the foundation of various schools and sects, resulting in the convening of a number of councils. Numerous documents show the great influence of the monasteries on Indian culture.

Laypeople still turned toward the jataka, narratives of the previous lives of the Buddha. In particular, they admired his great shows of generosity, patience, and energy. The supreme and perfect awakening attracted them more than did the sanctity of the monks. Concerned about their own spiritual, mythological, and religious needs, they created the figure of the bodhisattva, a personage who is no longer a guide but a savior. While the *shravaka* aspires to the state of arhat (sanctity), the bodhisattva experiences ten stages in the service of his brothers and thus postpones reaching his nirvana. In the eyes of laypeople, this personage becomes a subject worthy of admiration and devotion because he puts the salvation of others before all else. Moreover, a new doctrine in Buddhism developed, inspired by the inherent character of Buddhahood, the deep dimension of all things. Contrary to what the monks teach, it is believed that every individual participates in the essence of the Buddha in the intimacy of his or her own being, thus opening the way toward the supreme awakening. In this respect, people refer to the Mahayana (or Large Vehicle), which carries a great number of beings to salvation.

Fig. 3.11 The third *stupa* at Sanci in India. Note a *harmika* (scenic overlook) at the top, including a parasol, as the symbol of kingship. A balustrade at the middle permits the faithful to walk around in procession as a rite of worship (circumambulation). Stupas are places for pilgrimage and cultic ritual.

Fig. 3.12 A bodhisattva in the temple of Candi Sari in Java, Indonesia.

In this transformation, that which had been the law of karma yields to the possibility that the merits obtained by the bodhisattva are transferred to the faithful, thereby allowing a belief in prayer and cult. Thus, together with the Buddhism of meditation, a Buddhism of faith was born. These two coexist to the present day.

Buddhism in China

Buddhist missionaries made their way to China during the first century CE along the Silk Road, preaching to both common people and to learned Daoists (sometimes, Taoists; those who follow the Dao—"the way"—which is central to one of the main philosophic and religious expressions of China). Listening to them, these Daoists felt that the missionaries were preaching a religion with the Buddha as its powerful god. This misunderstanding resulted in the first success of Hinayana Buddhism, or Buddhism of the Small Vehicle, in China.

The fall of the Han dynasty in 220 CE was followed by a period of instability, which opened the way to Mahayana missionaries, who favored voyages and pilgrimages to India and Ceylon.

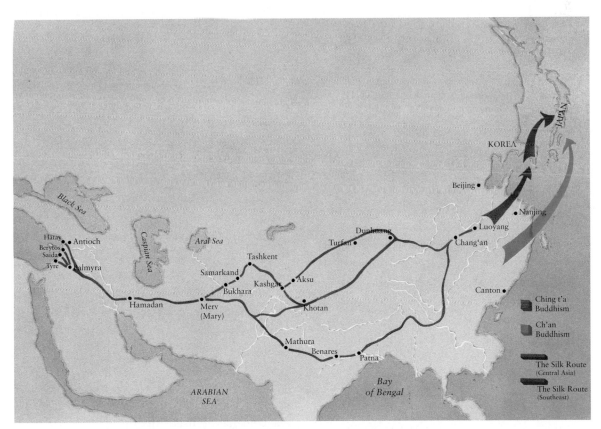

Fig. 3.13 The Silk Route in China. Buddhism spread along this route, from India through Afghanistan to China in the first century CE. Ch'an Buddhism passed directly from China to Japan, becoming Zen, while Ching-t'u Buddhism passed to Korea and Japan.

These links gave birth to an original Chinese Buddhism, which included aspects of both Hindu doctrines and Daoist teachings, and led to the formation of two Buddhist schools.

Ch'an (which became Zen in Japan) is the Chinese form of the Buddhism of meditation. Drawing on the Large Vehicle and on Tao, the masters Tao Cheng (360–434) and Sang Chao (384–414) taught that the nature of Buddha is a hidden treasure to be sought in every living being. In accordance with this belief, reading Buddhist texts or performing acts of piety is not required, but rather one must stop the work of the spirit to allow the inner light that will bring about the enlightenment to flow. During the great persecution carried out by Emperor Wutsung in 845, devotees of Ch'an were forced to lay low, but the belief was revived and strengthened after the storm of persecution ended.

One of the great Buddhas of the Mahayana (emanations of an originary, celestial Buddha, of whom Gautama, the historic Buddha, is a manifestation) known as Amitabha was already known in China in the second century. Ching-t'u, the school known as that of the Pure Land or of the Western Paradise, began and developed devotion toward this Buddha, who was considered as sovereign in paradise. The contacts of this form of mystic Buddhism with Christianity and the Indian devotion of the bhakti, addressing gods close to humanity, led its disciples to practice the cult of Amitabha. This belief system emphasized the importance of living a high moral life, including adoration of statues, permanent thanksgiving, a religion of love, and a tranquil happiness that prepared the way to paradise after death. This form of Buddhism soon migrated to Korea, Japan, and Vietnam.

Tibetan Buddhism and Lamaism

Tibet, "the roof of the world," with its great spaces and profound silence, was found to encourage religious thought. The pre-Buddhist religion, known as Bon, consisted of a complex of practices concerning the spirits (shamanism), nature cults, and magical rites, which may appear cruel to modern Westerners. In 779, the monk Padmasambhava came from the Kashmir and founded the great monastery of Bsam-yas, where many Buddhists gathered from various places to translate their Sanskrit texts into Tibetan. It was the foundation of the Buddhist sect known as the "old believers" or "red hats," who were later dispersed during a persecution between 803 and 842.

In 1042 CE, a second period of development began when the monk Atisha reached Tibet from his native Bengal. Together with other monks from India and Kashmir, he founded many monasteries and reorganized monastic life to include a monastic hierarchy, with the lamas or religious leaders as its aristocracy. This Buddhism of the Large Vehicle included both married and celibate monks.

The monk Tsong Khapa, born in 1357 in eastern Tibet, introduced yet another reform. Returning to the Buddhism of Shakyamuni, he made his monks wear yellow tunics and hats. He dictated their daily activities and insisted on celibacy, the practice of confession, fasting on prescribed days, and festivals. In 1578, a new title was conferred to the religious and political leader of Tibet—Dalai Lama, "ocean teacher." A monk, he was considered a reincarnation of Avalokiteshvara, a heavenly bodhisattva who has refused nirvana in order to look after humans with particular care and attention. Placed at the height of the social scale, the

Fig. 3.14 The sculptured grottoes of Dazú in Sichuan, China, are an expression of Ching-t'u Buddhism.

Fig. 3.15 Fifteenth-century monastery at Thiksey in India, a typical example of a Himalayan monastery.

lamas are revered religious masters who enjoy great privileges. All intellectual life is concentrated in the monasteries—holy places where the cult is celebrated in a rather rich liturgical framework featuring an extraordinary variety of rites. Tibetans also use divination and oracles to explain events in their lives.

Since 1949, Chinese Communists have invaded Tibet, imprisoning and executing thousands of monks and forcing many other thousands to marry. Of 3,700 great monasteries, which used to house more than 200,000 monks, more than 3,650 have been destroyed. Only a few hundred Tibetan monks remain.

Fig. 3.16 The fourteenth Dalai Lama of Tibet (born Tenzin Gyatso in July 1935). At this ceremony at the monastery at Namgyal in northern India, he holds a *dordje* in his hands, the symbol of Tibetan Buddhism.

Much of the cultural wealth of the country has been annihilated, causing irreparable damage to the heritage of humankind.

Buddhism in Japan

Chinese Buddhism arrived in Japan by way of Korea a thousand years after its founding. There it encountered the Shinto, "the way of the gods," a Neolithic religion built on the presence of kami, powerful supernatural beings. The emperor Shotoku Taishi (574–622 CE) built the first monasteries and embraced the new religion, which gave the country a new moral structure and a world vision, although restricted to the ruling class. In the eighth century, there developed an original form of Japanese Buddhism called Ryobushinto, which was an amalgam of Shinto and Buddhism, the encounter between the kami and the bodhisattva. In an attempt to achieve an equilibrium between these "two halves of a cloven piece of wood" and thus encourage national unity, the authorities embraced this new religion. In this preoccupation to adapt to the needs of particular epochs, however, schools and sects proliferated, centering on the two areas of devotion and meditation.

The Buddhism of devotion searched for its way at first in chanting, in prayer, and in ecstasy, and later in the doctrine of Jodo (Pure Land). An outstanding figure of Jodo, the monk Honen (1133–1212 CE) taught the Nembutsu, a practice of simply calling on the name of Buddha, constantly and with deep devotion, to obtain salvation. The Nembutsu led the believers to achieve the Buddhahood. Honen's disciple, the monk Shinran (1173–1262 CE), broke the law of celibacy for monks and denounced study as a means to achieve wisdom, steering Buddhism in the direction of a popular monotheism.

While the Buddhism of faith as preached by Honen and Shinran was diffusing, Zen (a Buddhism of meditation) was being organized at Kamakura, where a great number of monasteries were located. Zen proclaimed awakening without preparation. Its main practitioner was the monk Dogen (1200–1253 CE), who believed that Buddhahood was an innate feature of human nature to which one must only awaken. Through the practice of Zazen, "sitting meditation," the disciple achieves awakening. Each disciple must liberate his spirit from every

Fig. 3.17 A Zen garden in Kyoto, Japan. These gardens are created of rocks and sand that are carefully raked.

tie and overcome all mental agitation to achieve satori, an illumination that is an intuitive vision. Zen has been applied to the art of war, the tea ceremony, the art of gardening, and to painting.

The Bodhisattva, Savior and Saved

The Vow of the Bodhisattva

May I be the protector of the abandoned, the guide of those who walk and, for those who aspire to reach the other bank, the boat, the dam, the bridge; may I be the lamp for those who need a lamp, the bed for those who need a bed, the salve for those who need a salve. . . . Just as the earth and the other elements serve the multiple uses of the innumerable beings scattered in infinite space, so may I be useful in any possible way to the beings who inhabit this space, until everyone is liberated. (Santideva, *The Way to Light*, 111)

This text clearly summarizes the vow and the ideal of the bodhisattva, savior created by the Mahayana Buddhists at the beginning of our era, standing in contrast to the arhat of the Hinayana Buddhists of the preceding five centuries. Achieving the highest level of Buddhist compassion, which he transforms into an aspiration for universal awakening, the bodhisattva renounces his own immediate definitive liberation through the awakening to look after other beings.

Such a profound compassion makes him a "saved savior" who penetrates the hearts, responds to the various spiritual needs of all creatures, and reaches down to the human caravan to carry its burden of suffering. This path starts with a vow, which lies at the origin of the numerous merits that the bodhisattva will accumulate, a reserve made available to the other creatures and from which they can draw, through their devotion toward these saviors. The first among them is Avalokitesh-vara, "a great ocean of virtues worthy of every homage."

Thus, in parallel with the Buddhism of meditation, there developed a Buddhism of devotion with a cult of saviors.

◆ STUDY AND DISCUSSION QUESTIONS

1. Why do you think modern or contemporary Buddhism is a more attractive religious tradition than it was in the nineteenth century? Discuss the meaning and import of the idea of "awakening" in your discussion.

2. Consider how Buddhism took hold in various parts of Asia and how its expression in these varied cultures differs. Evaluate these differences, and draw any parallels to another religious tradition that is practiced throughout the world.

3. Review and explore further the life of the Buddha. Is Gautama's life history a compelling one for you? In what ways is or isn't it?

◆ KEY TERMS

Amitabha

Ananda

anatman

arhat

aryasatya

Ashoka

bhagavan or bhagavat

bhikshu

bodhi

bodhisattva

Buddha

cakra

Dao, Daoism

dharma

dhatu

duhkha

jnana

karma

lama

marga (path) astangamarga (eight paths of perfection)

nirvana

parinirvana

prajna

Samadhi

samgha

samsara

Santideva

satya

skandha

stupa

sutra

Sutrapitaka

Vinayapitaka

◆ FOR FURTHER READING

Boucher, Sandy. *Opening the Lotus: A Women's Guide to Buddhism*. Boston: Beacon, 1998.

The Dalai Lama. *The Path to Tranquility*. New York: Penguin, 1998.

Kinnard, Jacob. *The Emergence of Buddhism*. Minneapolis: Fortress Press, 2011.

Monius, Anne E. *Imagining a Place for Buddhism*. New York: Oxford University Press, 2001.

Morreale, Don, ed. *The Complete Guide to Buddhism in America*. Boston: Shambhala, 1998.

Suzuki, D. T. *Manual of Zen Buddhism*. New York: Grove, 1960.

Tamura, Yoshiro. *Japanese Buddhism: A Cultural History*. Translated by Jeffrey Hondu. Tokyo: Kosei, 2000.

CHAPTER 4

Jainism

Andrea R. Jain

Introduction

The Jain tradition is grounded in a discipline aimed at conquering life as we know it based on our day-to-day experiences. In fact, the term *Jain* is derived from the Sanskrit term *jina*, or "conqueror." *Jina* is a title ascribed to the great teachers of the Jain tradition, who are believed to have become spiritual "conquerors" through withdrawal from bodily action and social engagement, which cultivated a life of nonviolence. So Jains, in short, are followers of the conquerors. But this in no way means that Jain identity is monolithic. In any evaluation of the Jain tradition, it is necessary to consider the cultural forces that have shaped its history and development. Only then do the many ways of exemplifying Jain identity become clear.

The Jain tradition emerged as a new religious movement instigated by an ascetic world-renouncer, Vardhamana Mahavira, who was perceived as a great hero for his ascetic ability to conquer the path toward ultimate truth and achieve liberation from the cycle of rebirth.[1] Even though the path toward liberation as modeled by Mahavira is rigorous, the Jain tradition did not become a static, insulated community. Rather, it has been persistently dynamic, as Jains have constructed ideas and practices in response to the shifting trends of cultural

TIMELINE

BCE

ca. 490–410	Life of Mahavira, "The Great Hero"

CE

156	Completion of *Shatkhandagam*
4th c.	Compilation of Jain texts in *Tattvartha Sutra* by Umasvati
4th–5th c.	Schism between Shvetambara and Digambara sects
7th c.	Massacre of Tamil Jains in Madurai
1658	Building of Digambara Jain Lal Mandir temple in Delhi
1868	Building of Jain temple in Mumbai
ca. 1970	Chitrabhanu is first Jain to leave renouncer order and travel abroad
20th c.	Jains emigrate to East Africa, the United Kingdom, and North America

contexts. The tradition has offered various ways of being Jain and benefiting from that identity, from merit for worshipers of the *jina* as well as other Jain renouncers to worldly benefits for the worship of deities to programs for social reform and yoga. Yet underlying the various ways of being Jain lies a shared commitment to philosophical dualism, an evaluation of the world as permeated with life, a commitment to nonviolence, and a valorization of the ascetic ideal as modeled by the *jina*, who are believed to have conquered all mundane dimensions of life. Though Jain identity is plural, all Jains follow the conquerors.

Attaining Enlightenment and Release

Jains consider Mahavira, the Great Hero (*mahavira*), to be the most recent of twenty-four *jina*. Twenty-four *jina* are born into the world per time cycle—which occur endlessly—and each one reignites the eternal Jain teachings in the world.[2] A *jina* is also called a *tirthankara*, or "maker of the ford," a reference to the superior knowledge that functions as a "ford" from entrapment in samsara, the cycle of rebirth, to release from that cycle. A Jain is someone who ascribes total authority with regard to correct knowledge, correct vision, and correct behavior to the twenty-four *jina* of the current time cycle.

According to Jain doctrine, the ultimate goal is to attain enlightenment, a state in which one knows all things in existence. Subsequently, one attains moksha, or "release," from samsara, which occurs upon the enlightened person's death and entails instant movement to the top of the cosmos, where one remains in a state of pure knowledge, energy, and bliss for eternity.

According to Mahavira's biographers, the Great Hero attained enlightenment after he renounced the wealth and status of his royal family and spent years in withdrawal from society engrossed in ascetic practices. He renounced all of his belongings, including

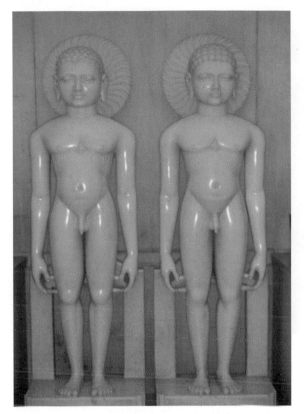

Fig. 4.1 Icons of jina meditating in the standing posture.

Renouncing Worldly Ways

Historically, the Jain tradition can be traced back to an ascetic culture of world-renouncers that arose in present-day northern India, beginning around the seventh century BCE. Renouncers deem life and its activities such as those of family, work, and play mundane (as opposed to spiritual); that is, they are ultimately unsatisfactory because they only reflect conventional truths that shift according to time and place. In short, renouncers maintain that there is no ultimate truth to be found in mundane life. They "renounce" that life and embark on an exclusively spiritual path, which they believe to lead to ultimate truth. Renouncers vary with regard to their ideas about ultimate truth and the practices deemed necessary to realize it, but they all agree that to some extent the spiritual path requires ascetic practices, techniques for freeing oneself from conventional desires, needs, and social conditioning. Most Indian renouncer traditions also agree that that freedom ultimately results in liberation from the cycle of rebirth.

Early Development

The Jain tradition came into being with the initiatives of Mahavira (ca. 490–410 BCE), who greatly influenced the emergent ascetic culture when he started a new religious movement that rejected the orthodox ritual culture established by the social and religious elites of his time, the authorities of what would come to be known as Hinduism.

From its beginnings, even during Mahavira's lifetime, the Jain tradition reflected popular trends regarding worship styles and rituals. Mahavira lived in a devotional culture in which

clothing, because he believed those things were mere distractions from the spiritual path. One day, after fasting from food and water for two and a half days, completely naked, his bare skin exposed to the heat of the sun, Mahavira squatted down in a meditative posture. It was in that ascetic state that he became enlightened. He was omniscient, meaning that he directly and simultaneously perceived all things in existence. In the Jain tradition, this superior knowledge is called *kevala-jnana*, or "knowledge isolated [from karmic obstruction]." Mahavira became a kevalin, "one who has achieved absolute isolation." Jains strive to emulate the life of Mahavira in order to become a kevalin like him.

Fig. 4.2 Icons of the twenty-four jina in a Jain temple complex.

laypeople worshiped renouncers. Mahavira and his disciples would have been attractive objects of devotion because of what would have been perceived as their heroic asceticism.[3] By participating in the popular devotional culture, Mahavira and his disciples attracted many people to the new religious movement.

Mahavira's closest disciples, *ganadhara*, are believed to have produced texts based on Mahavira's teachings and to have maintained the development and growth of the earliest Jain community after their teacher's death. In the following one thousand years, the Jain community quickly grew in northern India. By the third or second century BCE, Jains had accommodated regional deities, participated in mainstream literary traditions, built temples, and acquired socioeconomic power through trade and aristocratic alliances as far south as the Tamil region. This was especially the case in urban centers, where commerce was strong, because Jains were concentrated in the merchant class.[4]

Divisions and Migrations

By the fourth or fifth centuries CE, Jains split into two major sects: Digambara, or "sky-clad," and Shvetambara, or "white-clad." These names

Fig. 4.3 An icon of Mahavira sitting in meditation.

refer to their dress: whether their male renouncers renounce all clothing or wear white robes. Shvetambaras, moreover, attribute authenticity to a scriptural canon they believe can be traced back to Mahavira's lifetime, whereas Digambaras reject that canon as inauthentic and instead maintain that all early Scriptures were lost. Perhaps most significantly, Shvetambaras and Digambaras disagree on the spiritual status of women.[5] Although both agree that birth into a female body is a sign of unbeneficial karma from a past life, Shvetambaras believe that it is possible for women to attain enlightenment, whereas Digambaras do not.

The debate over this issue reflects the general misogyny that permeates much of Jain literature, especially prior to the modern period. Historians believe there to have been more nuns than monks as early as Mahavira's lifetime, so renunciation on the part of women has always been central to the tradition. Yet nuns are always subordinate to monks, and it is the leading monks who define correct ascetic practice. Furthermore, nuns did not contribute to the Jain literary tradition until the modern period.

In the fourth century CE, a Jain by the name of Umasvati wrote a text, the Tattvartha Sutra (Sutra on the Meaning of the Real), which provides a concise articulation of the central Jain doctrinal positions and came to be authoritative for both Shvetambaras and Digambaras. The Tattvartha Sutra functions as an authoritative resource on Jain doctrine to the present day. Nevertheless, different interpretations of Jain doctrine, usually with regard to renouncer praxis or ritual style, have resulted in the establishment of several subsects.

The Digambara community grew in present-day southern India until it reached its peak there between the fifth and seventh centuries

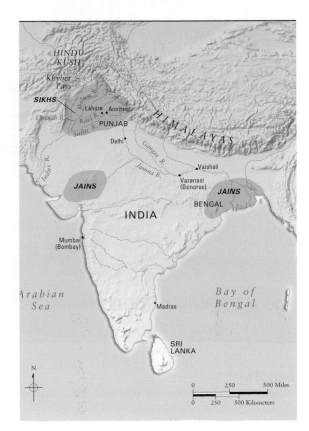

Fig. 4.4 Map showing the concentration of Jains in India today.

CE. In the medieval period, the Shvetambara community continued to grow in the north. But beginning in the thirteenth century, the Jain community decreased in number when mass conversions of Digambaras to Shaivism (devotion to the Hindu deity Shiva) took place in southern India. Then, from the sixteenth to the nineteenth centuries, Shvetambara numbers decreased in the north, as many Jains converted to Vaishnavism (devotion to the Hindu deity Vishnu).[6]

In addition to the estimated 4.2 million Jains living in India today, there are an estimated 100,000 Jains living outside of India (mostly in the United Kingdom and North America).[7]

Fig. 4.5 Jain Digambara renouncers.

Teachings

Jains believe that karma, a material substance that accumulates to the soul as a result of all actions over many lifetimes, perpetuates both rebirth and ignorance of ultimate truth. There are many types of karma, each of which depends on the qualities of the actions that resulted in them, such as intention and consequence. Most living beings are perpetually entrapped in a state of ignorance because karma obscures their perception of things. Only the kevalin, the enlightened one, perceives ultimate truth, the way things really are.

The kevalin's superior knowledge includes an awakening to the eternal distinction between two things: jiva and ajiva. The jiva, or "life monad," is the unchanging, eternal self or soul, characterized by pure knowledge, energy, and bliss. Every living being has a jiva. Ajiva is the perpetually changing stuff—our mundane experiences of day-to-day life—that makes up the cycle of rebirth as we know it. Karma is in the category of ajiva and is the force that entraps the jiva in the form of material bodies over and over again in the cycle of rebirth.

Because the jiva is entrapped in the cycle of rebirth, the path to liberation is rigorous ascetic work over many lifetimes, which limits the accumulation of karma and burns karma already bound to the jiva. Jains are well-known for maintaining an ascetic ideal, modeled by Mahavira, whereby the human must conquer the mundane dimensions of life through processes of withdrawal from bodily action and social engagement.

Correct forms of asceticism are determined based on their conformity to the vow of ahimsa, or "nonviolence." Ahimsa is the foundation of the Jain ascetic ethic and is directly linked to the body. In fact, *himsa*, or "violence," is the result of all bodily action: breathing, walking, eating, coughing, and so on. Whether we see them or not, living beings of every size are present in the earth, water, fire, and air. They get injured or destroyed not only when a person consciously kills something for the sake of food, protection, or some malicious intent but also when a person performs the most simple of actions, such as taking a step or a breath. Ultimately, every living being suffers the violence of death. So all living beings are both agents and subjects of violence. Because all bodily action involves violence, ahimsa requires the cessation of bodily action. In other words, it requires a nonactive nonviolence, an ethical stance believed to be possible for humans only in an advanced degree. When the renouncer achieves this level of bodily control, karma stops accumulating to the jiva and karma already bound to the *jiva* begins to burn away. The culmination of this path of purification is moksha.

Ascetic Ethic

Asceticism is a term used to describe a systematic program of self-discipline and self denial in which immediate gratifications are renounced in order to attain a higher spiritual state.[8] It is believed that Mahavira prescribed five ascetic vows that functioned as the basis of advancement along the spiritual path through purification from karma. The *mahavrata*, or "Great Vows," begin with ahimsa. The other four are *satya* ("telling the truth"), *asteya* ("restraint from stealing"), *brahmacharya* ("celibacy"), and *aparigraha* ("restraint from attachment"). Because of the preeminent status of ahimsa in Jain ethics, the other four vows are considered extensions of or elaborations on this one. In other words, the adoption of the other four vows serves to help one maintain the vow of ahimsa. Jain renouncers must adopt the vows and implement them in every moment of their lives.

In addition to the five vows, Jain renouncers must regularly engage in a number of ascetic practices. These include the conscious adoption of an attitude of equanimity and repentance, praise to the twenty-four jina and to one's teacher, meditation involving dissociation from the body and limitation of action, as well as vows to abstain from specific forms of bodily activity, such as the consumption of food, in the future.

The degree to which Jains adopt the five vows and ascetic practices occurs along a wide spectrum. There are, after all, more Jain laypeople (nonrenouncers) than Jain renouncers. Whereas renouncers take the vows literally, laypeople fulfill the vows to the best of their abilities as participants in normal life. On the one hand, a layperson may have sex within the confines of marriage, drive a car and consequently destroy thousands (even millions) of living beings along the way, own a home and run a business, which necessitates some level of attachment, and so on. Laypeople implement the vows by avoiding "unnecessary" harm caused by such acts as meat-eating or acting out in physical aggression toward living beings. On the other hand, the renouncer will not only avoid eating meat and acting out in physical aggression but will also take care in every step so as not to crush the living beings below his or her feet, adopt strict celibacy and thus avoid even lustful thoughts, withhold from social and business interactions, and renounce all personal belongings.

Social Ethic

Although the ascetic ethic is believed to lead to the ultimate goal of the Jain tradition, moksha, many Jains also value things necessary for

Fig. 4.6 Jain Shvetambara Terapanth nuns.

success in day-to-day life such as well-being, health, and wealth. And even though Jain doctrine may seem incompatible with a social ethic that prescribes right action, since the path of purification requires withdrawal from bodily action and social engagement, Jain identity has always entailed a transformation of ahimsa into a social ethic for laypeople.

The Jain tendency to transform ahimsa into a social ethic is evident in the fact that lay Jains are especially known for providing financial support to hospitals and animal welfare organizations. One example can be witnessed in the Gujarati town of Palitana, where a group of lay Jains established a large medical camp for twenty-five thousand people with disabilities. BBC journalist Sanjoy Majumder reports on the camp: "At the medical camp in Palitana town the spiritual becomes practical: doctors fit patients with artificial limbs and calipers. Some are given crutches and wheelchairs. People with hearing problems are given special aids and taught how to use them."[9] He quotes Asha

Mehta of the Ratna Nidhi Charitable Trust, the organization responsible for establishing the camp: "Our Jain faith teaches us to reach out to the underprivileged."[10] Clearly, an ascetic ethic is not the motivating factor for such philanthropic activity. Rather, it is a social ethic and, more specifically, an interpretation of ahimsa in terms of compassion for others.

Another example of Jains transforming ahimsa into a social ethic is the institution of animal hospitals (*pinjrapole*) in India. The most famous of all such hospitals is the Birds' Charity Hospital in New Delhi, devoted solely to caring for sick, injured, and dying birds. These birds are often mangled, paralyzed, or blinded and in a great deal of suffering. Many of them eventually die in the hospital, but sometimes their lives are saved, and they are released back into the world.

Today, Jains are constructing new and creative ways to expand the Jain community by linking Jain ideas and practices to ethical movements that are increasingly popular in the global religious market, such as antiwar/ peace, animal rights, vegetarian, and ecological movements. These Jains are especially concerned with an interpretation of ahimsa that deems it preeminent in dictating how society should function and what the human disposition should be toward the earth and the life that permeates it. For example, the theme of the JAINA (Jain Association in North America, an umbrella organization for Jain societies) 2010 annual convention was "ecology," and the Dakshin Bharat Jain Sabha (South Indian Jain Society) supports social-reform movements in India. Most recently, the Dakshin Bharat Jain Sabha has received widespread attention for its advocacy work at the national level in India aimed at getting minority status for Jains.

Devotional Ritual

So being Jain is often about worldly contingencies, pursuits, and benefits. This is reflected as much in Jain ritual culture as it is in the Jain social ethic. Devotional ritual primarily occurs in the form of puja, worship of an icon, which is showered in various substances that are considered pure, such as water, milk, and flower petals. Although some Jains reject icon worship, the majority of Jains worship the jina as well as various deities in this way. On the one hand, deities are believed to reciprocate the devotee with worldly blessings, such as health or wealth. On the other hand, ideologically, jina are considered liberated from the world for eternity and thus no longer capable of personal, mutually beneficial engagement with devotees. So Jains are not supposed to worship them with the hope of gaining worldly rewards. Rather, they should worship the jina because the jina functions as a model of the ascetic ideal necessary to

attain moksha. In practice, however, the icons of jina are often associated not only with the ascetic ideal, but also with auspicious powers to transmit worldly benefits.

The simultaneous pursuit of worldly benefits and the ascetic ideal is common in Jain worship spaces. In fact, the more an object of devotion represents the ascetic ideal, the more worthy it is of worship. Jain ritual culture thus includes the regular recitation of the *Pancana-maskara*, or "Five Homages," mantra, in which Jains express their homage to revered renouncers, including omniscient teachers, liberated souls, and all living renouncers. Furthermore,

Fig. 4.7 A fifty-five-foot tall icon of the Jain kevalin, Gomateshwara Bahubali, in Shravanabelagola, Karnataka, India. This is an important Jain pilgrimage site where, every twelve years, Jains participate in a ritual called the Mahamasthak Abisheka, in which they consecrate the icon with various libations (here, turmeric water).

the worship of living renouncers is believed to result in a transmission of punya, or "merit," from the renouncer to the devotee. Punya is a form of karma, but it is advantageous karma insofar as it results in worldly benefits. Such karma is distinct from disadvantageous karma, *papa*, which may result in ill health or poverty. Thus when the devotee offers the renouncer an abundance of worldly gifts, such as food, he or she receives merit, which then results in worldly benefits.

Jain ritual culture is not exclusively concerned with worldly benefits. Some ascetic rituals aim at liberation from the world. On the ascetic end of the ritual spectrum, one finds *sallekhana*, or "scouring out the body." *Sallekhana*, also called *samthara*, or "deathbed," is a ritual death by fasting, and this is considered the ideal way to die in the Jain tradition. One voluntarily partakes in *sallekhana* by ritually decreasing one's consumption of food and water while simultaneously focusing the mind on the jiva and thus burning an immense amount of karma immediately prior to death. Whereas from a non-Jain point of view this may seem like an extremely violent way to die, Jains insist that *sallekhana* is not violent, nor is it suicide, because it does not involve psychological weapons or passions, such as fear or depression, nor physical weapons, such as knives or guns. In fact, *sallekhana* is considered the least violent way to die because it requires the limitation of nearly all bodily action and thus the limitation of violence.[11]

Fig. 4.8 A decorated icon of the jina, Mallinatha. Shvetambara Jains believe that Mallinatha was the only female jina, whereas Digambara Jains believe that Mallinatha was a male jina.

Jain "Renouncers" in the World

Since the beginning of the second half of the twentieth century, strategies to expand the Jain community by linking Jain ideas and practices to popular movements in the global religious market have become increasingly common, even though such movements stray from the orthodox Jain ascetic ideal. Some Jain renouncers have even taken the lead in the global spread of Jain ideas and practices by constructing and disseminating Jain systems of modern yoga and meditation.

Efforts on the part of renouncers to globally disseminate Jain ideas and practices required radical breaks from Jain doctrine about renouncer praxis. For example, according to Jain orthodoxy, renouncers are not allowed to travel by means of mechanical transportation, but can only travel by foot. They are also not allowed to leave India under any circumstances. Yet, in the 1970s, two Jain Shvetambara monks, Chitrabhanu (b. 1922) and Sushil Kumar (1926–1994), separately left India by plane and traveled to the United States.

Chitrabhanu became the first Jain to leave his renouncer order and travel abroad. When he arrived in the United States, Chitrabhanu struggled to attract disciples but gradually began receiving support from Americans interested in his guidance to the Jain American community and non-Jain Americans interested in learning from Indian religions. Chitrabhanu teaches a "nonsectarian" Jain message that focuses on meditation. He also prescribes a vegan diet based on a Jain ethical mandate against the food industry's torture and slaughter of animals. Today, his Jain Meditation International Center, in New York City, still exists, and he and his disciples continue to teach there and at other religious centers around the world.[12]

Sushil Kumar also broke Jain rules regarding renouncer praxis, going to the United States in 1975 to disseminate Jain ideas and practices. Like Chitrabhanu, Kumar often referred to his teachings as "nonsectarian." He syncretized Jain ideas with various yoga techniques and established a temple and retreat center in Blairstown, New Jersey, where he taught what he called "Arhum Yoga."[13]

Another Jain renouncer, Mahaprajna (1920–2010), of a Jain Shvetambara sect called the Terapanth, did not consider Chitrabhanu and Kumar's unorthodox acts acceptable for a Jain renouncer, but he also wanted to adapt to the global religious market.[14] In 1975, Mahaprajna introduced *preksha dhyana*, literally, "concentration of perception" but most often translated as "insight meditation." He prescribed *preksha dhyana* as a universal meditation and yoga system that could resolve widespread problems due to people's lack of health. In order to avoid being declared unorthodox by renouncers, beginning in 1980, the Terapanth introduced a new order of proselytizing novice renouncers called the saman.[15] The saman make up an order of intermediary renouncers—intermediaries between

Fig. 4.9 Female saman gather in preparation for Mahaprajna's birthday celebration in Ladnun, Rajasthan, India.

full renouncers and laypeople—who are charged with the mission to travel throughout the world in order to spread Jain ideas and practices primarily by teaching people *preksha dhyana*.

Deep Meditation: Knowing All Conditions

For insight into the Jain tradition, consider the following account of Mahavira's enlightenment from a Jain text called *The Limbs of the Teaching*:

> Then [Mahavira] formed the following resolution: I shall for twelve years neglect my body and abandon the care of it; I shall with equanimity bear, undergo, and suffer all calamities arising from divine powers, men or animals. . . . The Venerable Ascetic Mahavira passed twelve years in this way of life; during the thirteenth year . . . in the field of the householder Samaga, in a northeastern direction from an old temple, not far from a Sal tree, in a squatting position with joined heels exposing himself to the heat of the sun, with the knees high and the head low, in deep meditation, in the midst of abstract meditation, he reached Nirvana, the

complete and full, the unobstructed, unimpeded, infinite and supreme, best knowledge and intuition. . . . . He was a Kevalin, omniscient and comprehending all objects, he knew all conditions of the world.[16]

Mahavira argued that asceticism was necessary for enlightenment, hence he is believed to have achieved enlightenment in an extreme ascetic state. He went without food or water for two and a half days, crouched down in the squatting meditative posture, was completely naked, and was exposed to the hot sun as he rejected the protective shade of a tree. Mahavira's ascetic state resulted from his conscious choice, since he understood that this was necessary for advanced spiritual progress.

The Jain ascetic ideal is intimately linked to Jain philosophical dualism, the belief that there are two distinct, opposing categories of existence. When Mahavira achieved enlightenment, he immediately experienced direct knowledge of the soul as eternally distinct from the material world, including the body. Because the soul remains entrapped in the material world as long as one is subject to basic bodily desires and needs, the Jain seeks to conquer the body through the asceticism modeled by Mahavira.

◆ **STUDY AND DISCUSSION QUESTIONS**

1. Consider the institution of Jain animal hospitals, or *pinjrapole*, in India. Can you imagine strategies not mentioned in this chapter that Jains might use to apply their commitment to ahimsa toward ethical action?

2. Reflect on the Jain ritual of *sallekhana*. Is this a violent or nonviolent way to die according to your own cultural ideas about violence and acceptable and unacceptable ways to die? Why or why not?

3. Are there cultural analogues to the concepts of *papa* and *punya* in your own culture? If so, how are your concepts similar and how are they different?

◆ **KEY TERMS**

ahimsa

ajiva

Digambara

ganadhara

jina

jiva

karma

kevala-jnana

kevalin

mahavrata

moksha

pancanamaskara

papa

pinjrapole

preksha dhyana

puja

punya

sallekhana/samthara

samsara

Shvetambara

tirthankara

◆ FOR FURTHER READING

Babb, Lawrence A. *Absent Lord: Ascetics and Kings in a Jain Ritual Culture*. Berkeley: University of California Press, 1996.

Carrithers, Michael, and Caroline Humphrey, eds. *The Assembly of Listeners: Jains in Society*. New York: Cambridge University Press, 1991.

Cort, John E. *Jains In the World: Religious Values and Ideology in India*. New York: Oxford University Press, 2001.

Dundas, Paul. *The Jains*. New York: Routledge, 2002.

Jaini, Padmanabh S. *Jaina Path of Purification*. New Delhi: Motilal Banarsidass, 2004.

Laidlaw, James. *Riches and Renunciation: Religion, Economy, and Society among the Jains*. New York: Oxford University Press, 1995.

Vallely, Anne. *Guardians of the Transcendent: An Ethnography of a Jain Ascetic Community*. Toronto: University of Toronto Press, 2002.

◆ NOTES

1. *Ascetic* is a term used to describe the following: "A voluntary, sustained, and at least partially systematic program of self-discipline and self-denial in which immediate, sensual, or profane gratifications are renounced in order to attain a higher spiritual state or a more thorough absorption in the sacred." Walter O. Kaelber, "Asceticism," in *Encyclopedia of Religion*, ed. Lindsay Jones, 2nd ed. (Detroit: Macmillan Reference USA, 2005), 1:526. This definition implies the dichotomy that exists between "sacred" and "profane" according to the analysis of Emile Durkheim. Durkheim argues that the sacred is antagonistic to the profane. Emile Durkheim, *The Elementary Forms of Religious Life*, trans. Carol Cosman (1912; New York: Oxford University Press, 2001), 236. He further argues that the distinction between the sacred and profane can only be defined by their heterogeneity. Durkheim, *Elementary Forms*, 38. In the Jain tradition, this heterogeneity is most explicitly expressed in the duality of *jiva* (sacred) and *ajiva* (profane).

2. In addition to Mahavira, only one other *jina* may have been a historical figure. Parshva, the twenty-third *jina* of the current time cycle, is traditionally believed to have lived around two centuries before Mahavira and to have prescribed a similar ascetic practice to that of Mahavira. Mahavira is traditionally believed to have been a part of the ascetic community that descended from Parshva and to have further developed Parshva's teachings. However, the quality of the evidence suggesting that Parshva was indeed a historical figure is highly debated among historians.

3. Paul Dundas, "Conversion to Jainism: Historical Perspectives," in *Religious Conversion in India: Modes, Motivations, and Meanings*, ed. Rowena Robinson and Sathianathan Clarke (Oxford: Oxford University Press, 2003), 130.

4. Smita Sahgal, "Spread of Jainism in North India between circa 200 BC and circa AD 300," in *Jainism*

and Prakrit in Ancient and Medieval India: Essays for Prof. Jagdish Chandra Jain, ed. N. N. Bhattacharyya (New Delhi: Manohar, 1994), 216. Some speculate that Jains became concentrated in merchant classes because this occupation made it possible to avoid the violence associated with other occupations, particularly agriculture.

5. For a detailed discussion of this debate, see Padmanabh S. Jaini, *Gender and Salvation: Jaina Debates on the Spiritual Liberation of Women* (Berkeley: University of California Press, 1991).

6. Dundas, "Conversion to Jainism," 142.

7. For data on Jains in India, see Government of India Census Data 2001, accessed May 13, 2011, http://www.censusindia.gov.in/Census_Data_2001/India_at_glance/religion.aspx. For data outside of India, see Paul Dundas, *The Jains* (New York: Routledge, 2002), 271.

8. For a definition of *asceticism*, see note 1.

9. Sanjoy Majumder, "Faith and Charity in Indian Temple Town," *BBC News Gujarat*, January 9, 2010, accessed February 10, 2010, http://news.bbc.co.uk/2/hi/south_asia/8448290.stm.

10. Ibid.

11. Today the adoption of *sallekhana* requires the approval of a guru, and it is usually only adopted by those already advanced in age or terminally ill and thus considered relatively near to death. There are some, though rare, exceptions to this rule. In 1987, a Shvetambara Terapanthi *mumukshu* ("one who is desirous of emancipation"; refers to aspiring nuns) claimed to be possessed by a *bhut* (malevolent spirit). She believed that the only way to escape the *bhut*'s torture was through ascetic practice. This eventually led to her adoption of *sallekhana* with the permission of her guru, Acharya Tulsi.

During her fast, she was initiated as a renouncer. She then fasted unto death. She is celebrated by renouncers and laypeople as a symbol of the triumph of asceticism over materiality. For a detailed account, see Anne Vallely, *Guardians of the Transcendent: An Ethnography of a Jain Ascetic Community* (Toronto: University of Toronto Press, 2002), 132–36.

12. For more on the Jain Meditation International Center, see *Jain Meditation International Center*, www.jainmeditation.org.

13. The center, Siddhachalam Jain Tirth, established by Kumar in 1983 in Blairstown, New Jersey, is still active today. See *Siddhachalam*, http://www.imjm.org/common/index.php.

14. For a discussion of this sect's acts of adaptation in attempt to globally disseminate Jain ideas and practices, see Andrea R. Jain, "The Dual-Ideal of the Ascetic and Healthy Body: Modern Yoga, the Jain Terapanth, and the Context of Late Capitalism," *Nova Religio* 15, no. 3 (February 2012): 29–50.

15. Saman is derived from the Sanskrit word *shramana*, which means "striver," and is used as an epithet for world-renouncers. It is used in the sense of one who "strives" for release from the cycle of rebirth. Although four *samana*, or male saman, were initiated in 1986, almost all saman are *samani*, or female saman. The first initiation of semi-monastics in 1980 included six *samani*. Today, there are 103. Of the four *samana* initiated in 1986, only two remain *samana*. The other two have undergone full initiation into the renouncer order, and there have been no additional initiations of *samana* since 1986.

16. Hermann Georg Jacobi, ed. and trans., *Acaranga*, in *Jaina Sutras*, parts 1 and 2 (Charleston, SC: Forgotten Books, 2008), 2.15.25.

CHAPTER 5

Sikhism

Nikky-Guninder Kaur Singh and Todd Curcuru

CHAPTER OUTLINE

Introduction	Rites of Passage
Celebrating a New Life Phase	Sikhism in a Global World
Art and Ornamentation	The Opening of the Guru Granth
History	*Study and Discussion Questions*
Scripture	*Key Terms*
Doctrine	*For Further Reading*
Worship	*Suggested Websites*

Introduction

The word *Sikh* means "disciple" or "student" (from Sanskrit *shishya*, Pali *sekha*). With their spirit of adventure and entrepreneurial skills, Sikhs have migrated from their homeland—Punjab, the land of the five rivers—throughout India and around the globe. There are more than 23 million Sikhs today. Evolving historically and geographically between southern and western Asia, Sikhism is currently the fifth-largest religion in the world. Its origins can be traced to Guru Nanak (1469–1539), and it developed through his nine successor Gurus within a rich pluralist environment of northwestern India. Sikhs believe in one divine being. Their sacred space is called the Gurdwara. Their sacred text is the Guru Granth, which is the center of all their rites and ceremonies. Both Sikh men and women keep the five symbols of their faith given by their tenth Guru, Gobind Singh (1666–1708), popularly called the "five *k*'s" (see below, "The Khalsa"). Sikh men can be recognized by their colorful turbans and beards, and Sikh women by their neatly braided and styled hair, by their long shirts (*kameez*), loose trousers (*salvar*), and flowing scarves (*dupatta*). The marker of their identity is the surname "Singh" (for men) and "Kaur" (for women). Sikhs greet one another (whether hello or goodbye) by

TIMELINE CE	
1469–1539	Life of Guru Nanak, the first Sikh prophet
1563–1606	Life of fifth guru, Arjan Dev
1621–1675	Life of ninth guru, Tegh Bahadur
1666–1708	Life of tenth guru, Gobind Singh
1699	Gobind Singh founds order of Khalsa
1708	Guru Granth Sahib installed as Guru
1780–1839	Maharaja Ranjit Singh and establishment of Sikh kingdom
1849	British rule in Punjab as Sikh rule comes to end
1919	Massacre at Amritsar by British forces
1947	Sikhs forced to leave Pakistan for India
1999	Millions of Sikhs celebrate three hundredth anniversary of founding of the Khalsa

joining their hands and saying *Sat Sri Akal* ("Truth is the Timeless One").

Celebrating a New Life Phase

Harinder Singh's mother is the first to get up in their family. She bathes and goes to the tiny room where the holy book rests. She opens it up and adorns it in pink silks. She then goes to the kitchen, and with her head covered and feet bare, she starts to make *karahprashad*. With her lips, she recites sacred verses, while with her hands, she vigorously combines equal amounts of water, sugar, butter, and flour in a pan on the stove. Soon the father joins her. They take turns stirring, but their voices melodiously join in the recitation. Once the mixture acquires a solid consistency, they ceremoniously carry the aromatic sacrament to their prayer room and place it beside the sacred volume. Then together the parents wake up their ten-year-old son. It is his first day at the junior high school! They

lovingly dress him up in the school uniform— grey pants, white shirt, blue tie. Reciting "*waheguru waheguru*," the mother braids her son's long hair and puts it in a bun, tucking it neatly in a small sapphire-blue turban. All dressed

Fig. 5.1 A Sikh man offering the traditional Sikh greeting, "Sat sari akal."

Fig. 5.2 A visitor at the Golden Temple, Amritsar, India.

from the last verses of the CD—"constellations beyond constellations"—Harinder excitedly enters his school.

Art and Ornamentation

Sikh art is aniconic; it does not display images of any deities, and even the images of the historical gurus are not exhibited in their sacred space, which would be the presence of their holy Scripture. The most ubiquitous visual Sikh image, ੴ, is used extensively as a form of ornamentation in arts, crafts, and architecture. It can be seen on gateways, walls, and windows of homes, shrines, and shops. The image is elaborately inscribed in silk, marble, steel, and gold. It is embroidered on oxen covers and precious canopies; it is embossed on books and on

up, they go to the prayer room, bow before the holy book, say their prayers, and partake of the delicious *karahprashad*. Soon the phone rings. It is his granny, sitting miles away on her farm in northern India, giving Harinder her good wishes. He doesn't quite follow her Punjabi, but he is very happy that she remembered his special day. After the family has a breakfast of pancakes with powdered sugar and syrup, the Mom drives to her job at the college library, and Dad drives Harinder to school before taking the train to Manhattan. The morning hymn Japji— recalling the divine being shared by humans across religions and cultures—plays on the CD. The preparation and distribution of the *karahprashad* was a special celebration for launching Harinder on his new phase of life, but the rest pretty much happens to be their daily morning routine. Trying to imagine the huge world

Fig. 5.3 A rare nineteenth-century Tanjore-style painting depicting the ten Sikh Gurus and Bhai Bala and Bhai Mardana.

earrings and pendants. Without confining the divine in any way, the rhythmic unity sustained by the numeral one, the syllabic oan, and the unending geometric arc launches the spectator toward an all-encompassing infinity. Its inherent openness permeates Sikh art and forges innovative patterns.

Janamsakhi illustrations constitute the earliest form of Sikh art. Their brightly painted scenes portray the founder guru carrying his progressive message to people from different religious and social backgrounds. In various scenarios, he delivers his message about the importance of truth, the futility of empty rituals, the value of honest work, and the submission to the divine over any other agent. Numerous artists triumph in relaying the impact of his lessons. A glance at Guru Nanak with crimson blood dripping from the bread offered by a wealthy man in his left hand, and nurturing milk dripping from the bread offered by a humble carpenter in his right, leaves a lifelong imprint on the value of honest labor.

During the reign of Maharaja Ranjit Singh, Sikh art received unprecedented royal patronage. The Maharaja's tolerance promoted harmonious coexistence among Muslims, Hindus, and Sikhs, and his patronage extended to artists of all religious denominations in his vast domains, resulting in many spectacular creations. He provided countless opportunities for folk vitality to develop into refined art. During his prosperous reign, there was the construction of magnificent forts, palaces, gurdwaras, mosques, and temples; enormous production of gold and silver objects; designing of precious jewelry; issuing of coins; crafting of exquisite arms; and creation of luxurious tents, canopies,

Fig. 5.4　A view of the prayer hall (Darbar Sahib) enshrining the Guru Granth at the center of worship.

Fig. 5.5 Close-up of the Guru Granth, the holy book of the Sikhs.

caparisons, and large woolen shawls that could slip through a tiny ring. Centers such as Lahore, Amritsar, Srinagar, Multan, and Sialkot produced artifacts for the Maharaja and his court. The highlights include the embellishment of the Golden Temple, the bejeweled canopy for the Guru Granth, the golden volume of Sikh scripture inscribed in ink mixed with gold-diamonds-emeralds, the gold throne made by Hafez Muhammad Multani that is now at the Victoria and Albert Museum in London, exquisite jewelry for both men and women—including the legendary Kohinur diamond, now in the Crown Jewels in London.

European visitors to India like the artists Emily Eden and August Schoefft were so dazzled by the Sikh kingdom that they re-created it magnificently in the language of colors. Emily Eden even sketched Ranjit Singh's horses decorated with precious emeralds. On a huge canvas, Schoefft vividly painted the Sikh court with over sixty people from multiple religions and ethnicities. When the dethroned Dalip Singh arrived in London, Queen Victoria commissioned painters and sculptors to depict her exotic subject. In fact, during the week that he was modeling for the German painter Franz Winterhalter (July 10–17, 1854), the queen sat across with Prince Albert and composed her own sketches of the teenager.

The cultural and political shifts of the twentieth century generated a new momentum, with many men and women creating exciting works. The most famous is Amrita Sher-Gil, daughter of a Sikh father and a Hungarian mother. In her short life span (1913–1941), she transformed the course of Indian art. The prodigious young female artist took upon herself the challenge of bringing in a bold new aesthetic with an existentialist realism to Indian painting. Other famous painters include Thakur Singh (1899–1976), Sobha Singh (1901–1986), Phoolan Rani (b. 1923), Arpita Singh (b. 1937), Arpana Caur (b. 1954), and the Singh Twins (b. 1966).

Fig. 5.6 *The Dalip Singh* (1854). Royally commissioned portrait by Franz Winterhalter (1805–1873).

Sobha Singh's great masterpiece is a portrait of Guru Nanak—inspiring comfort and serenity in the audience. In this composition, which is now deeply imprinted in the Sikh imagination, the guru's face with his white beard is tenderly bent, his turban and robe are a soft yellow, his eyes brim with spirituality, and his hand gestures a gift of blessings. The prints of this painting are extremely popular and serve as a prime marker of a Sikh site.

The Singh Twins are creating an exciting new multicultural perspective. By collaborating together, the sisters have created a genre of painting they call "Past Modern." It is a skillful reworking of the traditional Indian miniature style with their own postcolonial diasporic experience in a multicultural England. Their works are hugely popular and elicit much thought. For example, *The Last Supper* (see fig. 5.7) depicts their Sikh family having a Christmas feast, and the entire scene overflows with icons, food, clothes, and items belonging to the West, the East, and the Middle East. As the father sitting near the decorated Christmas tree carves a big turkey, a cousin wearing a T-shirt with an Egyptian pharaoh tries to catch a spilling bottle of Coke. A plurality of images from different religions—Guru Gobind Singh, Lord Buddha, Lord Ganesha, the Virgin Mary, the Taj Mahal—fill the space around the sumptuous table spread with English and Indian delicacies. The backdrop is Leonardo daVinci's *The Last Supper*, evoking the significance of Christmas often lost in its commercial hype. And the typical plump snowman outside the window happens to be a sleek Sikh with a saffron turban and black beard! Facing the Christmas party, he introduces themes of hybridization, globalization, and postmodernity in Sikh art.

History

We will now explore the history of the Sikh religion by looking at its beginnings, the Khalsa ("the community of the pure"), and the Sikh kingdom.

Beginnings

Sikh religion begins with the birth of its founder, Guru Nanak, in 1469. Though there is not much historical documentation, we learn about his life from the Janamsakhis ("birth stories"), which were orally circulated sometime after the death of the guru, in 1539. Similar to the narratives of Buddha and Christ, the Janamsakhis show Guru Nanak as divinely configured,

Fig. 5.7 *The Last Supper*, The Singh Twins. Image copyright The Singh Twins, www.singhtwins.co.uk.

underscore that all human beings are equal. As a little boy, he refuses to go through the rite of passage reserved for upper-caste boys in his society. Instead of an external thread worn on the bodies of the twice-born Hindu males, he proposes a thread made of the inner fiber of compassion for everybody. In words enshrined in Sikh Scripture, he even condemns the customary practices that subjugated women—*purdah* (the segregation and veiling of women), *sati* (upper-class widows obligated to burn alive on the funeral pyre of their husband), and taboos associated with menstruation and childbirth. Criticizing the prevalent "dos and don'ts," Guru Nanak opens the way for celebrating an egalitarian humanity.

After his revelatory experience into the one divine, the Janamsakhis continue, he travels

whose knowledge and inspiration were able to create a new religion. We hear about how most dangerous elements of nature protect him (such as a cobra offering its shade for Nanak to sleep), and are even controlled by him (Nanak stops a boulder hurled at him with the palm of his hand). When he died, the shroud that should have been covering his body was simply hiding a bed of flowers, which both Hindus and Muslims then carried away to cremate or bury, according to their respective death rituals.

From his birth to his death, the Janamsakhis portray Nanak as rejecting the prevalent confines of caste, gender, religion, and ethnicity only to

Fig. 5.8 Guru Nanak with his parents from the B-40 Janamsakhi (dated 1733; printings published by GNOU, Amritsar).

Fig. 5.9 Ornate ceiling, with inlaid gold and precious stones, of the Golden Temple, Amritsar, India.

widely with his musician companion, Mardana, who is a Muslim. As Mardana plays his rabab, Nanak bursts into powerful verse exalting ultimate reality, literally, *Ikk Oan Kar* ("One Being Is"). His usage of the numeral one affirms the concept of the divine shared across religions. On his long journeys, Guru Nanak not only met holy men from different cultures and religions but also had meaningful conversations with them. At one point, he climbs up a mountain where a group of venerable holy men are sitting in a circle. Their shaved heads, lengthened ear lobes, long earrings (*kan-phat,* "ear split"), and ash-smeared bodies indicate their arduous Hatha yoga practices and ascetic ideals. Nanak begins to discuss with them their human responsibilities. He urges them to return to normal social life and perform their civic duties. Wherever he went, people were influenced by the content of his message and the simple style of his communication. Many began to call themselves his "Sikhs" (disciples).

He eventually settled on the banks of the River Ravi. The first Sikh community grew in this beautiful landscape, with Guru Nanak at the center. Men and women came to hear the Guru's words and to practice the values of equality, civic action, and inclusivity. Engaged in ordinary occupations of life, they denied monastic practices and affirmed a new sense of family. Their pattern of *seva* (voluntary service), *langar* (cooking and eating together irrespective of caste, religion, sex, or status), and *sangat* (congregation) created the blueprint for Sikh doctrine and practice.

The Khalsa

The tenth and final Guru, Gobind Singh, established the Khalsa ("community of the pure"). Through a radical choreography of social equality, he concretized the Sikh ideal of the one inclusive divine. For the new-year celebrations of 1699 in Anandpur, he invited men and women from far and near. He

Fig. 5.10 This scene shows both Sikhs and non-Sikhs being fed for free at a Sikh langar. People sit in continuous rows to demonstrate that all are of the same status in life.

prepared a drink by stirring water in a bowl with his double-edged sword while reciting sacred hymns. His wife, Mata Jitoji, added sugar puffs, mixing the strength of steel with the sweetness of sugar. The first five who took this *amrit* drink constitute the founding members of the Khalsa family. These initiates came from different classes, geographic regions, and professions, but they sipped *amrit* from the same bowl. This was a spectacular enactment of their spewing out hegemonic structures and pledging to fight against social oppression and injustice for the sake of liberty and equality. In Sikh memory, the guru also revoked the oppressive patriarchal lineage by giving the surname "Singh" (meaning "lion") to the men and "Kaur" (meaning "princess") to the women. In the new family of the Khalsa, everyone was to share the same name and worth. Their strong sense of identity was amplified by the five external markers:

Kesha, uncut hair—denoting the way of nature, most often wrapped in a turban for men.

Kangha, a comb tucked in the hair to keep it tidy, in contrast with recluses who keep hair matted as an expression of renunciation.

Kirpan, a sword symbolizing self-defense and the fight against injustice.

Kara, a steel bracelet worn around the right wrist. The steel of the bracelet represents spiritual courage, and its circularity reminds the wearer of the unity, infinity, and proximity of the divine.

Kaccha, short breeches worn by soldiers at the time of the tenth guru, stand for chastity and moral restraint.

Just before he passed away, in 1708, Guru Gobind Singh initiated a phenomenon unique to the history of religion: he identified the sacred *book* as the *body* of the gurus for perpetuity, and so the Guru Granth has been venerated for generations.

Fig. 5.11   Nineteenth-century lithograph depicting Sher Singh, the Maharaja of the Punjab, and his entourage on a hunt, passing a group of Sikh ascetics (lower right).

The Sikh Kingdom

Due to internal battles in the Punjab and external invasions by Afghans and Persians, the period following Guru Gobind Singh was fraught with enormous hardship for the Sikhs. However, by the middle of the eighteenth century, they became a major political force, and at the end of the century, they established a state of their own. In 1799, Ranjit Singh, the nineteen-year-old leader of a Khalsa band, peacefully seized power in the city of Lahore. Guided by his mother-in-law, Sada Kaur (1762–1832), he integrated twelve warring Sikh bands into a sovereign state and was crowned Maharaja in 1801. Known as the Lion of the Punjab, Ranjit Singh ruled for forty years. He created a formidable army and added Multan, Kashmir, and Peshawar to his kingdom. His court represented unparalleled pageantry and brilliance. He wore the world's largest diamond (the Kohinur) on his right arm. The Maharaja remained a devout Sikh who built and renovated many shrines. Even his foreign employees had to live by the Sikh code: they had to wear their beards long and refrain from eating beef and from smoking tobacco. After Waterloo, several soldiers who lost their employment with Napoleon—including the Frenchman Allard and the famous Italian-born Ventura—came to work for Ranjit Singh. But just a decade after his death, the Sikhs lost their enormous kingdom to the British. For a short period, his wife Maharani Jindan (1817–1863) served as regent for her son. She was famous for her sharp intelligence and acute statesmanship, and the British were in awe of her. Eventually they imprisoned her, and her young son Dalip (1838–1893) was converted to Christianity and exiled to England.

The Maharaja's diamond was cut down to fit Queen Victoria's crown. Generations of heroic Sikhs began to serve the British Army, valorously fighting in Europe, Africa, and Asia. Sikhs formed a major part of the imperial army in World War I.

Scripture

Just before he passed away, Guru Nanak handed his compositions to his disciple Lahina and appointed him as his successor. In this way, the message and mission begun by the first was carried through ten living Gurus. Concerned about the needs for his expanding community, the fifth guru, Arjan, compiled the Scripture in 1604. This 1,430-page volume includes not only the voice of his predecessor Sikh Gurus but also that of the Hindu and Muslim holy men, many of whom were harshly discriminated against only because of their biological birth into a low class. By including diverse voices, the Sikh sacred book offers a paradigmatic expression of the collective human spirit. Its universality is the hallmark of Sikh identity.

In poetic form, the Guru Granth expresses the desire for the infinite one. Rather than the languages of Sanskrit and Arabic, which had been used by the Hindu and Muslim religious elite, it uses the vernaculars accessible to the masses. Guru Arjan's goal was to provide deep insight into the nature of the divine and to explore how one might come to attain and

Fig. 5.12 An eighteenth-century illustrated page of the Guru Granth.

live with this understanding. He put most of the verses into musical measures to enhance their aesthetic beauty. The artistic technique channels the metaphysical divine into the deepest human recesses. Sikh Scripture begins with Guru Nanak's celebration of the infinite one (see final segment) and ends with Guru Arjan's analogy of the text as a platter that holds three dishes: truth (*sat*), contentment (*santokh*), and reflection (*vicar*). The editor-compiler thus perceived the volume as something accessible and necessary for everybody: it holds knowledge of the universal truth, brings emotional sustenance to each reader/hearer, and promotes social interaction with fellow beings through mutual reflection. The ingredients were to be savored and absorbed—not merely swallowed—so that their literary nutrients would create a peaceful mode of existence for his community and for future generations. Literature, like all art, has profound influence in shaping worldviews, attitudes, and behavior. In order to bring about a moral transformation in their discordant society, the gurus offered sublime poetry. They did not give any rules or prescriptions. In aesthetically uplifting rhythms, their lyrics evoke love for the divine and inspire people to act morally toward their fellow beings. Translations of selected verses can be accessed in an anthology of Punjabi lyrics titled *Of Desire Sacred and Secular* (IB Tauris, 2012).

Doctrine

Sikhs believe in the one divine reality (*Ikk Oan Kar*) permeating each and every finite creature and simultaneously transcending all space and time. The primary numeral one, with its soaring geometric arc, is a universal modality that everyone can tap into. This infinite one is beyond gender. It is named Truth, and it is the creator of all beings. But more important than the belief in the one is the living of truth. Consequently, there is no division between the sacred and the secular, or between religion and ethics.

Without prescribing rules, Sikh Scripture teaches readers and hearers to stay attuned to the universal truth every moment. Such a consciousness naturally produces ethical behavior. Morality is not fostered in some distant cave or once a week in a religious space; rather, it is practiced in everyday nitty-gritty acts, within the immediate world of family, classes, sports, and profession. Human life is precious. The world is good. Rather than shift attention to a heaven or eternity after death, Sikh Scripture draws attention to actualizing moral, aesthetic, intellectual, and spiritual potential within this ordinary temporal and spatial world. The common Sikh exclamation *Waheguru* surges with the wonder and magic (*wah* + *guru*) of the divine proximity felt here and now.

The Sikh religion deems five psychological propensities harmful to the human race—lust, anger, greed, attachment, and pride. These are so-called robbers residing within who steal the precious morality with which humans are equally endowed. Their root cause is *haumai*, literally, "I-myself." By constantly centering on the selfish I, me, and mine, individuals are split from their divine core, and they are split from people around them. This is when inequities and hostilities take over.

These are overcome by hearing about the divine one (which is why Scripture is so important), keeping that one constantly in mind and loving the infinite one. (Nanak articulates this triple process as *sunia, mania, man kita bhau*.) Love opens emotionally clogged arteries and fosters respect for and joy with fellow beings. The Sikh theistic perception is relevant today:

only when we get a real feel for that *oneness* we all share will we be able to live responsibly and implement our social, political, economic, and environmental policies. If we align ourselves with That One, we will take constructive steps toward equality, health care, education, and ecosystem for our global community.

Worship

Whether in shrines or at home, the holy volume is the center of Sikh worship. It is treated with the highest respect, always draped in silks and brocades (called *rumala*), placed on quilted mats, and supported by cushions. A canopy hangs over it for protection, and a whisk is waved over it by an attendant. Such cultural symbols as the whisk and the canopy for royalty affirm the sovereign status of the scriptural guru. Men and women remove their shoes and cover their heads before they come into its presence. Every morning, the sacred book is ceremoniously opened, and in the evening folded together and then carried to a special place for its nightly rest. Religious practices include seeing and bowing before it and sitting in its proximity (*darshan*); reading the passage that it randomly opens up to as the personal message for the day (*hukam*); singing its verses (*kirtan*); remembering historical moments and making wishes for the future while standing up before it (*ardas*); and savoring in its presence the warm dish made of flour, sugar, butter, and water (*karahprashad*).

Sikh sacred space is the *gurdwara* (literally, door/*dwara* to the guru) with the scriptural guru as the focal point. In India and in diasporic communities, gurdwaras serve as resources for information, assistance, food, shelter, and fellowship. The Golden Temple emerging out of a shimmering pool in Amritsar is the most popular Sikh shrine. Its four doors symbolically welcome people from all classes, faiths, and ethnicities. The view of the building merging at once with transparent waters and radiant sunlight sweeps the spectator into a sensory swirl. A visitor to the Golden Temple gets a feel for

Fig. 5.13 The Golden Temple, Amritsar, India. It is the spiritual and cultural center of Sikhism.

Fig. 5.14 Entrance to the Golden Temple, Amritsar.

Guru Nanak's vision of the infinite one. And its kitchen puts his perception into practice. About eighty thousand visitors daily eat meals prepared by enthusiastic volunteers, and over weekends, almost twice as many are served! The *New York Times* calls it the "world's largest free eatery."

Rites of Passage

Four rites of passage mark significant events in Sikh life. As always, the Guru Granth is the presiding agent.

Name-Giving. Children are named in consultation with the sacred text. While its spine rests on cushions, it is reverently opened at random, and the child receives a name that begins with the first letter appearing on the left-hand page.

Amrit Initiation. This is the Sikh initiation rite, which essentially reenacts Guru Gobind Singh's historic birth of the Khalsa. It marks devotion to the faith and ideals of equality and justice.

According to the Sikh ethical code (*Rahit Maryada*), "Any man or woman of whatever nationality, race, or social standing, who is prepared to accept the rules governing the Sikh community, has the right to receive *amrit* initiation."

Wedding. The Sikh rite of marriage is called *Anand Karaj* ("bliss event"). No words or gestures are directly exchanged between bride and groom. As the wedding hymn (*lavan*) is read from the Guru Granth, the couple circles it four times. After each circling, both bride and groom touch their foreheads to the ground in unison—a gesture of their acceptance of each other with the textual guru as their witness and constant companion. During the fourth round, the congregation of family and friends showers the couple with petals.

Death. Sikhs cremate their dead. The closest male relatives and family friends carry the body of the deceased on a stretcher to the funeral ground. Following ancient customs, the eldest son lights the funeral pyre. Relatives collect the ashes and bones (called *phul*, "flowers") and immerse them in the flowing waters of a river or stream. In the home of the deceased, family members take solace from the reading, hearing, and the physical presence of the Guru Granth.

Sikhism in a Global World

The British annexation of the Punjab in 1849 offered Sikhs opportunities to become a part of the imperial workforce and to migrate to distant lands. A substantial number served in the British army in a variety of countries, and many were employed as soldiers and clerks in British colonies on the Malay Peninsula and in East Africa. In the late nineteenth and early twentieth centuries, advertisements by steamship companies and recruitment to work on the Canadian Pacific Railroad attracted many Sikh men to the North American continent. There were barely any Sikh women in this early group of immigrants, and the Sikh men often married Spanish-speaking women on the western rim, creating a biethnic community erroneously termed "Mexican-Hindus" (also "Mexidus"). Since the relaxation of immigration laws after World War II, and especially after the elimination of national quotas in 1965, there has been a dramatic surge in the Sikh population, both male and female, all across North America.

The first generation of Sikhs had been concerned about social and economic success, and they tried to keep their religion in their homes and places of public worship. But now they are more self-conscious and are deeply involved in

Fig. 5.15 A Sikh wedding. This bride and groom, with their families and friends, are seated in the presence of the Guru Granth.

exposing their faith to the larger society. Following the discrimination many Sikhs faced after 9/11, young Sikhs are seriously taking the responsibility to educate the general public. Mainstream media projections instilled such fear and hate for anybody with turban and beard that more than two hundred Sikhs have been victims of hate crimes in the USA since 9/11. In that first week of backlash, a bearded and turbaned Mr. Balbir Singh Sodhi, a Sikh gas station owner in Phoenix, was murdered in blinding rage. Since then, young Sikh men and women are enthusiastically providing legal assistance, educational outreach at the federal and state levels, and legislative advocacy to protect the civil rights of Sikh Americans. The community has played a very important role in promoting the academic study of Sikhism and is also very actively engaged in educating the general public.

The diasporic landscape serves as a rich resource for innovative ventures. In metropolises around the world, Sikhs come into contact with other diasporic communities of southern Asians, Caribbeans, Africans, and Irish. Their children grow up in multiethnic and multifaith neighborhoods. Modern Bhangra is an exciting consequence of the social contacts and cultural crossovers between Punjabi youth and their Afro-Caribbean peers who happened to live close by in places like Southall and Birmingham in the United Kingdom. Traditionally performed in the Punjab during harvest festivals and weddings, Bhangra dance music is being fused with Western pop, hip-hop, house, rap, and reggae; its distinctive drumbeat is being synthesized with drum machines, live percussion, and other modern instrumentation; its Punjabi language is being mixed with English. The novel sounds and rhythms, and the pancommunal, antiracist politics of Bhangra are empowering for the youth and help them reach a wide audience. With their creative energy, young Sikhs are combining their inheritance—"their parents' drumbeat"—with the

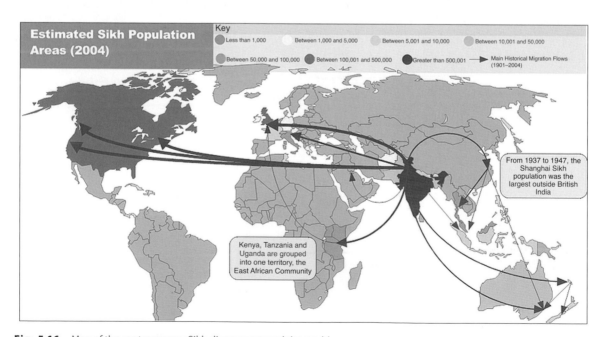

Fig. 5.16 Map of the contemporary Sikh diaspora around the world.

cultures around them, and they are generating an exhilarating music and dance form, which is becoming quite popular around the globe.

Along with an urgent sense of responsibility, Sikhs today are committed to exploring their tradition. Musicians, novelists, short story writers, fashion designers, filmmakers, and so on are creating innovative arabesques with *other* cultures they encounter in their postcolonial world. Their works offer a meaningful insight into the colorful past that connects Sikhs from Singapore to Montreal. Most subtly, they bring up the complex strands of nostalgia, adaptation, hybridization, and multiculturalism that are woven into the present reality of the diasporic experience. And their introspective artistic designs provoke reflections on the future of Sikhism in a rapidly shifting world.

A popular example of this diasporic reality is the film *Bend It Like Beckham*, directed by Gurinder Chadha. She is the first British South Asian woman to direct feature films. As in many of her other films, Chadha's camera sensitively explores ethnic, racial, religious, and gendered identities. But this classic coming of age comedy with its feel-good quality is acutely sharp. "Bending the ball" is actually bending one's conventional roles so that dreams can come true. The images of Guru Nanak and David Beckham frequently flash across Chadha's screen, juxtaposing the protagonist's Sikh heritage with her Western dream. Her family wants her to get educated, married, and take care of domestic matters, but Jess wants to play soccer. When Jess is called a "Paki" during a match, she experiences her father's exposure to racism and exclusion when he wanted to join the cricket team on arriving in Britain. The airplane flying above their home, moreover, is a trope for their relocation. With its clash between tradition and modernity, and the generational conflict of the parents' desire to preserve their home culture while the younger generation seeks to assimilate into the West, Chadha's film has an international appeal.

The possibility of seeing people like themselves in mainstream cinema is a self-affirming phenomenon for Sikhs. It is therefore quite an exciting time for them. They are becoming proud citizens who celebrate their heritage with great jubilation across the globe at numerous cultural and academic venues. And they are making new ones. The air is especially abuzz with excitement around Baisakhi, the Sikh New Year (in the spring) and for Guru Nanak's birthday (in the autumn). Huge Sikh processions with colorful floats carrying their sacred Scripture and depicting different aspects of Sikh life are becoming a familiar sight in cities around the world. Guru Nanak's birthday was celebrated in the White House for the first time in 2009. Indeed, Sikhs are a vibrant part of the "patchwork heritage" praised by President Obama in his historic inaugural address.

The Opening of the Guru Granth

The first hymn in the Guru Granth is the Japji. Recited each morning, it is the quintessence of Sikh philosophy and practice. Its prelude celebrating the singular creator recurs frequently in the text and on the lips of the devout:

> There is One Being
> Truth is Its Name
> Primal Creator
> Without fear,
> Without enmity
> Timeless in form
> Unborn
> Self-existent
> The gift of the Guru.

Japu

Truth before time
Truth within time
Truth here and now
Says Nanak, Truth is evermore.

Thought cannot think it,
    nor will a million thoughts,
Silence cannot silence it,
    nor will seamless contemplation,

Greed is not made greedless,
    not by the wealth of the whole world,
Though a thousand mental feats become
    a million,
    not one can go with us.
How then to be true?
    How then to break the wall of lies?
By following the Will,
    Says Nanak, this is written for us.

◆ STUDY AND DISCUSSION QUESTIONS

1. What is the concept of the divine in Sikhism? How does it relate to other conceptions of divinity in your or other religious traditions?

2. What is the center of Sikh worship and practice? Can you draw parallels to other religious traditions and their reverence of sacred texts and sacred space?

3. What is the relevance of Sikhism in modern times?

4. What do you share with Sikhs?

◆ KEY TERMS

gurdwara
Guru Granth
Ikk Oan Kar
Janamsakhis
karahprashad
langar
man
man kita bhau
mania
sangat
sat santokh vicar
Sat Sri Akal
seva
Sikh
sunia
waheguru

◆ FOR FURTHER READING

BOOKS

Cole, Owen, and Sambhi, Piara Singh. *The Sikhs: Their Religious Beliefs and Practices*. Boston: Routledge & Kegan Paul, 1978.

Goswamy, B. N., and Caron Smith. *I See No Stranger: Early Sikh Art and Devotion*. New York: Rubin Museum of Art, 2006.

Jakobsh, Doris, ed. *Sikhism and Women: History, Texts, and Experience*. New Delhi: Oxford University Press, 2010.

McLeod, W. H. *Guru Nanak and the Sikh Religion*. Oxford: Clarendon, 1968.

———. *Historical Dictionary of Sikhism*. Lanham, MD: Scarecrow Press, 2005.

Singh, Gurharpal, and Darshan Singh Tatla. *Sikhs in Britain: The Making of a Community*. New York: Zed, 2006.

Singh, Harbans. *Encyclopedia of Sikhism*. Patiala: Punjabi University, 1992–1998.

Singh, Nikky-Guninder Kaur, ed. *The Name of My Beloved: Verses of the Sikh Gurus*. New Delhi: Penguin, 2003.

———. *Of Sacred and Secular Desire: An Anthology of Lyrical Writings from the Punjab*. New York: I. B. Tauris, 2012.

———. *Sikhism: An Introduction*. New York: I. B.Tauris, 2011.

◆ **SUGGESTED WEBSITES**

www.nytimes.com/slideshow/2010/08/29/world/asia/INDIA.html

www.srigranth.org/

www.sikhiwiki.org

www.SikhFoundation.org

www.advancedcentrepunjabi.org/eos

Daoism

Lawrence E. Sullivan

Introduction

Daoism (also spelled Taoism—see glossary) is an important feature of religious life in China today, just as it has been for thousands of years. Daoism cultivates wisdom and physical well-being, including longevity and even physical immortality. In the Daoist view, the human being is an image of the universe. Energies that drive the universe, which is the active cosmic body, also empower the human body, which is active in religious ritual, physical discipline, and in mental exercise. Daoism offers practices for the body and understandings for the mind. Together these practices and ideas provide access to the Dao, the supreme source of all reality. Breathing, movement, healing, and nutrition are physical exercises that preserve and increase vital energy. Meditation, interior hygiene, and philosophy are mental exercises that produce effective visions of renewal. Daoism nourishes itself on contrasts, starting with its intention to foster wholeness without striving for it.

Over centuries, Daoism has generated folk festivals for community celebrations and has compiled Scriptures and developed philosophies for individual study. Daoism integrates routine practices into everyday life and at the same time produces mystical and magical

TIMELINE

BCE

ca. 1750–1100	Shang Dynasty (ancient traditions)
ca. 1122–221	Zhou Dynasty
ca. 600–300	Life of Lao-zi
ca. 365–290	Life of Zhuang-zi
221–206	Jin Dynasty; emergence of immortality movements
206–220 CE	Han Dynasty; early Daoist sects

CE

618–907	Tang Dynasty; Daoism and Buddhism influences
960–1280	Northern Daoist sects flourish
1445	Daoist canon of Scripture (The *Daozang* or *Tao Tsang*) published
1950	National Association of Daoism (in Beijing, China)
1966–1976	Daoist temples and books destroyed during Cultural Revolution in China
1990	Daoist temples reestablished

techniques linked to extraordinary religious experiences. By mastering numerous spirits and identifying gods by name, Daoist leaders have established separate movements within Daoism. After achieving immortality, these leaders transmitted their rites and teachings to their followers. An official collection of Daoist texts, the *Tao Tsang*, was published in 1926 in Shanghai. The *Tao Tsang* was collected in 1445 CE in 1,120 volumes, but an earlier collection of these texts, burned by Kublai Khan in 1281 CE, was even longer. This is the rich and complex tradition of Daoism.

Dividing the New Fire: *Fen-Deng*

In the brief meditation call *fa-lu*, the Daoist high priest purifies the hearts and minds of the devotees. The meditation empties them of images and spirits that crowd inside, in order to make space for the Dao. New fire is lit by striking sparks from fresh flint: the first ceremonial candle of the Daoist religious rites is set aflame to renew the cosmos. Then the new fire is carefully divided in a rite called *Fen-Deng*. The first candle brings to light the visible Dao, known as *Taiji*, the power of primordial breath associated with the highest level of the natural world and linked to the realm of thought. The first candle also stands for *San jing*, the ancient spirit who governs heaven. Next, the fire of *Taiji* is used to light a second candle, whose flame makes visible the soul that lives within the loving human heart. This second candle represents *Ling-bao*, the spirit who rules the earth, the central level of the cosmos. Finally, fire is passed to a third candle associated with the watery underworld of the cosmos as well as the human midsection, with its gut instincts and intuitions. The third candle stands for the spirit *Daode*, who

The three bear the ten thousand things.
The ten thousand things
carry the *yin* on their shoulders
and hold in their arms the *yang*,
whose interplay of energy
makes harmony.

(from *Lao Tzu, Tao Te Ching* by Ursula
K. LeGuin. © 1997 by Ursula K. LeGuin.
Reprinted by arrangement with Shambhala
Publications, Inc., Boston, www.shambhala.
com)

Fig. 6.1 A prayer and an offering of incense sticks are common Daoist devotions, as Daoists seek the best site in which to pray, following the ancient art of geomancy or "feng shui."

rules water and rebirth. The *Fen-Deng*, though a simple set of gestures, reenacts the emergence of the world from the *Dao*, a process described in the forty-second chapter of the *Dao de jing*:

The Way bears one.
The one bears two.
The two bear three.

Fig. 6.2 A silk tapestry of the Eight Immortals who in Daoist tradition obtained immortality by following different paths.

Fig. 6.3 A sign of devotion and prayer in a Daoist temple in Hong Kong.

Through the *Fen-Deng* and its ritual actions, human beings participate in the powerful relationships that emerge from the Dao on every level of existence.

Renewal and Union: Planting and Eating the Elements

Two important rituals oppose each other like bookends. The first rite is often called *Suqi*, and it is performed during the first day of the *Jiao* renewal festival. During the *Suqi*, the five basic elements are planted. The second ritual of the opposing pair is called *Daojang* or *Cheng-jiao*, performed during the last day of the renewal festival, when the five elements are harvested and eaten. Around the time of the winter solstice, for example, these two rites are used to open and close the *Jiao* festival of renewal.

During the opening *Suqi*, the ritual leader sets five bushels of rice in an order that outlines the whole world: a bushel set in the east, another in the south, west, north, and center of the world. In each bushel he then plants a basic element: wood, fire, metal, water, and earth respectively. These "elements" are composed of magical signs drawn on five colored silk cloths: green, red, white, black, and yellow respectively. Standing in the "center of the world," the Daoist ritual master makes an arrangement with the spiritual forces of the universe to obtain a good seedtime, growing season, and rich harvest along with health and happiness for all.

The *Daojang* (or *Cheng-jiao*) ritual, held on the final day of the festival, culminates the ritual year in many Daoist temples. The ritual leader reenacts the limping dance steps of Yu, the ancient mythical figure who rescued the world from the primordial flood. In the course

Fig. 6.4 The Five Elements. Earth is at the center, the point of intersection. The oriented elements are associated with colors; parts of the body; the east, south, west, and north; and mythic animals such as the dragon, bird, tiger, and tortoise.

of the dance, the ritual leader "harvests" the magical crop that has sprung from the five elements planted in the bushels. Through powerful meditation, the leader absorbs the five elements into the five main organs of his inner body: liver (ingesting wood from the east), heart (fire, south), lungs (metal, west), kidneys (water, north), stomach (earth, center). In this rite, the body is the world; the Dao is made visibly present in the center. This experience of mystical union with the Dao achieved in rituals is the high point of the cycle of rebirth.

Change through Time

Various forms of Daoist practice and thought appear throughout its long history. Already in the beginning of the imperial era (221 BCE–220 CE), systematic writing on Daoist ideas such as *taiping*, "great peace," described this ideal of perfect harmony among all of the world's

realities. The *Tianshi* (Heavenly Master) tradition, which promised to achieve the "great peace," based itself on the thought of Zhang Dao-ling in the second century and that of his grandson in the third century. Over the centuries, Chinese rulers depended on Daoist leaders, who communicated directly with Lao-jun, a deity identified with Lao-zi, who was credited with writing the *Dao de jing*. The Heavenly Master tradition changed from the fourth century onward in ongoing contact with southern China. One transformation, for example, was called *Shangqing* Daoism, and it based its changes on revealing visions received from *shenren*, divine beings or immortals living on mythical mountains. *Shenren* had the power to appear, disappear, and multiply, changing at will by perfecting the techniques of alchemy and visualization. They dwelled on the Isles of the Blessed in Kun-lun, the heavenly mountain that one climbed along the path of self-perfection. From these mystical vantage points, the *shenren* enter *Dongtian*, the holy caves that provide access to the inner womb of the earth, where the immeasurable treasures of health and revealed wisdom are hidden. From the fourth century onward, *Lingbao* Daoism fostered public liturgies that linked individuals with nature and with society on a common path toward salvation. Mongol rule, which began in the twelfth century, as well as the Ming and Qing dynasties, suppressed Daoist groups and other religious organizations. During this period of repression, a separate mystical form of Daoism emerged that stressed the importance of individual meditation. Daoist liturgical and mystical practices continue today, even though Daoism was outlawed in the People's Republic of China for a period during the mid-twentieth century.

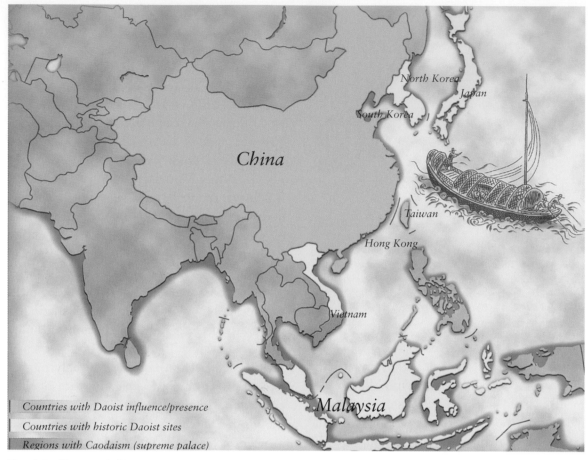

Fig. 6.5 The spread of Daoism as an organized religion, including Caodaism in Vietnam.

Dao

The Chinese word *dao* means "way" in several senses of the word: a road or path, a way of life, a discipline or method to follow closely. In Daoist religious thought, *Dao* means a teaching, doctrine, rule of conduct, or valuable speech. The idea runs in two different directions at the same time. On the one hand, Dao is a power that transcends any reality, including the human mind: Dao is inconceivable and unnameable. As the mystery of all mysteries, it remains impossible to describe, incomprehensible. On the other hand, Dao is the ground of reality, the inexhaustibly fertile womb where all reality runs through its cycle of conception, gestation, and birth and to which all realities return in their cycles of death and rebirth. Thus Dao is both a force beyond any single expression in nature and, at the same time, the force that flows within tangible nature, propelling it to change. Dao therefore embraces reality at its widest reach, both inward to the smallest speck of material existence and outward beyond all

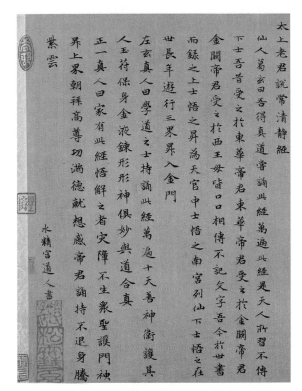

太上老君說常清靜經
仙人葛玄曰吾得真道當誦此經萬遍此經是天人所習不傳
下士吾昔受之於東華帝君東華帝君受之於金闕帝君
金闕帝君受之於西王母皆口口相傳不記文字吾今於世書
而錄之上士悟之昇為天官中士悟之南宮列仙下士悟之在
世長年遊行三界昇入金門
左玄真人曰學道之士持誦此經萬遍十天善神衛護其
人玉符保身金液鍊形形神俱妙與道合真
正一真人曰家有此經悟解之者災障不生眾聖護門神
昇上界朝拜高尊功滿德就想感帝君誦持不退身騰
紫雲
水精宮道人書

Fig. 6.6 From the Daoist Sutra of Constant Purity and Tranquility, that had been transmitted orally beginning with Lao-zi. It teaches that with the detachment of passions one will have a clear mind and a peaceful heart.

material expression. Natural reality is a ceaseless cycle spinning outward from the Dao to all creatures, and cycling back to the dao for renewal, in keeping with the turning of the seasons in nature.

Attuned to nature, human beings unite eternally with the Dao. The way of the Dao is especially evident in water: its flow, vitality, irresistibility, clarity, effortlessness, and shape-shifting conformation to the terrain. Water adapts to the sky, the earth, and the underworld, taking on distinct forms in each of these realms. Rulers and wizards who bring such diverse planes into fruitful contact are said to possess the power of the Dao and bring human beings into communication with powers in heaven and on earth. Throughout Chinese history, kings manifest the power of Dao by performing rituals that ward off disaster and renew nature through contact with the heavenly Dao.

Fig. 6.7 Painting of a Daoist master meditating on a rocky promontory, where the idea of emptiness gives birth to and nourishes everything.

Lao-zi

Lao-zi, the great and wise sage, holds a special place in Daoist thought and practice, where he plays several different roles. He is described as the author of the fundamental text of Daoism; he is also seen as a cosmic power and a divine figure. Already by the first century BCE, Lao-zi was regarded as the author of the *Dao de jing*, the principle book of Daoism and known also as *The Lao-zi*. Some ancient writings link Lao-zi to Lao Dan, "Old Man Tan" from whom Confucius apparently sought advice and instruction. The *Zhuang-zi*, written around 320 BCE and attributed to an author of the same name, describes Lao Dan as an archivist from the Court of Zhou (1111–255 BCE). This identification of Lao-zi with Lao Dan was developed in the first full-length biography of Lao-zi written by Sima Qian (145–86 BCE), who tells the story of Lao-zi leaving the Zhou kingdom around the time of its downfall. Disillusioned by the realm's inability to cultivate goodness, Lao-zi moved westward through the Han-gu Pass toward Tibet. At the Han-gu Pass, a gatekeeper named Yin Xi asked Lao-zi to write down his ideas about Dao and De. In three days, Lao-zi wrote the *Dao de jing* ("The Way and the Power of the Way"), a work written in five thousand characters on two scrolls. Scholars think that various authors contributed, right up until the last part of the third century BCE, to the text as it is known today. The *Dao de jing* remains the basic book of Daoist thinking. Moreover, the ideal teacher-student relationship is based on the model relationship that existed between the archivist-teacher Lao-zi and his gatekeeper-disciple Yin Xi. By 165–167 CE, the emperor Huan allowed sacrifices to be offered to Lao-zi, who by then was revered as a primordial being, as ancient as the chaos that existed before the

Fig. 6.8 Lao-zi is represented in a popular print as the Supreme One. He holds the diagram of the cosmos with the eight trigrams and the symbol of yin and yang, as symbols of immortality decorate his robes.

world emerged. After undergoing significant transformations, the ancient Lao-zi descended to the human realm to serve as sage counsel to the wisest kings of China.

For centuries it was debated whether Lao-zi had also transformed himself into the Buddha after his westward journey in order to bring barbarians knowledge of the "Way of the *Dai*." In one way or another, then, Lao-zi came to be seen as a savior and deity, the very source of the Dao from the beginning, who moved between the worlds of heaven and earth. In troubled times, his followers awaited his return to rescue them from oppression. The events of history were explained by using Lao-zi's absences and reincarnations to write about periods of prosperity and depravation. Lao-zi became a microcosm of the larger universe, embodying the Dao and serving as the mother of all things, the origin of all creation. Lao-zi encouraged the confession of sins and other forms of ritual purification as means of moral and physical cure. Taking Lao-zi as their example, Daoist meditators pictured themselves as the universe and, in their contemplative visions, journeyed throughout their inner landscape to quicken life forces on every plane. In this way, Daoist meditation focuses on the disciple on the *zhenshen*, the "true body" of Lao-zi, and on the landmarks changed by his passing. Similarly, the ritual actions of the Daoist priest during the *Jiao* renewal ceremony regenerate the embryo of the Lord Lao-zi inside the participating devotees and thus bring the entire community to salvation.

Oppositions and Phases: Yin/Yang and *Wu Xing*

Yin and yang are basic aspects of the Dao, as are the *Wu Xing*, the Five Elements or Five Phases. These terms are used to classify the relationships and realities that compose the world as Daoists see it.

Like the shady and sunny slopes of the same mountain, yin and yang are complementary opposites of the same reality. Sometimes symbolized as a dragon and a tiger, yin and yang are locked in a never-ending cosmic struggle that accounts for the dynamic developments of the visible world. The space of the world and the space of the body can be mapped in terms of yin and yang. The underworld of fire and water, associated with the belly in the human body, is a region of pure yin, divided into nine numbered sections, each one ruled by a destructive leader. The numbers are arranged in a magic square. At death, the souls move toward the yin realm, where they are purified. Religious practitioners and spirit mediums contact the souls there and give voice to the desires that were never satisfied in life. The uppermost realm of heaven, associated with the head in the human body, is pure yang. Dead souls journey toward heaven when properly cleansed in the underworld and ritually assisted by the living. The earth sits in the middle level, corresponding to the chest in the human body; here yin and yang mix together and overlap. In this central realm, Daoists carry out rituals that enliven the world and advance souls along their path by paying the required tolls to gatekeepers, who control the path to their destiny.

The *Wu Xing*, or Five Phases, bear the names of the five basic material elements, each also possessing a number: (1) water, (2) fire, (3) wood, (4) metal, and (5) earth. These named elements are the basic influences that shape the world. Their names are the categories used to classify all kinds of relationships and realities: foods, directions, seasons, animals, colors, body parts, tastes, social activities, and so on. These categories organize philosophical thinking as well as such practical matters as eating a balanced diet harmonized with the seasons and the healthy functioning of the body.

Qi and *Wu Wei*: Vital Energy and Pure Effect

Qi can mean "moist breath" or "vapor," referring to the vital energy that enlivens all beings in the cosmos. *Qi* is a central concern in Daoist religion and philosophy. Managing *Qi* so that it is aligned with and fed by the forces of the universe is the major aim of the techniques of self-control cultivated in Daoist meditation, ritual, diet, gymnastics, medicine, and philosophy. *Qi*, as a power of the *Dao*, streams throughout the cosmos and throughout the individual. Unhealthy habits and moral faults reduce the flow of *Qi*. But rigorous training of mind and body clear the channels and open the sluice-gates for the flow of *Qi*. Daoist practices maximize the flow of vitalizing energy, evident in philosophical wisdom and in physical health. Long life and even physical immortality can be the ultimate outcomes of the cultivation of *Qi*. *Qi* streams unimpeded when the individual is in a state of *Wu Wei*, a condition of creative quiet, as when a pool of water lies clear and still. *Wu Wei* consists of two opposed conditions that coexist at the same time: supreme relaxation and supreme creativity. *Wu Wei* is the condition of pure effect, an effectiveness never disrupted by striving. Human beings achieve *Wu Wei* only because they are open to the Dao, for *Wu Wei* cannot be created by human thought. Instead, it arises when the deeper unconscious mind contacts the life that is lived beyond the tension between separate forms and beyond the distraction of separate intentions. Like water that settles into cracks and crevices, *Wu Wei* appears effortless. It wastes no energy on process or display; no energy is spent on anything other than effect.

Life-Cycle Rites

The power of the Dao manifests itself in the cycles of growth and renewal marked by the sun and moon, the gestation and growth of plants and animals, and in the procession of the seasons. Above all, Daoists mark the time of human life and the annual life of the cosmos by celebrating rituals at the major punctuation points. The human life-cycle has five phases, corresponding to *Wu Xing*, the five elemental phases: birth, growth, marriage, old age, and death. At

Fig. 6.9 Vapor rises from an incense burner toward Heaven, the most immaterial aspect of energy, of which matter is one of the most condensed forms.

each phase, special rituals are performed. Death rituals, for instance, can be very elaborate. They begin at the moment of death, when white paper is set over the body and, at the same time, actions are performed near the ancestral shrine in the home. During the funeral, money offerings are made and incense is provided to assist the spirit of the deceased on its journey through the tollbooths and roadblocks of the underworld. Relatives enact scenes of the ideal burial, sometimes performing as many as twenty-four episodes that demonstrate the devotion children should have for honored parents. A model house is made of paper, including furniture and fixtures. A willow branch symbolizing the soul of the dead relative is brought back from the cemetery and installed on the family altar in the home. On the seventh, ninth, and forty-ninth days after the burial, additional ceremonies are held (as they may be also on the first and third anniversaries of death). The Daoist priest may accompany the deceased soul on a dramatic journey through the underworld, escorting it through the various gates of hell and conducting it past the demonic gatekeepers. At the proper moment, the paper house and other decorations are set afire.

Ritual Rhythms of the Year: The Calendar

The yearly cycle of ceremonies swings back and forth between the odd, festival months marked by yang and the even, working months of agricultural labor marked by yin. Farmwork and festivals alternate with one another because the festivals fortify the laborers and strengthen the growing crops. Some calendrical festivals stand out as more notable than others. The most important festival is the lunar New Year festival that takes place on the first day of the first month. In the most auspicious way, it ushers in the New Year and the forces of renewal. Families unite in special meals honoring their ancestors and their living elders. Special foods, with names and meanings particular to the occasion, are prepared in memory of the dead: special offerings are made at the family altar. The Festival of Light (first month, fifteenth day) marks the first full moon of the New Year with processions of lanterns and floats as well as special dances and poetry recitals. The Lustration Festival (third month, third day) responds to the powers evident in the bright days of spring by offering sacrifices, special foods, and the cleaning of graves. These activities continue

Fig. 6.10   A Daoist priest in Macau.

Fig. 6.11 Chinese New Year celebrations end with the Festival of the Lanterns, as at the Temple of Earth in Beijing, China.

until 105 days after the winter solstice. Summer Opening Day rituals (fifth month, fifth day) protect against sickness and maintain the health of children by performing ritual exorcisms and invigorations. Seven Sisters Day (seventh month, seventh day) celebrates the eternal courtship of the mythical spinning girl and her beloved cowherd boy.

On the fifteenth day of the seventh month, Daoists hold a preharvest festival at which all the souls of the dead are honored. For the duration of the festival rites, the deceased souls are freed from hell to attend the festive ceremonies. Special foods are set before them, just as the living enjoy their banquet. The Autumn Moon Festival is a harvest festival and thanksgiving feast held on the fifteenth day of the eighth month. Round mooncakes are the hallmark food of the occasion, which is also marked by the recitation of poetry. Various winter festivals are held from the ninth month, ninth day until the eleventh month, eleventh day. This is the time when one is most likely to find celebrations of the *Jiao* renewal festival.

"Mindful of Little Things": *Dao de jing*, Chapter 64

The following selection is drawn from *Lao Tzu, Tao Te Ching*, by Ursula K. LeGuin. © 1997 by Ursula K. LeGuin. Reprinted by arrangement with Shambhala Publications, Inc., Boston, www.shambhala.com.

Chapter 64

It's easy to keep hold of what hasn't stirred,
easy to plan what hasn't occurred.
It's easy to shatter delicate things,
easy to scatter little things.
Do things before they happen.
Get them straight before they get mixed up.

The tree you can't reach your arms around
grew from a tiny seedling.
The nine-story tower rises
from a heap of clay.
The ten-thousand-mile journey
begins beneath your foot.

Do, and do wrong:
hold on, and lose.
Not doing, the wise soul
doesn't do it wrong,
and not holding on,
doesn't lose it.
(In all their undertakings,
it's just as they're almost finished
that people go wrong.

Mind the end as the beginning,
then it won't go wrong.)

That's why the wise
want not to want,
care nothing for hard-won treasures,
learn not to be learned,
turn back to what people overlooked.
They go along with things as they are,
but don't presume to act.

◆ STUDY AND DISCUSSION QUESTIONS

1. Reflect on the way fire (and other material forces in our world) is used in Daoism. Do you see similarities with other religious and secular events and ceremonies?

2. Discuss how the twin tracks of understanding the *dao*—as a "way" and as a "doctrine" or "rule". Explain how the connection to water brings deeper meaning for practitioners of Daoism.

3. Consider the multiple ways that "balance in life" is practiced and achieved by those who follow Daoism.

◆ KEY TERMS

(The Chinese words are written in pinyin, the official system of spelling used in the People's Republic of China and used throughout the world. Alternate spellings, long known in English usage for common terms, are provided in parentheses, including the word Tao (for Dao), from which derive words such as Taoism and Taoist.)

Dao (Tao)
Dao de jing (Tao te ching)
Dongtian
Fa-lu

Fen-Deng
Festival of Light
Jiao Festival
Lao-zi (Lao-tzu)
Lingbao
Lunar New Year Festival
Lustration Festival
Qi (Ch'i)
Shangqing
Taiji
Taiping
Wu Wei
Wu Xing
Yin and Yang
Yü
Zhuang-zi (Chuang-tzu)

◆ FOR FURTHER READING

Boltz, Judith. *A Survey of Taoist Literature*. Berkeley: University of California Press, 1986.

Eliade, Mircea, ed. *The Encyclopedia of Religion*. New York: MacMillan, 1987. See the related articles, especially in volume 3 and volume 14.

Girardot, Norman. *Myth and Meaning in Early Taoism*. Berkeley: University of California Press, 1983.

Lagerwey, John. *Taoist Ritual in Chinese Society and History*. New York: Macmillan, 1987.

Lao, D. C., trans. *Tao Tzu: Tao te Ching*. Baltimore: Penguin, 1963.

Lao Tzu, and Tao Te Ching: A Book about the Way and the Power of the Way. A new English version by Ursula K. LeGuin, with the collaboration of J. P. Seaton. Boston: Shambhala, 1997.

Robinet, Isabelle. *Meditation Taoiste*. Paris: Dervy livres, 1979.

Saso, Michael. *Blue Dragon, White Tiger*. Honolulu: University of Hawaii Press, 1990.

———. "Chinese Religions," in *A New Handbook of Living Religions*, edited by John R. Hinnells, 445–78. New ed. London: Penguin, 1997.

Schipper, Kristofer. *Le Fen-Teng: Rituel taoiste*. École Francaise d'Extrême-Orient, 1975.

Schipper, Kristofer. *The Taoist Body*. Berkeley: University of California Press, 1993.

Welch, Holmes. *The Parting of the Way: Lao Tzu and the Taoist Movement*. London: Methuen, 1958.

CHAPTER 7

Confucianism

Yong Huang

Introduction

Confucianism is one of the three main religions in China, together with Daoism and Buddhism. It later spread to other Eastern Asian countries such as Japan, Korea, and Vietnam. In the contemporary world, it provided moral and spiritual resources for the economical miracles in Japan as well as the so-called four little dragons: Singapore, South Korea, Hong Kong, and Taiwan. While there has been debate about whether Confucianism can be properly regarded as a religion, several salient features of this tradition qualify it as such. Its adherents believe in Heaven, or Shangdi, Lord on High, as the ultimate reality that controls natural and human events, rewarding the good and punishing the evil. Its organization is constituted by the political institution of the state. The emperor is regarded as the son of Heaven and so is not only responsible for the political government but also for the religious worship of Heaven. Ancestor worship, which is practiced by everyone, is an important religious activity of Confucianism, as it is believed that there can be communication between the dead and the living. The sage (*shengren*) is the ideal person. Although throughout history only very few have been recognized as sages, it is the belief of Confucianism that everyone can become a sage.

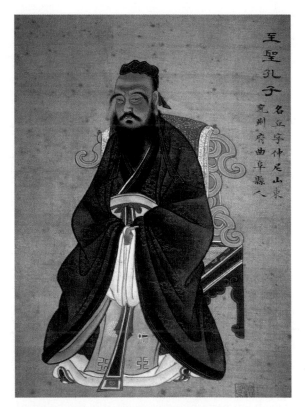

Fig. 7.1 Confucius (551–479 BCE).

Confucius and Confucianism

The term *Confucianism* refers here to the tradition we are discussing, as it clearly indicates the relationship between Confucius and this tradition. However, it is important to note that this term is a Western creation, not a translation of any existing Chinese term. It is supposed to refer to what Chinese people call *Rujia*, or the school of *Ru*, or simply Ruism. While Ruism as a school is certainly also inseparable from and would not exist as we know it today without Confucius, there are at least two senses in which Ruism preceded Confucius, and so it is more appropriate to regard this tradition as Ruism than Confucianism.

First, while it is true that among the existing literatures, the term *ru* first appears in Confucius's *Analects*, where Confucius asks his students to try to be a superior (*junzi*) *ru* instead of an inferior (*xiaore*) *ru* (*Analects* 6.13), this very fact shows that *ru* already existed before Confucius. The term *ru* has the meaning of soft,

Fig. 7.2 Chinese characters spelling Confucius's name.

originally two chapters in a later edition of the *Book of Rites*, written by Confucius's students. The Five Classics, including the *Book of Poetry*, the *Book of Documents*, the *Book of Change*, the *Book of Rites*, and the *Spring and Autumn Annals*, however, all existed before Confucius, although Confucius did spend time editing them, to a great or lesser extent, in his later years.

Westerners coined the term *Confucianism* from the name of the person Confucius, which is the Latinized form of Kong Fuzi (551–479 BCE), a person living in ancient China during the Spring and Autumn period (722–481 BCE). Kong is the family name, while Fuzi is an honorific means of address, meaning master. His given name is Qiu, literally meaning "mountain," as his parents, after he was conceived, prayed for a son at the Mountain Ni, about 30 kilometers southeast of the present-day Qufu of Shandong province. His official name is Zhong Ni, where Ni refers to the name of the mountain, while Zhong indicates that he was the second son in his family. Most frequently, however, he is addressed as Kongzi, where *zi* means the same as *fuzi*, "master."

gentle, and elegant, or a person with such qualities. *Ru*, as a social class, existed as far back as in the Yin dynasty, functioning as priests of Yin people. After the succession of the Yin dynasty by the Zhou dynasty in 1046 BCE, this class continued to exist, to run funerals, perform rituals, and teach the six arts (*liuyi*) necessary for political leaders: rites, music, archery, charioteering, writing, and mathematics. Confucius himself was a *ru*. When he was young, he supported his family by running funerals for others.

Second, in the Confucian canons, there are so-called Five Scriptures and Four Books. The Four Books are indeed *Confucian*. They include the *Analects*, primarily the sayings of Confucius collected and edited by his students after he died; the *Mencius*, primarily the sayings of Mencius, whose importance is second only to Confucius in the Confucian tradition; and the *Great Learning* and the *Doctrine of Mean*,

Fig. 7.3 The Chinese character for *Ru*.

Fig. 7.4 *The Book of Change*, one of the Confucian classics, written on silk, from the Han Tombs in Mawangdui.

of the state of Lu, where many of her clan members lived. Their life was hard, and Confucius had to do chores to help his mother make ends meet when he was young. After his mother died when he was only seventeen years old, Confucius had to rely entirely on himself. However, without a fixed teacher, Confucius set his mind to learning when he was fifteen. By thirty, he had begun to accept students, becoming one of the earliest teachers outside the official schools in Chinese history. It is said that, throughout his life, he had more than three thousand students, and over seventy of them were accomplished. His teaching focused on ritual (*le*) and virtues (*de*) as illuminated in the classics, with which a state was supposed to be run.

The height of Confucius's own political career was his appointment as the minister of justice and, briefly, the acting chief minister in the state of Lu. With some successes, his political ideals, to rule the state with ritual propriety and virtues, were fundamentally unacceptable to the power holders of his home state. Thus he eventually had to give up the position, after which he started fourteen years of travel among other states, selling his political ideals to their rulers, with no success. He acknowledged that he was like a homeless dog during these years. Without hope, he returned to his home state at his old age, devoting himself almost entirely to teaching and editing classics, for which he has been remembered up to the present day.

After Confucius died, Confucianism developed into several different schools, due to different understandings of Confucius's teaching by his different students. The two most prominent Confucian schools are the school of Mencius (371–289 BCE) and that of Xunzi (298–238 BCE). Confucius's most important teachings are on humanity (*ren*) and ritual propriety; Mencius developed the former, while Xunzi focused

While a descendant of the royal family of the Yin dynasty (1300–1046 BCE), Confucius had a tough childhood, as the status of his family had declined to the lowest of the noble class, *shi*, or literati, by Confucius's time. When Confucius was three years old, his father died, and his mother left the Kong family in the small town of Zou, where his father served as the governor, and brought Confucius to Qufu, then the capital on the latter. The most important disagreement between the two is their views of human nature (*xing*): Mencius claimed that it is good, while Xunzi argued that it is bad. Mencius understood human nature to be what distinguishes humans from animals, while Xunzi regarded it as the natural tendency human beings are born with.

Transformative Encounters with Other Traditions

During the Warring States period (480–222 BCE), Confucianism was one of the so-called one hundred schools. While Mohism was

Fig. 7.5   Confucian Temple in Qufu, Shangdong, the site of Confucius's birthplace.

its main rival in the early part of this period, Legalism, whose greatest synthesizer, Han Fei, was a student of Xunzi, presented the most serious challenge to Confucianism. As a matter of fact, the first unified Chinese dynasty, the Qin dynasty (221–206 BCE), adopted the Legalist ideals of government. In order to exclude heresies, with Confucianism as its primary target, it initiated the notorious "burning of [Confucian] books and burying of Confucians." It was in the second unified Chinese dynasty, the Han dynasty (206 BCE–220 CE), which adopted the policy of "promoting Confucianism alone and banning all other schools," that Confucianism replaced Legalism as the state ideology. In this process, Dong Zhongshu (179–140 BCE), a Yin Yang Confucian, played an instrumental role in politicizing Confucianism and developing a systematic Confucian cosmology.

In the ensuing periods, with rise of Neo-Daoism, the so-called learning of the mysterious (*xuanxue*), as well as the Daoist religion, and the introduction of Buddhism into China, Confucianism lost its monopoly or even preeminence, as Buddhism became the dominant religion in the Sui (581–618 CE) and Tang (618–907 CE) dynasties. It was in the Song dynasty (960–1279) that it regained the status of state ideology, with the rise of Neo-Confucianism, normally regarded as the second main stage in the development of Confucianism, which continued until the beginning of the Republic era (1911). The unique feature of Neo-Confucianism lies in its meeting the challenge of Daoism and Buddhism, which are both strong in metaphysics, by providing a metaphysical foundation for classical Confucian moral values, partially by drawing on the very resources of Daoism and Buddhism. There are two main schools of Neo-Confucianism, the school of principle (*lixue*), with Zhu Xi

(1130–1200) as its greatest synthesizer, and the school of heart-mind (*xinxue*), with Wang Yangming (1472–1528) as its culminating figure. The influence of Neo-Confucianism went beyond China to other Eastern Asian countries such as Japan, Korea, and Vietnam.

In the Republican period, Confucianism was criticized as the root source of the weakness and backwardness of China under the threat of modern Western powers; and in much of the Communist rule since 1949, Confucianism was rejected as the ideology of Chinese feudalism, the target of the Communist revolution. It was in Hong Kong and Taiwan that the third stage in the development of Confucianism occurred, the so-called Contemporary New Confucianism, marked by the historic "Manifesto on Chinese Culture," by Zhang Junmei, Xu Fuguan,

Tang Junyi, and Mou Zongsan on January 1, 1958. The main task of Contemporary New Confucianism is to meet the challenge from the West by arguing for the compatibility of Confucianism with science and democracy. Such a tendency has been developing in mainland China since 1980s.

Rules of Ritual Propriety

Confucian rules of propriety cover almost every aspects of human life. They may be divided into two groups. The first is moral norms, stipulating appropriate actions for different social roles so that rulers can act as rulers, ministers as ministers, fathers as fathers, and sons as sons. While such rules of propriety appear to be external,

Fig. 7.6 *Three Laughing Men by the Tiger Stream*, a Song Dynasty painting illustrating the theme "Confucianism, Daoism, and Buddhism are one." In the picture are Daoist Lu Xiujing (left), Confucian official Tao Yuanming (right), and Buddhist monk Huiyuan (center, founder of Pure Land) by the Tiger stream.

Confucianism claims that they are created by sages not only according to human emotions and desires but also to guide and channel them to their appropriate expression and satisfaction to avoid excess and deficiency or deviation from their appropriate path.

The second is rituals governing various communal events, including rituals for worship, for celebration, for diplomatic matters, for military events, and for mourning and funerals. Among them, rituals for worship are the most important; three rituals perform three functions. The first is to pray to the gods and spirits for protection and happiness; the second is to give thanks to the gods and spirits for the protection and happiness provided; and the third is to report to the gods and spirits when important political and military events take place. It is important that one only worship one's appropriate god and spirit. For example, only the emperor can worship Heaven (*tian*), while feudal lords can only worship earth, and common people can only worship their ancestors. There are also rituals for worshiping gods and spirits for different trades, including those for scholars to worship Confucius and some of his early students.

Fig. 7.7 The *Book of Rites*, one of the Confucian classics, describing different ritual propriety on different occasions.

Heaven: Transcendent, Immanent, and Immanently Transcendent

While ritual is the most salient religious practice of Confucianism, Heaven is the most typical theological concept in Confucianism, although it has not always meant the same thing throughout its history. In pre-Confucius Confucianism, particularly as recorded in the Confucian classics the *Book of Documents* and the *Book of Poetry*, Heaven is regarded as a transcendent, personal being. For example, it is claimed that Heaven gave birth to the multitude of people; that to protect common people, Heaven made for them rulers and teachers so that they might be able to secure the peace of the world; that Heaven hears and sees as our people hear and see and approves and manifests its awesomeness as our people approve and manifest their awesomeness. This personal and transcendent character of Heaven continued in early Confucianism. For example, Confucius says that it is Heaven that knows him (*Analects* 14.37) and produces the courage in him when he is in danger (*Analects* 7.22), that people cannot destroy a pattern that Heaven does not intend to destroy (*Analects* 9.5), and that he is puzzled by the inscrutable ways of Heaven (*Analects* 3.24).

In Neo-Confucianism, Heaven lost its personal and transcendent character. Instead, it becomes identical to Principle (*li*), the trademark concept of Neo-Confucianism to refer to the ultimate reality of the universe. While nothing can exist without Principle, Principle is not outside of the things. In this sense, it is entirely immanent. By "Principle," Neo-Confucians does not mean any fixed entity but the life-giving activity, or creativity, manifest in the universe and the ten thousand things in the universe. This apparently metaphysical concept does acquire some religious meaning when Neo-Confucians regarded it as divine (*shen*) in the sense that the life-giving activity is mysteriously wonderful and unpredictable.

In Contemporary New Confucianism, Heaven is regarded as immanently or internally transcendent in contrast to the Christian God, which is externally transcendent (the world here and God there) as well as the nonreligious view, which lacks any idea of transcendence at all. Heaven is right within the ten thousand things of the universe as their essence, not as what they actually are but as what they ought to be. As it is within the ten thousand things, it is immanent; but as it carries things from what they are to what they ought to be, it is transcendent. It is in this sense that the theology of Heaven in Contemporary New Confucianism is primarily moral. While the essence of humans, as the distinguishing mark of being human, is virtue, no actual human being is fully virtuous. Heaven is the unceasing transcending activity within humans from what they actually are to what they ought to be.

"Don't Turn the Other Cheek"

Jesus famously urges people not to resist an evil person: "If someone strikes you on the right cheek, turn to him the other also. And if someone wants to sue you and take your tunic, let him have your cloak as well. If someone forces you to go one mile, go with him two miles" (Matt. 5:39-41). Confucius's teaching is very different. When asked what he thought about repaying injury with a good turn, Confucius responded: "If so what do you repay a good turn with? You repay an injury with uprightness (*zhi*), but you repay a good turn with a good turn" (*Analects* 14.34). While the exact meaning of uprightness with which one ought to repay an injury is subject to scholarly interpretations, it is clear that Confucius does not approve repaying injury with a good turn. The reason behind this can be seen from the following anecdote.

Fig. 7.8 Temple of Heaven. Complex of fine cult buildings (fifteenth century), symbolizing the relationship between earth and heaven.

Once Zengcan, one of Confucius's students, famous for his virtue of filial piety (*xiao*), harmed plants while he was weeding. His father became excessively angry and hit him with a large stick until Zengcan became unconscious. After recovering, he went to see his father, saying that he deserved the punishment and expressed his concern about his father's health, as he might be exhausted by hitting him so hard. Then he went to his room, singing while playing zither, to assure his father that he was fine. Zengcan thought he was practicing the filial piety that his master taught him, and so he had the story told to Confucius. Instead of praising Zengcan, however, Confucius blamed him, asking him to learn from the sage king Shun, also famous for his virtue of filial piety.

Shun's mother died when he was very young, and his father remarried and had a younger son, Xiang. All three hated Shun, frequently causing trouble for him and even attempting to kill him; Shun, meanwhile, still maintained his filial piety to his parents and loved his brother, willing to accept any appropriate punishments when he made mistakes. However, he made sure that he would not let his parents kill him, as they indeed attempted. For example, once, his stepmother asked him to dig a well. When it was deep, she and her son started to dump the dirt in the well. However, Shun had already dug a tunnel out in advance and so was able to get out safely.

Confucius explained that Shun tried to avoid being killed by his parents and brother not because he was scared of death but because, if he allowed them, they would have done something immoral. So by avoiding being killed, Shun actually helped prevent his parents from committing an evil act. So Confucius told Zengcan that, to follow the example of Shun, when his father intended to hit him so hard for such a minor fault, which was obviously wrong, Zengcan should get away, so that his father would not have the opportunity to commit this wrongdoing (*Kongzi Jiayu* 15; 103). The important idea is that a person who wants to be virtuous should help others become virtuous, and a person who is not willing to do immoral things should help others not do immoral things. This is the unique Confucian golden rule (*Analects* 6.30).

"Love Virtue as You Love Sex"

Confucius once complained, "I have never seen one who loves virtue as one loves sex" (*Analects* 15.13). The ideal person in Confucianism is not merely the one who does the right thing but the one who also loves doing it, finds joy in doing it, and becomes effortless in doing it. For Confucius, to know what is moral is not as good as to do what is moral, and to do what is moral is not as good as to find joy in being moral (*Analects* 6.20). In Confucius's view, moral cultivation starts from reading the *Poetry*, from which one's moral sentiments can be stimulated; as such moral sentiments are unstable, they need to be regulated by rules of propriety; as one will feel externally constrained when one's action is regulated by rules of propriety, one's moral cultivation can be accomplished only by music, through which one becomes natural in performing moral actions. It is important to point out that not only do music (*yue*) and joy (*le*) share the same Chinese character, but their meanings are also closely related. Mencius makes this particularly clear: the essence of music (*yue*) is to take delight (*le*) in the virtues of humanity (*ren*) and rightness (*yi*), naturally resulting in joy (*le*). As soon as the joy arises, one's moral action cannot be stopped; as it cannot be stopped, one cannot help but dance with feet and wave with

Fig. 7.9 Confucius visits Nanzi (from the film *Confucius*), the wife of Duke Ling of Wei. As Duke Ling spent too much time with his wife and neglected governing his state with virtue, Confucius remarked, "I have never seen a person who loves virtue as he loves sex."

hands even without realizing that one is doing the moral thing (*Mencius* 4a27).

This ideal is reflected in the famous passage in which Confucius describes the milestones of the process of his own moral development: "At fifteen I set my mind on learning; at thirty I took my stand; at forty I came to be free from doubts; at fifty I understood the decree of Heaven; at sixty my ears are attuned; and at seventy I followed my heart's desire without overstepping the line" (*Analects* 2.4). The meaning of each of these stages is not entirely clear, but what is most important is the last stage, at which Confucius can act on his heart's desire without violating any moral principles. It is the highest stage of one's moral cultivation because at this stage, one does not need to worry about any external rules of morality, not because at this stage one has acquired a privileged exemption from the constraints of such rules, but because such rules are no longer needed, as whatever one likes to do, without any consideration of such rules, is

precisely what these rules would require one to do. To use Mencius's term, at this stage, one no longer merely practices humanity and rightness but practices from humanity and rightness (*Mencius* 4b19). In the former, humanity and rightness are still seen as something external that one practices; in the latter, however, they become something internal to oneself.

In the *Great Learning*, one of the four books of Confucianism, there is a similar exhortation: "Love the good as you love the beautiful color and hate the evil as you hate bad odors." This is a great analogy. One does not need to be told, or need to make a calculated deliberation, or to make any forced effort in order to love beautiful colors and hate bad odors. As soon as one sees beautiful colors, one loves them, and as soon as one smells bad odors, one hates them. As a matter of fact, one cannot recognize any colors as beautiful unless one loves them simultaneously and cannot regard any odors as bad unless one hates them at the same time, and vice versa.

Derive an "Ought" from the "Is"

"Ought" and "Is" are often regarded as belonging to two very different categories. The former is about value, while the latter is about fact, and it is almost universally believed, particularly since David Hume, that an "ought" cannot be derived from an "is." In other words, from what something is, we cannot know what something ought to be. However, this is not a dogma that Confucianism accepts. As we have seen, the ideal person in Confucianism loves virtue as he or she loves sex. In other words, human beings ought to be virtuous persons. But why ought human beings to be virtuous? Of course, this "ought" does not come from the fact that all human beings "are" actually already virtuous, which is obviously not empirically true on the one hand and, if true, would make the "ought" claim pointless, on the other.

However, the Confucian claim that humans ought to be virtuous is indeed based on the fact of what human beings essentially are, particularly in their difference from beasts. In a stark contrast with the Western tradition, which almost universally regards rationality as the distinguishing mark of being human, Confucianism regards virtue as what distinguishes humans from animals. This is made most clear by Mencius, whose view on this issue has since become the official doctrine in Confucianism. Mencius states that everyone has a heart that cannot bear to see the suffering of others. To prove this, he says that, seeing an infant about to fall into a well, everyone has a heart of commiseration and an urge to save it, not in order to befriend its parents, nor to be praised by villagers, nor to avoid a bad reputation. "It can be seen from this," says Mencius, "that one who does not have the heart of commiseration is not a human; one who does not have the heart of shame is not a human; one who does not have the heart of deference is not a human, and one who does not have the heart of right and wrong is not human." He then further claims

Fig. 7.10 The Gates of Politeness, Temple of Mencius, Zoucheng.

that these are the respective four sprouts (*siduan*) of the cardinal Confucian virtues, humanity, rightness, propriety, and wisdom (*Mencius* 2a6).

Since the four virtues are distinguishing marks of being human, then every human being ought to be virtuous. Anyone who lacks one or more of these virtues, just for that reason, is a defective human being, is someone a human being ought not to be. So "ought" not only can but also should be derived from "is," as it is clear that we cannot claim that a particular person is a good human being (what one *ought* to be) or a bad human being (what one *ought* not to be) unless we know what a nondefective human being *is*. This is similar to our value judgment of a plant or an animal, as we cannot claim that a particular tree or wolf is a good tree or wolf (what it *ought* to be) or a bad tree or wolf (what it *ought* not to be) unless we know what a nondefective tree or wolf *is*.

The Political Is Also Personal

The contemporary liberal tradition makes a strict division between the political and the personal. On the one hand, "the personal is not political": the function of government is limited to the public sphere, while people's life in the private sphere, particularly within family, is "protected" from governmental interventions. On the other hand, the political is not personal: the function of government is limited to establishing social institutions regulated by just laws and public policies but has nothing to do with the types of persons living within these institutions, whether they are virtuous or not. While feminism has challenged the claim that the personal is not political, Confucianism poses a threat to the claim that the political is not personal.

There is a famous claim in Confucius's *Analects*: "If you lead people with political measures and keep them in order with punitive laws, the common people will stay out of trouble but will have no sense of shame; if you lead them with virtue, and keep them in order with propriety [*li*], they will have a sense of shame and not make trouble" (*Analects* 2.3). Here Confucius makes it clear that what kind of government you have will affect what kind of people you will have. If the state is governed by punitive laws, then even when people obey them, they may have no sense of shame, as they obey laws not because they think it is the right thing to do but because they want to avoid punishment. As a matter of fact, such laws tend to encourage people to find ways to do things they prohibit without being caught.

In contrast, Confucius proposed two ways of government to ensure the people governed will be virtuous. The first is government by virtue. It requires the ruler to be a virtuous person. In Confucius's view, the ruler can be compared with wind, while common people can be compared with grass, where grass bends in the direction the wind blows (*Analects* 12.19). In other words, if the ruler is virtuous, common people will become virtuous, and if the ruler is vicious, one cannot expect common people to

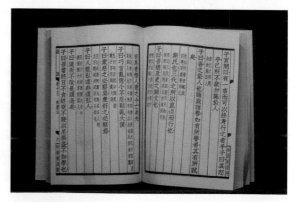

Fig. 7.11 Copy of *The Analects of Confucius,* a record of sayings mostly by Confucius.

be virtuous. It is in this sense that Confucius says, "To govern is to be correct. If you set an example by being correct, who dares to remain incorrect?" (*Analects* 12.17). So this idea of government is close to the Daoist idea of government without action, and Confucius himself says that "to govern with virtue is like the north polar star, which remains at its place while all other stars turn toward it" (*Analects* 2.2).

The second is government by rules of propriety. Rules of propriety, just like laws, provide people with action guides. However, while one will be punished if the person violates the law, one will not be punished but will feel shame if rules of propriety are violated. For Confucius, rectification of names (*zhengming*) is the essential to government by rules of propriety: "The ruler ought to act as a ruler, and minister ought to act as minister, father ought to act like a father, and son ought to act like a son" (*Analects* 12.11). So there are clear specifications for different roles in society, without which people will not even know where to put their hands and feet.

Love with Distinction (*Ai You Chadeng*)

In Confucianism, humanity is the leading virtue. The fundamental meaning of humanity is to love people. Thus, when one of his students asks what humanity is, Confucius responds that it is "to love people" (*Analects* 12.22). Mencius also states that a person of humanity loves people (*Mencius* 4b28). However, what is unique about love in Confucianism is its conception of family love as paradigmatic. In the *Analects*, it is said that "filial piety and brotherly love are the root of humanity" (*Analects* 1.2). In the *Doctrine of the Mean*, there is a similar claim that "humanity is the characteristic element of human beings, and its most important aspect is to love your family members" (*Zhongyong* 20.5). Mencius also holds that the most important duty one has is to one's parents (*Mencius* 4a19). It is in this sense that Mencius directly links humanity to family love: "Loving one's parents is humanity" (*Mencius* 7a15).

To say that family love is the beginning of *ren* does not mean that one should not love people outside one's family, as it is important for Confucians to extend one's love for family members to members of other families. However, one of the central ideas of Confucianism is love with distinction. In his argument against Mohism, which advocates impartial love (*jian ai*), Mencius claims that "the Mohist idea of universal love amounts to a denial of one's father" (*Mencius* 3b9), in the sense that one would not be able to love one's father unless one could either simultaneously or subsequently love everyone else. He further questions whether a Mohist truly believes that a man loves his brother's son in the same way as he loves his neighbor's newborn baby (*Mencius* 3b9). While Confucius himself did not live to see this debate, he would certainly agree with Mencius that one's love for parents is and should be different from one's love for others. When told by the governor of She about an upright person in his village who witnessed against his father for stealing a sheep, Confucius responds that "an upright person acts differently in my village: father does not disclose the wrongdoing of his son, and son does not disclose the wrongdoing of his father" (*Analects* 13.18).

There are several justifications for this love with distinction in Confucianism. First, family love is the root of one's love for others in the sense that one's love for others is a natural growth from it. Thus, when one's family love and one's love for others come into conflict, it is more important to preserve one's family love. Second,

Fig. 7.12 Disciples holding bamboo slips (the book form of ancient China) chant the much-quoted lines of the *Analects*, "All those within the four seas can be considered one's siblings," during the Opening Ceremony of the Games of the XXIV Olympiad, August 2008, in Beijing.

appropriate love requires one's knowledge of the object of love. Since clearly one knows one's family members better than other people, one's love for one's family member is more likely to be appropriate than one's love for others. Third, family is the basic unit of society, and a good society consists of well-functioning families.

Cultivating Learning and Friendship: Excerpts from the *Analects* of Confucius*

Is it not a pleasure to learn and practice what is learned? Is it not delightful to have friends come from afar? Is one not a superior person who does not feel hurt when one is not recognized by another? (*Analects* 1.1)

A person of humanity, wishing to establish one's own character, also establishes the character of others, and wishing to be prominent oneself, also helps others be prominent. (*Analects* 6.28)

*Author's translation of excerpts

With coarse rice to eat, with unboiled water to drink, and with bent arms for a pillow, there is still joy. Wealth and honor obtained through unrighteousness are but floating clouds to me. (*Analects* 7.15)

Superior persons bring the good things of others to completion and do not bring the bad things of others to completion. The inferior persons do just the opposite. (*Analects* 12.16)

Superior persons seek harmony, not homogeneity, with others, and inferior persons seek homogeneity, not harmony, with others. (*Analects* 13.23)

Superior persons seek occasions to blame themselves, and inferior persons seek occasions to blame others. (*Analects* 15.20)

There are three kinds of friendship that are beneficial and three kinds that are harmful. Friendship with the upright, with the truthful, and with the well-informed is beneficial. Friendship with those who flatter, with those who are meek and compromise with principle, and with those who talk cleverly is harmful. (*Analects* 16.4)

◆ **STUDY AND DISCUSSION QUESTIONS**

1. Heaven is the most religious concept in Confucianism. Explain how the meaning of Heaven changes from classical Confucianism, to Neo-Confucianism, and to contemporary Confucianism.

2. Unlike Jesus, Confucius does not advise us to turn the other cheek. What is his main reason, and what ought we to do to wrongdoers according to Confucius?

3. Why does Confucius think that it is not enough just to do virtuous things? And what does Confucius mean by saying that one also ought to love cultivating virtue as much as one loves sex?

4. What is the Confucian view of the goal of government, and how do Confucians think this goal can be reached?

5. What is the Confucian conception of love with distinction, and why does Confucianism prefer love with distinction to impartial love for all?

◆ **KEY TERMS**

Ai You Chadeng (love with distinction)
de (virtue)
jian ai (impartial love)
junzi (superior person)
li (Principle)
li (propriety)
liuyi (six arts)
ren (humanity)
ru (Confucian)
sheng (sage)
shi (scholar-official)
siduan (four sprouts)
sishu (four books)
tian (Heaven)
Wujing (the five Scriptures)

xiao (filial piety)
xin (heart/mind)
xing (human nature)
xioaren (inferior person)
yi (rightness)
zhengming (rectification of name)

◆ **FOR FURTHER READING**

Angle, Stephen C. *Sagehood: The Contemporary Significance of Neo-Confucian Philosophy*. Oxford: Oxford University Press, 2009.

Bell, Daniel A. *China's New Confucianism: Politics and Everyday Life in a Changing Society*. Princeton: Princeton University Press, 2010.

Bol, Peter K. *Neo-Confucianism in History*. Cambridge, MA: Harvard University Asia Center, 2010.

Ching, Julia. *Confucianism and Christianity: A Comparative Study*. New York: Kodanshan International, 1977.

Confucius. *Analects*. Translated by D. C. Lau. *Analects*. Middlesex, UK: Penguin, 1979.

Fingarette, Herbert. *Confucius: The Secular as Sacred*. Prospect Heights, IL: Waveland, 1998.

Hall, David, and Roger Ames. *Thinking through Confucius*. Albany: State University of New York Press, 1987.

Huang, Yong. *Confucius: A Guide for the Perplexed*. New York: Continuum, 2012.

Ivanhoe, Philip J. *Confucian Moral Self Cultivation*. Indianapolis: Hackett, 2000.

Levenson, Joseph R. *Confucian China and Its Modern Fate: A Trilogy*. Berkeley: University of California Press, 1968.

Mencius. Translated by D. C. Lau. Middlesex, UK: Penguin, 1970.

Makeham, John, ed. *Dao Companion to Neo-Confucian Philosophy*. New York: Springer, 2010.

———. *Lost Soul: "Confucianism" in Contemporary Chinese Academic Discourse*. Cambridge, MA: Harvard University Asia Center, 2008.

Tu, Wei-ming. *Centrality and Commonality: An Essay on Confucian Religiousness*. Albany: State University of New York Press, 1989.

Yao, Xinzhong. *An Introduction to Confucianism*. Cambridge: Cambridge University Press, 2000.

Yearley, Lee. *Mencius and Aquinas: Theories of Virtue and Conceptions of Knowledge*. Albany: State University of New York Press, 1990.

CHAPTER 8

Shinto

Lawrence E. Sullivan

Introduction

The word *Shinto* refers to native Japanese religious ideas and practices that date back to the earliest recorded history. Shinto is still practiced by tens of millions of Japanese, particularly at special moments in their life: birth, naming, coming of age, school exams, marriage, moments of community celebration, and times of crisis. Ironically, the name *Shinto*, designating native Japanese religious life, derives not from the Japanese but from the Chinese words *shin tao*, meaning "the way of the gods," a term that appeared in the eighth century, after Buddhism and written language were introduced to Japan from abroad. The term *Shinto* was probably coined in reference to the Japanese religious life that existed before the arrival of Buddhism and Chinese religious influences. In fact, from the earliest written records onward, many Shinto practices reflect an awareness of being a response to religious life from outside Japan. The Japanese equivalent phrase for Shinto is *kami-no-michi*, meaning "the way of the kami." Kami are powerful beings, affecting people's lives in special ways and at special places and moments, but are primarily linked with the very first forces that shaped the world when Japan and its people originated.

TIMELINE
BCE

ca. 660	Time of legendary Emperor Jimmu
ca. 350	Ritual worship of sun and fertility

CE

ca. 350–550	Unification of clans and kami worship
552	Introduction of Buddhism to Japan
712	Writing of the *Kojiki*
797	Writing of the *Nihon Shoki*
ca. 1650–1850	Shinto scholarly revival
1868–1912	The Meiji Restoration and modernization of Japan
1882	Beginning of state Shinto
1945	Conclusion of state Shinto
1946	Emperor Hirohito rejects title of divinity

The term *Shinto* covers a wide range of action and thought concerning the kami. Shinto shrines (*jinja*) can be found in every city and town, whether in great parks or on small shelves in private homes, whether on mountaintops or along the water's edge. Shinto organizations or sects (*kyoha*) affect the social life of many people; and Shinto folk practices (*minzoku Shinto*), such as placing protective charms in one's car or home, shape the daily habits and outlooks of urban as well as rural populations. Shinto rites are performed in private homes and in public street festivals. Shinto ceremonies purify new building sites and construction, as well as satellites and ships. Special Shinto rites protect professionals and artists as well as newborns and high school students taking college entrance exams. This chapter describes Shinto ideas and rituals that link the kami, the natural world, and the Japanese people.

Growing Up with Shinto

When a newborn infant is brought to a Shinto shrine for the first time, it is an important event for her and for her entire family. Many Shinto rituals mark important passages in the human life cycle. At each stage, life is renewed and strengthened by fresh contact with the kami, who shaped the world, making it vital and strong. The first visit to a shrine often occurs ceremonially on the thirtieth or hundredth day of life. The child may be named in the first ceremonial visit. Dressed in an outsized robe, the newborn is brought to the shrine by parents and relatives for the ceremony of the first visit (*hatsumiyamairi*), when he or she is brought under the special protection of kami. In the past, such kami were associated with the *ujiko*, the kin group to which the family belonged. Today the kami to whom the newborn is presented are likely to be associated with a nearby shrine.

Fig. 8.1 Near the Heian shrine in Kyoto, Shinto devotees hang folded pieces of paper onto fences, which contain prayers of purification, before entering sacred space.

The renewal that comes with "first visits" to a Shinto shrine may be relived each year, after midnight of New Year's Eve. During the New Year's season, Japanese purify themselves to begin the new cycle of time. Visiting shrines, they greet the kami with a loud handclap, make an offering , and bow to show their respect.

On the fifteenth of November, children who are three (*san*), five (*go*), and seven (*shichi*) years of age are brought to the shrine grounds to mark the *shichigosan* ritual. Thanks are given for their lives to date, and prayers are offered for their protection and continued health and growth. In addition, special ceremonies are held each year at home and community shrines for young girls on the third day of the third month (March 3) and for boys on the fifth day of the fifth month (May 5) in order to foster their growth and well-being. At age twenty (voting age in contemporary Japan), they may visit a Shinto shrine to celebrate the ceremony of *Sei-ajin no Hi*, a day to mark their transition into adulthood. Most young people also celebrate important ritual phases of their marriage ceremonies at Shinto shrines.

Invigorating Life

Every winter, the city of Konomiya celebrates an elaborate festival called *Hadaka Matsuri*. Ten thousand chanting men, costumed in white breach-cloths and colored headbands, process through the freezing streets, tossing water on

Fig. 8.2 Some of the thousands of lanterns in the shrine of Kasuga (Nara), which means "Spring Day." Lanterns are lit in spring, celebrating the new cycle of life.

themselves drawn from barrels along the road-side. Many come by bus or train from far away, sponsored by their companies or hometowns. Teams of twenty to thirty men carry bamboo trees decorated with white paper and special rope. In a noisy din, they pour into the plaza outside the principal Shinto shrine, dancing shoulder to shoulder, whirling in circles to symbolize the rice grains ground beneath a mill-stone, and swirling like the winds that pollinate the waving rice plants. The atmosphere is emotionally charged and boisterous; thick clouds of steam rise above the milling men.

The dramatic festivities center on men aged forty-two years, the peak year of a man's life, according to local custom. (Women are believed to reach this peak slightly sooner, at age thirty-eight.) The underlying idea is that the powers of a man's life grow and accumulate until his forty-second year, after which they decline and dissipate. This turning point is risky for the men involved and also for the communities around them. The natural world, it is believed, could

also be affected by the change in their energies. Unless the moment is handled through careful attention to Shinto ritual, it could become an unlucky time (*yakudoshi*), when misfortune could affect the man, his family, and community in the form of illness, poor crops, or bad luck.

Tens of thousands of spectators, bundled in winter jackets, line the frosty procession routes and the plaza. As the teams of forty-two-year-olds stream past, the gawking crowds, especially women and children, strain to touch the men in order to transfer their weakness and faults onto them. The men sometimes tear off a tiny swatch of cloth from their headband and pass it to those who have touched them. Toward sunset, when all the men have gathered in the plaza, an extraordinary moment occurs. Without announcement, the *shin-otoko* ("god-man"), a man chosen by lot and purified through weeks of fasting and ritual isolation, slips out of the shrine and runs a gauntlet through the lengthy plaza. To be selected *shin-otoko*, a living *goshintai*, is a great honor. All the men strain to touch him in order to transfer to him the weaknesses placed on them by the crowds. Since the *shin-otoko* is indistinguishable from all the other men in the crowd, and since no one knows when he will step into the plaza, there are false alarms and cries of "There he is!" and "No, over there." The *shin-otoko* often fears for his life and, in his preparations, dreams of being torn apart limb from limb. He too has heard rumors that, in the past, men in his position have died during the festival. After racing through the entire plaza, he dashes, as quickly as the thick mass of men allow, back to the shrine. The crowds disperse. Late that night, in a ceremony reserved for Shinto priests, the priests drive away the divine man, expelling him into the darkness by pelting him with symbolic "stones" (actually tiny pieces of light pine wood). The *Hadaka*

Matsuri purges men and communities of their weaknesses, both physical and moral. Ridding the community of its faults in this way, it is believed, purifies the people and reinvigorates both life and land.

Kami: Powers of Life in the World

The word *kami*, which lies at the heart of Shinto, is often translated by foreigners as "gods." But kami differ from deities found in most monotheistic or polytheistic religions. Kami can be any superior powers that are extraordinary and inspire special awe. The kami manifest *musubi*, a deep and mysterious power associated with creation and the harmony that supports the natural world. The will of the kami is present in

Fig. 8.3 Dancers perform bugaku dance to gagaku court music in Shinto celebration.

Fig. 8.4 In this painting by Hokusai, a flutist contemplates the mountain. Shinto believers admire the manifestations of creative forces in the world.

human life through *makoto*, which means truthfulness, the willingness to live life in accordance with powers that surpass human understanding. Human beings receive life and its blessings from the kami. That is why life is sacred. A true and pure heart (*magokoro*), which is the Shinto ideal, remains always aware of the power of the kami at work in human life and in the life of the world.

In Japanese myths, the kami appeared divided into two categories, those associated with heaven and those with earth. Later, kami came to be associated with many powers of nature (springs, mountains, waterfalls, rivers, and other notable places). Although associated with specific places (such as trees, remarkable

stones, caves, waters, mountain peaks, or cliffs), the kami remain mysterious and vaguely defined forces that descend on on their *goshintai* ("divine bodies") but whose reality and power also pass beyond them. *Goshintai* are the physical images or objects on which kami descend and with which specific kami become identified. The range of objects functioning as *goshintai* includes such items as jewels, mirrors, swords, stones, or trees, and also human imagery as presented in statues and paintings. The *goshintai* function as a focus of worship in a shrine and allow for a direct encounter between the faithful and the kami to whom the shrine is dedicated. Emperors, and sometimes deified ancestors or heroes, have also occasionally

Fig. 8.5 A Shinto shrine that enshrines the nature spirit of sweet potatoes as *kami*.

Early Shinto and Its Buddhist Influence

Shinto has changed over time, especially due to contact with religions originating outside Japan. In Japanese records of the eighth century, the principle kami, called ujigami, protected each clan and its territory. Sometimes, the *ujigami* was a divine, life-giving ancestor who founded the clan. When the nation unified under the imperial clan, its founding deity and ancestress, Amaterasu-O-Mi-kami, began to be worshiped beyond the imperial family palace. Myths about Amaterasu, among other matters, were gathered by Emperor Temmu (672–687 CE) and set down in writing soon afterward: the *Kojiki*, "Record of Ancient Matters," dating to 712 CE, and the *Nihon Shoki*, "Chronicles of Japan," dating to 797 CE, were both written in Chinese characters. Between the eighth and twelfth centuries (the early Heian period), Shinto shrines were organized into a national system, based partly on native Japanese practices and partly on Chinese models. In 927 CE, the *Engishiki* appeared in fifty volumes, including ten books on rules and prayers for Shinto shrine organizations and ceremonies. For example, the *Daijo-sai*, the Great Thanksgiving, was celebrated during the enthronement of a new emperor, and gifts of new cloth—changes of ceremonial clothing—were offered to the imperial ancestor kami at the onset of each summer and winter. To this day, Shinto reflects its association with groups, such as the clan, the village, the corporation, and the nation.

Early Shinto leaves little evidence of permanent shrines. Kami were believed to visit ritual sites near rivers, mountains, trees, or remarkable stones and to leave afterward. Later, permanent structures sheltered devotees and

been identified as kami. Finally, kami are linked with ideals, concepts, and abstractions. Even where kami are associated with built spaces such as shrines, they are not always considered permanent residents but rather as transient beings, called down for special occasions and sent away after receiving offerings and prayers. Over the centuries, people have described how kami might take possession of animals (such as foxes or badgers) and even domestic pets like dogs and cats. These animals, in turn, when empowered by the kami, might take possession of human beings. An *ujigami* (somewhat like a household or family god) is a deity associated with a group of related kin, who once resided in the same village (*ujiko*).

Fig. 8.6 Main building of the Izumo Shrine, whose design reflects ancient granaries.

housed kami and their *goshintai*. Early shrines resembled rice granaries. To learn the will of the kami, ancient Japanese studied patterns of lines on tortoise shells or cracks on the burnt shoulder bones of deer. They received the kami's messages in dreams and trances of possession, when kami were believed to enter them.

Buddhism from Korea and China influenced Shinto, beginning in the mid-sixth century, when kami were set in Buddhist temples to protect the Buddhas. Later, the kami were seen as beings progressing toward Buddhist enlightenment. Prayers were offered for the kami at Buddhist shrines to propel them through the cycle of rebirths to full Buddhist liberation.

During the Kamakura period, from the twelfth to the fourteenth centuries, specific kami were treated as incarnations of enlightened Buddhas. On Mount Hiei, for example, the Shinto deity Enryaku-ji was an incarnation of Shakyamuni Buddha. Thus Buddhist images appeared in Shinto shrines and vice versa.

Later Influences and Developments

The fourteenth-century *Jinno Shotoki* recorded instructions on kami worship and public practices and remained in effect until the nineteenth

Fig. 8.7 Hachiman, originally a Shinto agricultural deity, was taken up by Buddhism as a protector of the land, and so is represented here as a Buddhist monk.

century. Shinto, however, continued to change. A mystical Shinto emerged in the fifteenth century at the Yoshida shrine in Kyoto, affected by Daoism and Shingon, a Buddhist experience reserved for the initiated. At Yoshida, the Urabe family of Shinto priests celebrated fire ceremonies to purify the heart or mind (*kokoro*) through

the power of Taigen Sonjin, whom they recognized as Kuni no Tokodachi no Mikoto, a kami present at the creation of the universe.

Confucian thought also influenced Shinto thinking and practice. Yamazaki Ansai (1618–1682), relying on other thinkers in the Edo period such as Yoshihkawa Koretaru (1616–1694), emphasized the Confucian process of cultivating Shinto virtues within the self: purity of mind, prayerfulness, devout precision (*tsutsushimi*), and faithful loyalty to the imperial family.

Norinaga Motoori based his Revival Shinto (*Fukko Shinto*) on research of the seventeenth-century Kokugaku, School of National Learning. Motoori sought to restore ancient Shinto by separating it from the other religious influences that had changed it. One of this disciples, Atsutane Hirata (1776–1843) studied ancient texts as well as Catholic thought and claimed that Ame-no-minaka-nushi was the kami who ruled the universe and stood separate and above all others. He proposed new ceremonies and prayers.

During the Meiji period (1868–1912), the Japanese government outlawed some Shinto

Fig. 8.8 An 1895 replica of the Heian shrine in Kyoto, the earliest imperial palace of the city dating back to 794.

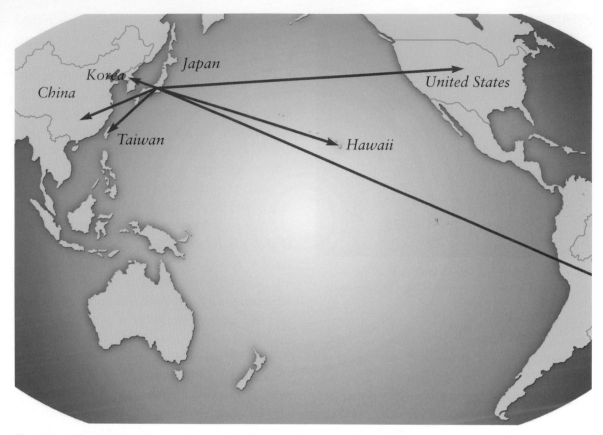

Fig. 8.9 Although Shinto is primarily Japanese, it has spread geographically, especially following World War II into the Hawaiian islands. Shinto movements are also found in China, Korea, Taiwan, the United States, and Brazil.

folk practices, like divination and healing, and tried to make *Fukko Shinto* (Revival Shinto) the official religious belief of Japan. An Imperial Rescript on Education proclaimed Shinto the official basis of the state, stressing the divine nature of the Japanese emperor. The Meiji government separated Buddhist practices, ideas, and shrines from those of Shinto, centering Shinto life on shrines (*jinja*). Shinto and the government remained linked throughout the military buildup of the twentieth century and World War II. After the war, the occupation government dissolved official ties between Shinto and the state. The emperor himself declared he was not divine. On occasion, as

when World War II soldiers are memorialized at the Yasukuni shrine in Tokyo, public debate still focuses on the relationship between the state and Shinto.

For three hundred years, Shinto subdivisions, or sects (*kyoba*), have appeared, reflecting influences from diverse Shinto thinkers as well as from Buddhism, folk practice, Daoism, Confucianism, and Shugendo (the religious life associated with the sacredness of mountains). Thirteen sects, some of which became large religious movements, received official recognition during the Meiji period and still exist. For example, Tenrikyo, Kurozumikyo, and Konkokyo stress healing and model themselves on the practices of their founders, whereas Fusokyo and Ontakekyo stress the worship of mountains and the powers derived from them. Shinto affects new religious movements in Japan today. Given its history, Shinto is likely to continue its evolution in the future.

Purification

Purity places one into relationship with the pure beings, the kami on whom depend the meaning of life and the solidarity that governs the natural world and human society. Even if one avoids gross physical and moral pollution, life needs periodic purification because it is inevitably soiled by natural calamity, personal misdeed, and social mishap. The kami themselves, in the days of myth, had to deal with the disruptions of the rascal kami Susano-o and his antisocial antics. When the mythical figure Izanagi tried to bring his wife Izanami back from Yomi-no-kuni, the land of the dead, he first purified and fortified himself by withdrawing from the company of the other kami and washing himself in a river.

Purity is periodically restored through ritual acts, many of which are performed at Shinto shrines. When visitors enter a shrine, before they stand before the kami, they perform a cleansing (*misogi*) at the shrine entrance by rinsing their mouths and washing their hands. Over the centuries, and perhaps under the influence of Buddhism, Shinto purification came to include both interior purification (*naishojo*, purification of heart and mind) and exterior purification (*geshojo*, purification of the body). Whole communities used to purify themselves through abstinence (*imi*), fasts, and other spiritual exercises that are now more often reserved for priests. Attendance at dramatic spectacles

Fig. 8.10   Before entering the Heian shrine in Kyoto, girls perform the purification ritual, symbolizing passage from an impure world to a sacred space of beauty

that drive out or destroy evil beings also serves to cleanse and revitalize the community.

Such purification through exorcism (*oharae*), the expulsion of what is unclean, including evil spirits, is an important Shinto practice. Described in the first Shinto literature of the eighth century, it is a tradition that continues today. *Oharae* exorcisms dispel the evils that disrupt society and overcome the negative consequences of sickness, dreams, death, and disaster. *Oharae* purification takes many forms, including ritual dramas, tossing salt, sprinkling water, walking through a ring made of special leaves, and waving a special branch overhead. Since strong, pure beginnings link new undertakings with the creative forces of the kami, professionals and corporations frequently commission purification ceremonies when constructing a building, launching a ship, opening a factory, or beginning a new business.

Shrines

The presence of kami is marked by Shinto shrines, which range in size from large complexes with many buildings to small objects on shelves in homes. Shrines (*jinja*) are intimately connected to woods, waters, hills, and fields that are considered part of the shrine area. Entrance to a shrine is through one or more *torii*, a stately gateway with a double-lintel overhead. A *simenawa*, or large ceremonial rope strung alongside the gate, also indicates that one is entering a sacred enclosure. The visitor's pathway soon leads to a basin (*mitarasi*) overflowing with water, where visitors wash their hands and rinse their mouths. Shrines often separate the inner sanctuary, which is hidden or closed to the public, from the outer shrine, which is more visible and accessible to visitors. In the outer area may be a hall where purification ceremonies take place, a welcome room where visitors can gather, a shrine office, and a building that houses special treasures. These are public spaces for routine use. Further inside are places linked with ceremonies and celebrations: the hall of worship (*haiden*), hall of sacred dance (*kaguraden*), and hall of offerings (*heiden*). These places are available, on a more restricted basis, to those participating in ceremonies or making offerings. The innermost sanctuary, set apart from easy view, is mostly for the priests (*kannushi*) or *miko*, women specially

Fig. 8.11 The giant torii at the entrance of the Meiji shrine in Tokyo. Its presence emphasizes a space sheltered from the competition and struggles of daily life.

prepared for ritual roles. The innermost sanctuary contains items directly associated with the kami, such as precious jewels, mirrors, swords, wooden statues, or other precious objects covered in silk and enclosed in containers. These items are called *goshintai* (literally, "kami bodies") and are usually seen only by the head priest of the shrine.

Shrine visitors greet the kami with a solemn clap of the hands, bowing respectfully beforehand and afterward. The visitors may offer a coin, rice wine, fruit, or other gift. They write petitions of need on special pine tablets and tie small white papers to the branches of bushes. Many visitors also try their luck by drawing fortune sticks out of a special container. In homes that observe Japanese traditional practices, families may keep a *kamidana*, a shelf devoted to kami who protect the family. This small shrine is the center of household prayers and offerings, which can occur daily. The home shrine may include amulets (*o-mamori*) obtained during pilgrimages to *jinja* shrines or to the *jingu*, the few special Grand Shrines.

Amulets (*o-mamori*) obtained at shrines are also given to friends and relatives or placed in cars for protection. Special foods (sweets, teas, wild plants, or herbs typical of the shrine area) may be brought home as well.

The Ritual Calendar of *Matsuri* Festivals

Shinto festivals (*matsuri*) celebrate special occasions in the calendar, often linked to agriculture (planting seeds, transferring slips, opening sluice gates, harvesting crops, or storing and distributing the harvest). The largest *matsuri* occur at the great turning points in the spring and autumn seasons: in the spring to offer the *kinensai*, the prayer for success of the new crop cycle, and in the fall to pray the *niinamesai*, or Thanksgiving for harvests. *Matsuri* vary greatly but share an overall pattern.

Fig. 8.12 The carrying of *mikoshi* (a portable Shinto shrine) at the Asakusa Sanja Festival, Tokyo, Japan.

Worshipers and priests purify themselves, after which the head priest leads solemn greetings (such as bowing and clapping) before the place where the kami is enshrined. The priest then opens the doors to the innermost sanctuary. At this point, the kami's *goshintai* may be carried through the neighborhood in grand procession. To the delight and awe of the spectators, kami move through the area on *mikoshi*, special litters on poles carried by teams of devotees. Parade or not, the chief priest presents the kami food offerings: fruits of the sea (fish, seaweed) or land (fruits, vegetables, rice, even birds). In the past, cooked foods were offered, which the kami shared with devotees. Today, mostly raw foods are given with thanks. The priest chants prayers (*norito*) modeled on those in the *Engishiki*, a tenth-century collection. The kami are honored and entertained with music and dance. *Matsuri* festivals typically combine solemnity with merrymaking. Varieties of entertainment can involve horse racing, mountain climbing, log rolling, sumo wrestling, parades with floats, archery contests, and tugs-of-war, singing, drum ensembles, and masquerades. Prayers are offered by the general population, who often place branches of the *sakaki* tree before the kami. When the offerings are removed and the kami restored to its original place, the doors are closed again. The chief priest offers a last prayerful greeting and the ceremony ends. Then the festival meal (*naorai*) starts. In ancient times, the *naorai* meal was a special communion between kami and worshipers. The food, given to the kami, shared in their power. By eating it, devotees absorbed the kami's power into their own bodies. This sense of communion is still preserved in the plentiful drinking of sake at *matsuri* and in the Thanksgiving feasts carried on in the imperial household and in some shrines.

Fig. 8.13 Sunrise over the Wedded Rocks (the divine primordial couple) on Ise Bay. The rocks represent the union of the creator of *kami*. The adjoining rope of rice straw, which weighs over a ton, is replaced periodically.

Transfer of the Sun Deity at Ise

A special focus of Shinto life can be found at the three national Grand Shrines (*jingu*), of Izumo, Atsuta, and Ise, a town on Ise Bay. All year long, pilgrims stream to Ise from all over Japan to pay respects to Amaterasu, the sun deity, who is enshrined there. She is the founding ancestress of the Japanese imperial family. The Ise Grand Shrine is commonly regarded as the most ancient shrine in Japan, said to have originated in the mythic era, when the earth was new. Archaeology reveals that the innermost shrine at Ise existed as early as the third century; and the outer shrine dates at least to the fifth century. They are completely rebuilt every twenty years. The task is enormous, for some two hundred buildings are remade, as are their ritual implements and ornaments. The refashioning cultivates traditional arts and crafts in each generation.

Toward the close of each twenty-year period, ceremonies and pilgrimages multiply. Thousands of pilgrims in ceremonial garb may be seen hauling in white stones to pave the new building sites. The ritual activities of the *Shikinen Sengu* culminate in a solemn nighttime ritual, when Amaterasu-O-Mikami, with her ritual objects, is transferred from her old to her new home. Shrouded within a portable enclosure of white cloth, surrounded by torchbearers, and accompanied by priests playing eerie sounds on ancient musical instruments, Amaterasu slowly moves to her new quarters. Her image is never seen, for it is transported as a reflection in a covered mirror and never brought into open view. During the ancient times described in myth, the kami used a mirror to coax the sun deity from the cave where she had withdrawn into hiding, plunging the world into darkness. She came forth to see her own reflection. The mirror and the sounds of the celebrating kami enticed the life-giving sun deity to reenter the world. The mirror at Ise, reflecting the unseen Amaterasu, is a mystery wrapped in an enigma: even as it emerges from the old shrine to make the several-hundred-year journey to the next abode, it remains covered and closed in a container, which, in turn, is ringed round with a white cloth.

A Ritual Prayer

HIRANO FESTIVAL
("Hirano no matsuri")

By command of the Emperor,
I humbly speak in the solemn presence
Of the Great Sovereign Deity
Who has been brought hither from Imaki
    and worshipped:

In accordance with your desires, oh Great
    Sovereign Deity,
In this place, The shrine posts
Have been broadly set up in the bedrock
    below,
The crossbeams of the roof
Soaring towards the High Heavenly Plain[1]
And [a shrine] established as a heavenly
    shelter,
As a sun-shelter,
And I (office, rank, surname, and name)
Of the Office of Rites,
Having been designated as "kamu-nusi"[2]
Do present the divine treasures:
Bows, swords, mirrors, bells,
Silken awnings, and horses have been lined
    up in rows;
Garments of colored cloth, radiant cloth,
Plain cloth, and coarse cloth have been
    provided;
The first fruits of the tribute presented
By the lands of the four quarters have been
    lined up:
The wine, raising high the soaring necks
Of the countless wine vessels filled to the
    brim;
The fruits of the mountain fields—
The sweet herbs and the bitter herbs—
As well as the fruits of the blue ocean—

The wide-finned and the narrow-finned fishes,

The seaweeds of the deep

And the seaweeds of the shore—

All these various offerings do I place, raising them high

Like a long mountain range, and present.

Receive, then, tranquilly, I pray, these noble offerings;

Bless the reign of the Emperor as eternal and unmoving,

Prosper it as an abundant reign,

And grant that he may abide for a myriad ages.

[Thus praying] I fulfill your praises

Thus I humbly speak.

Also I humbly speak:

Guard, I pray, the princes of the blood, the princes,

The courtiers, and the many officials here assembled

Who serve [the emperor];

Guard them in the guarding by night

And the guarding by day,

And grant that they may serve in the Emperor's court

Ever higher, ever wider, always prospering

Like luxuriant, flourishing trees.

[Thus praying] I fulfill your praises

Thus I humbly speak.

An imperial messenger recited this ritual prayer (*norito*) at the Hirano shrine in Kyoto during the fourth and eleventh months of the year. The prayer and offerings were made to a kami brought to Hirano from the town of Imaki. The kami is asked to bless the imperial court with peace, health, and abundant long life. Recorded during the tenth century, such *norito* continue to serve as models for Shinto prayer today.

◆ **STUDY AND DISCUSSION QUESTIONS**

1. Assess the relationship that practitioners of Shinto have with nature and natural forces, drawing on the role and action of kami and how this relationship may inform an approach to environmentalism.

2. Think about the wide variety of private and public shrines and discuss their significance and value for sustaining religious belief. Why are shrines often integral elements in a religious tradition?

3. Despite Shinto no longer officially being tied to the state of Japan, public debate continues about the idea of a state religion. In what ways can a relationship—strong or weak—between religion and the state be valuable or harmful, or both?

◆ **KEY TERMS**

Amaterasu-O-Mi-kami

Ame-no-minaka-nushi

Daijo-sai

Engishiki

Enryaku-ji

Fukko Shinto

geshojo

goshintai

Hadaka Matsuri

haiden

hatsumiyamairi

imi

Ise
Izanagi
Izanami
jingu
jinja
kaguraden
Kamakura period
kami
kami-no-michi
kamidana
kannushi
kinensai
Kojiki
kokoro
Kokugaku
Kuni no Tokodachi no Mikoto
kyoha
magokoro
makoto
matsuri
miko
mikoshi
minzoku Shinto
misogi
mitarasi
musubi
naishojo
naorai
Nihon Shoki
niinamesai
norito
oharae
o-mamori
sakaki
Seijin no Hi
shichigosan
Shikinen Sengu
shin tao
shin-otoko

Shingon
Shugendo
simenawa
susano-o
torii
tsutsushimi
ujigami
ujiko
yakudoshi
Yomi-no-kuni

◆ FOR FURTHER READING

Aston, W. G., trans. *Nihongi: Chronicles of Japan from the Earliest Times to A.D. 697*. 2 vols. 1896; repr., Tokyo: 1972.

Bock, Felicia Gressitt, trans. *Engi-Shiki: Procedures of the Engi Era, Books 6–10*. Tokyo: Sophia University, 1972.

Hardacre, Helen. *Shinto and the State, 1868–1988*. Princeton: Princeton University Press, 1989.

Hariuki, Kageeyama, and Christine Guth Kanda. *Shinto Arts: Nature, Gods, and Man in Japan*. New York: Japan House Gallery, 1976.

Hirai, Naofusa. *Japanese Shinto*. Tokyo, 1966.

———. "Shinto." In *The Encyclopedia of Religion*, edited by Mircea Eliade, 13:280-94. New York: Macmillan, 1987.

Kasulis, Thomas P. *Shinto: The Way Home*. Dimensions of Asian Spirituality. Honolulu: University of Hawaii Press, 2004.

Kitagawa, Joseph M. *Religion in Japanese History*. New York: Columbia University Press, 1966.

———. "Preface." In *Norito: A New Translation of the Ancient Japanese Ritual Prayers*, translated by Donald L. Philippi, vii–viii. 1959; repr., Princeton: Princeton University Press, 1990.

Philippi, Donald L., trans. *Norito: A New Translation of the Ancient Japanese Ritual Prayers* 1959; repr., Princeton: Princeton University Press, 1990.

————, trans. *Kojiki*. Princeton: Princeton University Press, 1969.

Picken, Stuart D. B. *Shinto: Japan's Spiritual Roots*. New York: Kodansha International, 1980.

Shinto as Religion and as Ideology. Special volume of *History of Religions*, 1988.

Sokyo, Onon. "The Concept of Kami in Shinto." In *Proceedings of the Second International Conference for Shinto Studies: Continuity and Change*. Tokyo: Kokugakuin University, 1968.

Tsunetsugu, Muraoka. *Studies in Shinto Thought*. Translated by D. M. Brown and J. To. Araki. Tokyo: Ministry of Education, 1964.

◆ **NOTES**

1. "High Heavenly Plain" refers to *takam-no-bara*, where the heavenly kami live, a world different from the visible world of human beings.

2. The *kamu-nusi* is the title of the Shinto priest who is in charge of ceremonial life at a shrine and performs certain ceremonies. Today he is called *kannushi*.

CHAPTER 9
Judaism

Lawrence E. Sullivan

Introduction

Judaism is the way Jews of the Hellenistic world described their manner of serving God. Other Jews at other times and places have used different terms, which some prefer today. Still, Judaism is the term used widely and respectfully by most Jews and non-Jews alike to designate the religious life of Israel, God's holy people. Judaism, in all its varieties, is a way of life observed by Jewish people for nearly 3,300 years, beginning when God chose Abraham, the ancestral father of Israel, from among all the nations. The Jewish people consider themselves descendants of Abraham and Sarah, Isaac and Rebekah, and Jacob and Leah and Rachel, Bilhah, and Zilpah.

Judaism is dedicated to observance of the Torah, a word that means "teaching." Torah refers to all of the Hebrew Bible, especially the Pentateuch (the first five books), as well as to the oral teachings and lore that constitute Jewish tradition. Two forms of Torah, one written and the other oral, emerge from the covenant relationship God established with the people of Israel through Moses around 1200 BCE.

Today the culture of Judaism flowers in the realm of ideas, sciences, professions, and the arts, leaving an impressive mark on human history today, as it has for millennia. Throughout the world, there are about 17 million Jews,

TIMELINE

BCE

ca. 1800	Abraham, the first patriarch
ca. 1260	The exodus, the Hebrews' flight from Egypt under Moses
ca. 1000	Jerusalem established as capital of Israelite kingdom under David
961–922	First temple completed under Solomon
721	Northern kingdom defeated by Assyria
587–539	Destruction of the first temple; Israelites exiled to Babylon
538–515	Israelites return from Babylon
515	Dedication of the second temple in Jerusalem
ca. 430	Torah read to public by Ezra

CE

70	Destruction of the second temple in Jerusalem by the Romans
90	Completion of the canon of Hebrew Scriptures (the Tanakh)
133	Bar Kokhba leads Jewish revolt in Rome
ca. 200	Completion of the Mishnah
ca. 400	Completion of the Palestinian Talmud
ca. 600	Completion of the Babylonian Talmud
1470	Spanish Inquisition begins
ca. 1800	Beginning of the Reform movement in Europe
1896	Theodor Herzl, father of Zionism, publishes *The Jewish State*
1937–1945	The Holocaust (Shoah); attempt to destroy much of European Judaism by the Nazis
1948	Israel founded as modern independent Jewish state
1967	Arab/Israeli War

of whom more than 7 million live in North America, over 3.7 million in Israel, and some 3.5 million in Europe and states of the former Soviet Union.

Outside of the Jewish community, few are familiar with its rich and varied religious traditions. Relations between Jews and non-Jews have suffered because of this ignorance. Throughout their history, Jews have borne the brunt of misunderstanding and persecution precisely for being who they are: their defining adherence to their religious lifeways and their faithfulness to their distinctive covenant with God. In opening a chapter on Judaism, readers do well to recall that little more than fifty years ago, from 1937 until 1945, there was a systematic attempt in Europe to completely exterminate the Jewish people using the full force and fury of the modern nation-state. There is a pressing need to know Judaism better.

Jewish religious life is extraordinary; it stands out in human history. To understand

Fig. 9.1 A torah scroll from the synagogue in Madrid, Spain.

how Jews have constantly reshaped their way of life around faithfulness to the God who has chosen them turns one away from blind prejudice toward an enriching appreciation. Given the historical depth and social complexity of Judaism, and given the many different ways that Jews themselves describe their core beliefs and practices, this chapter provides a brief study of key, important events and ideas.

Bar Mitzvah: Becoming Subject to the Commandments

This boy is undergoing his bar mitzvah, an important ceremony in his life and in the life of his community. *Bar mitzvah*, meaning "son of the commandment," is the name of a ritual observed when a Jewish boy reaches the age of thirteen years plus one day. A similar celebration, called the bat mitzvah, is celebrated among some Jews for the girls who have reached twelve years plus one day in age. For a *bar mitzvah*, the boy's family and friends celebrate his passage into responsibility for study, prayer, and observance of the law. They also celebrate the renewal of the community and the transmission of the Torah to a new generation. For the first time, the boy rises to recite the words of Torah before the congregation in worship. The scroll is taken out of the ark and opened to the proper section for the day. The boy intones the ancient Hebrew Scripture in the traditional manner and addresses an interpretation to the congregation. As signs and reminders of his responsibilities, he receives the *tallit*, or prayer shawl, and tefillin, two small leather containers holding passages from Exodus (13:1-10 and 13:11-16) and words form the Shema (Deut. 6:4-9; and 11:13-21). One of the tefillin (meaning "prayers") is fixed on his head with a leather strap; the other is bound to the upper part of his left arm (if he is right-handed), opposite the heart. From now on, dressed and equipped as an attendant of the Divine King in his court, the young man counts as one who can form a *minyan*, the group of at least ten men required to form a synagogue community for worship.

Mitzvot (plural, "commandments") play a major a role in the life and identity of Jews as individuals and as community members. Even *mitzvot* developed in rabbinical teaching derive their authority and creative power from God (Deut. 17:9-11). All commandments stem from the Torah God has revealed. The rabbis remarked on some 613 commandments given to the chosen people in the Torah, including

Fig. 9.2 Jews praying at the Western (Wailing) Wall, Jerusalem. The wall is the remains of the temple built in the first century BCE and evokes the roots of Jewish history.

the Decalogue given to Moses on Mount Sinai. They took note as well of seven universal *mitzvot* given to all humankind in the days of Noah. Given that all of life is to be lived under God's command, many halakhic norms are considered *mitzvot*. Certain areas of life stand out as especially marked by *mitzvot* that characterize Jewish life: circumcision of males; prayer; keeping Sabbath as a holy day; sexual relations and marriage; study of Torah; food and diet; the *mezuzah* (small receptacle that contains hand-written biblical passages on parchment) that marks the doorway to a Jewish home and other doorways within; festivals (*chagim*); and *tzedakah*, a word that literally means "uprightness" or "righteousness" and refers especially to generous contributions to charity, avoidance of gossip, and comforting of mourners.

Fig. 9.3 The remains of the Synagogue of Gamla, known for Jewish resistance against Rome in 68 CE. It is located east of the Sea of Galilee, at the conjunction of the Golan Heights, the Sea of Galilee, and the Jordan Valley.

Israel, the Holy People of God: Biblical Foundations

The religious life of Judaism is rooted in the life and history of the Hebrew people, who first appear in history as nomadic tribes moving through the upper regions of the Arabian desert, in the shadows and margins of the great empires of Egypt, Sumer, Akkad, and Phoenicia.

The life of the Hebrew people, beginning with the call of Abraham after 2000 BCE, is recorded in the Hebrew Bible, whose Pentateuch (first five books) was compiled after the destruction of the temple in 586 BCE and in response to captivity in Babylon (586–528 BCE).

The people of Israel returned from exile in the years 538 to 515 BCE and, drawing on a variety of sources, composed most of the Hebrew Bible as we know it during that and the following period (538–333 BCE). The Pentateuch, known also as the Torah of Moses, therefore reflects the pattern of Israel's experience of exile from and return to Israel (seen also as the suffering caused by alienation from God and the reconciliation marked by renewal of right relationship with God). In this light, the Hebrew Bible tells the story of the exodus of the Israelites from Egypt, led by Moses, around 1260 BCE, the settlement of twelve tribes in Canaan, and the establishment of a kingship, led first by Saul and then by David, the latter of whom was from the southern tribe of Judah and who

Fig. 9.4 Scene from an open-air bar mitzvah in Jerusalem.

established Jerusalem as a religious center. There David installed the ark of the covenant and his son Solomon (961–922 BCE) built the fabulous temple. Later the nation split into two kingdoms, Israel in the north and Judah in the south. These were conquered by Assyria (in 722 BCE) and Babylon (in 587 BCE), and the temple of Solomon was destroyed. The pattern of exile and return, well established in the time of Ezra (450 BCE), framed an abiding inquiry about how best to observe the covenantal conditions that God set forth in giving the land to the chosen people. One outcome of the constant inquiry was an abundant and varied Jewish religious literature, including a translation of the Torah into Greek (250–200 BCE).

The fact that Torah includes methods for inquiry and ongoing development is essential, for it means that the traditions of Torah are open-ended and remain the responsibility of each successive new generation in history. Defining Torah as ongoing inquiry changes the nature of reading the Bible: not only is the Bible the story of the Hebrew people and their

relationship with God, but it is also a story about the revelatory nature of existence in time. The eternal being of God enters a vital relationship with his finite creatures of temporal existence. God reveals his purposes in the world of time, through the changes and struggles of his chosen people in history, especially in the unique and unrepeatable events of salvation that disclose his law and teaching. Key figures of the Hebrew Bible—Adam, Noah, Abraham, Moses, Nehemiah—appear in distinct circumstances of major significance: the Garden of Eden, the universal flood, the exodus from Egypt, the captivity in Babylon, the restoration of the temple. God reveals himself in his extraordinary deeds, exemplified by the way he raised his mighty hand to lead the people out of Egypt (Deut. 6:22). History was reviewed and recorded in the Bible in light of God's extraordinary actions in history. In promising to be faithful to his people and in insisting that they review the meaning of his will in all circumstances, God thus transforms the life of the observant inquirer in each generation into a

Fig. 9.5 Symbol of the Ark of the Covenant and other Jewish symbols.

manifestation of his will and an event of salvation history.

Diaspora

Diaspora means "dispersion," referring to the way in which Jewish people became scattered like seeds, far from the land of Israel. Early Jewish records take note of those who serve God while living outside the Land of Israel in the midst of peoples who worship other deities. Such was the experience of Abraham in the last days of the Sumerian kingdom and that of Moses in Egypt, called to lead the chosen people toward the promised land, which he never entered.

In 587 BCE, Jerusalem fell, and Jews entered captivity in Babylon. Some returned fifty years later, but others stayed to form a Jewish community within Babylonian society. When Alexander the Great "conquered the world" two centuries later, Jews further dispersed throughout his empire, taking residence, for

example, in Alexandria. Jewish scholars there translated the Bible into Greek. Other emigrants settled in Antioch, Rome, and the cities of the Greco-Roman world. Throughout the Hellenistic world, Jews preserved their faith by forming synagogue congregations that studied and obeyed the Torah, supported the temple in Jerusalem, abided by decisions of the Sanhedrin there, and made pilgrimages to Jerusalem if possible. Jewish intellectuals, like Philo Judaeus (20 BCE–50 CE), read Greek and Roman philosophy in the light of faith and vice versa. After the fall of Jerusalem in 70 CE and its destruction in 135 CE, Jews entered a period of great dispersion throughout the wider world.

Jewish life reflects the experience of Diaspora. In addition to use of the major literary languages of Hebrew, Greek, and Latin, and the many languages of the lands inhabited by Jewish minorities, for instance, there evolved specifically Jewish languages whose sounds were written down using letters from the Hebrew alphabet but whose languages arose from unrelated vernaculars such as Judeo-Arabic, Judeo-Persian, Ladino, and Yiddish, in lands where Jews lived. Diverse influences are reflected in Jewish practice. For example, in traditional prayer life the Kaddish that the congregation prays in response to a sacred reading is recited not in Hebrew but in Aramaic, reflecting the days of the second commonwealth and rabbinic period.

Although Jews often made prominent contributions to the societies in which they lived, they remained minorities. Their treatment at the hands of rulers and populace alike was often based on misunderstanding and open hatred. They were repressed by law and on many occasions massacred in large numbers, as occurred in York in 1190 and in association with the outbreaks of plague in 1348. Notwithstanding moments of fruitful interaction with non-Jews,

Fig. 9.6 Scale model of the Second Temple. This elaborate model, located at Holy Land Hotel in Jerusalem, re-creates the temple from the reign of Herod the Great, c. 20 BCE.

Jews frequently became targets of injustice, expulsion, and persecution. They were formally expelled from Spain in 1492 and from Portugal in 1497, causing these Jews, called Sephardim, to scatter to the Middle East, North Africa, Holland, northern Europe, and South America. These expulsions echoed earlier ones of Ashkenazi Jews from Lithuania (1495) and Germany (1348–1350) into Poland.

In the span of seven years, from 1938 to 1945, six million Jews were deliberately killed for being Jews; one third of the world's Jewish population was exterminated. Whether and how the meaning of such an event can be attained in the light of election by God are matters of grave concern and debate in Judaism today.

Messianic themes of various sorts—from political redemption to spiritual renewal—are reflected in Zionism, the movement that facilitated the return of Jews to Palestine in the modern period. Throughout the centuries of Diaspora, Jews nourished the hope of return to Israel. When that Scripture-based hope merged with the rise of nineteenth-century nationalism, it found expression in the writings of Moses Jess and Theodor Herzl. In 1896, in response to growing antisemitism, Herzl published *The Jewish State* and organized a Zionist Congress in 1897. The nation-state of Israel was established in 1948.

Election: God's Chosen People

"The Lord God has chosen you to be a people for his own possession" (Deut. 7:6). God's selection of Abraham was renewed with his descendants, the people of Israel, throughout history. God's faithfulness to his promises is displayed in the signs of election that appear throughout Israel's history. The Lord spared the

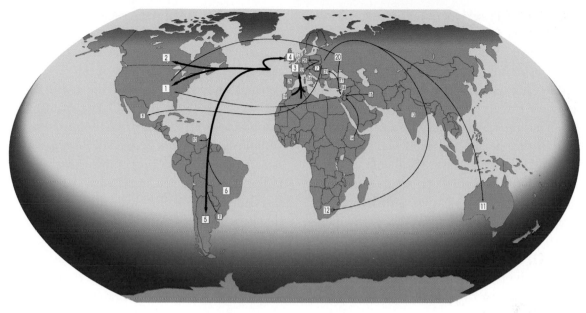

Fig. 9.7 The Jewish Diaspora.

1	USA	5.72 million		14	Ethiopia	18,000
2	Canada	330,000		15	Iran	35,000
3	France	670,000		16	Italy	35,000
4	United Kingdom	360,000		17	Turkey	21,000
5	Argentina	250,000		18	Syria	4,000
6	Brazil	130,000		19	Morocco	17,000
7	Hungary	75,000		20	The Former Soviet Union	1.76 million
8	Mexico	40,000		21	Romania	30,000
9	Uruguay	44,000		22	Switzerland	21,000
10	Venezuela	17,000		23	The Netherlands	28,000
11	Australia	70,000		24	Belgium	41,000
12	Republic of South Africa	105,000		25	Germany	42,000
13	India	7,000		26	Spain	13,000

lives of Israel's firstborn when the heads of all other lineages in Egypt were visited by death and plagued by destruction. The Lord chose to set them free from bondage in Egypt; elected to reveal to them his own nature, name, and will at Sinai; agreed to establish a kingship in Jerusalem and set that city as a light to the nations, beaming like a sanctuary lamp in the world-temple he had created. It was the Lord who renewed his election of Israel after exile, signified by the reconstruction of the temple and the renewal of his covenant.

Religious Jews know themselves to be a people set apart by election and Torah, the will of the God they serve: not an impersonal force of nature nor a first principle of philosophy but a divine personality with a revealed name, the source of all holiness and uprightness, who created in the beginning an orderly and good universe and revealed in time his command about action within it. Above all, Jews are a people set apart by the one and only God who chose them by name in a singular way. God entered a special relationship with them, a covenant agreement binding on both parties. Out of reverence, ancient Jewish custom avoids pronouncing directly the name of God revealed to Moses: YHWH, or the double *yud* in Hebrew, which comes to be pronounced not as written but as Adonai, meaning "My Lord."

The meaning of chosenness has been a constant question in Judaism. During certain periods, Jews remained faithful to their election by separating the community from the corruption of the neighboring religions. At other times, as in Europe from the twelfth to the eighteenth centuries, gentiles in the majority forced Jews to live in walled ghettos with gates locked at night. How Jews should maintain the distinctiveness that signals their election today is a question among Jews, religious or secular. The varying answers to that question have, in part, given rise to several branches of practice, which will be discussed later in this chapter. Judaism is not primarily a set of beliefs. Jews do not say a common creed, for instance. There exists a general mandate to think broadly and debate interpretations. Rather, Judaism emphasizes concrete practice to observe God's will: rite, custom (*minhag*), and a life ordered by the Torah. An observant Jew unites a life of necessary actions with a life of religious practice in line with God's intention in electing Israel: to elevate all of the benefits of life to the level of holiness, to sanctify them by uniting them with God's will.

A major instrument for hallowing the world is the Jewish religious calendar, which begins with R'osh ha-Shanah, New Year, in late September. The first ten days of the year are for penance and reflection, and the tenth day is known as Yom Kippur, the Day of Atonement, emphasizing repentance and forgiveness. In autumn, Succoth, the Festival of Booths, recalls Israel's time of wandering in the wilderness and at the same time celebrates with thanksgiving the fruitfulness of the earth. In midwinter, at the eight-day festival of Hanukkah ("Dedication"), also known as the Feast of Lights, Jews celebrate the ritual cleansing of the temple at Jerusalem in 165 BCE, after a revolt by the Maccabee brothers obtained religious freedom. Each night, they light an additional candle on the *hanukkiyya* to commemorate the miracle when a small cruet of oil burned for eight nights. In late winter or early spring, the carnival-like feast of Purim ("lots") celebrates the victory of the Jews of Persia over Haman, who advised the enemy king. The *megilla* (scroll of Esther) is chanted in the synagogue, to the accompaniment of much deliberate noise and merry-making, especially whenever Haman's name is mentioned. The religious year is renewed in Pesach, Passover, in the spring, commemorating the liberation of the people of Israel from captivity in Egypt. The principal celebration takes the form of a ritualized meal, the seder, where family and friends read and talk about the story of Israel's deliverance. The gathering of Passover also resembles the symposium held in the ancient Greek world, where philosophers (literally, "lovers of wisdom") assembled at a meal to probe and experience issues of deepest concern. Shavuot ("weeks") occurs fifty days after Pesach to commemorate the giving of the Torah on Mount Sinai. In addition to these feasts, many Jews observe at least five daylong

Fig. 9.8 A family celebrates a seder meal during Passover.

fasts throughout the year, especially on *Tish b'Ab* (the ninth day of the month of Ab), which commemorates the day Babylonians destroyed the first temple and Romans destroyed the second. The primary emphasis in ceremonial life is to observe the command "to remember and not to forget" God's saving interactions with Israel.

Current debate about election and observance is animated by increasing rates of intermarriage between Jews and gentiles and by trends toward secularization in modern society. Talk of election and its meaning is shadowed by the unspeakable event of the Holocaust.

Sources of the Torah: Law, Teaching, and Observance

One view of the Torah, meaning God's will for the Jewish people, refers to tradition transmitted in an unbroken chain from Moses to Joshua, to the Hebrew elders and prophets, to leaders like Ezra and Nehemiah of the mid-fifth century BCE, to the earliest rabbis mentioned in the Talmud. A different view of Torah, sometimes called a liberal one, sees the tradition develop over time, blending faithfulness to what was received from the past with creativity to the changing circumstances of present and future. Either view of Torah's revelation and transmission recognizes certain authoritative expressions of Torah that stand out above others. The twenty-four books of the Hebrew Bible form

Fig. 9.9 The Sefer Torah, containing the books of the Pentateuch. From the Synagogue Or Hachaim, Jerusalem.

three sections: the Torah (the Pentateuch, or first five books), *Neviim* (the Prophets), and *Ketuvim* (Writings or Hagiography). The written Torah refers especially to the first five books of the Bible, which are also simply called the Law of Moses. By the mid-fifth century BCE, the reading of written Torah was a central feature of public worship (Neh. 9:3). Torah also includes oral teachings that are both legal and nonlegal in character as well as methods for ongoing development of the Torah tradition.

Next to the Bible, the Talmud is the classic text of Judaism, an authoritative source of tradition and the principal text of rabbinic Judaism. There exist two Talmuds, both written in the Aramaic language. The Talmud is rabbinical commentary on the Mishnah. (Dealing with less than forty of the sixty-three treatises in the Mishnah, however, it does not comment on all six orders of the Mishnah.) The Talmud Yerushalmi (called the Jerusalem or Palestinian Talmud) was composed at the end of the fourth century CE. The Babylonian Talmud, longer and more ambitious in scope, was edited at the end of the fifth century CE and is more authoritative. The two broad headings of most Talmudic concerns are Halakhah (dealing with law, rite, and customary practice) and Aggadah (dealing with theological and ethical argument as well as narrative and folklore).

The Mishnah is a topical law code in six parts with sixty-three subdivisions and formed over a long time, which, some believe, extends back in the Near East to the time before the formation of the Bible and reaching forward to the second century CE. Tradition attributes compilation to Rabbi Judah the Prince, the patriarch of the Jewish community of Palestine. The Mishnah's authority lies in revelation alongside the Pentateuch: it describes itself (in the tractate *Abot*, regarding founders and their sayings)

Fig. 9.10 A page from a nineteenth-century Russian Talmud.

as an expression of Torah revealed on Sinai and transmitted *in oral form* from the time of Moses until its inscription in the Mishnah. Its message: behind all the hierarchical manifestations, seen in the great chain of being in the world, lies the one, true, and holy God. In practice, the Mishnah is an authoritative source for rabbinic teaching and inquiry in Tannaitic, or early rabbinic, Judaism. The Mishnah's view of holiness and sanctification reflects priestly and Levitical concepts rooted in temple rite and calendar, as reflected on by philosophical sages after the Roman destruction of the temple.

Many other written works, too numerous to mention, influence tradition. They include: the commentary on the Bible and Talmud by Solomon ben Isaac, known as Rashi (1040–1105), and two works by the philosopher Moses Maimonides (1135–1204), known as Rambam. His *Mishneh Torah* ("review of the Torah") organizes Jewish law and includes issues basic to faith, such as conditions for the messianic age. And Maimonides's *The Guide for the Perplexed* reworked Jewish theology in the light of Aristotle. Later, Rabbi Joseph Caro (1488–1575) prepared *Shulchan Arukh* (the "Prepared Table"), the most influential code of law and ritual, which includes customs from Spanish and Middle Eastern cultures. Rabbi Moses Isserles (1525–1572) added customs of central and eastern Europe.

Authority: Prophet, Priest, Rabbi

The authority that guides and governs the religious life of the Jewish community has changed over time, in regard to form, function, and spiritual emphasis. The prophet, the priest, and the rabbi ("teacher") exemplify shifts in authority that mark the various epochs of Judaism.

Prophet

The biblical prophets spoke for God in order to challenge the state of affairs on earth. Several kinds of prophets appeared, especially from the eighth to the sixth centuries BCE, when they played a central role in Israel. Bands of unnamed wandering prophets, associated with King Saul and his madness, deliberately induced ecstasy through dance and music. Other kinds of prophets like Elijah or Nathan

confronted kings with dramatic oral statements that questioned the moral caliber of the king's own actions. Still other prophets like Amos, Jeremiah, and Isaiah composed written analyses of injustice, inequity, abuse of power, decadence, and religious hypocrisy. The prophets insisted on a life of genuine observance of God's commands, especially the command that humans establish justice, mercy, and holiness throughout the land and that kings foster the well-being even of their lowliest subjects. At times, courageous prophets announced God's decision to rebuke his wayward people in order to instruct them by means of calamity and defeat at the hands of enemy nations (Amos 3:2). Assyria sacked the northern kingdom in 722 BCE, and Nebuchadnezzar of Babylonia carried

Fig. 9.11 In this stained glass window by Marc Chagall, Jeremiah, having warned the people of the Babylonian conquest, is incarcerated as a defeatist. Located in the Union Church, Tarrytown, New York.

the leaders of the southern kingdom into exile in 587. During such destructions, captivities, and exiles, the prophets steadfastly announced that the faithful remnant of Israel would be set free and vindicated.

Priest

When Ezra the scribe, leading some 1,700 Babylonian Jews back to Jerusalem after captivity, assembled the people to renew the spiritual life of the community, he read them a book of the law. They bound themselves to observe its codes of holiness and place the priests of the temple at the center of their renewed religious life. A new state was begun with power vested in the priests, an office with roots in ancient Israel. To this day, lineages of priests (*kohen*, pl. *kohanim*) can be traced. The high priest was descended from Zadok, the priest appointed in King David's time. Living in the temple at Jerusalem, the high priest ruled both the state and the religious life of the nation. Religious life became highly centralized around the temple and also around the calendar of festivals and fasts. Above all, religious life revolved around the priests, Levites, and scribes who functioned there. The priests and scribes centered on the temple undertook a massive literary effort, particularly in the fifth century BCE, copying and compiling writings of prophets, old and new, and composing complete biblical works that expanded, revised, and added materials drawn from a variety of sources and genres. Eventually, the schools of scribes would give rise to the learned Pharisaic schools and their rabbis of the first century BCE. The Pharisees, in turn, produced the works of teaching, writing, and legal inquiry that would guide Jewish life for millennia after the destruction of the temple.

Rabbi

After the destruction of the second temple of Jerusalem, in 70 CE, authority shifted away from the temple-based priests who presided over rites of sacrifice to the teachers (rabbis) directing study of Torah. In turn, the synagogues where Jews assembled to study under a rabbi became central to worship. Indeed, the Talmudic texts edited in the fourth and fifth centuries organize and elevate study in such a way as to transform the process of human inquiry into a form of worship and interpretation into an extension of God's revelation. Under rabbinic authority, Jews fused rigorous questioning with pious devotion to constitute a single process of religious life, one that maintains its vitality and focus after two thousand years.

Messianism

Prophetic sayings that originally referred to the kings of the ancient kingdom of Judah gave rise to speculation concerning a Messiah, the righteous king whom God would choose to overthrow wicked oppressors and rule Jews and the wider world with justice and mercy. The Hebrew word *mashiach* means "the anointed one." In the Bible, the title indicated kings, high priests, or those elevated to places of honor. From the time of the Babylonian captivity, "messiah" designated especially the one who will redeem God's chosen people from oppression, exile, suffering, and degradation. Acting as a mighty warrior, the messianic king would lead his chosen people in battle and fulfill the other authoritative roles of prophet, priest, and teacher. At the same time, the value of suffering became increasingly clear over the course of biblical history, especially through the preaching of the prophets.

After 70 CE and the destruction of the second Jerusalem temple, the title "Messiah" denoted the one who will gather up Jews from the Diaspora. Exactly how such salvation would be achieved has been a matter of great excitement and discussion. Was the Messiah to be a political figure who would elevate the nation of chosen people over their enemies on the world stage? Was he to be a spiritual leader who would renew the moral purity and force of the chosen people? Was the scale of the Messiah's accomplishment to be national, worldwide, or even cosmic? Would God himself intervene directly as the messianic agent in human history to create conditions of freedom, moral order, and happiness, or would the Messiah be a human leader? Would the transformations brought by the Messiah create a world never seen before or restore a condition that already existed, for example, in the time of King David? In fact, would the messianic age dawn in this world or only after this world is brought to an end?

Since the dawn of the Messianic age is signaled by trial, persecution, and suffering, and since Jews have often suffered such circumstances in history, no age has had its shortage of self-proclaimed messiahs. Christianity began as a Jewish movement declaring Jesus the messiah. Soon afterward, in 133 CE, Bar Kokhba (meaning "Son of the Star") was proclaimed the Messiah and led a revolt spurred on by Rabbi Aqiva, a leading religious authority of the day. Roman forces responded with force, undertook sweeping reprisals, and outlawed Jewish religious observances. The most dramatic and widespread messianic initiative occurred in the seventeenth century. Sabbethai Zevi (1626–1676), a young Kabbalist from Smyrna in Turkey, declared himself messiah at age twenty-two. Driven out by enraged rabbis, he traveled to Salonika, Constantinople, Palestine, and Cairo

before returning to Jerusalem with fanfare until he was expelled. Nathan of Gaza (1643–1680), then twenty years old, acted the part of Elijah, the prophet whom tradition expected to be the forerunner of the Messiah. Sabbethai Zevi returned to Smyrna in triumph in 1665. From there, his movement spread through Europe. In 1666, under threat of torture and death by the sultan in Adrianople, he converted to Islam. Those followers who did not abandon his cause sought to make sense of his apostasy by invoking a theory of "sacred sin," going so far as to suggest that the Torah would be brought to its messianic fulfillment only through actions that might appear immoral on their outward surface but, because of their inner meaning and intention, actually accomplished redemption.

In the last decades of the twentieth century, many of the followings of the Hasidic Rabbi M. M. Schneersohn, known as the Lubavitcher *Rebbe*, thought that he might be the messianic redeemer. He sought to renew religious fervor and observance by encouraging them to teach and practice in the public realm in order to persuade less observant Jews to return to religion. His family migrated from Eastern Europe to New York City, where he died on June 12, 1994, at age ninety-two. At that time, there was expectation that he might lead the chosen people back to the Holy Land. Among some followers, there is still high hope that he might somehow return from the grave to do so.

Mysticisms: Merkabah, Kabbalah, Hasidism

Alongside law and observance, Judaism includes vibrant mystical experiences. Merkabah mysticism is based on extraordinary visions. During the mystical journey, the visionary visits

Fig. 9.12 Students in a Hasidic school that follows the teachings of Rabbi Schneersohn, whose portrait is seen hanging on the wall.

hekhalot, seven palaces or halls where heavenly beings dwell, and then contemplates the very throne and chariot of God. There the mystical voyager encounters Metatron, an angel with human characteristics, identified as the biblical personality Enoch. All those in the family line that descends from Adam to Noah die except for Enoch, whom "God takes" (Gen. 5:18-24) and, according to tradition, rises to the rank of an angel. Metatron-Enoch becomes a focus of mystical and apocalyptic literature. Most *hekhalot* texts date from the third to the sixth centuries CE, although aspects of Merkabah mysticism date back to the second century BCE.

Kabbalah, meaning "tradition," is a different form of Jewish mysticism. The word refers to a special mystical tradition hidden from public teaching. Kabbalists held that God is boundless (*Ein-soph*). However, in the course of creation, a "breaking of the vessels" (*shevirat ha-kelim*) containing the prime matters of darkness and light (evil and good) occurred, and there was a withdrawal or contraction (*tsimtsum*) of God into himself. Kabbalah aims to overcome fundamental divisions and restore—at every level of the heart, soul, and world—the unity that existed among all realities in the beginning. The idea is expressed with great power by Abraham ben Samuel Abulafia (1240–1291), a Sephardic Kabbalist who sought union with God, and by Moses of León (1250–1305), who composed the *Sefer ha-Zohar* (the Book of Splendor), the best-known book of the Kabbalah. It encourages an allegorical reading of the Bible, discovering the mystical meaning of names and letters. This goal of healing rifts and restoring oneness is called *tikkun*, and it is in accord with two other aims of Kabbalah: *kavvanah* (contemplation through meditation) and *devekut* (clinging to God in a mystical union with the divine). Each of these ends serves as a means to the other two. Isaac Luria (1534–1572) and his disciple Hayim Vitale organized Kabbalistic ideas into an elaborate system.

Kabbalah attunes itself to the mystical dimension of grammar, numbers, names, tones, and other corresponding realities found in revelatory writings. Letters of the alphabet reveal commandments and the name of God in the written form and also reveal God to the Parasidics (people in a state of mystic delight) on a level of mystic experience. *Hekhalot* literature and the *Sefer Yetsirah* ("Book of Creation," composed around the third or fourth century) provided Kabbalists a basic worldview: ten *sephirot* (corresponding, some say, to the Ten Commandments, among other realities) make up the universe. Each sphere contains its own modes of bring. Taken together, the *sephirot* contain all imaginable forms of existence in this universe. The *sephirot* (and the realities in them) are connected to one another via twenty-two paths (corresponding to the twenty-two letters of the Jewish alphabet). Just as letters and numbers can be combined and recombined to refer to one and all kinds of realities, so also can the mystic enter the transformative power of numbers, letters, names, and signs to contact the realities they signify.

By uncovering the mystery of the scriptural text, the Kabbalist unveils the divine light hidden in the words and letters. Recombinations of

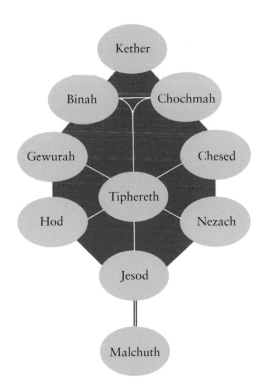

Fig. 9.13 Diagram of God's ten divine emanations (sephirot) with their most common attributes, connected by twenty-two channels that correspond to the letters of the Hebrew alphabet.

visible letters correspond to inner changes that enlighten the mystic's entire being in ecstasy. In this way, humans become microcosms reproducing within themselves the macrocosm of the larger world. Humans can become one with all things, including the divine being. Some Kabbalists speculate there are several spiritual universes that sustain one another: (1) *atsilut* (emanation) made up of ten *sefirot*, which, in sum, compose the mythical man Adam Kadmon; (2) *beriyah* (creation), with the seven mystical palaces (*hekhalot*) and the merkabah; (3) *yetsirah* (formation), where all the hosts of angels reside; and (4) *asiyah* (making), which is the perfect, normally invisible model of the visible world seen by humans. The last years of the twentieth century witnessed a revitalization of interest in Kabbalah and enthusiasm for mystical experiences predicated on Kabbalistic learning and practice.

In eighteenth-century Poland, Israel ben Eliezer (born around 1700), more commonly known by his title Baal Shem Tov or simply Besht, launched a vital religious movement called Hasidism (from the word *hasid*, meaning "pious one"). When rabbinic leaders of Judaism in eastern Europe, such as Elijah of Vilna, condemned Hasidism for not stressing Talmud and asceticism, Hasidic Jews set up their own synagogues. They ignored the established rabbis and turned to *zaddikim* ("the righteous ones") as their leaders. *Zaddikim* descend from their ecstasies for the benefit of their communities. Using extraordinary power acquired in their heavenly ascents, they work wonders on behalf of others. Hasidism has spread throughout the Jewish world and is present as a notable influence in Europe, North America, and Israel. Hasidism stressed that God is everywhere, and it centers spiritual life on the joy that comes from union with God (*devequt*). Ascent of the

Fig. 9.14 A Hasidic family dressed in holiday clothing, standing in front of the Western (Wailing) Wall in Jerusalem.

soul into God's divine light (*aliyat ha-neshamah*) can occur in the most ordinary activities, even when eating or sleeping. Though Hasidism performs dramatic songs and dances, they hold that directing one's mind toward union with God transforms all physical actions into worship.

The Spectrum of Observance

Jewish practices vary by region, family, and the branch of Judaism to which one belongs. Customs cover all aspects of life, from tearing blades of grass and tossing them over one's shoulder at the end of a visit to the cemetery, to covering mirrors or not wearing leather shoes during the seven-day (*shiva*) period of mourning after death. Custom governs greetings, clothing, and prayer. As noted, prescribed behavior is heightened at Sabbath and holy days.

Kashrut is a special area of food observances, instructing Jews to avoid restricted foods and to prepare and serve allowable foods properly. The Bible links dietary laws to holiness: "You shall be holy people to me; therefore you shall not eat any meat that is torn by beasts in the field." The Talmud details the complexities of *kashrut* in a special tractate called *Chullin*. Regulations govern ritual slaughter (*shechitah*), examination of the animal and internal organs (*bedikah*), and preparation of the meat (*kashering*). Generally speaking, Orthodox and Conservative Jews today observe standards of *kashrut*. Reform Judaism leaves matters to individual judgment.

The eighteenth century saw change in the relationship between Jews and non-Jews. The 1789 Declaration of the Rights of Man by the French Revolution was symptomatic of the change, for it declared all human beings equal before the law, including Jews. Notwithstanding setbacks and antisemitism, Jews increasingly faced decisions about how they wanted to relate their social and religious life to that of non-Jews.

As early as 1843 in Frankfurt, Germany, and in the 1870s in America, Reform Judaism introduced new views of worship, observance, and texts. Reform Judaism emphasizes the unity of religion and ethics, dedicating itself to establish peace, eradicate poverty, and achieve social justice. The teachings of the Torah should remain the source of Reform Jewish life but—and here was the important innovation that opened to change—they should be adapted to the needs of each age (other works and traditions of interpretations, such as the Talmud, should be diminished in status). Some Reform Jews today believe that their heritage should not be lived in overtly religious practices. Rather, Judaism should be reworked so that the spirit of those historical religious practices yields ethical principles, psychological truths, political commitments, and wisdom, all of which would have universal standing and transform civil society into a just, peaceful, and healthy world that sustains the well-being of the common good.

Conservative Judaism was founded by leaders like Sabato Morais and Solomon Schechter, both of the Jewish Theological Seminary in New York (opened in 1886), to conserve traditions set aside by Reform initiatives. In 1918, Mordecai Kaplan established a synagogue in New York as a center for Reconstructionism, a movement that stems from Conservative impulses and yet includes more liberal, naturalistic, and anthropocentric philosophies of religion.

Those who observe tradition discuss what accommodations, if any, should be made to modernity in regard to forms of education, engagement with the state, family organization, and even personal hygiene and dress codes. Orthodoxy, associated with the 1896 founding of the Isaac Elchanan Yeshiva (now Yeshiva University), is a numerically strong branch of modern Judaism, although it took shape later than the Reform, Reconstruction, or Conservative branches. Modern Orthodox embrace any cultural benefit that is not expressly forbidden by God's revealed teaching. Other Orthodox reject such accommodation. In turn, others reject Orthodoxy, saying that it is undemocratic

Fig. 9.15 A self-service restaurant for kosher food in Jerusalem. The word *kosher* means suitable or fit, indicating food that has been prepared in a ritually fit manner according to Jewish tradition.

and anti-intellectual, unwilling to work with science and history. Still, the distinctive religious life of Judaism is not being irreversibly eroded by modern society. On the contrary, many Jews (and some gentiles) whose families were unacquainted with strict observance rediscover observant Jewish religious life, for example, when they move from their secular homes to attend secular colleges and encounter lively traditional practices through the Hillel House on their college campus. There is lively ferment at every level of Jewish culture today, a search for the meaning of Torah. Notwithstanding differences, all branches of Judaism embrace plural forms of response to God's revelation and election. On the one hand, they cling to the covenant made with Moses on Mount Sinai by keeping the Torah, and on the other hand, they hold fast to the messianic promises granted to King David on Mount Zion. Keeping Torah and living in hope of promised salvation, Jews know they collaborate with God in redeeming the world.

The Shema: A Prayer for All Time

Here are selections from the Shema, an ancient prayer of special power and prominence in Jewish life. The Shema is composed of three biblical passages (Deut. 6:4-9; 11:13-21; Numbers 15:37-41). Jewish men are required to recite the Shema twice each day, morning and evening. Individuals recite it before sleeping and on the brink of death. For thousands of years, the Shema has been the last word on the lips of Jewish martyrs, who followed the example set by Rabbi Akiva, martyred in the second century. A ruling in that same century obliged Jewish parents to teach the Shema to their children as soon as they began to say their first words.

Hear, O Israel! The Lord is our God, the Lord alone. You shall love the Lord your God with all your heart and with all your soul and with all your might. Take to heart these instructions with which I charge you this day. Impress them upon your children. Recite them when you stay at home and when you are away, when you lie down and when you get up. Bind them as a sign on your hand and let them serve as a symbol on your forehead; inscribe them on the doorposts of your house and on your gates. (Deut. 6:4-9)

If, then, you obey the commandments that I enjoin upon you this day, loving the Lord your God and serving Him with all your heart and soul, I will grant the rain for your land in season, the early rain and the late. You shall gather in your new grain and wine and oil.

Therefore impress these My words upon your very heart: bind them as a sign on your hand and let them serve as a symbol on your forehead, and teach them to your children reciting them when you stay at home and when you are away, when you lie down and when you get up. (Deut. 11:13-14, 18-19)

The Lord said to Moses as follows: Speak to the Israelite people and instruct them to make for themselves fringes on the corners of their garments throughout the ages; let them attach a cord of blue to the fringe at each corner.

Thus you shall be reminded to observe all My commandments and to be holy to your God. I the Lord am your God, who brought you out of the land of Egypt to be your God; I, the Lord your God. (Num. 15:37-38, 40-41)

◆ **STUDY AND DISCUSSION QUESTIONS**

1. Discuss why the idea of "commandment" is so deeply a part of the meaning of Judaism, especially as the idea is reflected in the Torah and in the bar and bat mitzvah ceremonies for young boys and girls.

2. Consider and reflect on the experience of Diaspora for the Jewish people and their frequent minority status in societies, and how this experience informs their religious faith and practice.

3. Review the three major branches of Judaism— Orthodox, Conservative, and Reform—and account for their different beliefs and practices. Do you see parallels in other religious traditions?

◆ **KEY TERMS**

Aggadah
antisemitism
ark
Ashkenazi
circumcision
Conservative Judaism
covenant
Diaspora
Halakhah
Hasidism
Hellenism
kashrut
Lubavitcher
midrash
minhag
minyan
Mishnah
mitzvot
mysticism
observance

Orthodox Judaism
Passover (Pesach)
Pentateuch
rabbi
Reconstructionism
Reform Judaism
R'osh ha-Shanah
seder
Sephardim
shiva
Talmud
Torah
Yom Kippur
Zionism

◆ **FOR FURTHER READING**

Bloch, Abraham P. *The Biblical and Historical Background of Jewish Customs and Ceremonies*. New York: KTAV, 1980.

Chouraqui, André. *L'amour fort commune la mort*. Paris: de Rocher, 1998.

———. *Pensée juive*. Paris: Presses universitaires de Paris, 1997.

Eliade, Mircea, Eugene B. Borowitz, Mark R. Cohen, Jane S. Gerber, Raphael Patai, Martin A. Cohen, Ivan G. Marcus, Steven J. Zipperstein, and Leon A. Jick, eds. *The Encyclopedia of Religion*, 5:127-205. New York: Macmillan, 1987. s.v. "Judaism." A series of articles covering Judaism across time, space, and cultures, by Eugene B. Borowitz, Mark R. Cohen, Jane S. Gerber, Raphael Patai, Martin A. Cohen, Ivan G. Marcus, Steven J. Zipperstein, and Leon A. Jick, with many cross-references to other relevant articles throughout the encyclopedia.

Fackenheim, Emil L. *To Mend the World: Foundations of Post-Holocaust Jewish Thought*. 1st Midland ed. Bloomington: Indiana University Press, 1994.

Glazer, Nathan. *American Judaism*. Rev. 2nd ed. Chicago: University of Chicago Press, 1989.

Idel, Moshe. *Hasidism: Between Ecstasy and Magic*. Albany: State University of New York Press, 1995.

———. *Kabbalah: New Perspectives*. New Haven: Yale University Press, 19900.

Kugel, James. *On Being a Jew: What Does It Mean to Be a Jew? A Conversation About Judaism and Its Practice in Today's World*. San Francisco: HarperSanFrancisco, 1990.

Levenson, Jon D. *Resurrection and the Restoration of Israel: The Ultimate Victory of the God of Life*. New Haven: Yale University Press, 2006.

———. *Sinai and Zion: An Entry Into the Jewish Bible*. New York: Winston, 1985.

Lieberman, Saul. *Studies in Jewish Myth and Jewish Mysticism*. Albany: State University of New York Press, 1993.

Neusner, Jacob. *Judaism without Christianity: An Introduction to the Religious System of the Mishnah in Historical Context*. Hoboken: Ktav Publishing, 1991.

———. *The Mishnah: A New Translation*. New Haven: Yale University Press, 1987.

———. *The Mishnah: Introduction and Reader*. Philadelphia: Trinity Press, 1992.

Rudavsky, D. *Modern Jewish Religious Movements: A History of Emancipation and Adjustment*. 3rd ed. New York: Behrman, 1979.

Scholem, Gershom G. *The Origins of the Kabbalah*. Princeton: Princeton University Press, 1991.

Seltzer, Robert M. *Judaism: A People and Its History*. New York: Macmillan, 1989.

Soloveitchik, Haym. "Rupture and Reconstruction: The Transformation of Contemporary Orthodoxy," *Tradition* 28 (1994): 64–130.

Wolfson, Elliot R. *Through a Speculum That Shines: Vision and Imagination in Medieval Jewish Mysticism*. Princeton: Princeton University Press, 1994.

CHAPTER 10

Early Christian Foundations

Julien Ries

Introduction

This chapter provides an overview of the first four centuries of our era, when the early Christian church established its firm roots in the ancient world. The limits of this period are provided by two books: the first is the Acts of the Apostles, which records the events of the first thirty years of Christian life and evangelization, while the second is marked by *The City of God*, written by St. Augustine between 412 and 426 CE, which covers the vast extent of history.

Born among the people of Israel, from whom it inherited the ideas of the promise and of prophets, early Christianity soon went its own separate way since the paschal community retained a very vivid experience of the mission imparted by the risen Christ and confirmed by the Holy Spirit on Pentecost Day. Under the leadership of the apostles, the gospel spread rapidly until, at the beginning of the second century, the Greco-Roman world started to react. Some Christian writers, called apologists, from a Greek word meaning "to defend," strongly criticized the idols and their cults, although they insisted on Christians' civic

TIMELINE

BCE

37	Herod installed as king of Judea
ca. 7	Birth of John the Baptist
ca. 6	Birth of Jesus

CE

26	Ministry of John the Baptist
ca. 27–30 (33)	Ministry of Jesus (death of Jesus, ca. 30–33)
49	Council of Jerusalem
35–62	Missionary work of the apostle Paul (death of Paul, ca. 62–64)
64	Persecution of Christians under Roman emperor Nero
66–70	Gospel of Mark, the first Gospel, is composed
70	Destruction of Jerusalem and the temple during Jewish-Roman war
80–90	Gospel of Luke and Acts of the Apostles composed
80–85	Gospel of Matthew composed
90–100	Gospel of John composed
165	Martyrdom of Justin Martyr, early church father
ca. 250	Dura-Europos, earliest Christian church
313	Constantine, Roman emperor, makes Christianity legal in Roman Empire (Edict of Milan)
325	Council of Nicaea
381	Council of Constantinople
405	Jerome completes the Vulgate (Latin bible)
410–416	Augustine writes *The City of God*
451	Council of Chalcedon

allegiances. In spite of persecutions, Christian values managed to penetrate society: the new culture of the new faith spread in a society prepared by Hellenism, which encompasses fundamental Greek cultural elements in the ancient world. The third century saw the affirmation of a Christian way of life. This chapter begins by showing the progress of the church during the first two centuries.

The Roman Empire had a religious foundation that became accentuated in the third century with the emperor's being viewed as a god. The emperors tried to react against internal crises and external threats in various ways, including the relaunching of the sacred: the cult of the emperor and the cults of the protecting gods. Christians became the victims of the new ideology and of the persecutions that arose from it. In 313, however, Constantine confirmed an edict at Milan that allowed religious liberty. The church continued to organize itself and to react against Gnosticism and

Fig. 10.1 Fourth-century Christian mosaic at the Aula Theodoriana, Aquileia, Italy, representing Jesus as "The Good Shepherd," leading persons away from sin.

From Apostolic Paschal Community to the First Christian Communities

Following the events of Easter, which took place toward 30 CE, the apostles, together with some of the disciples of Jesus who had been frightened and scattered by the events that had unfolded on Golgotha, started once again living a communitarian form of life they had lived with their master. In the Acts of the Apostles, Luke describes this specific context and the activities of this enthusiastic group of followers, who were conscious of the presence of the risen Christ among them during meeting, meals, and projects. An unprecedented event predicted by Jesus took place: the gift of the Holy Spirit, the creation of the church as an event in sacred history (Acts 2:1-4), which became known as Pentecost. After Pentecost, the apostles and the disciples formed a community assiduous in prayer, conscious of having received a permanent injunction to evangelize the world, and characterized by the remembrance of the signs and words of Jesus. They formed a community identifiable by the behavior of its members who diligently followed the teachings of the apostles, by its fraternal unity, and by the breaking of the bread within their houses, just as Jesus had asked them to do in remembrance of the Last Supper, which had taken place before his crucifixion.

A new people was in the making (Acts 15:14-18). The rapid succession of conversions brought about the opposition of the Jewish authorities, followed by the persecution and dispersal of the Jerusalem community. New communities were formed in the synagogues and even among pagans. Some collections of

Manichaeism, forms of religious-philosophical thinking that threatened to introduce errors into the Christian community. Moreover, during and after this time, it clarified the rules of faith to its opponents through doctrinal controversies and church councils. By the time it found its freedom, Christianity was woven into the fabric of society. The last five parts of this chapter describe the events of these two centuries.

In order to emphasize the fact that the first Christian communities did not consider themselves as followers of the dead master but rather of the Son of God who had risen from the dead, we do not begin with a biography of Jesus. The life of the Christian communities should therefore be considered—from their own point of view—as the life of Jesus himself, just as he had promised the disciples at his ascension into heaven following the resurrection: "Behold, I am with you at all times, even to the end of the world" (Matt. 28:20).

Fig. 10.2 Late second-century scroll of The Acts of the Apostles. Located at the Biblioteca Laurenziana, Florence, Italy.

the words of Jesus, soon integrated in the Gospels, which were still in the process of definitive formation, constituted a sort of memorandum of the oral tradition of those who had personally witnessed and intensely lived the faith. In Galilee and Syria, Greek-speaking Hellenistic communities lived side by side with Aramaic-speaking Judeo-Christian communities. Struck on the road to Damascus, Saul of Tarsus converted from being the persecutor of the new religion to its apostle. The word *ekklesia* came to refer to the real Israel: a religious and cultural concept that gave expression to the free choice of God and the unity among the believers within communities characterized by great social and ethnic diversities.

The rapid spread of the new religion in Palestine and in Syria, together with the numerous Judeo-Christian and Hellenistic communities existing side by side, caused tensions to spring up and grow. The Judeo-Christians wanted to impose circumcision and other Jewish Mosaic practices on new converts from paganism. In 49 CE, the incident at Antioch and the Council of Jerusalem brought the matter to an end (Acts 15:2-10; Gal. 2:11). The authority of the apostles and the firmness of Peter and Paul saved the unity of the newly born church, which they would confirm with their martyrdom in Rome under Nero. The fall of Jerusalem in 70 CE served to definitely sever Christianity from the government of Israel.

The Rapid Spread of Christ's Message

Shortly after its foundation, Christianity reached Antioch in Syria as well as Damascus,

Fig. 10.3 Bas relief of Peter and Paul, Paleo-Christian Museum, Aquileia, Italy. This sculpture shows Peter and Paul in embrace as "founders of Christianity."

where communities of Hellenized Christians established themselves. "At Antioch the disciples were called Christians for the first time" (Acts 11:26). It is from Antioch as well that, in 45 CE, a mission left for Asia Minor, which was to mark the start of the ministry of Paul, who was accompanied by Barnabas. They first turned to the Jewish communities, then to the proselytes and the pagans. Paul's strategy can be clearly seen in Acts 13. It also shows how, following the opposition and the refusal of the Jews, he slowly elaborated his own theology of conversion for the pagans.

In the forties, Jewish nationalism started to lose its patience and began exerting an ever-stronger pressure on Christian Jews. Thanks to Paul's efforts, the Christian message rapidly made its way into the pagan world. Following

the decisions taken at Jerusalem in 48 CE, Pauline Christianity dissociated itself completely from the temporal destiny of Israel. In 50 CE, Paul undertook a new missionary journey. Following stops in Asia Minor, he turned to Europe (Macedon, Achaia). After passing through Athens, in 51–52 he stopped at Corinth and then returned to Antioch by way of Ephesus and Jerusalem. Silas, Timothy, and Luke accompanied him in the foundation of these churches.

In the spring of 53, Paul left on another journey, passing through Galatia and Phrygia, before settling down for three years at Ephesus (54–57) to preach the gospel in the synagogues and to the pagans. Returning through Greece, he visited Macedon, Corinth with Titus, Tyre, and Miletus before arriving in Jerusalem in 58 CE in time for Pentecost. The Judeo-Christian

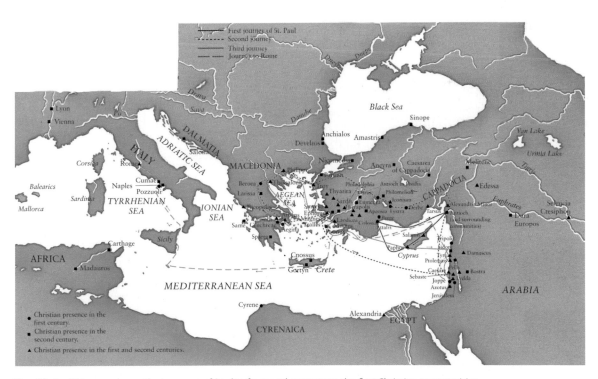

Fig. 10.4 This map shows the journeys of Paul to form and encourage the first Christian communities.

opposition to him had kept growing since 49 CE, and the nationalists arrested him. Eventually, after a number of adventures, he was martyred in Rome under Nero.

Toward 112 CE, Pliny the Younger, the governor of Bithynia in Asia Minor, wrote to Emperor Trajan about the Christians. Following inquiries, he had found that they were responsible for the decline of pagan sacrifices in the cities and in the country. Pliny confirms what is already known from the Apostolic Fathers: the extraordinarily rapid spread of Christianity starting from the end of the first century, the organization of the community, the celebration of the Eucharist on the Lord's Day, the shaping of Christian symbols and rituals, and the unity of the group living in a pagan world subject to Rome.

The Conflict between Pagans and Christians

In the second century, the extraordinary vitality of Christianity started to attract attention and to foster uneasiness since it was an odd religion, one that refused to worship false gods or false cults. This monotheism, the cult of a one and only God, was looked on as a dangerous form of atheism, similar to not having any god at all. Various rumors of strange Christian practices fed popular suspicion: the adoration of a donkey's head, the sacrifice of children, incest, and orgies. In 177 CE, Celsus wrote *Logos Alethes*, a "discourse of truth," which contemptuously referred to Christianity's origins, Jesus the founder, and the doctrine itself as being unworthy of a religion. He contrasted the "mystic madness of the Christians" with the values of other religions, Hellenic culture, and the wisdom of the barbarians. Born in 233,

the Neoplatonic philosopher Porphyry wrote a *Treatise on Divine Images* and a *Treatise Against the Christians*, the latter mostly lost, in which he attacked the Christian Scriptures, denied the resurrection of Jesus, confuted the sacraments, and reproached Christians for their disrespect to the statues of the gods. In the name of Hellenic culture, he asked for help against Christianity.

The Christian apologists picked up the challenge. Justin, a Greek philosopher who was martyred in Rome in 165 CE, wrote two *Apologies*, in which he refuted the accusations and attacked the idols, which he described as mere statues made by men and raised in temples as gods. He contrasted Jesus and the realization of the prophecies with the pagan gods, although he also found some common features in the two, the sign that "the seed of the Word is

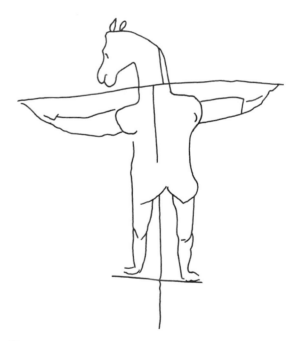

Fig. 10.5 Jesus depicted as a donkey in this second- to third-century drawing, ridiculing the Christian belief that a god could become man and allow himself to be killed.

innate in all mankind" (*Apol.* 2.8.1). Tertullian (155–225), who was born in Africa and was refined in Latin culture, wrote his *Ad Nationes* ("To the Nations") and *Apologeticum* ("Speech for the Defense"). An expert in law, he refuted the dominant accusations against Christians, asked for freedom of worship on their behalf, and then attacked the pagan gods, who could not feel either disrespect or homage. Like a good lawyer, he demolished the cult of the emperor, stressing the devotion of Christians who were to be found all over the empire and who constituted its force: "We have just been born and we have already filled the earth and all that belongs to you" (*Apologet.* 37.4). A contemporary of Tertullian, Minucius Felix also wrote a Christian apology in the form of a dialogue, titled *Octavius*. It listed both the attacks against Christians and firm replies based on proving the pagan gods were false.

Christian apologists made use of three approaches. The first is that of Philo of Alexandria, a first-century Jewish philosopher who made use of the deification of the elements, the stars, idolatry, zoolatry, and pagan mythology to highlight their baseness. It was the approach Latin apologists would later favor. The second approach was drawn from the ideas of the Greek writer Evemerus (ca. 340–ca. 260 BCE), according to whom the gods were only deified illustrious individuals. The apologists used this approach against the cult of the emperor. The third approach is taken from demonology, study of demons, which was extremely popular at that time. Various apologies showed how devils hide beneath the appearance of the statues of pagan gods. Augustine made use of these ideas in his *De civitate Dei* ("The City of God").

The popularity of the image of the Good Shepherd in early Christian art was the answer to the accusations of lack of piety and madness,

Fig. 10.6 Image of Jesus as "The Good Shepherd" in the catacombs of Saint Callixtus in Rome.

since it represented the concern and protection provided by the God of Christians.

The Enculturization of Christianity in the Hellenistic World

1. The Christians saw the value of Greek culture and its philosophers quite early. This tile mosaic from Syria of the first centuries CE shows the philosopher Socrates with other wise men.

At the end of the second century, Alexandria became the center of the gospel's encounter with Greek culture. In Alexandria, Clement, a convert to Christianity and a great traveler, joined the *Didaskaleion*, a Christian center of higher studies run by Pantaenus the philosopher, whom he would actually succeed toward 200. Making use of his excellent knowledge of Philo, Clement elaborated a vast project of catechesis that brought together the teachers of the Gospels, Greek philosophy, and some basic elements of Hellenism. His *Exhortation to the Greeks*, the *Protrepticus*, was a proposal to idolaters to convert but that presented the "new song" (instead of the fine melodies of Orpheus, the supreme singer in Greek mythology) instead of the pagan mysteries, the most widespread religious experiences of the time. Clement then analyzed the various philosophers, showing how they all provided evidence of divine transcendence. A philosopher and a humanist, he placed philosophy at the service of the knowledge of the Scriptures so as to lead to a scientific knowledge and to change mere opinion into certainty, which he calls the true *gnosis* ("knowledge"). Truth is the illumination of humanity and the world by means of the divine *Logos* ("the Word"), which came to renew the entire cosmos (*Protr.* 9–12). In using the vocabulary of *soteria* ("salvation"), so fundamental to Hellenistic thought, he developed the entire perspective of salvation through Christ. The *Stromateis* ("Tapestries") analyze the relationship between the new religion and profane science as a preparation for the gospel: philosophy, the gift of God to the Greeks; symbolism, which provides access to the divine mysteries; and initiation that is the introduction to penetrating the heart of the mystery itself.

Inspired by Jesus Christ, the Logos, Christians live in the image of God. Clement made Alexandria the center of Christian culture. Inherited from the primitive Christian church, the practices that still bear a Jewish imprint take on a Hellenistic garb. The heritage of rhetoric and of ancient philosophy was also assimilated thanks to Clement and his

Fig. 10.7 Third- to fourth-century Christian sarcophagus. Christians drew on Greek ideas that agreed with their new faith, and they used images of Greek philosophy, as on this sarcophagus.

successors. As a reaction to certain Encratite (i.e., radically ascetic Christian) tendencies in Palestine, which stressed the evil in matter, a form of Christianity emerged that conformed to the Hellenistic ideal of humanity. According to Jean Daniélou, "a process of sociological uprooting from Judaism" took place in Alexandria. Significantly, Christian iconography included Orpheus among the symbols that anticipated Jesus and his new song.

Christian Society in the Third Century

Among the documents most useful for understanding the developments in Christian society in the third century, pride of place must be given to the works of Clement of Alexandria, Origen, Tertullian, and Hippolytus of Rome.

Initiation to Christianity was through a catechumenate, which was organized systematically by the hierarchy and firmly installed by the end of the second century. A candidate had to pass an admission test, attend regular meetings for religious instruction, and receive a positive assessment of one's preparation. Administration of baptism was by means of a triple immersion in water followed by subsidiary rites and by receiving the Eucharist in the presence of the bishop. Baptism of children was already practiced. Together with public and private penance, there were also rites of reconciliation, an authentic sacrament that included the confession of sins to a priest. During the third century, the remission of sins became the subject of a controversy between strict and more permissive authorities.

The organization of the hierarchy was uniformly fixed: the episcopate, the presbyterate, and the diaconate, three orders that were conferred by the laying of hands by the bishop, a tradition that firmly respected the primitive apostolic tradition. A number of ministries were conferred by bishops but did not need ordination: widows who looked after sick people and deaconesses and virgins dedicated to teaching and supporting neophytes.

The Christian communities included various assemblies, the most important being the Eucharist on the "day of the Lord" preceded by prayer and concluded by the giving of the kiss of peace, a tradition that dates back to the earliest days. There were daily assemblies of the faithful with the priests and deacons for the purpose of praying and teaching, from which numerous homilies have survived. There was also the evening assembly, which took place at the time when the lamps were lit, sometimes

followed by an agape, which is a community meal. The ruins of the church of Dura Europos (256) and some frescoes show the first diffusion of Christian art connected with meeting places and sacred buildings.

Continuously growing in number, the Christians lived within society, sharing the same language, the same food, and the same dress. However, a style of Christian life also developed. Clement and Tertullian indicated the differences from a pagan way of life: a simple life without excessive luxury, food and wine in moderation without drunkenness or orgies, baths, shows, and sport but not pagan or immoral games. The family represented a cherished value: divorce and abortion were condemned, the education of children was greatly encouraged, and one was expected to stay away from all that was idolatrous. As far as civic duties were concerned, there was great reserve concerning the official cult, while military service was carefully evaluated with discrimination. Death represented the important moment not only for martyrs but also for every Christian. The catacombs and the cemeteries bear eloquent testimony to this reality.

The Cult of the Emperor and the Persecution of the Christians

The religious base of the Roman Empire became even more pronounced in the third century, when imperial power was given a sacred dimension. As a result of the great crisis brought about by the threats of the Persians, the German tribes, and civil wars, the emperors attempted to rectify matters with an energetic political transformation in a new religious climate: a profound sense of the sacrality of the world and of life; a sense of the divine

Fig. 10.8 A fresco in the catacombs in Via Latina in Rome, showing Samson beating the Philistines, which prefigures the story of Jesus expelling merchants from the temple.

expressed by the protecting gods of Rome; the sacred character of the emperor as a reflection of Jupiter; and a solar theology that made the emperor the son of *sol invictus*—"the invincible sun." The cult of Mithras, a solar god of eastern origin, contributed to this development. Christianity became incompatible with this cult of the emperor and of Rome.

Already in 249, Emperor Decius had issued an edict ordering all citizens to publicly show their devotion to the protecting deities of Rome, by means of incense and of sacrifice. These two acts of worship were meant to re-create political and religious unity throughout the empire. Most Christians refused to obey, and many were tortured and condemned to death. Supported by pagan public opinion, in 257 an edict issued by Valerian and Gallienus enjoined the bishops, the priests, and the deacons to sacrifice to the Roman gods. If they refused, they were to be punished with exile or death and the confiscation of all the wealth of the community in favor of the public treasury. The results of these persecutions are well-known: there were many martyrs, but also many apostates—deniers of their faith—and there was great fear for Christian unity for a time.

In 239, the tetrarchy was set up: the provinces of the empire were divided among Diocletian, Galerius, Maximian, and Constantius Chlorus. Motivated by the solar cult, a new sacralization of power opened the way for more persecution, first of the Manichaeans, the followers of a religion of Persian origin, and then of the Christians. Churches were razed to the ground, and bishops and leaders of the communities, especially in the East, in the regions of the Danube, and later in Africa were arrested and put on trial. Many people chose martyrdom, but many others preferred to apostatize. In the West, a sort of calm followed the abdication of Diocletian, but in the East, Galerius and Maximinus Daia started the persecutions afresh.

In 311, Galerius issued an edict of toleration that gave freedom for Christians to practice their cult, permission to rebuild their meeting places, and also requested them to pray for the safety of the emperor and the empire. In the East, Maximinus renewed the persecution. However, Constantine, who obtained an important victory on October 28, 312, on February 313 confirmed in Milan Galerius's edict of toleration. On June 13, 313, it was published in Nicomedia for the entire East, thereby extending religious freedom to all Christians in the empire.

Christian Thought Facing Gnostics and Manichaeans

From the second century onward, as Christianity spread in the countries of the Mediterranean, it started facing the opposition of the Gnostics. Gnosticism stressed the revelation of mystical knowledge to a select group, who would thus obtain insight into the mysteries of the heavens, God, humanity, and the way to obtain salvation. According to such a dualist gnosis—that is, one that includes two original principles of the world—humanity is a stranger lost in a wicked world. A divine spark is imprisoned in the matter of the body, and the human's soul must be reawakened through initiation to find its path to salvation.

It was Irenaeus of Lyons who first realized the peril of such teaching. In his voluminous *Treatise against Heresies* (ca. 180), he denounced the gnosis of the false name, confuted its errors, and contrasted it with the essential facts of Christianity: belief in the New Testament, which has been most faithfully conserved; the value of traditions that derived from the apostles and apostolic witnesses; the dogma—a Greek word meaning "doctrine" that designated a truth of faith—of a unique God who was responsible for creation by means of the Word; the announcement of the incarnation through the words of the prophets; the story of salvation; Christology—that is, the mystery of Jesus Christ as understood by the church; the theology of creation, of the incarnation, and of the redemption—that is, reflections on the manifestations of the one God; Christian anthropology; and the search for the real aspect

Fig. 10.9 Obverse of a Roman coin. New cults worshipped the emperor as ancient cults of the sun worshipped stars, hence the sun rays coming off the head on the coin.

of human beings, who were created in God's image and saved through Jesus.

Like Irenaeus, Tertullian attacked the Gnostic followers of Valentinian, who had preached his doctrine in Egypt and in Rome, but Tertullian also wrote a *Treatise against Marcion*, a Greek author and theologian who had founded an ecclesial community in Rome in 144. He explained the rule of faith, refuted Gnostic terminology, and created a Latin theological vocabulary. A disciple of Irenaeus, Hippolytus of Rome wrote a *Confutation of all the Heresies*, which by means of a comparative study between pagan thought and about thirty Gnostic doctrines, attempted to show that gnosis was a new form of Hellenistic paganism.

Born in 216, Mani spent his youth in the Judeo-Christian sect of the Elkesaites of Dastumisan in Babylon. He reevaluated the Gnostic texts and restructured them around the light-darkness myth and then founded a Gnostic church on the model of the Christian church. He presented himself as the personification of the Paraclete—the Spirit—foretold by Jesus and chose twelve apostles and seventy-two disciples. He then compiled his own Scriptures, in which he attempted to integrate Christian doctrines with those of Buddhism and Zoroastrianism. A religion of the book and a universal religion of salvation, Manichaeism presents itself as the real religion preached by Jesus and revealed to Mani by the Paraclete. The fathers of the church organized a systematic rebuttal against the propaganda of this sect, whose missionary zeal had extended to all parts of the empire and beyond. After a struggle that lasted a couple of centuries, St. Augustine, who had belonged to the sect for ten years, carried out the last great assault.

Fig. 10.10 A fresco from the catacombs of Commodilla in Rome. A portrait of Jesus is positioned between the alpha and omega, the first and last letters of the Greek alphabet. The message is that Jesus gives meaning to everything in life, from the first to the last.

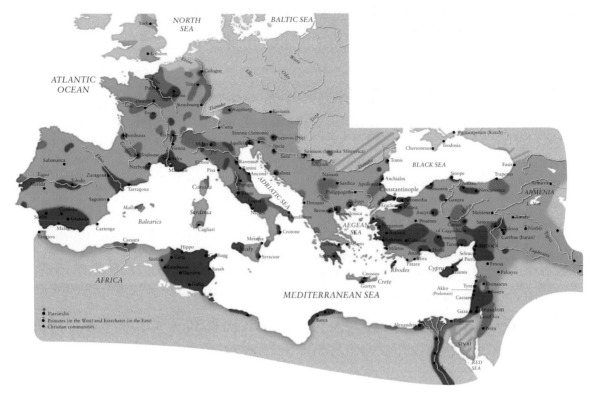

Fig. 10.11 The spread of Christianity in the third, fourth, and fifth centuries.

The Development of Christianity in Society in the Fourth Century

By the beginning of the fourth century, the church had already grown powerful within the Roman Empire. Bishops assisted by priests and deacons led the communities, while widows and consecrated virgins were given a special status. Conversions in the countryside meant the creation of parishes where the bishops sent priests to look after the faithful. Conversions also took place beyond the limits of the empire: Persia, Armenia, the Caucasus, Ethiopia, and among the Goths near the Black Sea.

Religious life was centered on the celebration of the Eucharist, which was celebrated solemnly on Sundays and also during the week. The liturgical calendar became defined: celebrations in winter revolving around the mystery of the incarnation and others in Easter centered on the resurrection. Different liturgies also took root in the East and in the West, each with its own characteristics influenced by the culture of the people. The churches legislated on their respective cults and on the administration of the sacraments. Thus adults were baptized during the Easter Vigil held Easter Saturday after sunset. The sacrament of penance remains of great relevance as a result of the public reconciliation of penitents. In 325, Sunday was declared a feast day.

The cult of the martyrs, already in practice in the second century, spread even further as a result of the great persecutions: the belief in the intercession of saints in heaven; the expectation of the manifestation of their miraculous powers; the belief in the resurrection of the body; and the veneration of relics. The celebration of the Eucharist took the place of the pagan funeral banquet (*refrigerium*) on the tomb of the deceased. The cult of relics came to assume great importance, and the church published directives to keep the devotion to saints within bounds.

Religious journeys known as pilgrimages became popular in the fourth century. Crowds made their way to the tombs and the sanctuaries of famous martyrs. They also visited holy sites known as martyria that were connected with the passion of Christ. These included Calvary, the Mount of Olives, and Bethlehem. Pilgrimage routes to Jerusalem were already established by 333.

Thanks to the influence of the pope and the bishops, the church attempted to bend its law and customs toward a greater justice and charity. Prisons were more closely monitored, slaves were liberated, treatment of prisoners was checked, infanticide was prohibited, charitable institutions were developed, and hospitals and nursing groups were founded, as well as an increase in the giving of alms.

Anthony, the father of monasticism, died a centenarian in the Egyptian desert in 356. His disciples had built their own quarters near his cell, thus becoming the first anchorites, or hermits. In 323, Pachomius had gathered around him a number of monks at Tabennisi in Upper Egypt and gave them a rule of common life: this marked the origin of coenobitism. The various forms of monasticism made their way to Syria, Asia Minor, Italy, and Gaul.

Constantine and the Conversion of the Empire

A Christian emperor, Constantine felt the responsibility to save Rome, but he also interested himself in spiritual matters, the salvation of the subjects that he felt he had been called to lead. He intervened energetically in the case of the Donatist schism in North Africa, which followed the great persecutions. The Donatists had refused to recognize those Christians who had denied the church during the persecutions. In spite of the intervention of both the emperor and the pope (Council of Arles, 314), the schism lasted for a whole century until the church in Africa was subsequently destroyed by the Vandals. In 325, Constantine convoked the Council of Nicaea, which condemned the heresy of Arius of Alexandria, who had called into doubt the divinity of Christ. In 381, the Council of Constantinople met to ensure the enactment of the decisions taken at Nicaea. Constantine played a decisive role in the building of basilicas and churches in the great cities of the empire and in the holy sites in Palestine.

The fourth century saw the flourishing of a Christian culture that stressed the values of the classical heritage, to which religious inspiration gave a fresh vigor. It was in this context that Emperor Julian, who succeeded Constantius II in 360, surprisingly reconverted to paganism and gave rise to a new persecution of the Christians, which ended with Julian's death in 363.

The second half of the fourth century is called "the golden age" of the fathers of the church: Athanasius of Alexandria (ca. 295–373), Basil of Caesarea (ca. 329–370), Gregory of Nazianzus (330–390), Gregory of Nyssa (332–394), Evagrius of Pontus (345–399), John

Fig. 10.12 Constantine, the Roman emperor who converted to Christianity, removed the threat of persecution within the Roman Empire.

Chrysostom (ca. 344/354–398/407), Theodore of Mopsuestia (ca. 350–428), John Cassian (ca. 365–435), Augustine of Hippo (354–430), Jerome (ca. 347–419), Ambrose of Milan (ca. 339–397), Marin of Tours (316–397), Damasus of Rome (ca. 305–384), and Hilary of Poitiers (ca. 315–367). All of these were great writers and fine stylists, in addition to being important theologians who gave the church a fundamental doctrinal base in both the East and the West. Most of them became bishops before their death. Their influence as theologians and bishops made this period crucial in church history. They provided the groundwork for an entire religious culture organized around faith and spiritual life—a culture that embraced all aspects of life.

The End of the Ancient World

Two cities have been founded by love: the earthly one by the love of self, even to the contempt of God; and the heavenly one by the love of God, even to the contempt of self. The former, in a word, glories in itself, the other glories in the Lord.... In the one, the princes and the nations it subdues are ruled by the love of power. In the other, the princes and the subjects serve one another in love. (Saint Augustine, *The City of God* 14.28)

In 410 CE, Augustine, a polished writer and the well-known bishop of Hippo in North Africa, started writing *The City of God*, a work of twenty-two books, which would take him fifteen years of his life. This monument of the literary culture of the late empire is also the first philosophy of history. A great authority on his own times, Augustine understood that pagan intellectuals were not interested in the modern cults but looked nostalgically back at the grandeur of ancient Rome.

Starting at the very origins of the story of humanity, Augustine refers to Cain, the builder of the early city, and to Abel, who is only a pilgrim from the celestial city, and whose mission is continued by Abraham and the people of Israel. By means of intricate symbolism about the states of antiquity, Augustine arrives at Rome and demonstrates the triumphal failure of the glory of conquests, of the thirst for power, of the disregard of man, and of the emptiness of idolatry and pagan cults. His prophetic vision

Fig. 10.13 From a Roman building in Maktar, Tunisia. Originally a gymnasium for young men, it became a Christian church.

embraces the entire horizon of human history, and he stresses the presence of a principle of growth that conforms to the Creator's plan in the development of humankind; this plan is at the origin of the history of Israel and will find its fulfillment in the coming of Christ. Thus human history has a meaning that can be discovered by means of the succession of events in sacred history and the words of the prophets. This causes Augustine to conclude that "the past centuries of history would have remained like empty jars if Christ had not come to fill them."

Fig. 10.14 Painting by Simone Martini of Saint Augustine, who wrote *The City of God*.

◆ STUDY AND DISCUSSION QUESTIONS

1. Discuss the kinds of motives and inspiration that attracted converts to Judaism and that saw the rise of Hellenized Christianity during the second and third centuries.

2. What elements figured into the growing Christian consensus that was developing toward the end of the second century, and evaluate the role of church councils and important thinkers, including Irenaeus and Tertullian, in the making of a Christian identity?

3. Trace in broad lines the changing underlying conditions that prompted the development of Christian thinking over the first four centuries, evident especially in the shifting forms in which the Christian message was conveyed (e.g., scriptures, apologetics, philosophical arguments): from Jewish origins to interactions with Greek and Roman religions and philosophies, to the changing fate of Christians under persecution and toleration by various powerful Emperors.

◆ KEY TERMS

aeon

agape

Apologists

apostolic tradition

Arian, Arianism

baptism

cemetery, coemeterium

coenobitism, coenobite

council

Donatism

Elkesaism

Encratism

Eucharist

Gnosticism

heresy

idolatry

initiation rites

Judeo-Christianity

Judeo-Hellenism

kerygma

Manichaeism

Marcionism

monasticism

mysteries

pagan, paganism

persecutions

pleroma

proselyte

refrigerium

remission of sins

sacrament

schism

tetrarchy

Vandals

Zoroastrianism

◆ FOR FURTHER READING

Borg, Marcus, and N. T. Wright. *The Meaning of Jesus: Two Visions*. San Francisco: HarperSanFrancisco, 1999.

Burridge, Richard A. *Four Gospels: One Jesus?* Grand Rapids: Eerdmans, 1994.

Chadwick, Henry. *The Early Church*. New York: Penguin, 1993.

Crossan, John Dominic. *The Birth of Christianity: Discovering What Happened In the Years Immediately After the Execution of Jesus*. San Francisco: HarperSanFrancisco, 1999.

Frend, W. H. C. *The Rise of Christianity*. Minneapolis: Fortress Press, 1984.

Horsley, Richard A. *Christian Origins: A People's History of Christianity*. Minneapolis: Fortress Press, 2010.

RELIGIONS OF THE WORLD

Johnson, Luke Timothy. *The Real Jesus: The Misguided Quest for the Historical Jesus and the Truth of the Traditional Gospels*. San Francisco: HarperSanFrancisco, 1996.

Hill, Jonathan. *Christianity: How a Despised Sect from a Minority Religion Came to Dominate the Roman Empire*. Minneapolis: Fortress Press, 2011

Newsome, James D. *Greeks, Romans, Jews: Currents of Culture and Belief in the New Testament World*. Philadelphia: Trinity Press International, 1992.

Raisanen, Heikki. *The Rise of Christian Beliefs: The Thought-World of Early Christians*. Minneapolis: Fortress Press, 2009.

CHAPTER 11

Roman Catholicism

Julien Ries

Introduction

In 410 CE, following the sack of Rome by Alaric's barbarian hordes and the subsequent Vandal invasions, Christianity looked on in dismay at the collapse of the empire and the dissolution of the Greco-Roman world. A melting pot of cultures, the church resumed its evangelical mission. The baptism of Clovis by St. Remigius in Reims, and that of Ethelbert by St. Augustine in Canterbury, assured the conversion of Gaul and England to Christianity. The acceptance of the gospel by the barbarians gradually led these peoples toward the emergence of the Carolingian Empire, rightly termed *regnum Christianitatis* ("Christian kingdom"), although feudal lordship came to exert undue power over local hierarchies. The foundation of the abbeys of Cluny (910) and Citeaux (1098), which ushered in the Cistercian reform, projected the Rule of St. Benedict, signaling a new vitality. This period of renewed growth expressed itself

TIMELINE
CE

ca. 33	Peter declares Jesus to be Jewish messiah
ca. 34	Paul converted to Christianity
49	Council of Jerusalem
64	Persecution of Christians under Roman emperor Nero
313	Constantine, Roman emperor, makes Christianity legal in Roman Empire (Edict of Milan)
325	Council of Nicaea and Arian controversy
382	Council of Rome under Pope Damasus I, establishing biblical canon
405	Jerome completes the Vulgate (Latin bible)
410	Sack of Rome by Barbarians
592–604	Pope Gregory the Great extends Roman Catholicism
800	Charlemagne crowned Holy Roman Emperor
910/1098	Founding of abbeys of Cluny and Citeaux
ca. 1000–1100	Construction of Romanesque churches under direction of Pope Gregory VII
1054	Split (schism) between Eastern and Western Christian churches (Orthodox, Roman Catholic)
1123–1215	Four Lateran councils
1182	Concordat of Worms
ca. 1100–1300	Crusades by the Catholic Church
ca. 1500	New basilica built in Rome under direction by Pope Julius II
1545–1563	Council of Trent
1869–1870	First Vatican Council
1962–1965	Second Vatican Council

in an unprecedented increase in the number of monasteries throughout Europe, a reform movement lead by Pope Gregory VII, the construction of Romanesque churches, and a surge of pilgrimages throughout the eleventh and the twelfth centuries. Indeed, the thirteenth century, with its Gothic cathedrals, its universities, its scholarship, and the rise of chivalry, which sublimated the warring spirit of the nobility, could well be described as the zenith of medieval Catholicism.

After an ebb in this dynamic impetus, sixteenth-century Europe enjoyed an extraordinary awakening during the Renaissance, a movement that began in Italy. This revival was characterized by a reappraisal of the humanities, a return to classical influences, sweeping geographic exploration, the invention of printing, and advances in the arts, literature, and the sciences. This renewal was vigorously sustained by a humanistic papacy but was offset by the resultant pagan tendencies that swept over Rome. Although these movements were counterbalanced by the appearance of a host of Christian humanists, the church was eventually challenged by the ideas of Luther, Calvin, and

Fig. 11.1 This sixteenth-century sculpture from Ormeau, France, represents the Jesse tree, or the genealogical chart that traces Jesus' lineage to the origins of Israel.

Henry VIII. Protestantism unleashed a veritable earthquake that produced a catastrophic breach within Christianity. Roman Catholicism responded with the Council of Trent, which issued momentous changes and effectively implemented a range of needed reforms. Still other challenges loomed large over the horizon in the form of absolutism, the Enlightenment, and political revolutions. Although a sense of alarm characterized the period between the seventeenth and the nineteenth centuries, Catholicism thrived through an aggressive missionary program that continued throughout the nineteenth century in Asia, Africa, and North America. During this period, the church also drew strength from the foundation of new religious congregations, a flourishing of charitable enterprises, and the consolidation of social Catholicism. Two world wars in the twentieth century left in their wake a devastated world that cried for reconstruction. The church again rose to the occasion. The Second Vatican Council, convened in 1962 by John XXIII and closed in 1965 by Paul VI, instilled a great sense of hope in the church and in believers throughout the world: hope in a unity between churches and harmony among nations—a true *Gaudium et spes*. Not since 1439, when the church tried in vain to reunite its Catholic and Orthodox branches and heal the schism that had kept them apart since 1054, had such a dramatic move toward unification been made.

Catholicism Today

The term *catholic* ("universal") denotes a fundamental characteristic of the Christian faith. Historically it defines the Christian church, which recognizes the primacy of the pope (the bishop of Rome), as distinct from other Christian denominations—Orthodox or the various Protestant churches. These denominations developed from the as yet unresolved tensions that erupted first between the East and the West toward the close of the first millennium, and later within the West itself throughout the second millennium. Fortunately, the dawn of the twentieth century saw the emergence of an ecumenical dialogue that, on the basis of a common heritage, tried to reestablish the church's original unity. Introduced by Pope John XXIII (1958–1963), and implemented by Popes Paul VI (1963–1978), John Paul II (1978–2005) and Benedict XVI (2005–), Vatican Council II

(1962–1965) projected to the world an image of a church that is sensitive to the needs of humankind, respectful of human liberty, in tune with humanity's initiatives, supportive of human anguish, and of service to human aspirations. The frequent intercontinental travels of Pope John Paul II, as well as those by Pope Benedict XVI, has exercised a great attraction among many peoples and has contributed greatly toward the maintenance of harmony and stability among nations.

During the second half of the twentieth century, the Roman Catholic Church was hit by the repercussions of a global crisis resulting from several factors: the grievous consequences of two tragic wars, the deportations and movement of entire populations, the demographic explosion of newly independent nations, the technological race of the industrialized countries, and the attempt by once underdeveloped states to attain the highest cultural achievements. Additionally, during the past twenty years, reports have surfaced of widespread sexual abuse committed by Roman Catholic priests over the past half century, as well as allegations of bishops concealing such practices as

the church's leadership sought to manage the crisis. An increasing secularization—as well as the influence of new ideologies and the debate over priority between development, humanization, and evangelization—led to a dearth of vocations and to a weakening of religious practice in the West.

In response, the Catholic Church has intensified its ecumenical, interreligious, and intercultural dialogues. Great attempts have been made for the enculturization of the gospel within Western society and within the varied and ethnic cultures of Latin America, Africa, and Asia, where the young churches are very active. The emergence and rapid expansion of new religious movements and communities has been quite remarkable. Invited to Rome on Pentecost eve on May 30, 1998, 350,000 adherents of these movements heeded Pope John Paul II's exhortation to a coordinated worldwide commitment of the church in the service of humanity.

At the dawn of the third millennium, the Roman Catholic Church offers to many the greatest of hopes—through its hierarchy and its social teaching, through its solicitude

Fig. 11.2 Ecumenical meeting at Assisi, Italy, in October 1986, where Pope John Paul II met with representatives of Christian denominations.

Prevalence of Catholics

Prevalence of Christians

Catholics within predominantly Christian areas

Significant Christian presence

Significant Catholic and Christian presence

Significant presence of Catholics

Fig. 11.3 This map surveys the current spread of Roman Catholicism.

toward the individual, and through the impact of its Christian anthropology, which remains grounded in the mystery of the incarnation and in the gospel message.

The Making of a Popular Religion—The Conversion of Western Europe

On August 24, 410, Alaric, king of the Visigoths, occupied Rome, a city recently devastated by his hordes. Now under barbarian rule, the empire was gripped by alarm. Yet, being a melting pot of cultures, the church continued with its work—restoring cathedrals and sanctuaries and pursuing its evangelical mission. After being crowned king of the Franks in 481, Clovis and three thousand soldiers converted to Christianity, establishing themselves in Paris and transforming Gaul into "the eldest

daughter of the church." In collaboration with monks from Lérins, Spain, and Africa, itinerant bishops went on to evangelize town and countryside. Theodoric the Great (d. 526), founder of the Ostrogoth kingdom in Italy, adopted the old administrative machinery of Rome, bringing together Catholics and Arians in a synthesis that remains amply reflected in such monuments as those at Ravenna. Toward the year 540, St. Benedict of Nursia compiled his Rule, which became the centerpiece of monasticism in Gaul.

It was, however, under that adept promoter of Christian thought, Pope Gregory the Great (592–604), that the fusion between Roman tradition and barbarian vitality was completed. He injected new vigor into the evangelization of the countryside—attending to the ordination of priests, and the establishment of episcopal or presbyteral teaching centers. He supported the work of monastic schools and distinguished himself among the founders of popular medieval religious life. Enhancement of civilization was a goal so strongly grounded within the church that the papacy became a "veritable rallying point for the Barbarian West" (Guy Bédouelle). In an age of a simple yet formidable faith, barbarian society produced innumerable saints. Pope Gregory had instructed the monks whom he had sent to England to "destroy the idols but to preserve the temples." His was indeed an authentic desire for an enculturization of the gospel that would have profound repercussions on pagan peoples.

In Italy, the Longobard invasion put such pressure on the church that numerous monks and priests emigrated northward into Europe. Meanwhile, in sixth-century Ireland, the church flourished by projecting itself from monasteries as centers of faith. From Ireland, St. Columbanus traveled into Scotland and from there, with twelve companions, arrived in Gaul, where he founded Luxeuil and undertook the evangelization of northern Europe. As a result, national churches sprang up, giving rise to a popular Christianity that nourished itself from Benedictine centers, which radiated peace, stability, and the valorization of work. This was indeed the birth of Christian Europe, which owed its origins to Benedictine monks from Italy and to the monks of St. Columbanus from Ireland.

The Church and the Challenges of History—Christianity Between Feudalism and Empire

The church experienced momentous changes under the Carolingians. In 732, Charles Martel stopped the Muslims at Poitiers, eventually forcing them back across the Pyrenees. Later, Martel's grandson, Charlemagne, restored

Fig. 11.4 Ruins of the ancient monastery of Skellig Michael, southern Ireland.

order within society and in 800 was crowned emperor by Pope Leo III in Rome. His collaborator, Alcuin, introduced Anglo-Saxon scholarship into Frankish schools and served as one of the great contributors toward a new awakening in literature, the arts, and theology. The church contributed greatly to this era of peace, and the accompanying cultural revival has been aptly termed the "Carolingian Renaissance." The emperor considered himself responsible for Christianity and its cohesion as guaranteed by dogma and the Roman liturgy. He saw to the nomination of bishops and regarded himself as both the custodian of doctrine and the defender of faith.

Toward the end of the ninth century, with the dissolution of the empire and the arrival of the Germanic emperors (Otto I was crowned Holy Roman emperor in 962), the church found itself at the mercy of feudal lords, who claimed for themselves exclusive rights to nominate bishops and administer ecclesiastical property. Throughout the tenth century, these feudal lords opposed the power of the papacy. Dioceses and parishes came to be offered to the highest bidder, and decay swept over the ranks of both clergy and laypersons. It was from the model monastery at Cluny, founded in 910, that the so-called Gregorian reform was implemented. Its name derives from the Cluniac monk who was elected pope as Gregory VII in 1073. This pope reaffirmed papal primacy, dispatched legates to enforce clerical celibacy, and prohibited the emperor from further nominations of bishops. When Emperor Henry IV deposed the archbishop of Milan, Gregory VII excommunicated him until he presented himself in penitential garb at Canossa. The conflict was only settled in 1182 by the Concordat of Worms between Pope Callixtus II and Emperor Henry V, which emphasized the distinction between

Fig. 11.5 Miniature from the codex of Mathilda of Canossa (1066–1115), where Mathilda is shown reconciling Emperor Henry IV with Pope Gregory VII.

church and state and affirmed the primacy of the spiritual power of the church.

The twelfth century was a dynamic time for Western Christianity. It was an era that witnessed special contacts with the East, a campaign of Crusades, and a revival of holiness and learning in which the universal use of Latin guaranteed the unity of Europe. Thanks to the influence of Cluny, the Rule of St. Benedict was adopted by almost all monasteries. Romanesque churches were built—houses of God for community and pilgrims, and the meeting place for God and humanity. Renowned for its pilgrimages and the veneration of saints and relics, the twelfth century is best remembered for its Romanesque symbolism, which drew its inspiration from the Bible and the universe, and

Fig. 11.6 The belfry tower at the twelfth-century Benedictine Cluny Abbey, France.

helped introduce humanity to the mysteries of religious faith.

Christ Recapitulates the Creation—The Great Centuries of Medieval Christianity

"Blessed be life under the crozier!" This popular medieval dictum encapsulates the social and religious sentiments prevalent in the twelfth and thirteenth centuries. People started to migrate into the countryside from nearby castles and monasteries, which had offered them shelter in times of invasion. These migrations, combined with the heavy demographic expansion of these two centuries, gave birth to the great European cities. The church sublimated the belligerent spirit of the chivalric orders, directing them toward mystical ideals as exemplified in the legendary quest for the Holy Grail. Thousands came forward to join in the Crusades with the intention of holding back the Muslim invaders and securing freedom for Christians in the Holy Land. This movement was animated by St. Bernard of Clairvaux (1091–1153), whose reform of Citeaux propagated a spirit of evangelical poverty, the principal exponents of which were St. Dominic and St. Francis of Assisi and their followers.

The image of Christ enthroned in glory came to dominate the portals and the stained-glass windows of Gothic cathedrals, where the high and sprightly vaults seem to reach into the skies in reflection of cosmic harmony. These cathedrals—particularly those at Chartres, Bourges, and Reims—created spaces of light, blending a complexity of features into a harmonious unity and leading humans toward their Creator. Throughout the thirteenth century, universities of learning grew in number and served as symbols of scientific fervor, reflecting the development of wisdom and progress. The church was the prime mover behind these institutions, injecting new vitality into the study of theology and philosophy and into the education of priests and the faithful. *Summae*, or comprehensive treatises, made their appearance in the thirteenth century, and include the noted work by St. Thomas Aquinas (1235–1274), which was based on a coherent and comprehensive system of philosophy that embraced within it the teachings of Aristotle as rediscovered by the Arabs. The life of the church was anchored within the theology of creation and the incarnation and was further nourished by the cult of saints and the phenomenon of pilgrimages. In 1274, the Second Council of Lyons made efforts to reconcile Eastern and Western Christianity.

Further divisions and ruptures shook Western Christianity in the fourteenth and fifteenth centuries. The dualistic heresies of incarnate, called *Devotio Moderna*, as exemplified in the feast of *Corpus Christi* and *The Imitation of Christ*; the recitation of the Holy Rosary; the doctrine of the assumption of the Virgin; numerous confraternities; the cult of saints and national heroes like Joan of Arc in France and Nicholas of Flue in Switzerland; and the veneration of charismatic figures like Raymond Lull (1315) and Nicholas of Cusa (d. 1464)—all of whom were imbued with a great sense of Catholicism.

The Dawn of Christian Humanism—The Church and the Challenge of Renaissance

Decimated by decades of war and plague and exhausted by emerging national rivalries, people yearned for a change. The achievements of Giotto (1266–1337), Boccaccio (1313–1375), and Petrarch (1304–1375) brought a surge of renewal over Italy. The decisive event was the Council of Florence, convened in 1439 to bring the East and the West together. The Byzantine faction, led by Cardinal Bessarione, obtained unexpected success and generated genuine enthusiasm among the Westerners. Latins and Greeks drew closer together following the fall of Constantinople to the Turks in 1453, just before the Platonic Academy was established at the court of the Medicis in Florence. This institution ushered in the Italian Renaissance, which soon spread throughout Europe, fueled by wealth, patronage, and the invention of printing.

During this period, new horizons unfolded before Western Christianity. In 1492, the Spanish *Reconquista* against Islam was completed with the victory at Granada, while on

Fig. 11.7 Main portal of Chartres cathedral, France. In Romanesque and Gothic architecture, the figure of Jesus is often surrounded by figures from the Old and New Testaments.

the Bogomils, the Albigenses, and the Cathars drove the church to establish the Inquisition, a tribunal created to supervise matters of faith and to lead people back to the church. Challenges to papal power forced Pope Clement V to seek refuge in Avignon (1309), marking the prelude to the Great Western Schism. From 1337 to 1453, an interminable war between England and France helped spread plague and terror. The threat of laicism, which aimed to subject the church to temporal power, ushered in an era of secularization. The people of God rallied against this challenge with expressions of faith that included the cult of Christ

October 12, Christopher Columbus set foot on the Bahamas in the Caribbean, at the same time that Portugal explored the coast of Africa. The papacy was elated. Julius II and Paul III commissioned Bramante and Michelangelo to rebuild the basilica of St. Peter. A series of humanistic popes patronized the arts and transformed Rome into a new city, influenced by the mythology and deities of pagan antiquity. This new Roman paganism and corruption led Fra Girolamo Savonarola to denounce Pope Alexander VI.

In 1485, Pico della Mirandola published his famous theses, which were preceded by an introductory text, *Oration on the Dignity of Man*. His was a veritable manifesto of Christian humanism, which looked on Christ as the paragon of wisdom. Great humanists like Marsilio Ficino (1433–1499), Thomas More (1478–1535), and Erasmus (1466–1536) insisted on a return to the word of God, the Holy Bible, and Christ. Conscious of the pitfalls of paganism latent in the Renaissance, these scholars created a humanism based on the gospel and laid the foundations for the joining of church and culture.

The discovery of new lands heralded an era of missionary activity, launched by a papal bull of Alexander VI in 1493. In America and Africa, the spread of Christianity did not encounter the organized structures found in the great religions of Asia. The collapse of local cults allowed the rapid conversion to Christianity of the peoples of Africa and the new Spanish-American world. In 1453, Nicholas of Cusa published his *The Peace of Faith*, a pioneering and thought-provoking work, which was the first to discuss the dialogue between Christianity and the various local cultures as conducted in Asia by St. Francis Xavier (1506–1552) and Matteo Ricci (d. 1620), and in America by Bartolomé de las Casas (d. 1556).

Fig. 11.8 Erasmus of Rotterdam (1466–1536). Depicted in this portrait by Albrecht Dürer, Erasmus was a leading Christian humanist during the Renaissance.

Missions, Charity, and Mysticism—The Church between Reform and Absolutism

In 1517, a German Augustinian friar named Martin Luther (1483–1546) began to teach about the need to purify the church's beliefs. He refuted a number of dogmas and ignored the sacraments, except baptism and the Eucharist. His abandonment of tradition led to a great schism. Luther's teachings about this "new faith" were adopted by the French layman John Calvin (1509–1564), who established a Protestant Church in Geneva. Except for pastors, this church had no hierarchy and was based on a biblical Christology and a rigid morality. In England, Henry VIII established Anglicanism, a new religion that came between Catholicism and Protestantism.

With entire nations embracing Protestantism, the Roman Catholic Church responded with a reform program that drew its inspiration from the three sessions of the Council of Trent (1545–1563). The conciliar decrees clearly reaffirmed the Catholic creed of Scripture, tradition, justification, original sin, the holy sacrifice of the Mass, and the sacraments. The council set in motion an ambitious program of reform, insisting, among other things, on the duty of residence for bishops and curates; priestly celibacy; the establishment of seminaries; the compilation of a catechism, missal, and breviary; as well as a renewal of preaching. Capuchins and Jesuits were enlisted to help the diocesan clergy in its pastoral work, especially in the German lands. The effect of these efforts began to be felt by the middle of the sixteenth century.

In 1555, the Treaty of Augsburg divided Europe into Roman Catholic and Lutheran areas; while the Treaty of Westphalia, which concluded the Thirty Years War (1618–1648), added a "Calvinist" faction to it. Jews were expelled from all countries, finding refuge only in the Papal States. Seventeenth-century Europe came to be dominated by state absolutism based on the principle of one king, one religion, and one law, replacing the long-forgotten Christian unity of medieval times. The church was thus confronted with an establishment that tolerated no rivalry. In France, Gallicanism vindicated the autonomy of the local church in its differences with Rome, especially under Louis XIV. Fully conscious of their absolutism, the various states unreservedly reaffirmed the necessary unity of religion and nation.

The church, however, made extensive progress both internally and externally. Religious life underwent a veritable and remarkable renewal under John of the Cross and Teresa of Avila in Spain; Charles Borromeo and Philip Neri in Italy; and the great founders Francis de Sales, Peter Berulle, Jean-Jacques Olier, and John Eudes in France. In combating political absolutism, the church proposed absolute charity, embodied in such figures as Vincent de Paul, a naval chaplain who founded the Sisters of Charity. On June 22, 1622, Pope Gregory XV established the Congregation for the Propagation of Faith (*De Propaganda Fide*), which provided a new missionary impetus. Its instructions of 1659 demanded the establishment of an indigenous clergy, healthy relations with political rulers, and respect toward local traditions, populations, and customs—thus furthering enculturization of the gospel.

Enlightenment, Secularization, and Persecution—The Church Confronted by Unbelief and Revolution

The eighteenth century distanced itself from the classicism of its predecessor and introduced European society to a new order of ideas and human relationships. The emergent middle classes brought with them a sharing of experiences, but their dominant egalitarianism led to a refutation of former traditions and privileges. In the absence of great Christian thinkers, public opinion came to be exclusively molded by the deistic philosophers such as Pierre Bayle and his *Dictionary*, Denis Diderot and his *Encyclopedia*, Jean-Jacques Rousseau and his natural religion of purely sentimental content, Voltaire, and the French Masonic movement with its concept of God as the "Great Architect of the Universe." In the wake of the French

Fig. 11.9 Jesuit mission in Latin America. This reconstructed building in Paraguay was one of the Catholic Jesuit order's global missions from the eighteenth century, offering Indians protection against local exploitation.

Enlightenment, Lessing established himself as the head of the *Aufklärung*, the German version of the Enlightenment. Completely divested of the supernatural, religion was made to rely solely on reason, accepting Christ but excluding his divinity.

Catholicism was caught unaware by a similar intellectual revolution that infiltrated its ranks. Drawing from Fénelon's search into the perfect love of God, with its complete disregard of evil, the quietism of Madame Guyon developed into a false practice of Christian life. The formation of the clergy and the religious education of the masses left much to be desired. The church was also shaken by the errors of Febronianism—a form of episcopalism that limited the primacy of the bishop of Rome to his particular diocese, transferred absolute primacy to a general council, and entrusted lay princes with the supervision over religious matters in their territories.

Influenced by the teachings of Voltaire, political Josephism secularized seminaries and religious orders and even legislated liturgical matters. Mounting hostility toward the Jesuits increased to the extent that, for the sake of good order, Pope Clement XIV was compelled to suppress the Society of Jesus on July 21, 1773. Subsequently, founders of religious congregations appeared, including John Eudes, Grignion de Montfort, and Alphonse Maria de Liguori.

In 1789, the French Revolution erupted in a bloody whirlwind and produced a "religion" of ridiculous cults, such as that of the Goddess of Reason, its deistic tenets, and its cult of the Supreme Being. Christianity answered the challenge, retaliating with the Wars of Vendée, the propagation of the cult of the Sacred Heart, and resistance to the Republic. The church was, however, weakened by a veritable hemorrhage of anti-Catholic persecution, which included the massacre and deportation of clergy and the spoliation and pillaging of the church's patrimony, which was destroyed and squandered. Church-state relations were restored only with a concordat between Napoleon and Pope Pius VII. Throughout the nineteenth century, following various national revolutions, a number of similar concordats were negotiated by the church for the sake of its faithful. Following the upheaval of the Industrial Revolution, the Catholic Church preached a social Catholicism till then unknown, characterized by Frederick Ozanam, Don Giovanni Bosco, Wilhelm Ketteler, Cardinal Mermillod, and Leo XIII (*Rerum Novarum*). At the height of the colonial revolution, the church sought to preach Christ through a host of catechists, teachers, medics, nurses, and instructors. One could indeed characterize the nineteenth century as the age of an authentic Catholic missionary epic.

Thought, Presence, and Action—Catholicism and Modern Challenges

Throughout the nineteenth century, the church came face-to-face with the doctrine of

Fig. 11.10 A marketplace in the Universal and Social Republic. A popular nineteenth-century print, this scene shows the belief in market forces following revolutionary activity, even if progress came on the backs of the working classes and the colonies.

positivism, to which Pope Pius IX responded by summoning the First Vatican Council (1869–1870). The council was brutally interrupted on September 20, 1870, by the invasion of Rome by the Italian army, in an attempt to annex the Papal States. The church's declaration on papal infallibility on July 18, 1870, led to the *Kulturkampf*, the German Empire's struggle to control the church, adopted later by Switzerland, France, and Italy. The victims of this anti-clericalism, successor to the Enlightenment, were the religious congregations and religious instruction.

Despite such setbacks, the church experienced a surge of vitality on many fronts, including its universities (Louvain, Dublin, Freiburg, and Paris); the Catholic press; an intellectual renewal led by such authors as Newman and Mercier; and a return to patristic studies, biblical exegesis, analysis of church history, and the study of non-Christian denominations (The Parliament of Religions at Chicago, 1893). Pope Leo XIII (1878–1903) opened new prospects with his insistence on the study of medieval sources of Christian thought, his promotion of social Catholicism (*Rerum Novarum*), and his renewed interest in the Eastern churches. Many intellectuals from different quarters came to embrace Christianity, among them Leon Bloy, Jacques Maritain, Ernest Psichari, Joris-Karl Huysmans, Charles Péguy, and Paul Claudel. Numerous religious and missionary congregations flourished, the latter addressing themselves specifically to spreading the faith in Asia and Africa. But the clash between Catholicism and the modern world led to the modernist crisis, with negative repercussions on the internal life of the church.

After the First World War, the church increased in prestige among public opinion and world leaders. It was the era of concordats

Fig. 11.11　Pope Leo XIII (1810–1903).

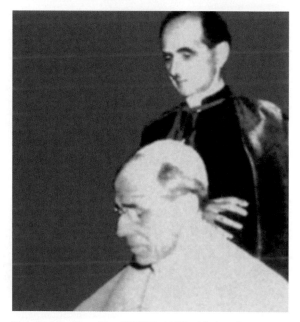

Fig. 11.12　Pope Pius XII (1876–1958) with then Secretary of State Giovanni Montini (future Pope Paul VI).

between church and state. The church also attained new freedom on the international platform with the creation of a Vatican city-state, which replaced the suppressed former Papal States. In the face of new ideologies, the church reaffirmed the primacy of the spiritual; it increased its social and charitable enterprises and offered its support to literature and the arts. Pius (1922–1939) established Catholic Action, a movement that injected youth with a vitality that was to have significant effects on church and society and that helped organize an elite Catholic corps. Pope Pius XI vehemently condemned Nazism and Marxism as oppressors of the individual and society.

Fig. 11.13 Soviet poster of the 1920s showing Vladimir Lenin, Soviet leader, sweeping Russia clean of priests, capitalists, and European heads of state.

The global tragedy of 1940–1945 left millions of young victims on the battlefields. In its aftermath, in the context of two politically opposed politico-ideological blocs, Pope Pius XII (1939–1958) made extensive use of the media to address the world's faithful and to proclaim the great principles that regulate the individual, the family, society, and peace. The papacy thus established itself as an influential element of global opinion, at a time when a group of political leaders bound together by a similar ideological program—Alcide De Gasperi, Konrad Adenauer, and Robert Schuman—were applying themselves to the reconstruction of a devastated Europe. The great thinkers who laid the future of Catholicism include Yves Congar, Henri de Lubac, Charles Journet, Hans Urs von Balthasar, Bernard Jungmann, and Teilhard de Chardin.

Light for the Church, Hope for the World—Vatican Council II

In 1959, with the Western world enjoying an economic boom in the aftermath of postwar reconstruction, Pope John XXIII (d. 1963) announced "a general council for the universal church." Launched on October 11, 1962, Vatican Council II worked through four sessions before its closure, under Pope Paul VI (1963–1978), on December 8, 1965. Its sixteen decrees addressed the pressing problems of the church and probed into its origins, constitution, organization, mission, and identity in the modern world. The council, which was attended by 2,500 bishops from all the continents and by non-Catholic and lay observers, was a watershed for the church and the world.

As a counterbalance to the ecclesiology of the First Vatican Council, the conciliar fathers

Fig. 11.14 Opening of the Second Vatican Council. On October 11, 1962, Vatican II convened in St. Peter's Basilica, Rome, Italy.

defined episcopal collegiality, stressing the episcopate as a sacrament and the church as a communion. The establishment of episcopal conferences became mandatory. Christian liturgy was highlighted as the expression of the salvific work carried on by the church, ensuring Christ's presence among God's people. The brief but rich text on religious liberty evaluated the dignity of humanity, endowed with reason, will, and responsibility, and committed to the search of truth. The council set in motion a dialogue between Catholics and other Christian and non-Christian denominations as well as with nonbelievers and the world at large. The documents that regulated these relationships were a novelty whose impact is still felt today. Their implementation was entrusted to pontifical secretariats specifically created by Pope Paul

VI, which included eminent personalities from various nations.

The implementation of conciliar reforms met opposition from conservatives, such as Mgr. Lefébvre, who provoked a schism in 1988 on the grounds that the liturgical reforms, episcopal collegiality, and the definition of religious liberty contradicted church tradition as defined by the Council of Trent. At the other extreme, a number of progressive thinkers upheld the council to outdo it, producing confusion among Catholics. In reality, the positive effects of Vatican II are still much in evidence thirty years after the event. The papacy enjoys enormous prestige and attracts immense audiences from all over the globe. In the wake of the important trips of Paul VI, the travels of John Paul II and Benedict XVI have mobilized whole populations and have exerted incalculable ecclesiastical and political influence. Today, Catholic vitality is best impressively reflected in those young Christian churches that have enthusiastically embraced the program of Vatican II.

A Catholic Teaching for the Modern World

The brief introduction to the pastoral constitution *Gaudium et spes*, which is here reproduced, bears ample evidence to the content, aim, depth, and solicitude behind the church's program in the service of humankind, both present and future. In solidarity with humankind, the church proposes an ongoing human dialogue in the light of the principles of the gospel, which have inspired humanity over the past two millennia. Solidarity, respect, and love toward all humankind are the hallmarks of the church's mission on earth.

Gaudium et spes

The joys and the hopes, the grief, and the anxieties of modern man, and especially the poor or in any way afflicted, are also the joys and the hopes, the grief, and the anxieties of the followers of Christ. . . . The community of Christians therefore feels truly and intimately linked with mankind and his history (n. 1).

Modern man wonders with admiration at his own discoveries and potential, but he also frequently raises anxious questions about the current trend of the world, about the place and role of man within the universe, about the meaning of his individual and collective efforts, and also about the ultimate destiny of reality and humanity. Hence, giving witness and voice to the faith of the whole People of God gathered together by Christ, this Council can provide no more eloquent proof of its solidarity with the entire human family with which it is bound up, as well as its respect and love for that family, than by engaging with it in conversation about these various problems. The Council brings to mankind light kindled from the Gospel, and puts at its disposal those saving resources which the church itself, under the guidance of the Holy Spirit, receives from her Founder. For the human person deserves to be preserved; human society deserves to be renewed (n. 3).

◆ **STUDY AND DISCUSSION QUESTIONS**

1. Assess the significance of religious movements and orders in the Middle Ages in providing direction and support of the expansion and definition of the Roman Catholic Church. Research the history of the medieval cathedral—including Chartres or Reims—and how the architectural designs brought meaning to the developing church.

2. Review the many challenges to the church during the Renaissance and Enlightenment, and discuss the ways the church responded, evaluating how successful—or not—the church has been in responding to challenges to faith and belief.

3. As you reflect on the impact of Vatican II, have you found that its reforms have resulted in a more effective or meaningful church in the world? Why or why not?

◆ **KEY TERMS**

Arians, Arianism
Benedict of Nursia
Bogomils, Bogomilism
Cathars, Catharism
Christian
Cistercians
congregation
Crusades
deism
Devotio Moderna
Febronianism

Gallicanism
Great Western Schism (1378–1417)
ideology
enculturization of the gospel
enquisition
Jansenism
Josephism
Kulturkampf ("cultural struggle")
laicism
modernist crisis, modernism
positivism
Propagation of Faith, Congregation for the
quietism
reform of Gregory VII (d. 1805)
secularization
social Catholicism
Vandals
Waldenses

◆ **FOR FURTHER READING**

Bokenkotter, Thomas. *A Concise History of the Catholic Church*. New York: Image/Random House, 2005.

Kee, Howard Clark, et al. *Christianity: A Social and Cultural History*. 2nd ed. Upper Saddle River, NJ: Pearson Prentice Hall, 1997.

Küng, Hans. *The Catholic Church: A Short History*. New York: The Modern Library, 2003.

O'Malley, John. *A History of the Popes; From Peter to the Present*. Lanham, MD: Sheed & Ward, 2010.

Vidmar, John. *The Catholic Church Through the Ages*. Mahwah, NJ: Paulist, 2005.

CHAPTER 12

Orthodox Christianity

Olivier Clément

Introduction

The Orthodox Church, along with Roman Catholicism and Protestant Christian denominations, is one of the three important expressions of Christianity. Its heritage of holiness and beauty, and of spiritual intelligence, is considerable. Like Catholicism, Orthodoxy is rooted in original, early Christianity and is considered to have been created by God with the incarnation and Pentecost. It was primarily developed in the Middle East and in eastern and southeastern Europe: this geographical area is often called the "Christian Orient (or East)." Zealous missionaries then brought it to the North Pacific and to Sub-Saharan Africa. But above

all, Orthodox Christianity (or Orthodoxy) has developed a presence throughout the West due to the extensive economic and political migrations of the twentieth century.

The separation (sometimes, the Great Schism) between Eastern and Western Christians, never completed, was a long process that began with the split between Rome and Constantinople in 1054 and lasted until the 1870 proclamation of papal infallibility, which was unacceptable to the Orthodox. This break was, and still is, the result of cultural and political issues, as well as partially theological differences about the Pope's primacy. These two different

**TIMELINE
CE**

843	Iconographic works restored to churches in the East
879–880	Ecumenical council at Nicaea, confirming Photius as patriarch of Eastern Church
ca. 900	Orthodox Church emerges in Russia
1054	Michael Cerularius, patriarch of Constantinople, excommunicated by Roman bishop
ca. 1100–1300	Crusades by the Catholic Church
1204	Sack of Constantinople further divides Eastern and Western Catholic Churches
1261	Latin occupation of Constantinople ends, with restoration of Orthodox patriarchs
1333	Gregory Palamas defends Orthodox spirituality; rise of Hesychasm
1453	The Turks overrun Constantinople; Byzantine Empire ends
1568	Pope Pius V recognizes key fathers (doctors) of the Eastern Church—John Chrysostom, Basil the Great, Gregory of Nazianzus, and Athanasius
1698	Consecration of first Orthodox Church in China
1794	Orthodox missionaries arrive in Alaska
1870	Roman Catholic papal proclamation of "papal infallibility"
1965	Pope Paul VI and Patriarch Athenagoras formally remove mutual excommunications (anathemas) of 1054
2008	Pan-Orthodox meeting in Constantinople

outlooks were complementary during the first millennium and could become so again. This may be a challenge for the future of Christianity.

Orthodox Christianity as the Major Religion: Greece

From the fifteenth century to the beginning of the nineteenth, Greece was absorbed by the Muslim Ottoman Empire, and it was the Greek church that maintained the country's language and culture (through "secret schools"). This is why, for Greeks, their country and church are inextricably linked. The faith is less important than a strong sense of membership. The Orthodox Church provides the framework for daily life in Greece. Time is measured by liturgical holidays. Rather than celebrating birthdays, for example, Greeks celebrate their saint days—the day carrying their first name—because the saint's name links them directly to the communion of the saints. For Theophany, on January 6, the holiday celebrating Christ's baptism in the Jordan River, priests, accompanied by a crowd, bless the sea and throw a cross in the water. The young people then must brave the freezing water to retrieve it. The Russians have a similar tradition, in which they break the ice on the rivers.

Easter is the holiest time of the year: "Christ is risen from the dead!" Each family gathers for a special meal of a lamb raised from birth. Transfiguration, August 6, is the holiday

Fig. 12.1 Central part of the royal door from a monastery of Gostinopol'e at Novgorod, St. Nicholas Church, Russia. Painted in 1475, these doors with colorful icons (iconostases), separate the nave and the sanctuary, where the altar is located.

festivities, Greeks enjoy popular dancing. The church and the state are not separate. Sometimes conflicts between the church and the state are pacified by monks from Athos—for instance, by sending a venerated icon to Athens, brought by some monks and solemnly received by members of the government.

This situation favors tendencies toward religious nationalism—indeed, demagogy. But it also favors the interweaving of daily life and culture with communitarian and liturgical life. (A major poet, Elytis, used the image of a Christian mountain and a pagan mountain in his significant work, "Athos and Pindus," where Athos, a mountain with connections to the twelfth-century hesychast spiritual Orthodox movement, represents the Christian mountain, and Pindus, a mountain consecrated to Apollo and the muses, represents the pagan mountain.)

Orthodox Christianity in the Minority: Diaspora, the French Example

During the twentieth century, for primarily political reasons (the exchange of populations between Greece and Turkey after the Russian Revolution, the Communist chokehold on southeastern Europe, and the conflicts in the Middle East), many Orthodox emigrated to the Western world. France was in the unique situation of having an elite group of Russian thinkers, intellectuals, and artists, called the "School of Paris." They made up two groups. One was enthusiastic about "religious philosophy" (Berdiaev, Bulgakov), and one was a revival of followers of Gregory Palamas, a thirteenth-century monk. This second group (Florovsky, Lossky, and Meyendorff) also focused on the study of

to bless the fruits of the summer. The country is scattered with sanctuaries for pilgrimages, and monasteries are often surrounded by Eden-like gardens. Rural areas are strewn with chapels, each maintained by a family. Many pre-Christian sacred places are venerated with different names: springs, consecrated to the Mother of God, "spring of life"; mountains have their own chapel to the prophet Elijah (on Mount Athos, it is a chapel to the Transfiguration). On these

Fig. 12.2 The Greek monastery of Amorgós. Leaning up against the rocks and almost rooted in the sea, it exemplifies the ties of local Orthodox Christianity to the Greek land.

the doctrine of the fathers of the church. Two centers of learning and thought opened: the Saint-Serge Theological Institute, in Paris, and Saint Vladimir's Seminary, near New York (to which the Greek-influenced Holy Cross Theological School was added in Boston).

The parishes played an essential social and spiritual role in the spread of this new Orthodoxy. They constituted meeting places for immigrants from different nations and their families. But the rise of Orthodox parishes in the West brought about a change to the vernacular—parishes began conducting services in their local languages: French, English, Dutch. In addition, books about Orthodox Christianity and spirituality were published in

France resulted in the creation of an assembly of bishops, led by a representative of Constantinople. But the autocephalous (self-governing) church established by Moscow in North America was not recognized by Constantinople, and in Canada and the United States, Orthodox Christianity remains divided.

History as Prophecy, Misfortune, and Fundamentalism

The story of Orthodoxy is one of deaths and resurrections. After the golden age of the

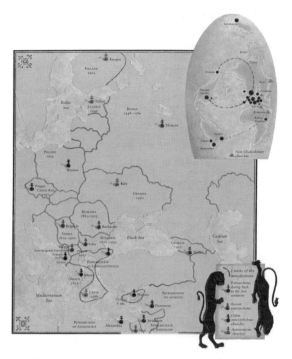

Fig. 12.3 Map of Orthodox patriarchates and churches. This shows the spread of Orthodox Christianity throughout Eastern Europe.

these languages. *Philokalia* (literally, "Love of Beauty"), an anthology of spiritual texts, was translated into Italian, French, and English. Necessary liturgical reforms began to take hold. This, in turn, little by little, brought about an awareness of the universality of Orthodoxy, within a context of personal experience and dialogue.

This gave an important ecumenical role to the diaspora. Nowadays, "The Jesus Prayer" ("Lord Jesus Christ, Son of God, have mercy on me, a sinner.") and, particularly, iconographic images themselves have become widespread far beyond the limits of Orthodoxy. Divided into "jurisdictions" depending on the traditional churches, the diaspora swings between nationalistic conservatism and the still timid development of local churches. A unification effort in

Fig. 12.4 The Cathedral of Saint Basil in Moscow, Russia. This national symbol in Red Square has always been a constant reminder of the Orthodox tradition, even during communist regimes.

fathers of the church and of Byzantine theology, most Orthodox countries (except Russia) were subjugated to Islam and crippled by Catholic proselytization and Uniatism. Orthodoxy was reduced to a rural monastic culture. During the eighteenth century, the Russian government, in an attempt to modernize itself, attempted to control the church: Peter the Great suppressed the patriarchate of Moscow and replaced it with a synod ruled by a high-level civil functionary. At the same time, the sultans scoffed at the patriarchate of Constantinople. The church's resurrection came at the end of the century with a powerful spiritual revival ("The Prayer of Jesus," the publication of the *Philokalia*, and the development of a charismatic "paternity"). This revival worked its way from Moldavia to Mount Athos in Greece, and Russia, following the north-south axis of Orthodox unity.

In the nineteenth century, a group of Russian spiritual leaders (called *startsy*) revived Orthodox monasticism. The interest in them expressed by major writers and philosophers further amplified the revival in Russia. The great writer Fyodor Dostoevsky took a modern look at theology through his explorations of the abyss of the soul, where he finds Christ as victorious over death and hell. Because of Dostoevsky's writings, the prophecy of Russian "religious philosophy" gained momentum and spread. But this revival, which culminated in the Moscow Council of 1917–1918, was crushed by the Bolshevik Revolution. Then came the time of martyrs—and of compromise. Orthodoxy revived once again after the collapse of Communism, but the invasion of American culture, the aggression of sects, and the blunders of other Christian groups contributed to

Fig. 12.5 The refectory of the monastery of Dionysiou, Mount Athos, Greece, where Saint Nikodemus the Athonite (1749–1809), who was responsible for compiling the *Philokalia*, took his vows.

a fundamentalist, anti-Western movement that rejected both ecumenism and liturgical reforms. Living thought and spirituality were rejected, and the church, unable to handle and understand modernity and the cultural changes, demanded protection from the government and, in turn, allowed itself to become politicized.

Theological Foundations

God, who revealed himself through the depth of the cosmos and through a people and his law, entirely manifests himself in the *divine-humanity* of Christ. Absolute personal existence, and therefore in communion, Christ, as human being at his maximum, is a universal existence. He carries all of humanity within him. He did not create evil, but he becomes incarnate to fight evil and give people, become again *created-creators*, the way to resurrection.

The "communion of saints," that is of the living, is the image and prolonging of divine existence itself. Jesus reveals that the divine abyss (about which we can only speak in "apophatic" nonlanguage, tending to the silence of the adoration) is, in reality, a paternal abyss, an abyss of love and liberty from which, through the Son, the Holy Spirit, the "giver of life," beams forth. God is so truly *one* that he carries within him, without separation, the mystery of the *other*. God is Trinity—absolute unity and absolute diversity at once.

God is Secret and Love, totally unknowable but totally accessible. The divine energies—the light of the Transfiguration and, through the Eucharist, of the coming of Christ at the end of time—make of the universe a burning bush, which our own blindness still veils. Sanctity means to bring to the surface of history this

secret incandescence to prepare for kingdom come.

Humankind is in the image of God; thus with their own freedom, together with grace, human beings can transform this image into a *resemblance*-participation; in this way, human beings can avoid the conditionings of the world, or change them. Humans are called to an existence guided by the Trinity—that is to say, in Christ and in the power of the Holy Spirit, they are called to carry all of humanity within themselves while also respecting the differences between people.

"Divine" energies, the light of the Transfiguration, penetrate and carry all things; "nature" is only as real as penetrated by "grace." The universe is called on to become Eucharist.

In our time, the Russian "sophiology" thinkers Solovyov, Florensky and Bulgakov have insisted on this omnipresence of Wisdom (*Sophia* in Greek), from the perspective of

Fig. 12.6 Icon of the Trinity, by Andrei Rublev (1425–1427).

a divine humanism capable of taking on both Eastern divinity and Western humanism, as Solovyov puts it.

The Church as Mystery and Misery

These theological foundations are part of the Orthodox concept of the church: body of Christ, temple of the Holy Spirit, and house of the Father. The church is a communion of faith and love because it is, first and foremost, made up of eucharistic communities. Permanent communion of these communities is assured by the presence among them of primates (important church leaders) charged with encircling life and love: metropolitans for regions, patriarchs for larger areas or different countries, and finally, primacy of honor and service of the ecumenical patriarch of Constantinople ever since the separation of Eastern and Western Christians.

All ecclesiastical processes must have a synodal aspect. Faith was, therefore, preserved during the first millennium by "ecumenical councils" (that is, held within the setting of the Roman Eastern Empire, which defined itself Christian and universal, thus ecumenical), which first specified the different aspects of Christ. Faith was also preserved by regional

Fig. 12.7 Fifteenth-century embroidery depicting the communion of the Apostles. Used during mass to cover the chalice, this cloth's images are called *anamneses*, meaning "memory," and differ from other representations of the Last Supper because they refer directly to the Eucharist.

councils finally recognized by all of Orthodoxy: in the fourteenth century, on how the essence and energies in God are distinguished yet united; in the seventeenth century, to situate Orthodoxy between Rome and the Reformation; and in the nineteenth century, to condemn religious nationalism. In our time, the primates of autocephalous (i.e., independent) churches gather in pan-Orthodox conferences and solemn assemblies in a conciliar perspective.

Still, all of this ecclesiastical development was compromised by the burden of history. Nationalism from the Balkan nations and Russia transformed the interdependence of autocephalous churches into juxtaposed independences. The church had difficulty reconciling this new freedom with the fact that it wanted the government's protection. Bishops form an oligarchy that is entered by co-optation; the patriarch, who in Russia condemns all change and reform, is an absolute monarch. The ecumenical patriarchate of Constantinople, weakened by history with the advent of Balkan autocephalous churches and the exchange of populations between Greece and Turkey, has difficulty playing its role on initiator, go-between, and coordinator.

The Liturgy, "Heaven on Earth"

It is first and foremost through liturgy that an Orthodox demonstrates his or her membership in the church. Surrounding the mystery of mysteries—the Eucharist, in which all is done by the Holy Spirit at the request of the priest and the people—is an ample hymnography that inserts biblical readings into a doctrinal and spiritual commentary. Thus the theology of the fathers of the church and councils transforms itself into poetry. Everything is chanted without any musical instruments, the music staying in the service of the word and using tones that bring to mind Greco-Roman antiquity and the Jewish religious service. The texts are woven with antinomies that reflect the fundamental antinomy between the inaccessible God and the Crucified. The liturgy is not only the proclamation of the word of God but also the anticipation of the kingdom via the mediation of a peaceful and luminous beauty—as the Russian envoys to Constantinople said in the tenth century, "heaven on earth."

The ecstasy of the resurrection lasts from Easter all through the feasts of the year, from

Fig. 12.8 A monk from Mount Athos plays the semantron, a wooden percussion instrument used to summon the faithful to liturgical services.

Sunday, "first and eighth day" of the week, eucharistic day, all through the week.

As soon as young children have been baptized/chrismated, they receive Communion. This event has been and continues to be very rare for adults. Liturgical languages, for example Slavonic in Russia, certainly steeped in poetry and mystery, have become incomprehensible to most. The most important prayers have, out of reverent fear, been transformed into "secret prayers." The congregants remain passive while the choir sings alone. Liturgy tends thus to become a sublime spectacle. Today, the situation is improving almost spontaneously in many parishes that, particularly in Russia, are also developing an important social role in the community.

The Icon

The veneration of saintly images was justified by the Seventh Ecumenical Council (Nicaea II, in 787). With the incarnation, which puts an end to the prohibitions of the Old Testament, God showed himself in the face of a man: "Whoever has seen me has seen the Father," said Jesus, in the light of the Holy Spirit. The celebrated icon by Andrei Rublev (1360–1430) represents the movement of love that both unifies and diversifies the Trinity.

The icon appeared around the sixth century, when the symbol designating "from the outside" a person's holiness or sainthood appeared in the person's face. The icon makes a personal presence arise. There is no visible light source,

Fig. 12.9 Celebratory mass at Monastery of Saint Daniil, June 1988. As the new see of the Patriarchate of Moscow, the Russian Patriarch Pimen concelebrates with other Orthodox patriarchs.

Fig. 12.10 An iconostasis (a wall of icons separating nave and sanctuary in a church) located in the Monastery of Kalenić, Serbia.

artists from being creative, nor has it prevented real innovations, provided they stay in the realm of *divine-humanity*. After the iconoclastic crisis of the eighth and ninth centuries, icons, frescoes, and mosaics became more and more hieratic—the focus was put on the divine. With the Renaissance in the fourteenth century, humanism was reaffirmed. During the modern era, artists created imposing masterpieces from Athos to Aleppo, reaching the apex of beauty and profundity of spirit in the frescoes of the Moldavian monasteries. After decadence in a later period, the art of the icon has been reborn again today, notably thanks to the "School of Paris" (Grigorij Krug and Leonid Uspenskij).

Monasticism and Hesychasm

Monks are essentially the "avant-garde" of the Orthodox Church; they have always prevented it from merging with "this world." There is only one monastic order, with no other end than contemplation, but with plenty of room for monks to pursue various personal vocations: from being in the community to being hermits, wanderers, and feigning madness. The monastic republic of Mount Athos in northern Greece, where monks gather from all around the Orthodox world, has experienced a renewed strength. The monks are rarely priests but are sometimes spiritual fathers (*startsy* in Russian), who have received the "discernment of the Spirit." For laypeople, they are role models and guides.

The axis of Orthodox monasticism is the hesychast tradition (from the Greek *hesychia*, meaning peace, calm, and silence of the union with God). "Art of arts and science of sciences," hesychasm uses a method that incorporates a psychosomatic aspect: hence, the invocation of Jesus' name using the rhythm of breathing,

nor shadow, nor "escape hatch": everything is lit up from the inside by God. The body is elongated, reaching toward the face, which in turn focuses on the gaze.

Starting in the fifteenth century, to demonstrate that the Christian temple was restarting and completing the temple of the Old Testament, a partition covered with icons, the iconostasis, both separated the sanctuary from the nave and bound them to each other as well.

The art of the icon, sober and measured, essentially theological, is a liturgical art that follows strict guidelines. This has not prevented sometimes of heartbeat, to favor the union of the mind and the heart (seen as the most central core of the being, where persons gathers themselves and go beyond themselves).

Hesychasm comprises, in general, three stages:

1. *Practice*: ascetic effort to liberate oneself from idolatrous passions and transform the energy that these passions use up into virtue. Virtues are divine-human; their synthesis, within Christ, is internal liberty and love.
2. *Physical theory*: contemplation of God's glory in people and things, vision of their spiritual essences rooted in the divine Word (*Logos*).
3. *Divine theory*: the embrace of the heart-spirit by the uncreated Light, which shines from the Father, through the

Son, into the Holy Spirit. Humanity becomes light, while turning toward the light's inaccessible source. This is "deification"—taking part in God's mercy and his resurrection to fight against evil.

An Excerpt by Father Sergei Bulgakov about His Conversion

The years were going by, and I could not find the strength to take the decisive step. . . . It remained this way until a strong hand raised me up. . . .

Autumn. A monastery hidden in the forest . . . , I had taken advantage of the opportunity to come here, with the secret hope of encountering God. But all resolve abandoned me. I attended Vespers, unmoved

Fig. 12.11   Monks working in the fields of Mount Athos, Greece, as part of the monastic program, analogous to many western Christian communities.

Fig. 12.12 A monk from Mount Athos in contemplation. In the background is the monastery of Stavronikita.

and cold. After the service, I left the church practically running. . . . I rushed in anguish toward the monastery, blind to everything around me, and I came to my senses . . . in a Starets' cell. I had been brought there—a miracle had happened to me. . . . At the sight of the prodigal Son, the Father hurried to meet him. I learned from him that all the sins of man amount to only a drop of water in the ocean of divine mercy. I left his cell pardoned, reconciled, trembling and crying. I felt as if I were being carried by wings into the church's enclosure. . . . I, too, had been affected by the Gospel that told of the pardon given to the woman who had greatly loved; and I was given a taste of the sainted Body and Blood of my Savior. (*The Everlasting Light*, translated from French, Lausanne, 1990, 25–26)

Text written circa 1910. Bulgakov, who was forty years old at the time of its writing, was a deputy in the Russian parliament. A former Marxist theoretician, he became increasingly attracted to Christianity.

Fig. 12.13 Photograph of Sergei Bulgakov (1871–1944). The son of an Orthodox priest, he was impressed by the rhythm of the liturgy and by a sense of the sacred land.

◆ STUDY AND DISCUSSION QUESTIONS

1. Consider the history of the Great Schism and assess those reasons that maintain separation between Western and Eastern Catholic Churches. Do you foresee any sort of accommodation or reunion?

2. Study a variety of Orthodox icons and describe the elements and features in each. Evaluate the value of iconography in both worship (liturgy) and sustaining personal belief (spirituality).

3. Review the role and importance of monastic orders in the Orthodox Christian Church. Discuss the claim that monastic orders are the "avant-garde" of Orthodoxy (maintaining separation or distinction from the earthly, temporal world), and draw any parallels to religious groups or personalities in other religious traditions that may serve a similar purpose for those traditions.

◆ KEY TERMS

antimony

apophatism

asceticism

Athos

autocephalous churches

baptism-chrismation

burning bush

council

diaspora

Easter

ecumenical

empires

fathers of the church

Gregory Palamas

iconoclast

iconostasis

kingdom

liturgy

nepsis

Orthodoxy

patriarch

Philokalia

Slavonic

starets

The Jesus Prayer

Uniatism

◆ FOR FURTHER READING

McGuckin, John Anthony. *The Orthodox Church: An Introduction to Its History, Doctrine, and Spiritual Culture*. Malden, MA: Wiley-Blackwell, 2010.

Meyendorff, John. *Byzantine Theology: Historical Trends and Doctrinal Themes*. New York: Fordham University Press, 1974.

———. *Catholicity and the Church*. Crestwood, NY: St. Vladimir's Seminary Press, 1997.

Pelikan, Jaroslav. *The Spirit of Eastern Christendom (600–1700)*. Chicago: University of Chicago Press, 1977.

Schmemann, Alexander. *The Historical Road of Eastern Orthodoxy*. Crestwood, NY: St. Vladimir's Seminary Press, 1997.

Ware, Timothy. *The Orthodox Church*. New York: Penguin, 1993.

CHAPTER 13

Protestant Christianity

Lawrence E. Sullivan

CHAPTER OUTLINE

Introduction

People of the Word: Bible, Preaching, and Song

The Changing Face of Protestant Christianity

"No Other Gods before Me": Luther and Zwingli as Leaders of Reform

Declare the Good News": The Mission and Method of Calvin and Wesley

Justified by Faith

The Priesthood of All Believers

The Protestant Principle

Faith and Order: Denominations, Polities, and the State

Radical Reform Sects: Piety, Apocalypse, and Mystical Experiences

"Knowledge of God and Knowledge of Self Are Connected"

Study and Discussion Questions

Key Terms

For Further Reading

Introduction

"Place God first, above all things." This is the prophetic message of all Protestant Reformers. On the one hand, the message was a rebuke, a *protest* in the manner of Old Testament prophets, against practices and beliefs of the Roman Catholic Church that, in the view of Reformers, obscured God's supreme power by posing as perfect and taking the place of God's authority. When church authorities present themselves as infallible or when sacramental actions, dogmatic beliefs, governing institutions, holy art objects, or philosophical certitudes appear ultimate or absolute, this idolatry should be criticized as

such and rejected. On the other hand, the Protestant message exhorted the believer to stand and give credible witness (*pro-testari*, "to testify") to the truth of God's saving grace. Different reformers made these points in distinct ways with long-lasting effects. Indeed, many Protestants are proud of the plural expressions that have blossomed as a result of the Protestant Reformation. In this chapter, the abiding insights and expressions that characterize Protestant belief and behavior are singled out for special attention.

TIMELINE CE	
1517	Martin Luther posts Ninety-Five Theses at Wittenberg
1521	Diet of Worms; Luther's excommunication
1521	Publication of Philipp Melanchthon's *Commonplaces* (Reformation teachings)
1522	Martin Luther publishes German translation of the New Testament
1529	Huldrych Zwingli, Swiss Protestant Reformer, debates Martin Luther at Marburg
1530	Diet of Augsburg, "The Augsburg Confession" (Luther's Protestant reform movement begins)
1533	Thomas Cranmer, archbishop of Canterbury, nullifies marriage of Henry VIII and Catherine of Aragon, defying the Roman Catholic Church
1534	Henry VIII becomes supreme head of the Church of England
1536	John Calvin publishes *The Institution of the Christian Religion* (the *Institutes*)
1541	John Knox brings the Protestant Reformation to Scotland
1549	Martin Bucer advises Thomas Cranmer on the Book of Common Prayer, first published in England
1563	Publication of the Thirty-Nine Articles of the Church of England (statement of faith)
1611	Publication of the King James version of the Bible
1618–1648	The Thirty Years War (Protestant/Catholic conflict in Germany)
1624–1681	Lifespan of George Fox, founder of the Quakers
1755	John Wesley publishes *Explanatory Notes Upon the New Testament* (establishing principles of the Methodist Church)
1948	World Council of Churches founded in Geneva

People of the Word: Bible, Preaching, and Song

Protestants are people of the word, as is evident in their regular common worship. On the Lord's Day, Protestants gather together to hear the word of God read before the congregation. Being the record of God's word made known in history, Sacred Scripture is the unrivaled source of revelation and authority, outweighing dogma, magisterial tradition, or the teaching of pope or bishops. Bible reading is the focal point of Protestant worship, where selections are recited aloud.

In response to God's word, worshipers usually offer words of their own—words of preaching, prayer, and praise. A minister or other leaders rise to preach a sermon based on the Scripture lesson of the day or give testimony to the word of God at work within them. The goals of the preached word and testimony are to enlighten the mind, warm the heart, and move the will of the listeners so that they might hear God's word and keep it. Such goals are arrived at only through the grace of faith, freely given by God. To that end, the preacher may call on God's Holy Spirit, who inspired the biblical text in the first place, to grace the listeners with the gift of faith in God's word.

diversity of Protestant expressions is evident in the range of Protestant music: from Johann Sebastian Bach to gospel choirs, Christian rock, and exuberant Pentecostal forms found among the various ethnic and indigenous peoples of the world today. The first book published by Puritan settlers in New England was a Psalter for singing the psalms in worship.

Christians believe that the one God revealed himself in Jesus Christ. Beyond the regular reading of the Gospels, most Protestants commemorate the words and deeds of Jesus Christ at suitable points in the life cycle of an individual or in the yearly calendar of the community: in baptism and in the Eucharist.

Fig. 13.1 A ceremony being held at the Episcopal Cathedral of St. John the Divine, New York City.

The congregation responds to God's presence in the biblical word with prayers and hymns. These vocal expressions offer praise, petition, and thanks. The congregation recites words in unison, expressing the conviction that a worshiping congregation is a fellowship of those who have like minds, united with the mind and body of Christ in a communion of saints.

Song plays a special role in Protestant prayer. Important Protestant leaders, such as Martin Luther, John Wesley, and Charles Wesley, composed hymns that still mark the worship in the denominations they founded. The

Fig. 13.2 Illustration of gospel singer, Bessie Griffin. African American spiritual music derives from its performance in church choirs.

The Changing Face of Protestant Christianity

The Protestant movement in Christianity generally refers to reform activities that began in sixteenth-century Europe. Unlike other Christian reform movements that sprang from the monasteries, religious orders, and leading bishops, many Protestant Reformers came from universities or academies. Great emphasis was placed on published writings and on the ability of the average worshiper to read those writings. Early Protestant writings are often linked to the widespread use of local languages and the standardization of national languages. Since then, differences in thought, practice, and social or national background have created some twenty thousand religious denominations, many of which are linked together in national or international councils or federations. Today, the greatest growth in numbers (if not in wealth and power) has been experienced not in the more highly educated northern Europeans and North Americans but instead in the less wealthy populations of Africa, Latin America, and parts of Asia (including China). Missionaries carried the Protestant message during the nineteenth and early twentieth centuries, where they often functioned with support from colonial governments.

However, the most significant transformation of Protestantism since 1900 has taken place in the spread of vibrant forms of Pentecostalism and other charismatic movements, which has occurred without state support. Following the experiences of the early Christians described in the first two chapters of Acts, Pentecostalism focuses on the dramatic religious experiences of conversion, sanctification, baptism in the spirit, revival, speaking in tongues, and healing. Launched from such places as Bethel Bible College in Topeka, Kansas, where Charles Fox Parham preached in 1901, and the Azusa Street Apostolic Faith Mission in Los Angeles, founded by Parham's African American disciple William Joseph Seymour, in 1906, the Pentecostal movement has spread throughout the world. The charismatic influence has even been felt in the so-called mainline Protestant churches. Since the 1950s and the gradual return of former colonies to their native leadership, Pentecostalism has been taken up by native groups, who have added their own particular influences. Of Mexico's 7 million Pentecostals, for example, one-third are Otomi Indians, while many of the more than 15 million Pentecostals in Africa belong to rapidly growing assemblies founded by native leaders.

"No Other Gods before Me": Luther and Zwingli as Leaders of Reform

Martin Luther (1483–1546) pioneered German Protestantism. Born in Eisleben, Germany, and raised in nearby Mansfeld, he entered the Monastery of the Hermits of Saint Augustine at the age of twenty-two, keeping a vow he had made to Saint Anne during a violent storm. He had already completed a master's degree at the University of Erfurt and had begun to study law. But he left legal studies to take up theology, receiving a degree in biblical study in 1509 from the University of Wittenberg, where he would later teach. Before completing his studies at the University of Wittenberg, he was sent to Rome by the monastery. In Rome, he was dismayed at how wordly the church had become. In his early years of teaching Scripture at the

Fig. 13.4 A portrait of Martin Luther (1483–1546).

on December 10, 1520. By 1521, the German legislature had declared him an outlaw. But Luther was not finished stirring up controversy. In 1525, the same year in which he married, he began to publicize his differences not with Roman Catholic authorities but instead with other Reformers. These disagreements continued and resulted in sharp divisions among Protestants at Marburg in 1529 and Augsburg in 1530, where the first Protestant confession of faith was produced. Because of his outlaw status, Luther himself could not be there, but his opinions were presented by other spokesmen, such as Philipp Melanchthon. From 1533 to 1536, Luther helped with the reorganization of the University of Wittenberg. Until his final days, Luther argued that only the Bible could provide an authoritative picture of God's goodness and grace.

Huldrych Zwingli (1484–1531) was born in Wildhaus, Switzerland, and studied in Vienna and Basel. He served as a pastor in Glarus and Einsiedeln before becoming a preacher at the Zurich Cathedral in 1518. He remained there for the rest of his life. Like Luther, he spoke out against indulgences and stated that the Bible was the ultimate guide for the Christian and the church. Zwingli believed that Christ's life and death provided the gift of grace—a gift that would take away all sin. For this reason, he rejected the Roman Catholic practices of penance and the idea of purgatory. He argued his views in his Sixty-Seven Conclusions, presented at the Council of Zurich in 1523, a meeting at which the council ultimately sided with the Reformation. However, Zwingli and Luther did not agree on all points. Zwingli believed that the Lord's Supper, or Communion, did not physically transform the bread and wine into Christ's body but instead changed the people participating in the Lord's Supper,

university (1515–1519), he had focused on the issues of sinfulness and saving grace. From his studies and his spiritual experiences, he came to understand a concept of God's righteousness, described by Paul in Romans 1:17, that did not agree with Roman Catholic practices, in particular the idea of indulgences granted by the church. Luther could not agree that salvation involved a kind of cooperation between God's grace and human work—he believed that salvation came only through God's grace alone, forgiving the sinful human being through a theology of the cross. On October 31, 1517, Luther published his ideas in a work titled Ninety-five Theses. In June 1520, the pope issued his response, condemning as wrong Luther's views in a statement known as *Exsurge Domine* (Arise, O Lord). Luther then took the radical step of burning this papal document in public transforming them into saints called by Christ to become members of his church. For Zwingli, this choosing and gathering of the saints by Christ is the true meaning of a church (which has heavenly, historical, and local manifestations), with Christ as a kind of invisible force making possible the visible, gathered church. In Zwingli's opinion, unlike the views of Luther or Calvin, Christ also serves as an authority over the government, which derives its power to govern from the will of the people whom Christ gathers as a church. Zwingli believed that government is founded on principles of justice revealed in the Bible and that through preaching, rulers should be taught these principles of biblical justice. In turn, the government rules over the church and is ultimately responsible for maintaining justice and order. Zwingli supported the suppression of the Catholicism in his part of Switzerland and also supported the movement, in 1526, to put down the Anabaptists, who disagreed with infant baptism and felt that local congregations, rather than larger churches or civil councils, should have the final say in decisions. Zwingli was killed in a battle with the pope's military forces.

Fig. 13.5   A portrait of John Calvin (1509–1564).

"Declare the Good News": The Mission and Method of Calvin and Wesley

John Calvin (1509–1564) was born in the Picardy region of France, where his father served as an attorney to the bishop of Noyon. Calvin earned a master's degree in theology at the University of Paris, studying there for eleven years before his father, after strong disagreements with the bishop, ordered his son to study law in Orléans. Calvin completed his law

degree in three years and, after the death of his excommunicated father, returned to Paris to study. In 1533, he was forced to leave the city when theologians at the university rejected the Lutheran ideas he had woven into a speech given by Nicholas Cop, the university's rector. In July 1536, he moved to Geneva, Switzerland, where he became the brilliant designer of a program of thought and action that included theology, social philosophy, training of ministers, and universal mission. He restructured the school system and established the University of Geneva. His preaching was so powerful that it resulted in Geneva's adopting a stricter moral code based on biblical principles. Calvin possessed a keen intellect, grounded in the humanists' tendency to prize primary sources—in his case the Bible—and favored practical applications of learning. In Calvin's view, the biblical message was a spiritual one, for the Scripture was inspired by the Holy Spirit and could only be interpreted through the work of the Holy Spirit. The goal of theology, in his view, was not to inspire abstract reasoning but rather to form a more pious, or spiritual, mind. In 1536, Calvin published a spiritual guide called *Institutes of the Christian Religion*, which emphasized that God created humans to be united with him through knowledge of God as the Creator and Redeemer. Calvin's idea was that the pious mind, formed by faith, would contain two kinds of knowledge: the knowledge of an invisible God, the hidden Creator of all things from nothing, and the knowledge of a visible God revealed in the history of redemption recorded in the Bible. At the center of these two kinds of knowledge is Christ, the sole mediator through whom God calls sinful individuals and then restores them to the life God intended for them. The Holy Spirit unites humans with Christ, inspiring in them this faith-knowledge that restores union with God. Not wanting to place power in the hands of hierarchical clergy, Calvin designed an organization that gave power to the local church, whose members elect their leaders. Local churches then send representatives to larger organizations and general assemblies. Calvin believed that churches should be free from governmental control. The Reformed and Presbyterian Churches came from this movement and contain the influence of Calvin's thoughts and practices.

John Wesley (1703–1791) studied at Christ Church, Oxford, and became a fellow of Lincoln College at Oxford after his ordination in the Church of England, in 1725. While tutoring at Oxford in 1729, he directed religious study groups, beginning with one formed by his younger brother Charles. The goal was to revive the spiritual life in these members of the Church of England (which King Henry VIII had created in separating from Roman Catholicism two centuries earlier). Through methodical study and reading the classic works of spiritual literature, Wesley and his students rededicated themselves to a Christian life modeled on the early church. The members of these study groups became known as "Methodists." For two years, John Wesley, with the assistance of his brother Charles and other Methodists from Oxford, carried out a ministry in Georgia, then an American colony. While Wesley felt that this mission was ultimate unsuccessful, he was impressed by the Moravians he met along the way. Under the guidance of Moravian Peter Böhler, Wesley had a dramatic spiritual awakening on May 24, 1738, during which he experienced Christ as his personal savior from sin and death. He changed his Methodist groups to more closely resemble the Moravian organizations, forming small bands of six members, consisting solely of men or women but never both, who shared spiritual experiences. He and his brother published emotional hymns and poems designed to testify to the warming of their hearts and draw other seekers toward the experience of Christ as their personal Lord and Savior. Wesley believed that, with the saving and perfecting grace of faith, Methodists could triumph over sin and show, through their own good deeds, the goodness of the Holy Spirit. Wesley published his sermons and outlined the purpose and manner of Methodist preaching in *Explanatory Notes upon the New Testament* (1755). He organized traveling preachers and commissioned laypeople, ordinary believers, to preach as well. His disregard for specific regional parishes, his use of lay preachers, and his organization of groups outside the control of church authorities all created tension with the religious leaders of the Church of England. In 1744, Wesley held the first of an ongoing series of annual conferences that became, many years later, the governing body of Methodism, a new denomination formally established after Wesley's death.

Justified by Faith

The apostle Paul wrote in his letters to the Romans and Galatians that "the just shall live by faith." This is an important phrase for Protestant thought, beginning with Martin Luther. In the Protestant view, faith is not simply agreeing with facts for which there is little evidence. Instead, faith involves a complete reorientation of personality, a total transformation in response to God. There is, of course, an intellectual aspect to faith—the knowledge, for example, that God is the infinite and omnipotent Creator who has revealed himself in the history of redemption. But, in truth, this knowledge is really beyond human understanding. Nothing within the sinful, finite self can render it conscious of God's infinite nature and mystery. Moreover, faith is never simply an intellectual understanding; it is also a stirring of the affections, resulting in acts of profound love and trust. And faith is also a revamping of the will, surrendering it to God and becoming thereby God's instrument of love in the world. Nothing within the unaided human self can propel it into the transformed condition of knowledge, affection, and will for which the human was created in the first place.

The energy and understanding that move humans toward this redemptive union with God come from the grace of faith alone. Through the grace of God in faith, humans are made right (*justum facere*), or justified. In this way, the Holy Spirit draws together the faithful Christian with the saving actions of Jesus Christ and so restores a right relationship with

Fig. 13.6 "Jesus Saves" is the title of the photograph by Wim Wenders. This Protestant place of worship highlights the saving action of Jesus.

God the creator as well as a right relationship with all other creatures in the world.

This faith is deeply personal, with its experiential knowledge that God is my God. This is why Protestant Reformers rejected the idea that faith, or ultimate justification, came from the routine practice of religious activities. A complete change of heart, through a direct experience of God's saving love, is the key.

For Protestants, sacred Scripture alone offers the authoritative experience of God's creative and saving love. The grace of faith is linked to reading the Bible, since the Bible and the saving events recorded in it are inspired by God's Spirit. The Spirit that hovered over the formless void at the time of creation, the Spirit that came down as tongues of fire on the first believers fifty days after Jesus' obedient death, is the same Spirit who speaks to the inner heart and soul, gracing the reader with the gift of faith. In this way, the word of God speaks to each human heart directly.

The Priesthood of All Believers

As a way to rebel against the abuse and corruption they saw in religious authorities, many Protestant Reformers insisted that all believers are priests. This means that all believers can intercede for one another in worship at the altar and before God in prayer. Christ alone is the high priest whose death guaranteed salvation for all who seek it. He is the only divine mediator between humans and God, and he should not be replaced by anyone else. Before him, all believers stand as equals. In addition, since the word of God speaks to each human heart in the grace of faith, there is no need for a church official to open the way to faith;

indeed, dependence on such human mediation may prove to be a misleading obstacle. Since faith is a deeply personal experience of God as Savior and Lord, no one else can take your place—you must believe for yourself. The priesthood of all believers is a position that carries antiauthoritarian implications or at least an ambiguity concerning the theological value of a separate and marked authoritative leadership. In many Protestant views, when the conscience and intelligence of the reader are graced by God's Holy Spirit, which is a personal event, the reader guided by Scripture can exercise a right of private judgment that takes precedence over the determinations of the community and the mandates of authority. By decreasing the importance of the professional priests, the Reformers also decreased the importance of the cult of sacrifice in the Christian community. Christ's sacrifice was offered once and for all. Instead of the daily holy sacrifice of the Mass as in the Roman Catholic tradition, the Protestant Eucharist, when celebrated at all, commemorates Jesus' Last Supper. Similarly, ordination to priesthood—recognized by Roman Catholics as one of seven sacraments instituted by Jesus—is not considered a sacrament in most Protestant groups. However, almost all Protestant groups have ministers, pastors, or professional clergy. The process of becoming a minister—ordination—formalizes the call to ministry from the congregation, in contrast to the Roman Catholic belief that priests' souls are impressed with a special character. Finally, the priesthood of all believers allows many different kinds of people to be called to serve as pastors or ministers, including (depending on the denomination) not only men trained in a seminary who remain celibate for life but a variety of men and women with different training and differing lifestyles.

The Protestant Principle

Protestantism is grounded in the abiding conviction that God alone is infinite and absolute; nothing in nature or history can be identified with God. Protestantism is dedicated to testify on behalf of God's unique sovereignty and to protest against any attempt to absolutize the finite, whether in the form of word, act, idea, person, institution, or any other cultural or material expression. This dedication is often called the Protestant Principle, and it is tantamount to a constant vigilance against idolatry. God must not be equated with any one concept or any sensible reality. And since one should love God with one's whole heart and mind, one must also safeguard against undue attachment to anything that does not point beyond itself toward God. Whatever in this world makes a claim of unreserved allegiance must be denounced as idolatrous (perhaps even diabolical) and set back in proper perspective. In this sense, the Protestant Principle recognizes that it carries forward the protests lodged by the prophets of ancient Israel who denounced idolatry. The vigilance of the Protestant Principle extends not only to the outer world of history but also to the inner world of human creativity and imagination, raising doubts about the value of images born in the human imagination and concretized in human culture. All human realities must be held accountable to God's judgment or criticism. Whatever is human is imperfect; nothing within temporal human history or thought is beyond the cleansing criticism grounded in loving knowledge of the one, eternal God. The experience of God's goodness is a deeply personal event that occurs deep within the individual self, where the word

Fig. 13.7 Title page of the Old Testament of Martin Luther's translation of the Bible into German, which was published 1523 in Wittenberg. Luther personally translated the Bible, permitting the freedom of reading sacred texts without regard for official interpretations.

of God speaks to each soul. The surest path toward this conversation wherein the loving heart of God addresses and awakens in faith the loving heart of the believer is the reading of the Bible, the inspired chronicle of God's grace. The Bible is God's living word, kept alive by the Spirit, who touches the grace-filled heart of the faithful reader. The Protestant Principle ensures that nothing profane should ever usurp the place of the divine God in the human heart or anywhere else in time or space.

Faith and Order: Denominations, Polities, and the State

A century after Martin Luther's death, hundreds of Protestant denominations already existed. By 1982, Christian sociologist David Barrett identified over 20,000 denominations in mainline Protestantism worldwide, as well as some 10,000 other organizational expressions

Fig. 13.8 Portrait of Henry VIII of England (1491–1547).

of Protestantism. Many of the 225 denominations within the Church of England (also known as the Anglican Communion or Anglicanism) would not call themselves Protestant but instead would see themselves as the church Catholic as it has taken shape on English soil (as opposed to the Roman Catholic Church). Because the Church of England broke with Rome under King Henry VIII in 1534 and then carried out many significant reforms culminating with those in the Acts of Supremacy enacted under queen Elizabeth I in 1559, other Anglicans do see themselves as part of the Protestant reform, and are viewed as such by Protestants, Roman Catholics, and religious scholars.

The divisions among Protestants have sometimes stemmed from national aspirations, such as those in the Church of England or the state-established Lutheran Church in Sweden, or from social identities, such as the African Methodist Episcopal Churches, which are parent organizations of numerous African American independent churches formed at the beginning of the nineteenth century in response to racial inequality within North American Methodism. At other times, divisions among Protestants have come from different theological views of authority. Protestants have generally looked to the Bible and the early Christian community for their systems of government and decision making. Protestants use several forms of government, including decision making by bishops, by elected elders or presbyters, by synods of bodies presided over by elders, or by local congregations acting independently. These forms vary in practice. For example, the governing authority in some Anglican and Lutheran churches centers on bishops consecrated in an unbroken chain of episcopal consecrations descending from the apostles. However, when other Lutherans and Methodists consecrate bishops to serve in positions of authority, they call forth individuals to serve for the greater good of the church without regard to this chain of apostolic succession. Overall, Protestants have been flexible in their forms of government. Having questioned authority in the form of the Roman Catholic Church, Protestants have understandably wanted a more flexible system for forming groups and establishing rules.

Whether ruled by an episcopacy, presbytery, synod, or congregation, Protestants have been forced to confront the question of the relationship between their own system of decision making and the authority of the local and state governments. Early reform movements, such as those begun by Luther, Calvin, and Zwingli, generally followed the state-establishment model set by the Holy Roman Empire, though on a much smaller scale. In England, Germany, Holland, Scandinavia, Scotland, and Switzerland, kings, legislatures, and other ruling powers established Protestant churches and then gave privileges of the state to them. As time passed, many Protestants favored the separation of church and state, particularly in light of the experience of later forms of Protestantism that, lacking the favor of the state, suffered repression even at the hands of Protestant states.

Today, many Protestant polities, or governing bodies, belong to the World Council of Churches, founded in 1948.

Radical Reform Sects: Piety, Apocalypse, and Mystical Experiences

Embodying the Protestant Principle, many Protestant sects have arisen to criticize the corruptions within church and society. Sects remain small, self-governing congregations, in deliberate contrast to larger churches that these sects view as too worldly. While church membership is usually the result of history or geography (being born, for instance, in a Lutheran family or state), sects ask for a special act of will on the part of new members. This usually involves a second baptism—baptism as a conscious act requested by an adult, rather than the baptism performed on infants. Such sects were called Anabaptists, meaning "rebaptizers." Anabaptists conducted an even more radical reform, using Scripture as the source not only of their faith but also of their decisions, forms of community, and daily habits. Anabaptists were persecuted by Catholics and Protestants alike. In 1534–1535, Melchior Hoffman, Jan Beukelssen (a tailor), and Jan Matthys (a baker) established a community in Münster, Germany, based on the biblical principles of polygamy and shared property. Their effort was crushed by a combined Catholic and Lutheran military action. Following this defeat, leaders like Menno Simons, a former Roman Catholic priest whose followers are known as Mennonites, directed their sects toward pacifist beliefs, not supporting any military action on the part of their government. Puritan and Separatist sects in England criticizes the established Church of England and favored separation of religion from the control of government. The first Baptist church returned to England in 1612 under the leadership of John Smyth after years of exile in Holland. Baptists received severe treatment in England through the seventeenth century. Under the leadership of William Brewster and William Bradford, Separatists from Scrooby in England moved to Leiden, Holland, in 1609 and then to Plymouth Colony in America in 1620.

There are many sects in this movement of Protestantism, known as the Radical

Reformation, and they are quite different from each other. They include the Quakers, or the Society of Friends, started by the English mystic George Fox (1624–1681), who stressed the value of sitting in silence during meetings. Later, Mother Ann Lee led a movement of Shaking Quakers, or "Shakers," from England to the United States, where men and women lived together in celibate communities that emphasized song and exuberant dance in worship. In Germany, Philip Spener (1635–1705) and Hermann Francke (1663–1727) formed small sects, known as Pietists, based on the quality of individual emotional experiences felt in response to Bible reading and prayer. The Moravian Brethren, who were founded in Germany in 1727 by Count Zinzendorf and emigrated to the American colonies soon after, owed much to Pietist influences and, in turn, influenced John Wesley, who began the Methodist movement in England and America.

Although some sects formed for theological reasons (such as Unitarians, who do not agree with the belief in the Trinity), most sects are based on three fundamental beliefs drawn from the New Testament: piety (the individual's strong emotional response to an awareness of faith and salvation); an apocalyptic belief that the kingdom of God will arrive soon; and mystical experiences of extraordinary visions, signs, and wonders.

Over the past centuries, evangelical revivals sparked by sects have rippled through the Protestant world, inspiring new combinations of beliefs and styles of worship. From the nineteenth-century mix of Radical Reform traditions (such as Baptists, Mennonites, Congregationalists, and Quakers) with Methodists (who were influence by Moravians), the Holiness churches have emerged; and these, in turn, have become the launching pad for the Pentecostalism active around the world today. As the

Fig. 13.9 Nineteenth-century lithograph shows Shakers in a community dance. Note the simple, austere design of the meeting room, which is consistent with their religious convictions.

center of active Christian populations moves away from the Northern Hemisphere of Europe and America and toward the Southern Hemisphere of Africa, Asia, and the Pacific region, the transformations of Protestant Christianity are likely to have a notable impact on the world's religious life in the third millennium.

"Knowledge of God and Knowledge of Self Are Connected"

The following passage is from the opening of John Calvin's *Institutes of the Christian Religion* (1560) volume 1, book 1, chapter 1. As noted above, Calvin's *Institutes* are a spiritual guide emphasizing that God created humans to be united with him through knowledge of God as the Creator and Redeemer.[1]

> Without knowledge of self there is no knowledge of God. Nearly all the wisdom we possess, that is to say, true and sound wisdom, consists of two parts: the knowledge of God and of ourselves. But, while joined by many bonds, which one precedes and brings forth the other is not easy to discern. In the first place, no one can look upon himself without immediately turning his thoughts to the contemplation of God, in whom he lives and moves (Acts 17:28). For, quite clearly, the mighty gifts with which we are endowed are hardly from ourselves; indeed, our very being is nothing but subsistence in the one God. Then, by these benefits shed like dew from heaven upon us, we are led as by rivulets to the spring itself. Indeed, our very poverty better discloses the infinitude of benefits reposing in God. The miserable ruin, into which the rebellion of the first man cast us, especially compels us to look upward. Thus, not only will we, in fasting and hungering, seek thence what we lack; but, in being aroused by fear, we shall learn humility. . . . Thus, from the feeling of our own ignorance, vanity, poverty, infirmity and—what is more—depravity and corruption, we recognize that the true light of wisdom, sound virtue, full abundance of every good, and purity of righteousness rest in the Lord alone. . . . Accordingly, the knowledge of ourselves not only arouses us to seek God, but also, as it were, leads us by the hand to find him. Without knowledge of God there is no knowledge of self. Again, it is certain that man never achieves a clear knowledge of himself unless he has first looked upon God's face, and then descends from contemplating him to scrutinize himself. For we always seem to ourselves righteous and upright and wise and holy—this pride is innate in all of us—unless by clear proofs we stand convinced of our own unrighteousness, foulness, folly, and impurity. . . . Suppose we but once begin to raise our thought to God, and to ponder his nature, and how completely perfect are his righteousness, wisdom, and power—the straightedge to which we must be shaped. Then, what masquerading earlier as righteousness was pleasing in us will soon grow filthy in its consummate wickedness. What wore the face of power will prove itself the most miserable weakness. That is, what in us seems perfection itself corresponds ill to the purity of God.

◆ STUDY AND DISCUSSION QUESTIONS

1. Review what it means by Protestants to be "people of the word." Consider the implications of this for how Protestants interpret biblical literature, and how or whether the role of mediators (for example, church leaders or biblical scholars) aids in biblical understanding.

2. Choose one of the major Reformers (including Luther, Zwingli, Calvin, or Wesley) and evaluate that person's role in the development of Christianity amid the growing diversity of Christian churches and practices (that is, in relation to Roman Catholicism and Orthodox Christianity).

3. Assess the implications of the Protestant Principle for personal belief and practice, and consider how belief and practice would be altered in the absence of the Protestant Principle.

◆ KEY TERMS

Anabaptists
apocalypse
commemorate
congregation
contemplation
denomination
depravity
disestablishment
dogma
episcopacy
Eucharist
excommunicate
grace
humanism
idolatry
indulgence
inerrantism
infallibility
justification
lectern
magisterial tradition
Mass
Mennonites
Methodists
minister
Moravians
mystical
omnipotence
Pentecost
polity
prelature
presbytery
purgatory
Quakers
redemption
synod

◆ FOR FURTHER READING

Barrett, David B., ed. *World Christian Encyclopaedia: A Comparative Study of Churches and Religions in the Modern World, AD 1900–2000*. 2nd ed. New York: Oxford University Press, 1996.

Forell, George. *The Protestant Faith*. Minneapolis: Fortress Press, 1975.

Hollenweger, W. J. *The Pentecostals: The Charismatic Movement in the Churches*. Minneapolis: Augsburg, 1972.

Janz, Dennis, ed. *The Reformation Reader: Primary Texts with Introductions*. 2nd ed. Minneapolis: Fortress Press, 2008.

Marty, Martin E. *Protestantism*. New York: Holt, Rinehart, and Winston, 1972.

Matheson, Peter, ed. *Reformation Christianity: A People's History of Christianity*. Minneapolis: Fortress Press, 2010.

Noll, Mark A., David W. Bebbington, and George A. Rawlyk, eds. *Evangelicalism: Comparative Studies of Popular Protestantism in North America, the British Isles, and Beyond, 1700-1990.* New York: Oxford University Press, 1994.

Pauck, Wilhelm. *The Heritage of the Reformation.* Rev. ed. New York: Oxford University Press, 1968.

Walls, Andrew. "Christianity." In *A New Handbook of Living Religions*, edited by John R. Hinnells, 55–161. New ed. London: Penguin, 1997.

Williams, G. H. *The Radical Reformation.* Philadelphia: Westminster, 1962.

◆ NOTES

1. This English-language excerpt is taken from John Calvin, *Institutes of the Christian Religion*, ed. John T. McNeill, trans. Ford Lewis Battles, Library of Christian Classics 20 (Philadelphia: Westminster Press, 1960), 35–38.

CHAPTER 14

Islam

Julien Ries

Introduction

Grounded in fourteen centuries of history, Islam is a religion and a community with an extraordinarily rich cultural heritage, with values and beliefs shared by millions of believers around the world. The religion was revealed to the prophet by Muhammad, an Arab caravan leader and a searcher of God rooted in his native Mecca. An enthusiast and a mystic, he was the bearer of a message resembling biblical monotheism. Muhammad discovered the one God, the God of Abraham, and he presented himself as the last prophet sent by God to humanity.

Muhammad proclaimed his revelation to his fellow traders on the caravans as well as to the merchants and bedouin (roaming desert tribes). He founded his first community at Medina, which served as a model for all future Islamic settlements. By the time of his death, Muhammad's message had already been received and accepted by thousands of believers. In a short time, this message was codified in the Qur'an, to which his companions and friends added the Sunna (or tradition). Over the centuries, the Muslim community has solidified around this message, on which all the political,

TIMELINE CE	
570	Birth of the prophet Muhammad
583	Muhammad's journey to Syria
595	Muhammad marries Khadija
610	Muhammad's call to prophethood on Mt. Hira (near Mecca)
620	Muhammad's night journey from Mecca to Jerusalem
622	The hijra, Muhammad's migration from Mecca to Yathrib (later, Medina)
629–630	Muhammad returns to Mecca; conquest of Mecca
632	Death of Muhammad; Abu Bakr selected as caliph
650	Written text of Qur'an is composed
691	Dome of the Rock in Jerusalem
732	Battle of Tours, stopping Muslim advance into France
750–945	The Abbasids, dynasty of caliphs
1058–1111	Lifespan of Sufi scholar al-Ghazali
1099	Catholic Crusaders conquer Jerusalem
1291	Muslim expulsion of Crusaders from Jerusalem
1453	Muslims conquer Constantinople, renaming it Istanbul
1492	Muslims expelled from Spain at surrender of Granada
1947	Independence of Muslim Pakistan from Hindu India
1967	Arab-Israeli War
2003	United States and allies invade Iraq following 9/11 attacks

social, and cultural institutions of Islam are based. Our account will describe the Prophet and prophetism, the Qur'an and the Sunna, the five pillars, and the one God as the basic elements of Islam.

Muhammad proclaimed the oneness and universality of his faith in the one God. He charged his successors to spread Islam throughout the world, and indeed the history of Muslim conquests and empires bears the marks of the tough origins of this culture, born among Arab caravanists and bedouin. Our account will only touch briefly on these historical aspects. At its beginning, Islam, like other social movements, found itself touched by violent forces, but it also had cultural and mystic aspirations that would flourish as the belief came into contact with other cultures and peoples.

Islam and Muslims Today

As we enter the twenty-first century, the world's Islamic population numbers around a billion. Of the 193 countries represented in the United Nations, 51 are Muslim and belong to the Organization of the Islamic Conference. As one of the great religions of the world,

Islam has produced an impressive civilization, as represented by its holy book (the Qur'an), its mosques, its writing, its literature, and its artistic forms and its traditions. It is a civilization that touches many different peoples, who despite cultural diversities, enmities, and rivalries share a common denominator: their faith.

Muslim devotees submits themselves to God through the practice of prescribed duties. Such adhesion binds them as believers before God and, as individuals, unites them with the community (*umma*).

This act of submission is based on the revelation received and transmitted by the prophet Muhammad, who, as "the prophet of the last times" and the last prophet to announce the mystery of God the creator and the merciful, also warns the imminence of divine judgment.

The Muslim affirms his faith in the *tawhid*, the oneness of God, creator and dispenser of all necessary things, Lord of the glory, to whom all praise is due. The signs of God (*ayat Allah*) provide humanity with the proof of creation and safeguard their belief, which they profess through the *shahada*, reinforcing belief in the singular God and in the definitive revelation received by Muhammad.

According to Islamic belief, human beings are creatures who received their souls through the breath of God and are therefore able to

Fig. 14.2 A Muslim man reading the Qur'an inside a Turkish mosque.

Fig. 14.3 These Muslims are washing themselves in a fountain at the Al-Qarawiyyin mosque at Fez, Morocco, before beginning their prayer.

respond to God. On earth, the human is the *khalifa* (representative) of God. It is from this relationship that the duties of the "five pillars" of Islam derive. These religious practices, when combined with the prescriptions of the community, guarantee adherence to the path toward God as well as harmony within the community (*umma*).

Thus the belief in the one God, upon which daily prayer, observance of Ramadan, and the pilgrimage to Mecca (the renewed affirmation of the religion's origins) are based, constitutes the grounding and motivating force that supports modern Islam.

The Spread of Islam

The birth of Islam occurred on the Arabian Peninsula and remained in this region until the first expansion, in the seventh century. Consisting mostly of deserts, the peninsula had a number of important cities that marked stopping places for caravans traveling between

Africa, Asia, and the Mediterranean, including Medina (Yathrib) and Mecca. The map (fig. 14.5) shows the historical spread of Islam under the caliphates and traces where Islam is prominently practiced. The map does not show the important Islamic presence in Europe or in North America. The immigration of Muslims gives rise to important religious communities and new mosques in the communities of the West.

According to the available data, 90 percent of the population in the following countries is Muslim: Afghanistan, Algeria, Saudi Arabia, Bahrain, Jordan, Iran, Iraq, Libya, Morocco, Mauritania, Niger, Oman, Pakistan, Western Sahara, Senegal, Syria, Somalia, Tunisia, Turkey, and Yemen. Smaller majority populations are also located in Albania, Bangladesh, Egypt, Guinea, Indonesia, Kazakhstan, Malaysia, Mali, Sudan, Turkmenistan, and Uzbekistan (see Joanne O'Brien and Martin Palmer, *Atlas*

des Religions dans le Monde [London: Myriad; Paris: Autrement, 1994).

The Prophet Muhammad and the Foundation Of Islam

Born in 570 CE, Muhammad was a member of the clan of Hashemites, who served as the keepers of the Kaaba, the principal pagan sanctuary of Mecca, and who traded via caravan with Syria. Having lost both his parents at the age of five, Muhammad was entrusted to his uncle, Abu Talib, with whom he later traveled as a guard. At the age of twenty-five, he married Khadija, a rich widow fifteen years his senior. Their sons died young, but their daughter Fatima went on to marry Ali, the fourth caliph.

At the age of forty, Muhammad received visions and a revelation (Qur'an 53 and 96), bringing about a profound change in his life.

Fig. 14.4 A school in Baghdad, Iraq. Traditional stories form part of the curriculum together with other subjects.

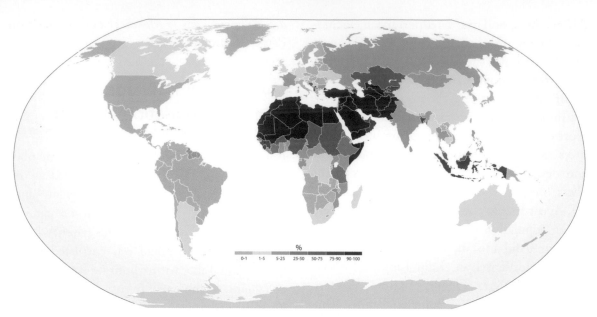

Fig. 14.5 Map indicating percetange distribution of Islamic populations throughout the world.

Fig. 14.6 Muslims perform Tawaf (circumambulating) at the Kaaba, in Mecca, Saudi Arabia.

Following this mystic experience, he proclaimed his message, emphasizing the might and goodness of Allah, and the divine justice that will bring either reward or punishment for humankind. From humans, God demands submission (*islam*) in the form of adoration, gratitude, faith, and prayer. A number of those who accepted this submission (Muslims) congregated around the Prophet, spurring opposition from other clans, who realized that the new message would bring about a social revolution. In 619, Khadija died and Muhammad remarried.

Faced with ever-growing opposition (Qur'an 37), Muhammad established contact with the oasis of Yathrib, where two Arab tribes and a Jewish tribe had settled. On July 16, 622, the Prophet and his followers left Mecca for this oasis, which was renamed al-Madina (Medina), or "the city." This migration, known as the *hijra*, marks the founding act of Islam as a community (*umma*). The *muhajir* is the term for those Muslims who left everything behind to serve God (Qur'an 8).

In Medina, Muhammad shaped his community with the first institutions: the

Fig. 14.7 Illustration of important meeting between Muhammad and a monotheistic shepherd.

organization of the economy and of prayer, the fight for survival, and for the conquest of Mecca. During this time, seventy-four expeditions were launched against caravans departing from Mecca. On January 11, 630, Muhammad entered Mecca in triumph, destroying idols both in the Kaaba and in private houses, and proclaimed a general amnesty. In doing so, Muhammad became the religious and political head of the new community founded on Allah, the one God.

The Conquests and the Expansion of Islam

Following a pilgrimage to Mecca in 632, Muhammad died. Abu Bakr (632–634), his father-in-law, was chosen as his successor (caliph). This event marks the beginning of the Islamic conquests in Syria and Persia. In turn, Abu Bakr was succeeded by Omar (634–644), who continued the military campaigns and

Fig. 14.8 Muslim horsemen from Abbasid manuscript, depicted as spreading the Islamic faith.

conquered Damascus in 636, and one year later Jerusalem. An energetic and realistic leader, Omar created military and civil institutions and paid particular attention to the financial organization of the Muslim community. Othman (644–656) collected the recollections of Muhammad and set the official text of the Qur'an. These three caliphs established the overlordship of the Umayyads, originally an aristocratic clan from Mecca, in the Near East. Ali (656–661), the fourth caliph and son-in-law of the Prophet, however, declared war against the Umayyads. Uniting his followers, the Shiites, he formed a legitimist Islam that demanded fidelity to God in opposition to the dynastic principle, which had become the prerogative of the Umayyads.

The Umayyad dynasty, which had established itself in Damascus first conquered North Africa and then Spain, where it had established the caliphate of Cordoba. Damascus, the capital of a powerful state, became the center for the spread of a new culture of Arabization and Islamization. The Shiite Muslims remained opposed to it, and on November 28, 749, Abu Abbas was nominated caliph in the mosque at Kufa. The Abbasids (750–945), another hereditary dynasty of caliphs, founded the city of Baghdad, the intellectual capital of the East, serving as a synthesis of the Arabic and the Iranian worlds, and as a great meeting place for the arts and sciences of the world. In 945, the Turks seized power, and the Seljuk Turks ended the Abbasid dynasty. The Shiites, however, continued to rule in Egypt for two centuries, forming the Fatimid dynasty of Cairo.

The Seljuk Turks conquered Anatolia and Syria, where they encountered the crusading armies of the West. These Turks belonged to the Sunni sect, that is, those Muslims who are faithful to the Sunna—the "tradition." In

Fig. 14.9 Helical minaret at Samarra mosque in Iraq. This minaret (from where calls to prayer are made) and the surrounding walls are all that remain of this mosque of the Abbasid period.

their wake followed an invasion by the Mongols, whose leader Tamerlane (1336–1405) later converted to Islam. The Ottoman Turks then set about on their expansion with the fall of Constantinople (1453), the invasion of the Balkans, the conquests of Syria and Egypt, and later of Iraq. With these advances, the Ottoman Empire extended from Vienna to the Nile, from Baghdad to Tunis, and would last for six centuries, marking the beginning of modern Islam.

The Qur'an, the Sunna, and the Sharia

For Muslims, the Qur'an is the word of God as revealed to and as proclaimed by Humannad. Supernaturally dictated and recorded by the inspired Prophet, this sacred book consists of 114 suras (chapters) and amounts to 6,226 verses, called *ayat Allah*—"the signs of God." Allah keeps the original, containing all revelation: *maktub*—"that which is written." Orientalists regard the Qur'an as a diary of the religious experiences, triumphs, and failures of the Prophet, augmented by a number of ancient pre-Islamic, Jewish, and Christian religious traditions.

The Qur'an records the primordial pact between Allah and humanity, which culminates in the covenant with Abraham. Following the death of Muhammad, many versions of his preaching and his deeds circulated among the people, but in 651 Caliph Othman collected all the existing texts and established a single, definitive, and official Qur'anic text. Subsequently, all the other versions were destroyed.

The deeds, words, and actions of the Prophet constitute a rule of life, practices, and beliefs: this is the Sunna, or the traditions. It follows the path of revelation and serves as a continuation, extension, and explanation of the Qur'an. To Muslims, Muhammad lived in a habitual prophetic state, and therefore all his words, actions, and judgments have a spiritual value similar to that of the Qur'an. The basis of the Sunna is the hadith, a message that can be traced back to Muhammad himself.

Fig. 14.10 A folio from the Qur'an in Kufic script. The title of the sura—the Qur'an is divided into 114 suras—is written in gold.

The sharia is the canonical law that includes all the dispositions of God concerning humankind. Deriving from the Qur'an and the Sunna, it describes the Islamic path for the community (*umma*) and for the faithful. This positive divine law applies to all social, religious, political, and private aspects of life. In the eighth and ninth centuries, Sunnism developed four great juridical schools (*madhhab*) to interpret the law, which remains the fundamental authority. Being of divine origin, the sharia makes it possible to confront secularization and gives a religious sense to a daily life steeped in the sacred.

Fig. 14.11 A tile from a seventeenth-century Turkish pulpit. One of the basic definitions of Islam is represented in the center: "There is no god except Allah and Muhammad is his Prophet."

Allah, God the Creator, the Judge, the Dispenser of Recompense

The word *Allah* derives from the pre-Islamic word *al-Ilah*, meaning "the God." Muhammad discovered the one God and proclaimed his oneness (Qur'an 112), affirming Allah as the creator of all things (*al-Khaliq, al-Bari*). In Islam, the creation serves as an affirmation of God's omnipotence and of the necessity for people to discover Allah through the signs of the universe: Abraham was the first to recognize these signs. The creator of humanity, Allah, will also give humans what they deserves on the day of judgment.

Unique and one in himself, Allah does not reveal his mysterious nature but may be discovered through his actions, which show his omnipotence in daily life. For the believer, Allah is the merciful (*al-Rahman*) and the clement (*al-Rahim*), two names found at the beginning of every sura of the Qur'an. Guided by a divine hand, humans have the duty to recognize God in the order of the world, where "everything will perish, except Allah" (Qur'an 28:88).

The perfections of God, understood through the signs and proclaimed in the Qur'an, lie in his "divine names." These ninety-nine names nurture Muslim devotion as believers meditate on and recite them with the help of a *subha* (rosary). Whole treaties are devoted to enumeration, analysis, and comment on these "most beautiful names of God," which include *al-Malik* ("the king"), *al-Quddus* ("the holy"), *al-Salam* ("the peace"), and *al-Khaliq* ("the creator").

Allah dispenses life and death as part of his omnipotence. After death, every human

Fig. 14.12 In this Turkish manuscript, prophet Muhammad is shown ascending to paradise, guided by the Archangel Gabriel.

must briefly come back to life for their particular judgment, after which follows the peace of the tomb. There each individual awaits the final resurrection and the universal judgment, during which all actions are weighed by Allah (Qur'an 43:16-18). The angels will assist Allah in the final judgment, during which all the secrets of the heart will be examined (Qur'an 86:9). According to the Qur'an, the faithful and virtuous will then cross the bridge of Sirat (26:66), which leads from the place of judgment to paradise, while all infidels will fall into hell below. The believers will then enter a garden without parallel, divided into seven layers.

This description of the final judgment may have been influenced by beliefs in Syrian Christianity and late Judaism, both of which were known to Muhammad.

The Prophets, Jesus Christ, Muhammad

In Islam, prophetism is linked to revelation. The Qur'an calls those biblical persons who have received a message from God *nabi*, whereas the word *rasul* refers to the Arabic tradition of "the guide."

Noah was the first to announce God, showing the people that monotheism was the only way to salvation. With Noah, God renewed the primordial pact. The builder of the Kaaba (the temple of Islam), Abraham is seen as the friend and first seeker of God, and as the first Muslim, serving as the prototype for monotheistic faith. He submitted himself to God to the point of accepting the sacrifice of his own son. The Qur'an also honors Moses and records both his call by God (Qur'an 28) and his mission to liberate a people enslaved in Egypt and to spread the message of the one God (Qur'an 20).

In the Qur'an, Jesus Christ is presented as one of the greatest of prophets; he is, however, a man, the son of Mary, a perfect Muslim, and an apostle of Allah. The text of the 15 Qur'anic chapters mentioning Jesus is clearly taken from the apocryphal Gospels. The Qur'anic text mentions the virgin birth of Jesus, his miracles, his book, and the announcement of a prophet who was to come after him. The Qur'an calls him the *rasul* of Allah and a *nabi*.

It was Muhammad's duty to announce the pure message of God and to communicate his revelation to all those who already had the Scriptures but who had altered them (Qur'an 2:91 and 98:1-4). He is therefore both a *nabi* and a *rasul* (one sent by God), charged with transmitting a religious law to which he too must submit, thus becoming the guide of the community (Qur'an 48:28 and 7:158). The Qur'an also assigns him a third mission—that of *nadhir*, "the one who warns" (Qur'an 50:2). As such, he must carry God's message to the nonbelievers so that they too may submit themselves to God. The Qur'an likens unbelief to deafness or blindness. Allah asks the Prophet to shun nonbelievers because they will be judged and punished (Qur'an 53:30 and 51:54), reserving divine mercy only for believers.

Fig. 14.13 An engraved stone from the portal of the Alhambra in Granada, Spain. The five fingers of the open hand symbolize the five pillars of Islam.

The Five Pillars of Islam

The fundamental practices of Islam, known as the five pillars, are obligatory acts of Muslims. They include the creed, prayer, charity, fasting, and pilgrimage, as described below.

1. The *shahada* is the keystone of Islam—the spoken testimony to the one God (Allah) and his Prophet (Muhammad). Each Muslim must proclaim: "There is no god except Allah and Muhammad is the messenger of Allah." It is the profession of the Muslim's faith.

2. Prayer is the expression of the monotheistic faith of humanity, who was created by

Fig. 14.14 A Muslim man praying on the bank of Lake Dal in the Indian Kashmir, facing Mecca.

Allah to serve for his adoration (Qur'an 109 and 110). Personal prayer, the main duty of the Muslim, is thanksgiving to God and memory of him. The ritual prayer (*salat*), said five times a day, is the liturgy (the divine office preceded by a call, ablutions, and by a proper preparation). If possible, this prayer should be said in a mosque.

3. Alms as required by law purifies the believer and increases his or her wealth in this world and in the afterlife. *Zakat* is a religious levy paid first at Medina. It is a social institution designed to benefit those in need, the poor, and travelers. The *sadaqa* is voluntary almsgiving offered by Muslims (Qur'an 9:103).

4. The fasting during *Ramadan* (Qur'an 2). Influenced by the Jews and especially by the Christians, Muhammad imposed a daytime fast during the month when he was granted his revelation, the ninth month of the Islamic lunar calendar. The fast must be followed strictly from sunrise to sunset and affects the entire community. The night between the twenty-sixth and twenty-seventh days is "the night of destiny" and is spent in the mosque to celebrate the Qur'an.

5. The pilgrimage, the *haj*, takes the Muslim to Mecca at least once in his or her life. It is modeled on the pilgrimage of the Prophet himself, taken in the tenth year of the Hijra, in the twelfth month, known as *dhu al-hijja*. From start to finish, the pilgrimage is immersed in prayer. Before leaving, pilgrims reconcile themselves with God, their fellow humans, and their family. When they arrive at the holy place, they don a particular garb (*ihram*) and then enter the great mosque. They must then walk around the Kaaba seven times, and run the path of Hagar the slave seven times, to commemorate her search for water for her son Ishmael, the firstborn of Abraham. On the ninth day, he participates in the catechesis on the plain of Arafat, followed on the tenth day by the sacrifice, which recalls the sacrifice of Abraham. The pilgrimage is meant to heighten solidarity among believers.

Islam: Society and Culture

Islam is a temporal community concerning itself with each believer's relationship with God and also with the relationships between the believers on a moral, social, and political level. Islam has no church, no priesthood, nor any human embodiment of spiritual power. The Qur'an is the book containing God's message, but it also serves as a code of religious and social life.

The *umma* is the community formed by religious, juridical, and political ties. The *jama* consists of all the believers united in their faith. Personal, family, and social life all assume a sacred character and are oriented toward an effort of expansion of the community in accordance with religious faith as outlined in the Qur'an.

The successor of Muhammad, the caliph, is a temporal sovereign charged with enforcing the precepts and ideals of the Qur'an as derived from Allah. These prescriptions concern both religious life and the organization of the Muslim city. Since he has the duty to lead the *umma*, the caliph also has a religious role. Although the *umma* is intended to reflect divine unity, it has assumed various forms throughout history, often endangering this unity. Indeed, after the death of the Prophet, this unity was shattered. The aim of Islam is to restore this ideal community.

Muhammad preached the one God to illiterate bedouin and desert tribes. The transmission of his message provided a foundation for the Arabic writing of the Qur'an and for all Islamic culture. In the ninth century, scholars in Baghdad translated the great Greek texts into

Fig. 14.15   The city of Ghardaia in the north Sahara in Algeria looks like a ship in the desert providing aid for travelers.

Arabic, marking the beginning of the golden age of Muslim thought. An initially intense flurry of translations was followed by the creation of philosophic, encyclopedic, and historical texts. In the great cities, there arose libraries, storehouses of invaluable treasures devoted to Islamic thought and tradition. Mathematics, the natural sciences, astronomy, geography, and (thanks to hospitals) medicine all underwent notable developments. Islam's artistic contributions to humanity can be seen in a diverse array of cities, including Cordoba, Granada, Mosul, Baghdad, and Palermo.

Muslim Mysticism: Sufism

Text by Al-Hallaj, which proclaims God within humanity.

> I have a friend whom I visit in my loneliness, a friend present even when invisible. You will never see me listening to Him trying to grab his language from noisy words. His words do not have vowels, nor speech, they are nothing like the melody of voices. It is as if I were a "thou" being addressed, and were so beyond the thoughts coming to my mind, in my essence, and for itself. Present, absent, near, distant, impervious to descriptions by qualities, He is more profoundly hidden to one's thoughts than profound conscience, more intimate than the flash of thought. ("The Diwan of Al-Hallaj," quoted from Roger Arnaldez, *Al-Hallaj ou la Religion de la Croix* (Paris: Plon, 1964, 129–30)

The word *Sufism* is derived from *suf*, meaning "wool," and recalls the white woolen habit worn by Christian monks. In Islam, Sufism is the search for God, an example of which is the

Prophet in prayer (Qur'an 17:79). This striving toward the divine continued among some Sufis in Iraq, Syria, Egypt, and the Khorasan into the eighth century. That era in Islamic history can best be illustrated by a woman called Rabiah, who lived a life of prayer and sang the pure love for God. In the ninth century, several schools of Sufism formed and attracted numerous novices. Yet these new institutions face harsh opposition. In 922, al-Hallaj was crucified in Baghdad for proclaiming that God lives within human beings. His contribution was decisive for the formation of the Sufi vocabulary.

Following this persecution, Sufism entered a phase during which its elders attempted to reconcile themselves with Muslim orthodoxy. Al-Ghazali, a mystic theologian who died in 1111, states that there is a proximity between God and humanity. In Andalusia, Ibn 'Arabi (1165–1240) provided a new impulse for Sufism. A philosopher, theologian, and founder of the doctrine of the "uniqueness of the being," Arabi was a renowned visionary who opened the way for the "Shiite mysticism of light and fire." He advanced the idea of a continuous creation, an effusion of the being, through divine compassion, that returns the being to its origins.

From the thirteenth century onward, several mystic movements (*tariqah*, "the way") formed around a founder and received the initiatory heritage uniting them with God. Each movement featured a well-defined hierarchical structure, rites of initiation, and practices that furthered each worshiper's search for God. Each brotherhood was marked by complete obedience to the rule, submission to the hierarchy, and secrecy. It is estimated that more than two hundred such movements have occurred in total. Sufism has continued to survive and exert influences within these movements.

◆ STUDY AND DISCUSSION QUESTIONS

1. Discuss possible reasons for why the idea of "submission" is the major theme of Islam, as opposed to other themes, such as salvation or community.

2. Compare and contrast the role of the "founder" of other monotheistic religious traditions, including Judaism and the diverse traditions of Christianity.

3. Assess the significance of a nation-state or country (in relationship with but also in contrast to the *umma*) being identified as a "Muslim" state or country, and what implications this may bring to both religious and civil society in that state or country.

◆ KEY TERMS

Abbasids
Al-Hallaj
Allah
caliph
clan
Druze
Fatima
Fiqh
hadith
haj
haram
hijra
Ijma
imam
Islam
Islamism
jihad

Kaaba
Ottoman
Qibla
Ramadan
Seljuks
sharia
Shiism
Sunna
Sunnism
tribe
Umayyads
umma
Ummat an-nabi

◆ FOR FURTHER READING

Ahmed, Akbar S. *Discovering Islam: Making Sense of Muslim History and Society*. London: Routledge, 2002.

Dawood, N. J., trans. *The Koran*. London: Penguin, 1993.

Esposito, John. *Islam: The Straight Path*. 3rd ed. New York: Oxford University Press, 1998.

Kaltner, John. *Introducing the Qur'an: For Today's Reader*. Minneapolis: Fortress Press, 2011.

Lawrence, Bruce. *The Qur'an: A Biography*. New York: Atlantic Monthly Press, 2007.

Nasr, Seyyed Hossein. *Ideals and Realities of Islam*. 2nd ed. London: Unwin Hyman, 1985.

Reynolds, Gabriel Said. *The Emergence of Islam*. Minneapolis: Fortress Press, 2012.

Schimmel, Annemarie. *Mystical Dimensions of Islam*. Chapel Hill: University of North Carolina Press, 1975.

CHAPTER 15

Zoroastrianism

Anthony Cerulli

Introduction

With a history dating back to the second millennium BCE in the steppelands of central Asia and eastern Iran, Zoroastrianism is one of the oldest world religions. In the twenty-first century, Zoroastrians continue their practices across the globe, as in the growing community of Burr Ridge, Illinois, in the western suburbs of Chicago. Yet Zoroastrianism is also one of the least well-known religions in the world today. Underlining the religion's theology and ritual praxis is a cosmological vision of an ongoing battle in the world between the Truth and the Lie (in the Avestan language *aša* and *druj*, respectively). Humanity is embroiled in the struggle between these ethical poles, and Zoroastrian doctrine requires that people must choose sides in the conflict. One either follows Truth, the principal Zoroastrian god, Ahura Mazdā, the "Wise Lord," or one follows the Lie, false gods and their ruler, Angra Mainyu, the "Destructive Spirit."[1] A follower of Ahura Mazdā, like his prophet Zarathuštra (see fig. 15.1), is said to be *ašāvan*, a "sustainer of Truth," whereas the supporter of Angra Mainyu is *drəgvant*, "possessed by Lie." The Zoroastrian opposition of Truth and Lie extends to all areas of human activity, depicted as dichotomies of order and disorder, good and evil, light and dark, and so on. In this sense, the tradition presents a dualistic cosmology. It also recognizes many gods and demons, although among them Ahura Mazdā is supreme.

The term *Zoroastrianism* is a nineteenth-century construct, and like other -isms, it suggests a tradition with teachings and practices that may be ascribed to a single founder—such as Buddhism and the Buddha and Manichae-anism and Mani. In Europe, for centuries the founder of Zoroastrianism has been known as "Zoroaster," from the Greek *zoroastres*, which is a translation of the Persian *zarathuštra*. Tradition recognizes Zarathuštra as a prophet and thus places Zoroastrianism alongside Judaism, Christianity, and Islam as one of the world's prophetic religions. Indeed, many Zoroastrians self-identify as Zarathushtis, "followers of Zarathuštra," rather than the traditionally used term in the West, *Zoroastrian*. In the last and present centuries, prominent religious

Fig. 15.1 A common image of the prophet Zarathuštra, dressed in white, bearded, and with a halo of sunlight.

institutions, such as the World Zoroastrian Organization (WZO), Zoroastrian Trust Funds of Europe, Inc. (ZTFE), and the Federation of Zoroastrian Associations of North America (FEZANA), have advocated the use of the term *Zarathushti*. Among Iranian Zoroastrians, the modern Persian form of the term is preferred, and so *Zartoshti* is also used to refer to someone who follows the teachings of Zarathuštra. This designation is prominent in the title of the important Zoroastrian organization World Alliance of Parsi and Irani Zartoshtis (WAPIZ). Historically, Zoroastrians have also been known as Mazdeans and Mazdayasnians, names based on the Old Iranian word *mazdā-yasna*, which means "one who sacrifices to (Ahura) Mazdā." Naturally, then, in literature on the religions of ancient Iran, we also find references to Zoroastrianism as Mazdaism and Mazdayasnianism.

A 2004 *Fezana Journal* survey estimated the number of Zoroastrians in the world to range from 124,000 to 190,000.[2] There are Zoroastrian communities all over the globe. A small Zoroastrian minority remains in Iran, where the tradition began, and where, over the last half century or so, there have been significant movements to celebrate Zarathuštra as a homegrown religious reformer who predated the Arabians and Islam. Certain archaic Zoroastrian symbols, such as the winged figure in the sun disk (*faravahar*—fig. 15.2), have also been recovered from the ceremonial capital of the Achaemenid Empire, Persepolis, and recognized in Iran and elsewhere as an important marker of pre-Islamic Iranian religion. In a 2004 FEZANA survey, there were an estimated 25,000 Zoroastrians living in Iran.

By far the highest number of Zoroastrians in the world today live on the Indian subcontinent, where they have had a sizable presence since the tenth century CE. An estimated 70,000 Zoroastrians live in India, where they are known as Parsis. (See the section titled "Parsis" below.)

Fig. 15.2 The *faravahar*. One of the best-known symbols of Zoroastrianism, Middle Persian *faravahar* derives from *fravaši*, an Avestan term meaning "spirit" or "soul" that exists before and after one's life. The earliest depictions of the Old Persian *fravarti* are thought to depict the face of the Achaemenid king Darius I (549–486 BCE). This suggests that the *fravarti* represents the *fravaši* (soul) of the king, hence giving ancient Persian kings a divinely-ordained authority.

Apart from Iran and India, there are also small Zoroastrian communities in the United Kingdom, North America, Australia, New Zealand, and Pakistan.

Living according to Truth

Zarathuštra's teachings in the *Gāthās* and elsewhere in the *Avesta* offer insights into the theology and ritual duties of Zoroastrians. Above all, there is a distinct concern for accepting what is good and true and rejecting everything that is evil and false, as seen in the Zoroastrian "declaration of faith" (*fravarāne*): "I profess myself a Mazdā-worshipper, a follower of Zarathuštra, rejecting false gods, accepting Ahura's instruction. I am one who praises the Holy Immortals (Ameša Spəṇtas), who worships the Holy Immortals. To Ahura Mazdā, the good, rich in treasures, I ascribe all things that are good" (*Yasna* 12.1).[3]

To live according to the Truth in Zoroastrianism, one must cultivate an unwavering trust in and earnest commitment to Ahura Mazdā, as well as an appreciation for one's spiritual descent from him. For instance, a Middle Persian Zoroastrian text, *The Select Precepts of the First Sages*, explains that every Zoroastrian should be able to address a series of probing, self-reflexive questions by the age of fifteen, the traditional age of initiation into the Zoroastrian community as an adult (see below, "Ritual Practice"). The first five questions and suitable answers are as follows:

> Who am I? To whom do I belong? From where have I come? To where shall I go back? From what stock and lineage am I?
>
> I am from the conceptual world; I was not from the visible world. I was created, I did not (always) exist. I belong to Ohrmazd (Ahura Mazdā), not to Ahreman [Angra Mainyu]. I belong to the deities, not the demons; I belong to the good, not the bad. I am human, not a demon; I am a creature of Ohrmazd, not of Ahreman.[4]

The Select Precepts then recounts a mythological line of descent for humankind extending back to the first man, Gayōmart, the first male-female human couple, Mahre and Mahryane, and a divine mother, Spendarmad, and father, Ohrmazd. Furthermore, it establishes for Zoroastrians a primeval distinction between Ahura Mazdā/the Truth and Angra Mainyu/the Lie. Zoroastrians should be attentive to Ahura Mazdā at all times in thought, word, and deed, while actively railing against the influence of Angra Mainyu and the bad things he and his cohort of demons produce in the world. To do this, *The Select Precepts* advises the following mental discipline: "Think of Ohrmazd: that he is, always was, and evermore shall be, his undying sovereignty, his infinity and purity; [and to think of] Ahreman: that he is not and will be annihilated."[5]

Steadfast belief in Ahura Mazdā forms the base of the Zoroastrian worldview, which in turn supports the day-to-day duties and practices of the Zoroastrian practitioner and religious community. Among the duties and practices mandated, *The Select Precepts* discusses marriage, procreation, cultivation of the land, and the respectful treatment of cattle. The faithful are to divide their lives into thirds: a third for religious instruction, a third for agriculture (or commerce), and a third for pleasure. The underlying principle of *The Select Precepts* is captured in a ubiquitous refrain many Zoroastrians regard as the basic message of Zarathuštra's teachings: through good thoughts, good words, and good actions, one will be rewarded by Ahura Mazdā and protected from Angra Mainyu.

Zarathuštra taught that every person has concrete choices to make in life. Either take up a path of the good and order, the path of Ahura Mazdā and *aša*, or follow the path of evil and disorder, the path of Angra Mainyu and *druǰ*. These choices effectively guide Ahura Mazdā's ruling on judgment day, mythologized in the critical passage across Chinvat Bridge and thus the course of a person's afterlife. The grand goal of the Zoroastrian religion is to equip all good men and women with *aša* in their thoughts, words, and deeds in order to fend off the forces of *druǰ*. People who have lived according to *aša* cross Chinvat Bridge and go to Ahura Mazdā's "paradise" (*pairidaēza*), where they live in bliss; people who have lived wickedly fall off the bridge and go to hell, where they live in misery until the end of the world.[6] The end of the world comes in an apocalyptic deluge of fire, at which point the good are rewarded with paradise and the wicked are scalded fiercely in hell for three days until the evil is burnt out of them. After those three days, Zoroastrian tradition says that everything will be forgiven, and a healing of the cosmos will commence. The world will become perfect, the Lie (*druǰ*) will be banished forever and never again have power on earth, and humans will be immortal.

The notion of community in Zoroastrianism effectively underlies the pursuit of living according to Truth (*aša*). At its core lies the question of whether or not outsiders are allowed to convert, or become assimilated, to the tradition. Historically, Zoroastrian identity has been tied to ethnicity and determined strictly along patrilineal lines. Because of a number of factors over the last century, such as the growing number of interfaith marriages among Zoroastrian women and low birthrates in Zoroastrian communities, there has been a precipitous decline in the Zoroastrian population worldwide. In response,

over the last century in India Parsi priests have quietly initiated the children of Parsi mothers and non-Zoroastrian fathers.[7] Questions about insider-outsider status and ways to reverse the tide of decreasing numbers are often the most controversial and pressing questions contemporary Zoroastrian communities face today. There is no uniform way for every Zoroastrian community to approach these issues, since Zoroastrianism does not have a universally recognized authoritative body—such as a synod of bishops in Christianity or ulema of imams in Islam—to mandate religious laws. Geopolitical and cultural circumstances each community faces have been and continue to be quite dissimilar; in response to specific needs, different religious institutions regularly take the lead in decision making. This has resulted in a rather broad range of interpretation of scripture and practice among Zoroastrians, which cover the ideological gamut from strict conservativism to radical liberalism. For example, today WAPIZ contends there was never a time in history when conversion to Zoroastrianism was condoned in any fashion, and thus it should not be allowed. Yet increasing numbers of self-identified progressive Zoroastrians call for leniency on issues of interfaith marriage and conversion.[8]

Cornerstone Texts: Avesta and Gāthās

Apart from countries where Zoroastrianism has been present for a long time, such as Iran and India, basic awareness of the religion is often limited to scholars, especially philologists and historians of religion.[9] Perhaps the most famous European intellectual to bring attention to Zoroastrianism and Zarathuštra in modern Western history was the German philosopher

Friedrich Nietzsche. In *Thus Spoke Zarathustra* (1883–1885), Nietzsche used the character of Zarathuštra "as a philosopher and poet . . . to engineer an epistemic break in the received history of Greek philosophy and Christian morality" in Europe. Nietzsche's Zarathuštra ran up against Western religious and cultural giants like Plato, Jesus, Descartes, and Kant.[10] Nietzsche famously had Zarathuštra proclaim that "God is dead" (*Gott ist tot*) to advance a new way of thinking about the frontiers of human morality and the Judeo-Christian concepts of good and evil. For Nietzsche, Judeo-Christian morality was imprecise, hence problematic, and neatly juxtaposed with Zarathuštra's overdetermined socioethical worldview of contrasting light and darkness, Truth and Lie, order and disorder, and so on.

For non-Zoroastrians, knowledge of Zarathuštra's teachings comes largely from extant translations of scripture and, to a lesser extent, scholarly writings and popular media. The Zoroastrian textual corpus is rather immense. The *Avesta*, and within it the *Gāthās*, are the textual cornerstones of the tradition.[11] The *Avesta* is a collection of books that are written in a language called Avestan and that go back to the second millennium BCE. The *Avesta* also contains translations of and commentaries on the oldest sources, written in a Middle Persian language called Pahlavi, which are known as the *Zand (Avesta)*.

The portions of the *Avesta* available today amount to about one-third of what was originally produced in ancient Iran. Our earliest description of the *Avesta* is in book 8 of the ninth-tenth-century CE Middle Persian text, *Dēnkard* ("Acts of the Religion"), in which twenty-one books are enumerated by name and category. The books are mostly liturgical manuals dealing with the *yasna*, "sacrificial worship." The *Avesta* is generally thought to have been composed in two historical stages of eastern-Iranian language development: Gathic or Old Avestan (in which the five *Gāthās* were composed) and Younger Avestan (the language in which the literature predominantly dealing with the *yasna* was composed). The Gathic portions of the *Avesta* are traditionally recognized as compositions of Zarathuštra; most of the Younger Avestan literature is presented as direct revelations from Ahura Mazdā to the prophet. Originally handed down orally through the ages, the *Avesta* was put to writing in the Avestan alphabet, which was invented solely for this purpose, around the fifth century CE. The following is a list of the various sections and books of the *Avesta*.

The *Gāthās* are the five "hymns" (also sometimes translated as "poems" or "songs") attributed to Zarathuštra and addressed to Ahura Mazdā.[13] In total, they amount to seventeen different hymns, which are arranged in the *Yasna* (Y) in five categories according to their different meters.

The *Gāthās* are not hymns of proselytization or a defense of the prophet's religious vision but are, rather, a set of inspirational songs meant to inspire and evoke already known theological ideas in worshipers of Ahura Mazdā. Many aspects of the *Gāthās* language, such as syntax and vocabulary, have for centuries defied scholars' attempts at translation and interpretation. The discovery and decipherment of the *Younger Avesta* and the Pahlavi *Zand (Avesta)* provide some clues to its often cryptic meaning, and a handful of recent publications have made great advancements in revealing the meaning of Zoroastrian Scripture to modern audiences.[12]

Historical Development

Nomadic Iranians arrived in southern central Asia and eastern Iran (around the north of present-day Afghanistan) circa 1500 BCE. The

The *Avesta*

Yasna	This is the name of the Zoroastrian texts used for recitation during religious rituals; this portion of the *Avesta* contains the *Gāthās*.
Vispered	("[Prayer to] All the Patrons") This is a ritual text dedicated to the six seasonal feasts and the seven holy days of obligation; special attention is given to the master of all patrons, Ahura Mazdā.
Khorde Avesta	("Little Avesta") This is a four-part miscellany of prayers to various deities: (1) Introductory materials, citing portions of the *Yasna*; (2) five "Praises" or "Prayers" (*Niyāyišns*) to the sun, Mithra, fire, moon, and waters; (3) five "Parts of the Day" (*Gāhs*): hymns praising the deities associated with morning, midday, afternoon, and night; (4) "Blessings" (*Āfringāns*) recited on behalf of the dead at the five days at the end of the year during festivals and to begin and end summer.
Sīrōzas	"Invocations" to the deities associated with the thirty days of the month.
Yašts	An assemblage of twenty-one prose hymns to the central Zoroastrian deities (*yazatas*), such as the Aməša Spəntas, Aša, Mithra, Haoma, the Fravašis, and others.
Videvdâd	("Law Repudiating the Demons") A twenty-two-chapter text on purity and purification rituals; important mythological stories are also in this work.
Assorted Smaller Religious Texts	On the afterlife and the soul; eschatology; law books on priestly activity and institutional organization of the religion; a catechistic manual; Zarathuštra's instructions to his patron Vištāspa; and Vištāspa's reply to Zarathuštra.
Assorted Fragments	These are fragments remaining from lost and existing Avestan sources in Middle Persian (Pahlavi) translations. A notable fragment is the *Frahang-i oim ek*, which is a lexicon of Avestan words and phrases and their Pahlavi translations.

The Gāthās

1. "Song of New Life" (*Ahunavaitī Gāthā*)—Y. 28–34
2. "Song of Wishes" (*Uštavaitī Gāthā*)—Y. 43–46
3. "Song of the Life-Giving Spirit" (*Spəntāmanyu Gāthā*)—Y. 47–50
4. "Song of the Good Command" (*Vohuxšathrā Gāthā*)—Y. 51
5. "Song of the Good Ritual" (*Vahištōišti Gāthā*)—Y. 53

earliest texts of the *Avesta* were originally composed among these people at this time. Texts in Young Avestan began to emerge around the ninth century BCE, continuing until approximately the fourth century BCE.

Zoroastrianism was well established in central and parts of southern Asia by the time the Persian king Cyrus overthrew the Median Empire and founded the Achaemenid Empire (ca. 550–330 BCE), which he ruled for nearly thirty years (see fig. 15.3). Since the nineteenth century CE, when the royal inscriptions of the Achaemenid kings were deciphered, scholars have vigorously debated about whether or not the Achaemenid kings and their subjects were

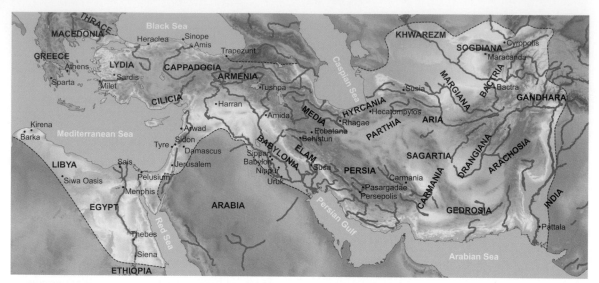

Fig. 15.3 Persia and the Achaemenid Empire ca. 500 BCE.

Zoroastrians. There is evidence in the inscriptions the Achaemenid kings commissioned that suggests the Achaemenids envisioned and actively sought to uphold a cosmology consonant with the *Avesta*. For example, the inscriptions refer to the *Avesta*'s dualistic vision of a world constituted by followers of the Truth or the Lie. Furthermore, the inscriptions portray the power and authority of the Achaemenid kings as entirely ordained by Ahura Mazdā.

Inscriptions of the Achaemenid kings Darius and Xerxes clearly state that worshiping Ahura Mazdā will bring rewards in the present lifetime and after death (see fig. 15.4). Iconography like the king standing before the sacred fire with the winged figure floating above (see fig. 15.2) suggests the Achaemenid kings envisioned themselves to be crucial intermediaries between humanity and Ahura Mazdā, supreme sacrificers in their own right just as Zarathuštra was.

For many people outside of academia, the idea that Zoroastrianism (or Mazdaism) was the official religion of three Persian empires—the Achaemenid Empire, the Arsacid (Parthian)

Empire, and the Sasanian Empire—is far less controversial.[14]

While Zoroastrianism was state-sponsored religion, because it was historically associated with Iranian ethnicity, many non-Iranian subjects did not convert to the religion. As a result, Zoroastrians across the three Persian empires coexisted alongside sizable groups of Jews, Mandaeans, Christians, Manichaeans, and, in eastern Persia, Buddhists. In 636 CE, at the

Fig. 15.4 Cuneiform royal inscriptions at Persepolis.

Fig. 15.5 Investiture of the first Sasanian king, Ardaxšīr I, by Ohrmazd at Naqsh-e Rustam. Ardaxšīr is on the left; his horse stands over the Arsacid ruler, Ardawān. Ohrmazd (Ahura Mazdā), whose horse stands atop Ahreman (Angra Mainyu), hands Ardaxšīr a circular ring, which symbolizes sovereignty.[15]

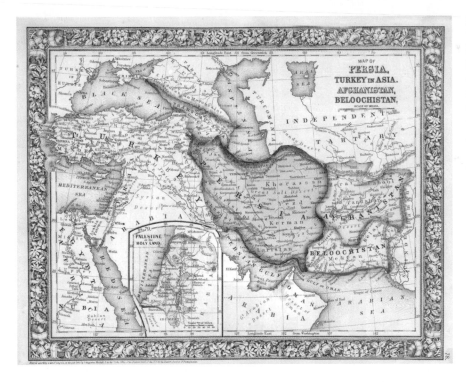

Fig. 15.6 Map of Persia, Turkey, Afghanistan, and Beloochistan [sic] prepared by Samuel Augustus Mitchell in 1886. In Persia, note the three locations, from north to south, of Khorassan, Yezd (Yazd), and Kerman, which factor predominantly in the emigration story of the Parsis from Iran to India.

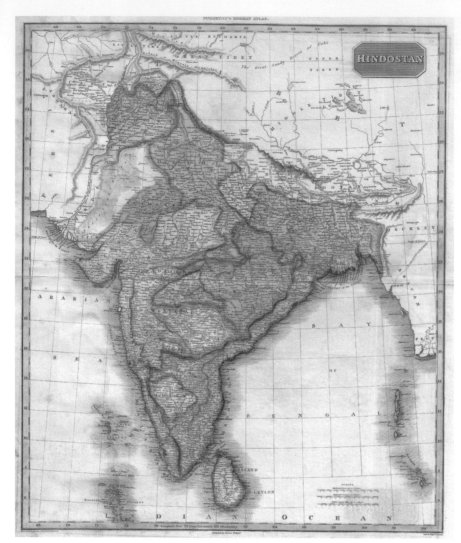

Fig. 15.7 Map of the Indian subcontinent ("Hindostan") prepared by John Pinkerton in 1818. Note the proximity of Persia to the northwest of what is present-day Pakistan and the Indus River Valley, as well as the western state of Gujarat and the Island of Diu, where the Zoroastrian emigrants from Iran arrived in the tenth century CE.

Battle of Qādisiyya, Muslims conquered Iran, forcing many Zoroastrians to hide their religious affiliation, convert, or emigrate.

Zarathuštra

Details of Zarathuštra's life have been debated for centuries. Some people have argued that he was a poet by profession. Others have called him a prophet or priest. Still others refer to him as a merchant. In all likelihood, he occupied a combination of these professions during his lifetime. In the *Gāthās*, Zarathuštra is called a *manthran*, "one who possesses sacred utterances [of Ahura Mazdā]." While many Zoroastrian practitioners recognize Zarathuštra as the composer of the *Gāthās*, some scholars have suggested that he heard these hymns rather than composed them. The literature is quite clear that he was a gifted sacrificer to Ahura Mazdā and that others should follow his example.[16] A suffix on the name of his father, Pourušāspa ("he who has grey horses"), naturally indicates that his father might have worked in an industry tied to horses. Zarathuštra's own name contains the word for "camel," *uštra*. These nominal markers have led some to suggest that Zarathuštra was from a merchant or agriculturalist class, not a priestly class, and that he chose, rather than inherited, a poetic-priestly profession. A common (though contested) translation for the Persian *zarathuštra* is "golden camel." This name could be understood as a kind of foreshadowing of his prophetic career as the reliable and tireless carrier, qualities identified with camels, of Ahura Mazdā's golden or dazzling message. Zarathuštra's family name was Spitāma, which William Malandra has translated as "brilliant or aggressive strength."[17]

The dates of Zarathuštra's lifetime are unclear. Some place his life as early as 1700 BCE, while others place his lifetime a millennium later. Looking at the connected linguistic histories of ancient Iran and India, scholars have noted similarities of language, mythology, and ritual found in the *Avesta* and the Indian *Rig Veda* to posit that Zarathuštra lived around 1200 BCE. The *Rig Veda* has enjoyed more attention from scholars over the last two centuries than the *Avesta* has, for unlike the *Avesta* the entire ten books of the *Rig Veda* are intact today. It has therefore been dated, not to mention its meanings have been amply pored over and discussed, with more certainty than the Iranian materials. Indologists usually date the *Rig Veda* conservatively around 1400–1200 BCE.

Zarathuštra's homeland is also uncertain. He might have been from the Caucasus region, eastern Iran, or central Asian countries such as Bactria and Margiana. Details of his childhood are vague. His mother's name was Dugdōwā,

and a common story passed down through tradition states that when Zarathuštra was born he was laughing. There are some miracle stories from his childhood, which narrate his thwarting of demonic influences among humankind. Most accounts of his life focus on the years between ages thirty and forty when he relocated to the "land of the Aryans," or Iran. In the *Young Avesta*, Zarathuštra is said to have had a wife, Hwōwī, and several sons. After relocating to Iran, he had seven revelatory encounters with Ahura Mazdā and other various divine figures that caused him to accept the Wise Lord's religion.

The Avestan term for "religion" is *daēnā*, which in the *Gāthās* means "good vision" and is closely associated with the Truth (*aša*). The term *daēnā* also refers to one's conscience or "self"; the term is also often mythologized as Daēnā, the goddess of religion. In the *Yasna*, *daēna* is recognized as an object of veneration alongside the speech and doctrine of the prophet: "We worship Zarathustra's words, we worship Zarathustra's religion [*daēnā*], we worship Zarathustra's choice and doctrine" (Y. 16:2).[18]

After accepting the religion of Ahura Mazdā, Zarathuštra proclaimed it publically. In the course of his evangelization, he experienced many failures and setbacks. In time, a high-ranking "king" (*kavi*—also "patron") named Vištaspa, mentioned in the *Gāthās* as someone of "good thought," converted to Zarathuštra's religion. As Zarathuštra's patron, Vištāspa was instrumental in helping the prophet spread the message of the Wise Lord.

By most accounts, Zarathuštra lived until the age of seventy-seven. The manner in which he died, however, is debated. In some texts, such as the *Saddar Bundaheš*, he met a quiet and natural death in Iran. Other texts, such as the *Dēnkard* and *Greater Bundahišn*, state that a man named Brātrōrēs, a member of the *karapan* priestly class from Tūr, assassinated him.[19]

Zoroastrian Pantheon

Ahura Mazdā is the creator all things material and conceptual.[20] The goodness and wisdom of Ahura Mazdā are underscored in the sacred scripture far more than his omnipotence.[21] Ahura Mazdā's first creations were the seven Aməša Spəntas, or "Holy Immortals."

Curiously Ahura Mazdā himself is also one of septet he created, namely, Spənta Mainyu. As seen in the chart below, each Aməša Spən ta presides over and protects one of the seven universal creations in Zoroastrian cosmology. In the *Gāthās*, the six Aməša Spəntas other than Ahura Mazdā are indistinguishable from the parts of creation with which they are associated. Each Aməša Spənta also represents an aspect of Ahura Mazdā and an aspect of the good Zoroastrian devotee. These seven deities also operate as mediators between the faithful and Ahura Mazdā. (See chart below.)

The primary symbol of Zoroastrianism is fire (*ātar*). Fire is especially associated with the Holy Immortal, Aša Vahišta (the Best Order), who among the holy septet is the most connected to ritual activity, particularly the "offering to fire" (*ātaš-zōhr*). After fire, water is the next most purifying substance in Zoroastrianism. The significance of fire in the tradition is possibly linked to ancient Iranian fire cults and Mithra, the god of covenants, oaths, and truths. Mithra was later incorporated into the Zoroastrian pantheon, where he had retained a place of importance.

Ritual Practice

At the core of Zoroastrian ritual practice is *aša* and its upkeep. The task of keeping *aša* in one's every thought, word, and deed extends to every aspect of a practitioner's life. Devotees demonstrate *aša* through: telling in interpersonal relationships and business dealings, nonviolent engagements with nonhuman animals and the environment, as well as honest thinking in one's private time. Zoroastrianism is in this sense a way of life. But there are also specific ritual practices and initiation rites that must be performed in special places and under the command of religious authorities. The primary place of worship is the fire temple, called an Agiary

---

The Holy Immortals and Their Earthly Symbols

The Aməša Spəntas	Holy Immortals	Earthly symbol
Xšathra Vairya	Well-Deserved Command	sky; pestle and mortar; flint knife
Haurvatāt	Wholeness	water
Spənta Ārmaiti	Life-Giving Humility	earth; ritual enclosure
Amərətāt	Long Life	plants (esp. haoma)
Vohu Manah	Good Thought	cattle; sacrificial beast or offering
Spənta Mainyu	Holy Spirit	the just man and Zoroastrian priest
Aša Vahišta	Best Truth or Order	fire; ritual fire

Fig. 15.8 A fire temple in Yazd, Iran.

in India and Atashkadeh in Iran. Specially trained priests look after these temples and their grounds. Their duties include the upkeep of the sacred fires housed in the temples, ensuring they burn in perpetuity.[22] Today there are only eight fire temples that house the highest grade of consecrated fire, the "Fire of Victory" (Ātaš Bahram): seven are in India (in Gujarat and Mumbai) and one is in Iran (in Yazd). To install the fire, thirty-two specially trained priests, called *dasturs*, perform a yearlong ritual that brings together and purifies sixteen different kinds of lower-grade fires.

Most archaeological evidence suggests that Zoroastrians constructed fire temples in all manner of sizes and shapes throughout history.

Today fire temples are generally nondescript, with limited ornamentation on their exteriors. The principal purpose of a temple is not iconographical. It exists to lodge the sacred fire. In addition to the sacred fire, an active temple will almost always have a tank or stream of water on its grounds where the final act of the *yasna* ("sacrifice") is performed in an "offering to water" (*āb-zōhr*).

Zoroastrianism also has important rituals and prohibitions associated with the life cycle. For example, after giving birth, some Zoroastrian families require new mothers to refrain from all religious activities. New mothers are not allowed to go to the fire temple or funerals for a period up to forty days, when postpartum

Fig. 15.9 The initiation ceremony, known among Parsis as *navjote*, loosely meaning "new member of the religious community," and among Iranian Zoroastrians as *sedreh pushi*, "putting on the sudreh-shirt." In this photo, a Zoroastrian priest officiates a navjote.

girl and is traditionally celebrated at the age of fifteen. Modern Zoroastrian initiation is called *navjote* among Indian Parsis and *sedreh pushi* among Iranian Zoroastrians. *Navjote* often occurs at a younger age, sometime before puberty between the ages of seven and eleven, while *sedreh pushi* occurs a bit closer to the traditional age of fifteen.[24] The initiation ceremony is the same for boys and girls; it emphasizes a young person's ability to appreciate the pervasive presence of *aša* and *druj* in the world, and initiates make a commitment to take responsibility for their thoughts, words, and deeds. At an initiation ceremony, a priest welcomes the young boy or girl into the community publicly. He gives the initiate a sacred rope (*kusti*), which should be wrapped three times around the waist over a white cotton undergarment shirt (*sudreh*). The cotton material of the shirt is significant, for it is a marker of the Holy Immortal "Long Life" (Amərərtāt), who is associated with plantlife and the constant cycle of life. The *kusti*-rope must be made from the hair of a lamb, goat, or camel, and it is woven together in seventy-two strands, representing the sections of the *Yasna*. A priest must consecrate the *kusti*-rope and *sudreh*-shirt, and both should be worn every day. The rope should be tied and retied seven times a day, each time accompanied by prayers. The daily multiple wrapping of the rope three times around the waist is seen as a reminder to perform good thoughts, good speech, and good actions day to day. When the *sudreh* and the *kusti* wear out, they should be replaced.

Over the past three centuries, Zoroastrianism's funerary rites for the disposal of a corpse have attracted a great deal of attention, especially from Western scholars and travelers in India and Iran. In Zoroastrian theology, corpses are regarded as highly polluting. Death is seen as "a triumph for evil," when "the corpse demon

bleeding is typically thought to have ended.[23] Among Indian Parsis, a naming ceremony on the sixth day after a child is born is common. Iranian Zoroastrians do not observe this rite. Names for new children in all Zoroastrian communities are often taken from key figures in the *Avesta*, *Shāhnāma* (the national epic of Iran), and from prominent family members.

The Zoroastrian initiation ceremony marks the religious coming of age of a young boy or

Fig. 15.10 A Zoroastrian priest instructs a young boy on the tying of his kusti-rope during a navjote ceremony.

. . . was believed to rush into the body and contaminate all that came in contact with it."[25] Since dead bodies are impure, they should be handled with great care so as not spread their contamination. This includes not interring bodies in the earth, which would contaminate the Holy Immortal linked to the soil, "Life-Giving Humility" (Spənta Ārmaiti). A well-known example of how to dispose of a corpse properly occurs in the *Vidēvdād*:

> "Where, O Ahura Mazdā, shall we carry the body of a dead man, where lay it down?" Then said Ahura Mazdā: "On the highest places, Spitāma Zarathuštra, so that most readily corpse-eating dogs or corpse-eating birds shall perceive it. There these Mazdā-worshippers shall fasten it down,

this corpse, by its feet and hair, [with pegs] of metal or stone or horn. If they do not, corpse-eating dogs and corpse-eating birds will come to drag these bones on to water and plants."[26]

A ritually impure corpse should be disposed of in a manner that is least likely to corrupt the good creations of Ahura Mazdā, which includes water and plants. After the flesh of the corpse has been eaten and picked over by dogs and birds (two animals mentioned often in the *Vidēvdād* and other Middle Persian texts in this capacity), sunshine further purifies the corpse of its impure properties, including hair, nails, and bodily fluids. Afterward, the bones are collected and buried. The *Vidēvdād* also mentions the use of a special rooftop location on a house

Fig. 15.11 A *dakhma* in Yazd, Iran.

Fig. 15.12 A *dakhma* in Diu, India.

called a *dakhma*, which in 1832 Robert Murphy famously called a "tower of silence."[27]

Circular towerlike structures meant for laying out the dead for exposure to the sunlight and vultures, *dakhma* are still used among Parsis in Mumbai, India, and Karachi, Pakistan. In recent years, some Mumbaikars have criticized the practice as epidemiologically unsafe, since the birds feeding on the corpses often transport body parts throughout Mumbai. Increasing development of high-rise buildings overlooking *dakhma* rooftops has also brought much negative attention to the funerary practice. What is more, southern Asian vultures that have traditionally cleansed and disposed of the polluting parts of exposed corpses are no longer as common in greater Mumbai as they once were, leaving corpses left on *dakhma* rooftops unsanitized.[28]

Parsis

The Parsis in India constitute the largest population of Zoroastrians in the world today. There are Parsi communities all over South Asia, but the major centers are in and around Mumbai and the state of Gujarat. Mumbai is home to the Bombay Parsi Panchayat, a mostly charitable organization that also speaks on behalf of the worldwide Parsi community. Parsis in South Asia descend from the families of Iranian Zoroastrians who left Persia around the eighth to ninth centuries CE in search of religious freedom following the Muslim conquest of Iran.

The legendary story of the Parsis' migration abroad is contained in Bahram K.Q. Sanjana's late-sixteenth-century work, the *Story of Sanjan* (*Qesse-ye Sanjān*). According to Parsi tradition, in the early tenth century, a small band of

Zoroastrians from the town of Sanjan in southwestern Khorasan (see fig. 15.6) decided to flee Iran and persecution at the hands of the then dominant Muslims. Following the guidance of an astrologer, they made their way to the port of Hormuzd on the Persian Gulf, where they obtained a ship that took them to the Indian island of Diu. They stayed on Diu for nineteen years before resettling on the coast of Gujarat in western India, where they became known as Parsis, which means "someone from Persia" (see fig. 15.7). Most Parsis believe the emigration occurred in 916 CE and that the Parsis landed on Gujarati soil in 937 CE.

According to the *Story of Sanjan*, a Gujarati king, Jadav Rana, met the Zoroastrians who emigrated from Iran. Jadav Rana eventually granted the Persians permission to settle permanently and practice their religion freely in Gujarat. Some legends about the encounter of the local Hindu ruler and the Persian Zoroastrians say that the Parsis had to abide by five conditions to stay in India:

1. Parsi priests would have to explain their religion to the king.
2. All Parsis would have to abandon their Persian language and adopt the local language.
3. Parsi women would have to give up their traditional dress for the Indian sari.
4. Parsi men would have to lay down their weapons.
5. All Parsis would have to follow local marriage customs.

In general, the history of the Parsis in Gujarat is relatively peaceful. Indeed, from quite early on in their new Indian homeland, the Parsis excelled in mercantilism, especially in textile trading. They coexisted rather well alongside the Hindus in Gujarat, and when the Mughals arrived in India (ca. 1526 CE) and successfully ruled vast regions of the sub-continent, Parsis fought hard but in vain with Hindus against the Muslims. Yet Muslim rule in India was not as difficult on the Parsis as Muslim rule in Iran had been on Zoroastrians, and the Parsis in time thrived as a religious community and in business during the Mughal Empire.

To assist the newly established Zoroastrian communities in India, between the mid-fifteenth to the mid-eighteenth centuries, Zoroastrian priests in Iran (from Yazd and Kerman—see fig. 15.6) regularly sent letters to the Parsis in Gujarat regarding practical religious matters, such as ritual practices, marriage and divorce, purity and pollution, associations with non-Zoroastrians, and the like. These catechistic epistles are known as the *Persian Rivayats*.

Following the arrival of British traders in the seventeenth century, trade commerce in South Asia increased, and Parsis thrived as middlemen between Europeans and Indian agriculturalists, merchants, and landowners. The British established a base in Bombay (now Mumbai), and the Parsis too made this city the center of their community. They quickly became renowned especially for their shipbuilding abilities. A prominent Parsi shipbuilder from Surat, Lowji Nusserwanji Wadia (1702–1774), is seen as the architect of the Bombay dockyards, and the Wadia family of shipwrights and naval architects went on to control the dockyards until the nineteenth century.

Other Parsi families followed the Wadias' lead, and in 1939 Hormusji D. M. Darukhananwala published *Parsi Lustre on Indian Soil* to document Parsi entrepreneurs and their achievements. Parsis have been influential in Bombay, western India, and on the world business market, particularly in commerce, banking,

education, and industry of all sorts. Two of the most famous Parsi businessmen and Indian cultural leaders were Jamsetji Nusserwanji Tata (1839–1904), the famous industrialist and founder of what became the Tata Group of companies, and Dadabhai Naoroji (1825–1917), cofounder of the Indian National Congress, who famously coined the term *swaraj*, "self-rule," that Mahatma Gandhi later deployed in India's Independence Movement.

Factions developed among Parsis in the nineteenth century about how to best implement the teachings of Zarathuštra on the Indian subcontinent. For example, the Ilm-I Khshnoom movement adapted the teachings of Zarathuštra to the tenets of occult philosophy and Theosophy (with an emphasis on Tibetan esoteric Buddhism). These Parsis followed the teachings of Behramshah Shroff and the uniquely Indian religious principles of Jain, Buddhist, and Hindu design, such as vegetarianism, recognition of rebirth and redeath, among other things. Ilm-I Khshnoom especially gained adherents after the British left South Asia. At the same time, there are many Parsis who follow a more liberal, Protestant-style interpretation of Zoroastrianism. These Parsis were directly influenced by the presence of Western-style education in India brought by British colonialism.

A View of Creation and Divinity

We close this chapter with an excerpt from a hymn in the *Gāthās* (*Yasna* 44.3-16, from the "Song of Wishes," *Uštavaitī Gāthā*). This passage deals with the Zoroastrian view of creation and the divinity of the world, and it highlights Zarathuštra's directness and inquisitiveness before Ahura Mazdā.

(3) This I ask Thee, tell me truly, Lord. Who in the beginning, at creation, was Father of Order (Aša)? Who established the course of sun and stars? Through whom does the moon wax, then wane? This and yet more, O Mazdā, I seek to know. (4) This I ask Thee, tell me truly, Lord. Who has upheld the earth from below, and the heavens from falling? Who (sustains) the waters and plants? Who harnessed swift steeds to wind and clouds? Who, O Mazdā, is Creator of Good Purpose? (5) This I ask Thee, tell me truly, Lord. What craftsman created light and darkness? What craftsman created both sleep and activity? Through whom exist dawn, noon and eve, which remind the worshipper of his duty? . . . (7) This I ask Thee, tell me truly, Lord. Who fashioned honoured Devotion together with Power? Who made the son respectful in heed to the father? By these (questions), O Mazdā, I help (men) to discern Thee as Creator of all things through the Holy Spirit. . . . (16) This I ask Thee, tell me truly, Lord. Who will be victorious to protect through Thy teaching those who are the progeny in my house? As Healer of the world, promise to us a judge. Then let Hearkening come to him with Good Purpose, O Mazdā—to him whomsoever Thou dost wish.[29]

◆ **STUDY AND DISCUSSION QUESTIONS**

1. Who was Zarathuštra, and in which part of the world did he likely live? Discuss Zarathuštra's role in the history of Zoroastrianism, and explain why he is often compared to important religious figures in other world religions, such as Moses and Muhammad. Are such comparisons defensible? Why or why not?

2. Zoroastrianism presents a fairly clear view of the nature of reality, and the religion accordingly offers certain straightforward choices for Zoroastrian practitioners concerning how best to live in the world. Using some of the terminology presented in the chapter, how would you describe Zoroastrian cosmology and ethics?

3. Who are the Parsis? Identify two to three points in Parsi history that highlight some of the ways in which their experiences and practices of Zoroastrianism are different from those of Iranian Zoroastrians.

◆ **KEY TERMS**

Agiary

Ahreman

Ahura Mazdā

Aməša Spəṇtas

Angra Mainyu

aša

ašāvan

ātar

Ātaš Bahrām

Atashkadeh

ātaš-zōhr

Avesta

Dēnkard

drəgvant

druǰ

fravaši

Gāthās

gētīg

kusti

manthra

mēnōg
navjote
Ohrmazd
Parsi
Persian Rivayats
saošyant
Shāhnāma
sudreh
Yasna
Zarathuštra

◆ FOR FURTHER READING

Anklesaria, Behramgore T., trans. *The Holy Gâthâs of Zarathustra*. Bombay: H. T. Anklesaria, 1953.

Boyce, Mary. *Zoroastrianism: Its Antiquity and Constant Vigor*. Costa Mesa, CA: Mazda, 1992.

———. *Zoroastrians: Their Religious Beliefs and Practices*. London: Routledge, 2001.

———, ed. and trans. *Textual Sources for the Study of Zoroastrianism*. Chicago: University of Chicago Press, 1984.

Briant, Pierre. *From Cyrus to Alexander: A History of the Persian Empire*. Translated by Peter T. Daniels. Winona Lake, IN: Eisenbrauns, 2002.

Garthwaite, Gene R. *The Persians*. Malden, MA: Blackwell, 2007.

Gershevitch, Ilya. *The Cambridge History of Iran*. Cambridge: Cambridge University Press, 1985.

Hinnells, John R. *Persian Mythology*. New rev. ed. New York: Peter Bedrick Books, 1985.

———. *The Zoroastrian Diaspora: Religion and Migration*. Oxford: Oxford University Press, 2005.

Insler, Stanley, trans. *The Gāthās of Zarathustra*. Leiden: E.J. Brill, 1975.

Kellens, Jean. *Essays on Zarathustra and Zoroastrianism*. Edited and translated by Prods Oktor Skjærvø. Costa Mesa, CA: Mazda, 2000.

Kriwaczek, Paul. *In Search of Zarathustra: The First Prophet and the Ideas that Changed the World*. New York: Alfred A. Knopf, 2003.

Lincoln, Bruce. *Religion, Empire, and Torture: The Case of Achaemenian Persia, with a Postscript on Abu Ghraib*. Chicago: University of Chicago Press, 2007.

Luhrman, Tanya. *The Good Parsi: The Fate of a Colonial Elite in a Postcolonial Society*. Cambridge, MA: Harvard University Press, 1994.

Malandra, William. *An Introduction to Ancient Iranian Religion: Readings from the Avesta and Achaemenid Inscriptions*. Minneapolis: University of Minnesota Press, 1983.

Rose, Jenny. *Zoroastrianism: A Guide for the Perplexed*. New York: Continuum, 2011.

———. *Zoroastrianism: An Introduction*. London: I. B. Tauris, 2011.

Skjærvø, Prods Oktor. *The Spirit of Zoroastrianism*. New Haven: Yale University Press, 2011.

Stausberg, Michael. *Zarathustra and Zoroastrianism*. Translated by Margret Preisler-Weller. London: Equinox, 2008.

◆ NOTES

1. The name Ahura Mazdā has long been translated into English as "Wise Lord." In his numerous pioneering works on ancient Iranian religions, Prods Oktor Skjærvø has argued that "All-knowing Lord" is a better and more literal rendering. See, for example, *The Spirit of Zoroastrianism* (New Haven: Yale University Press, 2011), 13.

2. Laurie Goodstein, "Zoroastrians Keep the Faith, and Keep Dwindling," *New York Times*, September 6, 2006.

3. This passage from the *Yasna* is a slightly edited version of Mary Boyce's translation in *Zoroastrians: Their Beliefs and Practices* (London: Routledge, 1979), 35.

4. Translation from Michael Stausberg, *Zarathustra and Zoroastrianism: A Short Introduction*, trans. Margret Preisler-Weller (London: Equinox, 2008), 8.

5. Ibid, 9.

6. The standard English translation of Avestan *pairidaēza* and Old Persian *pairidaida* is "paradise." Bruce Lincoln has convincingly shown, however, that the original Persian meaning of these terms was literally "walled enclosure" and, generally, "walled garden or game park." These enclosures held important religious significance, he argues, and they were built throughout the Achaemenid Empire. See *Religion, Empire, and Torture: The Case of Achaemenian Persia, with a Postscript on Abu Ghraib* (Chicago: University of Chicago Press, 2007), 78–80, 83–84.

7. Jenny Rose, *Zoroastrianism: A Guide for the Perplexed* (New York: Continuum, 2011), 11.

8. For a compelling radio documentary on in the dwindling population of Indian Zoroastrians, i.e., the Parsis, and how the community at the turn of the twenty-first century was struggling to the stem the ebb of its numbers, consult Michael Sullivan, "Parsis," *All Things Considered*, National Public Radio, 28 December 2000, available at www.npr.org. For a concise overview of the ambit of religious political views in Zoroastrian communities today, see Stuasberg, *Zoroastrianism and Zarathustra*, 5–6.

9. For example, the work of Thomas Hyde, a late-seventeenth-early-eighteenth-century scholar of Oriental Studies at Oxford, especially *Veterum Persarum et Pathorum et Medorum religionis historia*, presented many in the West with a first glimpse of the ancient religion of Ahura Mazdā and Zarathuštra. Not long after Hyde's famous study, the work of A. H. Anquetil du Perron, a young French scholar who traveled to Gujarat, India, in the mid-eighteenth century to collect manuscripts and translate the *Vendīdād* ("The Law Repudiating the Demons"), was very influential in bringing knowledge of Zoroastrianism and Zarathuštra to people in the West.

10. Jenny Rose, *The Image of Zoroaster: The Persian Mage Through European Eyes* (New York: Biblioteca Persica, 2000), 2.

11. For the following details on the Avestan texts, I have generally followed the sketch of Jean Kellens, "Avesta: The Holy Book of the Zoroastrians," *Encyclopædia Iranica*, Online Edition, August 17, 2011, available at http://www.iranicaonline.org/articles/avesta-holy-book.

12. Foremost in this regard is Skjærvø's *The Spirit of Zoroastrianism*, which contains a number of masterful translations from the Avestan and Pahlavi sources.

13. On the *Gāthās*, see Helmut Humbach, "Gathas I," *Encyclopædia Iranica*, Online Edition, December 15, 2000, available at http://www.iranicaonline.org/articles/gathas-i-texts, and William Malandra, "Gathas II," *Encyclopædia Iranica*, Online Edition, December 15, 2000, available at http://www.iranicaonline.org/articles/gathas-ii-translations.

14. Alexander the Great overthrew King Darius and the Achaemenid Empire, which ushered in Hellenistic rule (the Seleucid Empire) in Persia for almost a century (ca. 331–247 BCE).

15. On the investiture of the first Sasanian king, see Touraj Daryaee, *Sasanian Iran (224–651 CE)* (Costa Mesa, CA: Mazda, 2008), especially 3–6, 10–15.

16. That said, some scholars have suggested that Zarathuštra is a mythical figure, and that a human founder of Zoroastrianism never existed. See, for example, the character analysis of Zarathuštra in Jean Kellens, *Essays on*

Zarathustra and Zoroastrianism, trans. P. Oktor Skjærvø (Costa Mesa, CA: Mazda, 2000), 83–94.

17. On the possible etymology of Zarathuštra's name, see William Malandra, *An Introduction to Ancient Iranian Religion: Readings from the Avesta and Achaemenid Inscriptions* (Minneapolis: University of Minnesota Press, 1983), 17–18.

18. Religion here and in later verses of the *Yasna* is something that, as Michael Stausberg has suggested, "can be 'chosen,' it can be 'praised,' it can be 'confessed,' one can 'gird' oneself with it, 'hear' (or 'understand') it, 'offer oneself' to it, but also 'renounce it.' One has to think, speak and act according to the *daēnā*. And one also has to 'remember it'" (*Zarathustra and Zoroastrianism*, 32). An excellent study of the Middle Persian (i.e., Pahlavi) concept of *dēn* in Zoroastrianism may be found in Yuhan Sohrab-Dinshaw Vevaina, "Enumerating the Dēn: Textual Taxonomies, Cosmological Deixis, and Numerological Speculations in Zoroastrianism," *History of Religions* 50, no. 2 (November, 2010): 111–43.

19. On the legends associated with Zarathuštra's violent death, see Mary Boyce, *Zoroastrianism: Its Antiquity and Constant Vigor* (Costa Mesa, CA: Mazda, 1992), 14–16.

20. The terms "material" (*gētīg*) and "conceptual" (*mēnōg*) are very important and much discussed in Zoroastrian theology and comology.

21. In the literature, in fact, Ahura Mazdā's power is frequently portrayed as limited by the forces, activities, and demonic cohort of Angra Mainyu, the evil principle in Zoroastrianism.

22. Initiation into the Zoroastrian priesthood among the Parsis can begin as early as age nine. There is a scholarly component to the process of becoming a Zoroastrian priest, involving the memorization of religious texts and purification rituals, and it can take up to three years to complete. After this initial stage, one is ordained with the title of Ervad. An Ervad priest is not entitled to work as a professional ritual priest, however. To perform professional ritual activities in the fire temples, a second ordination is required, at which stage one receives the title of Mobed. Above the level of Mobed is Dastur, which is the highest level of priesthood in the Zoroastrian tradition. Dastur priests are frequently consulted on issues of theology and ritual performance; on special occasions, they officiate marriage and funeral ceremonies. Dastur priests typically supervise the work of Mobed priests at fire temples with the Ātaš Bahrām fire. The New Persian term *dastūr* (MP. *dstwr*) has many meanings. Among other things, the term means "person with authority (or power)." It most often refers to authority or power of a religious nature and is frequently qualified by the phrase *dēn āgāh*, "well-versed in religious matters."

23. Rose, *Zoroastrianism: A Guide for the Perplexed*, 146.

24. Ibid., 148.

25. Mary Boyce, "Corpse," *Encyclopædia Iranica*, Online Edition, December 15, 1993, available at http://www.iranicaonline.org/articles/corpse-disposal-of-in-zoroastrianism.

26. Ibid.

27. The original meaning of the Avestan root *dakhma-* is unknown. Mary Boyce has suggested that "the Zoroastrian word 'dakhma' (coming through '*dafma' from an IE verbal root dhṃbh 'bury') meant originally, it seems, a grave." *Zoroastrians: Their Religious Beliefs and Practices* (London: Routledge, 1979), 13–14.

28. See Michael Sullivan, "Vultures in India," *Weekend Edition Sunday*, National Public Radio, December 17, 2000, available at www.npr.org.

29. Mary Boyce, ed. and trans., *Textual Sources for the Study of Zoroastrianism* (Chicago: University of Chicago Press, 1984), 34.

CHAPTER 16

New Religious Movements

Marie W. Dallam

Introduction

This chapter will raise several key issues relevant to understanding the range and scope of new religious movements (NRMs). It will consider what NRMs are, and it will explore some of the most common concerns about them. Because NRMs are so varied in history, belief, structure, and influence, the chapter deliberately uses a wide variety of examples from what can all be considered NRMs. No single group embodies every characteristic, and none can be singled out as representative of the entire phenomenon. There are, however, some common issues that arise across religious boundaries.

When most people hear the word *cult* today, they sense that something negative and harmful is being discussed. But this was not always the meaning of the word. The formal religious studies definition of a "cult" is a neutral descriptive term that refers to a small community of religious believers. The term *cult* derives from the Latin term *cultus*, referring to the ritual behavior that showed "care" (*cultus*) for a god, hero, or sacred precinct in the form of prayer, offerings, ceremonies, sacrifices, and other religious observances. For example, when people speak of the "cult of Saint Brigid," a

Celtic offshoot of the Roman Catholic tradition, they are using the formal religious studies definition to refer to a para-institutional worship group that is focused on the care of a particular saint.

Most people today are more familiar with a different use of the word *cult* that refers to a group of people who are thought to be following false religious teachings, who may be dangerous, and whose practice is generally illegitimate in nature. When people use the word this way, they sometimes describe characteristics of a group, and other times they describe the functions of a group, and still others use it as a combination of both. As a result, this particular use of the word *cult* is ambiguous.

These mixed uses of the term *cult* become problematic for those who want to look seriously at forms of religious belief and practice outside the mainstream without assuming a negative standpoint. Many scholars have determined that neutral terminology, which does not imply value judgments, is needed to describe religions that differ from majority practices. Today, most scholars prefer the term *new religious movements* to categorize groups that are outside of the mainstream. This term also helps overcome translation difficulties. In several languages used on the European continent, words that sound like the English *sect* are equivalent in meaning to the negative word *cult*. Hence, when someone says *sekte* in German or *secte* in French, the word holds approximately the same meaning that the pejorative *cult* does in English, rather than being an equivalent for the more neutral English word *sect*. A standard term, *new religious movements*, helps overcome these issues.

Fig. 16.1 A Church of Scientology in Los Angeles.

Fig. 16.2 Santeria practitioners in Havana, Cuba, participate in the Cajon de Muertos ceremony.

Bearing Witness to Repentance

The following characterization of a Jehovah's Witness helps to express the views of a person who joins a religion that is outside of the mainstream, as well as showing that "mainstream religion" is a relative concept.

"My husband Will and I are members of the local Kingdom Hall. I grew up Baptist, and he was sort-of a Methodist, but neither of us felt very strongly about our faith as young people. After a few years of marriage we were beginning to lose our close connection, and I felt very confused about my role in life. When a Jehovah's Witness rang the doorbell one afternoon and asked me, "Are you happy in your life today?" I was on the verge of tears, admitting, "No." She and her witnessing partner came inside, and they began to open my eyes to a new way of understanding God and my life through the Bible. Will and I began attending Congregational Bible

Study together on weeknights, and eventually we became regular attendees of the Public Meetings on Sundays. We appreciated the careful scripture study that Witnesses emphasized—we had never had all of our questions about God answered this way before! We grew closer as a couple, and our renewed faith also renewed our marriage. Together, we took steps to change some of our sinful habits, such as drinking. We sought repentance for our past sins, and determined that we both wanted to dedicate our lives to serving Jehovah above all worldly things. The following year, we were baptized at our District Convention.

"When Will's company offered him a transfer to Provo, Utah, we looked forward to a change of pace. But we didn't think about what a religious shock it would be! In our Brooklyn, New York, neighborhood, our religion was large, with many congregations to choose from. Other Witnesses lived in my neighborhood and there were often Witnesses I didn't know giving out literature near the subway. But in Provo, where most people are members of the Latter Day Saint Church, I feel like an outcast. People are not familiar with my faith and they treat it like it's something very strange. I made friends with a neighbor but when she found out that I don't vote because of my religious beliefs, she started giving me the cold shoulder. She also didn't understand that I could be a Christian and not celebrate Christmas. What's funny is that in New York I never felt unusual because of my religion, but in a different part of the country I suddenly feel like I'm part of an exotic group. Now I'm shy to even mention it to people. Nevertheless, I know that doing God's will is my primary purpose here on Earth, so I hope my faith will keep me strong as I continue facing new challenges."

This sketch demonstrates two points. First, the process of joining any religion is often gradual and involves careful thought and preparation. There are almost always distinct steps of commitment through which potential members test out what membership will mean for them personally, though outsiders may or may not be aware of that process. Second, the designation of particular religions as "unusual" or "normal" is extremely subjective and can depend on a wide variety of social factors. In this particular case, a simple geographical change made the woman suddenly aware that her faith group occupied a minority position relative to the surrounding population, and that shift resulted in her feelings of discomfort.

Reporting on the Children of God

In the United States in the 1970s, public fear exploded around a particular new religion called The Children of God (COG). Founded by a Christian pastor named Moses David

Fig. 16.3 Jehovah's Witnesses evangelize by going door to door, inviting people to discuss their message.

Fig. 16.4 An artistic replica of the Golden Plates, Breastplate, and Urim and Thummin as described by Latter-day Saint prophet Joseph Smith.

Berg, COG was an independent communal group that attracted young people to its vehement biblical message. COG had various beliefs and practices that made nonmembers uncomfortable, and popular media reports typically focused on its most outrageous aspects. Largely because of the imbalanced investigation and reporting, most members of the general public wound up with limited and negative impressions of the group.

Quotes from news sources demonstrate the unfolding public characterization of COG and offer a window into the outsider view in its first decade. For example, the *New York Times* reported in 1972 that parents said their children were kept in a "slave-like atmosphere" when they became members of COG. As one of many articles it published on the theme of

"deception" in COG, *Christianity Today* noted in 1973 that from the first time a new person encounters COG, "his mind is controlled by outside forces. . . . Fear is added as a motivating factor." In 1974, news sources across the nation printed details of an eighteen-month investigation of COG by the New York State Attorney General's office that declared COG was a "fraud-tinged cult" that encouraged young people to drop out of school, have "bitter hatred of parents," and become "subservient to the whims or desires" of COG leaders. The *Los Angeles Times* added its own impressions of the report by saying COG was guilty of "sexual abuse . . . rape, kidnapping, tax evasion, draft dodging, [and] brainwashing." Implying that COG members had something to hide, in 1975 the *Washington Post* characterized them as "vague, evasive, and obscure in answering questions. Their responses are identical as if cued. They have a talent for exaggeration."

Pressure stemming from all the negative attention in the United States caused the group to begin relocating overseas. Following a Christian missionary impulse, COG sent members to countries in Europe, Asia, and South America with the goal of permanently removing the group from the hostile American environment. Although this was successful in some places, in other locations the public reception was equally hostile. For example, *The Times* of London declared that COG practices used "prostitution as a means of conversion." In Thailand, reports insinuated that COG members were responsible for the murder of a *Bangkok Post* journalist who was publishing an article that referred to the group as "a parasitic cult of Bible-pounding automatons" who "preach hate."

Certainly, there were points of genuine contention between COG members and outsiders, as well as problems within the group itself. Over the years, COG underwent extensive self-scrutiny, which led to several phases of restructuring to eliminate ethical violations within the movement. Now called The Family International (TFI), the group has a clear mission and a carefully delineated governance structure to support it, but many people are only aware of its more sordid past. Popular media outlets are a main source of information for outsiders looking to understand unfamiliar groups, but inflammatory characterizations are unhelpful for gaining a balanced perspective. The press about COG in those early years turned into a more pervasive and generalized anticult hype in which stereotypes were taken to extremes. In response, sociologists David G. Bromley and Anson D. Shupe were compelled to publish a parody piece in an academic journal in 1979, titled "The Tnevnoc Cult." The article proceeded as a formal sociological description of a secluded group that had "totalistic control"

Fig. 16.5 A member of the Nation of Islam sells products including the newspaper, *The Final Call*.

over those who joined, required participation in "compulsory group rituals," had a "rigid, all-encompassing code of behavior," and caused "cult-induced personality changes." Careful, thoughtful readers were able to identify that this "communal, sectarian group affiliated with a large and powerful international religious organization" was in fact a description of a socially accepted form of monastic life: *Tnevnoc* is "convent" spelled backward. The article demonstrated how evaluations of religion cannot be made in a vacuum; a balanced understanding must include the perspectives of both outsiders and insiders, as well as awareness about the larger historical context.

Changing Approaches to New Religious Movements

Before studying NRMs themselves, it is important to understand how the academic world frames the subject. The interdisciplinary field of NRM studies encompasses many diverse religious groups and welcomes scholars from different areas of expertise: sociologists, historians, anthropologists, and specialists in particular cultures and subject areas. One of the challenges is in finding enough common ground, especially given that the boundaries of the term *NRM* can vary widely. Considering that so many religious groups can be categorized as NRMs, what exactly links the information to make it one area of study? A brief history of the terminology will help clarify what the term *NRM* tries to encompass.

Both academic and popular audiences have often evaluated newer religions simply by contrasting them with forms of organized religion with which they are already familiar. Sociologists of the mid-twentieth century contrasted "sects" and "cults" from "religion," using the origins of the group as their measuring stick. In other words, if a group began as a break-off from an established religion, it was considered a sect; if a group had started completely independently—for example, it was based on a new prophecy, a new teacher, or a new god—it was considered a cult. This definition seems good on the face of things but when considered more carefully it can be problematic. For example, the term *cult* winds up describing a large number of groups that are drastically different from each other but are lumped together merely because of the way they began. For example, Scientology, Theosophy, and Raelians would all be considered part of the same category, "cults," because they have independent origins, while the "sect" category would include groups like the Oneida Community, Christian Science, and Santeria because they all stemmed from more established religious traditions. With this definition, groups are categorized not by what they are today but on how they started, no matter how long ago, and there is no mode for change in the schema; hence, once a cult, always a cult.

A different approach to distinguishing cults and sects from established religions is to isolate particular attributes common across categories. Scholars have made numerous attempts at this, but most have been unsuccessful. Many attributes are either too vague to identify (e.g., the group is manipulative); other attributes don't actually describe anything because they are phrased in the negative (e.g., the members don't believe Jesus was God); some contain a confusing mix of attributes, such as beliefs and functions (e.g., they have a new sacred text and they are deceptive in recruitment); and other lists contain too much personal bias (e.g., they believe in a false god). Some scholars have argued that the single attribute of being *new* is

particularly relevant, thus referring to the actual chronological age of the group. Age is important because groups pass through predictable stages of social development as they grow; therefore, very different groups of a similar age may exhibit similar characteristics that can be compared. Although not all scholars agree with this idea, the term *NRM* grew out of this theory and became the term that stuck.

A more recent approach to categorization is a visual spectrum, in which established religions lie on one end, marginalized religions are at the other, and sectarian religions are located in the middle. With a spectrum, there is an assumption that religions may move in any direction based on changing circumstances; no group is ever permanently locked into a category. One important variable to consider when locating a group on the spectrum is the external society: where is the group geographically located, and what is the assumed religious culture in that place? A second important variable is the group's internal characteristics: what are the basic beliefs and practices, behaviors and rituals? When we consider the external society and the internal characteristics in combination, we can place a group on the spectrum to determine whether it is a marginalized religion, an established religion, or something in between. Its location can easily change, however, if a key belief or practice changes, or if the group moves from one geographic place to another. This model, though not without flaws, allows us to carefully consider what, for example, causes a group to be labeled a "cult" in 1940 but a "religion" in 2013, or labeled a "religion" in one country and a "sect" in another.

Rather than trying to settle definitional questions once and for all, scholars have politely agreed to accept that the NRM area of study includes a range of groups that can be new in

Fig. 16.6 Outdoor baptisms were especially popular during the "Jesus Movement" era of the 1960s–1970s.

age and/or marginal in social status. The expectation is that there is something to be gained by examining common experiences and developmental paths of these alternative forms of religion, and in the end, definitions should serve to focus individualized studies rather than to keep ideas apart.

Joining and Leaving New Religious Movements

Many people have tried to formulate theories about who joins NRMs, why they do it, and how it happens. Among these theories are that

weak or gullible people are tricked into joining; that educated and privileged people deliberately seek out countercultural lifestyles; that seeker "types" constantly join and leave new groups in repeating cycles; that people gravitate toward groups that help them deal with serious personal problems, such as emotional, psychological, or financial ones; and that youth dabble in NRMs as an experiment in finding themselves. None of these theories is universally or comprehensively true, yet surely people have joined NRMs for all of these reasons. It is statistically difficult to pinpoint answers to many affiliation questions. The concept of "membership" is not construed uniformly from group to group, people are not always able to express why they have joined, and stereotypes like "gullible" and "seeker" are objectively difficult to measure. However, several qualitative points can help explain factors that cause people to join and leave NRMs.

It is clear that relatively few people are born and raised in NRMs, and therefore most members deliberately join—a process called *affiliation*. Many people also later choose to leave NRMs, or disaffiliate. The affiliation process typically involves several steps that are common whether a person is joining a new religion, a mainstream religion, or some other kind of voluntary association. It often begins with a yearning for something different that causes a person to open himself up to new ideas and new people. Once the person has identified a group that interests him, he typically tests the waters with gradually increasing participation in activities, socialization with members, and education about the group's ideas, behaviors, and expectations. The initial yearning for something other is not always disclosed to friends and family, and it can exist as a latent desire for many years. As a result, it may appear that someone has "suddenly" joined an NRM, when

Fig. 16.7 Members of the Moorish Science Temple of America, one of the earliest organized forms of Islam in the United States, pose for a photo in 1928.

in fact his conversion is the culmination of a long internal process of exploration.

Like individual paths to conversion, disaffiliation can be motivated by many things. When a person begins to think about leaving a group, she must weigh the advantages of staying against the disadvantages in a kind of cost-benefit analysis, and for that reason the factors that affect her decision to disaffiliate are collectively called "exit costs." Such costs are frequently social and emotional, such as friends one might lose by leaving, but in cases of communal living these might also be literal financial costs. Whatever the impetus, available statistics suggest that the majority of people who leave gradually withdraw in an uncontested process, and that later on most look back on the experience and consider it to have been either positive or neutral.

Sometimes, however, people leave an NRM in a dramatic and contested way, possibly caused by their anger with something that has occurred in the group. These people may become "apostates": ex-members who find meaning and purpose in decrying the NRM and who seek recognition and validation for their perspective.

How much attention they garner depends on more than just the validity of their claims. Even among marginalized forms of religion, there are groups with more social legitimacy than others, and this can affect how much the general public will pay attention to apostates. Perhaps not surprisingly, there is often an inverse relationship between the amount of social clout an NRM has and the amount of public impact a single apostate can make. For example, a lone defector from a religious group that wields social power, such as the Latter-day Saint Church, will probably be ignored by the public. In contrast, an individual defector from the more controversial (and polygamist) Fundamentalist Latter-day Saint Church will likely be taken more seriously when she makes complaints about life inside the religion.

Does the Term *Brainwashing* Explain Anything?

The brainwashing explanation for why people join NRMs dates to the 1970s. Starting in the 1960s and lasting about a decade, there was an upsurge in religious fervor among young Americans, and many became involved in alternative religious practices. Rather than trying to understand what appeal these new religions held for their loved ones, or trying to learn about the new beliefs and practices and then evaluate them, some concerned individuals (especially parents) jumped to the conclusion that people had been manipulated into joining against their will. Trickery was the only explanation that they could envision for what they interpreted as drastic changes in religious belief and behavior.

Fig. 16.8   Hare Krishna devotees sing on the streets of Leipzig in hopes of interesting passersby in their faith.

Employing terminology that came from a 1950s study of POWs in Asia, writers began to call this process of involvement in NRMs "brainwashing," and it was considered a totalistic program of thought reform.

There is a scholarly divide over brainwashing. On one side, brainwashing proponents believe that it is a scientific process by which leaders and/or members of an NRM attack a person's sense of self in an effort to undermine their beliefs, their defenses, and their overall stability. Victims begin to do whatever they are told, unaware that they are no longer making freewill decisions. The process of brainwashing is believed to be supported by social and environmental conditions designed to cause stress, such as sleep deprivation and nutrition control. However, the evidence of thought-reform programs is anecdotal rather than statistically viable, and critics say the few studies available have been tainted by sampling bias.

On the other side, brainwashing opponents do not believe that a scientific process such as brainwashing exists within NRMs. Rather, they believe that most people make relatively independent decisions to join religions through conversion processes and that to claim their actions are caused by deliberate programs of thought reform is both disrespectful and simplistic. The brainwashing theory assumes that NRM joiners are always passive victims rather than active agents who make choices that other people might not agree with. While they accept that vulnerable people can sometimes be pressured or manipulated into making choices they would not otherwise select, they do not accept that it is possible to conduct mass-scale overhaul of people's entire thinking processes.

The prominence of the different points of view varies around the globe. In the United States, for example, testimony about scientific brainwashing is no longer accepted in courts and its proponents are in the academic minority, but in some European countries brainwashing is still touted as a potentially credible theory. In many ways, it is a politically charged ideological debate about scientific theories that have not been thoroughly tested. One of the reasons for the lack of testing is that brainwashing theory is approximate, at times appearing to describe the process by which people join NRMs and at others appearing to be a structure that causes people to stay in NRMs against their will. There are also clear ethical problems with trying to set up any study that could measure it. What is most important is that all people should have independence and autonomy to choose their own religious paths, no matter how unorthodox.

Charismatic Leaders

When some people use the phrase *charismatic leader*, they are referring to the religious studies concept of *charism*, or special, God-given powers. Many Christian traditions, for example, believe in gifts of the Holy Spirit, such as glossolalia and spiritual healing. Charism is found across religious divides: the charism of Elijah Muhammad of the Nation of Islam, for example, manifested itself as prophecy. Other people use the term *charismatic leader* in reference to the English vernacular *charisma*, which describes a very compelling person. In this sense, a charismatic leader is acknowledged to have special qualities that set him or her apart and that might include great intelligence, wisdom or insight, good speaking abilities, or simply a compelling personality. Leaders such as Billy Graham and Malcolm X can be considered charismatic leaders in this sense.

Fig. 16.9   Members of a neopagan group of Druids participate in a ritual at Stonehenge.

"Charismatic leaders" are no more ubiquitous in NRMs than in mainstream forms of religion. And regardless of which definition is used, a religious leader depends on the validation of followers to secure and maintain his or her position. If followers do not believe in the person's special gifts, or if they do not recognize that the person has exceptional qualities, that person cannot possibly be a successful leader. In the absence of a strong leader, people will fall away from the group, or they may turn to a different member for guidance—one who could ultimately ascend to the top leadership position. Charismatic leadership, then, is perhaps best understood as a quality of the relationship between a recognized leader and his or her most ardent followers.

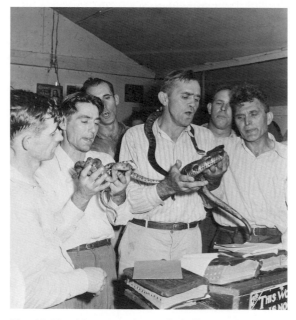

Fig. 16.10   A Pentecostal man who believes in the charismatic gift of snake handling engages in worship.

What people fear about charismatic leaders is that because followers validate their special qualities and seem willing to do anything asked of them, leaders may wind up having unrestricted power that they can then exploit for their own gain. This should be recognized as a potential problem in *any* religious group, no matter how old or new, mainstream or marginalized. It is normal for religious people to seek teachers and leaders, and it is normal for a person or small group of persons to occupy the places of power. But every power structure needs a system of checks and balances to ensure that the group is being run in a rational, thoughtful way rather than running on the whims of an individual under the guise of divine direction. The most dangerous sort of charismatic leadership can be found when individuals give over so much control to leaders that they cease thinking critically for themselves. Some Westerners would argue, for example, that a case like this was found with Reverend Moon of the Unification Church, who encouraged countless numbers of followers to enter into marriages that he arranged without personal knowledge of the individuals involved.

There is also a pattern of the routinization of charisma. The founding leaders of many NRMs have been considered charismatic in the sense of having a heightened connection to God, but as the religious group develops and stabilizes, the charisma appears to transfer to the office of leader and is no longer specific to the actual founder. Furthermore, while the charisma becomes more institutionalized, it concurrently diminishes in importance within the group. Routinization of charisma can be observed, for example, in the United House of Prayer for All People: founder Daddy Grace was considered to have a special connection with Jesus that included healing powers, but after his death in 1960 the quality was routinized. The title "Daddy" now signifies to followers that charismatic power has been held by successive House of Prayer leaders Daddy McCollough, Daddy Madison, and Daddy Bailey, but concurrently

Fig. 16.11 Jim Jones, the founder of the Peoples Temple, poses with children in Jonestown, Guyana.

Fig. 16.12 Members of the Unification Church are married by the Reverend Sun Myung Moon.

its members have deemphasized its importance. The routinization pattern can be observed as a historical trend in older established religions just as it can in religions that are chronologically young today.

Communal Living

Communal living is a lifestyle choice made by many new societies, not all of which are religious. Though there are many different types of communal arrangements, some of which hold all possessions in common and others in which some personal property is retained, in the West it is an inherently countercultural living arrangement, with the exception of forms such as monasteries and intentional communities.

NRM-based communes have been a particular concern for outsiders who are skeptical about unrelated people living in an intimate environment, and even more of a concern when all resources become common possession. Joining one's resources with those of a group means that, should the person later decide to disaffiliate, it may be financially difficult to achieve. However, communal living in NRMs provides constant support and reinforcement of a person's religious beliefs and lifestyle, which for many is an inviting and invaluable way to live.

Christian-derived NRM communes are based on the communal ideal articulated in the book of Acts (Acts 2:44-47 and 4:32-35). Such groups usually have numerous ways that they attempt to return to early Christian practices, and this typically includes an economic relationship. Jesus People USA (JPUSA), for example, is a communal NRM that sprang from the "Jesus Movement" of the 60s and 70s. Although today it has become a relatively mainstream form of Christianity, JPUSA still maintains a communal apartment building in Chicago that houses about five hundred members. They own businesses in common and pool resources in an effort to eradicate class divisions.

Communes based on Eastern religions often stem from close associations formed through following a particular guru. In the early years of the Hare Krishnas (ISKCON), for example, San Francisco followers of A. C. Bhaktivedanta Swami Prabhupada found that living together provided a strong structure for religious practice

and devotion. As Prabhupada's following grew, numerous ISKCON temples opened across the United States, and communal living became a more generalized teaching. Due to structural and financial changes, ISKCON's communal lifestyle eventually declined, and it is no longer the dominant model within the group; however, some of the most devout members still practice it today in centers all around the world.

Many utopian communities have been religious in nature: people who feel called by God to create not just a religious community but also a perfect society. Members are united by shared economics as well as a vision for the world, typically an example they are striving to set for others. Father Divine's Peace Mission

Fig. 16.13 Community celebration at ISKCON headquarters in Mayapur, West Bengal.

Movement, for example, which began in Sayville, New York, in 1919, was a multisite utopian community working to be an example of racial harmony, peaceful socialism, and cooperative effort. Small, self-organized groups of members opened cooperative businesses together and shared all work and profits in common. In an era when the United States was beset with economic crisis and increasing racial tension, the Peace Mission offered an alternative way to live stably in both urban and rural settings.

Violence and New Religious Movements

There are numerous examples of NRMs that have engaged in some form of violent behavior. These events receive much attention from the media, which may cause the public to incorrectly imagine there is a causal relationship between new religious ideas and violence. This is certainly not the case; extremism of all sorts can be found in any faith group, no matter how established or new, and very few NRMs ever engage in violent acts. However, sometimes the marginalized status of a group does correlate with additional social factors that, in certain combinations, can create an environment ripe for danger, abuse, or even large-scale violence. These factors can include, but are not limited to, isolation, high exit costs, dualistic thinking, direct persecution from outsiders, a leader with limitless power, and the belief in a coming apocalypse or world destruction.

Violence and abuse can be directed inward or outward. Internal abuse may be perpetrated by leaders against members, or sometimes by members against members, and it may be emotional, psychological, or physical. For example,

one could view the prohibition of all negative comments at Rajneeshpuram—theoretically a way to promote positive living—as a form of emotional abuse, because members feared they could be dismissed for speaking an honest, legitimate criticism. The practice of shunning can cause psychological abuse. For instance, when members of Sri Chinmoy Center chose to leave the group, they were completely shunned by all former friends and family members who remained. This meant that a dissatisfied person might stay in the group against their desires; for those who did choose to leave, there would obviously be a different kind of psychological pain. There are also cases of physical violence, such as when members of the Peoples Temple in Guyana were required to eat hot peppers or receive paddlings as punishment for transgressions. Escalated to an extreme degree, the Peoples Temple eventually engaged in the mass murder-suicide of its entire community.

External violence is that which occurs between a religious group and the outside world, though it may stem from either party. Aum Shinrikyo members, for example, initiated violence against the outside world when they carried out sarin gas attacks in Japan in 1994 and 1995. Their unprovoked attacks, which killed several and injured thousands, were intended as preemptive blows to an evil world that was on an inevitable path toward destruction, and also as mercy killings of the innocent. An example of external force initiated by outsiders against an NRM is seen with the Mt. Carmel community in Waco, Texas. When government agents sought to arrest religious leader David Koresh in 1993, the situation turned into a fifty-one-day standoff between members hiding inside the ranch and armed agents surrounding it. Agents tried to force members out using psychological pressure, such

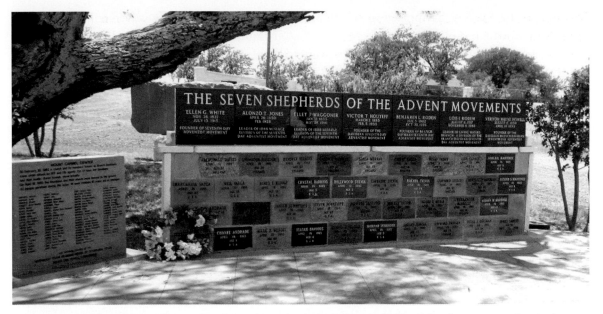

Fig. 16.14 A memorial pays tribute to Branch Davidians who died at Mount Carmel in 1993 and to seven prophets in the Adventist tradition.

as playing disturbing noises over loudspeakers and running tanks over their gravesites. When that failed to achieve the intended goal, agents turned to physical violence, using gunfire and nerve gas to force members out of their home. Tragically, most of the members died inside the ranch home when a fire ignited.

Numerous factors can create abusive and violent situations, and there is no simple checklist for avoiding or predicting it. Scholars have noted that the more internally fragile a religious community is, the more likely they may be to take drastic actions if persecuted. Repeated examples show that when ordered by outsiders to cease and desist, fervent religious believers are more likely to band together and hold a firm ground. For this reason, careful negotiations that are informed by people who understand and take seriously a group's religious worldview—no matter how unusual—are crucial for turning potentially violent situations into peaceful resolutions.

Last Chance before Heaven's Gate

Sacred discourse, often in the form of written text, has a role in every religious tradition. In many cases, religions are clearly separated from each other by the distinctly different texts that they hold sacred: for example, Baha'is use a text called the *Kitab-i-Aqdas*, and Scientologists use the writings of founder L. Ron Hubbard. In other instances, religions use the same texts but are separated from each other by their nuanced differences in interpretation, such as with Christian variations like Presbyterians, Methodists, Seventh Day Adventists, and Oneness Pentecostals. Yet another possibility is the use of old and new texts in a distinctive combination; this is the case with the primary-text excerpt below. This excerpt, which comes from Heaven's Gate, is technically a new sacred text that stands alone, but it is best understood in relation to the biblical Scriptures to which it refers and on which it elaborates.

The religious group that came to be known as Heaven's Gate was founded in the early 1970s by Marshall Herff Applewhite and Bonnie Lu Nettles. Heaven's Gate was a science-oriented NRM that combined, among other influences, interests in extraterrestrial life, Christianity, and millennialism. The group came to believe that the comet Hale-Bopp concealed an alien space-ship that could transport members to another planet. By shedding their physical shells, members' spirits would be able to access this space-ship and move on to a "level above human." The group made various attempts to reach out to others, hoping to entice as many people as possible to prepare for this opportunity; the text below is an example of one of these efforts. Thirty-nine members of Heaven's Gate committed suicide in March 1997, when the comet was passing closest to Earth; their expectation was that they could ascend to the ship unhindered by the limitations created by physical bodies. (Excerpt from Heaven's Gate text, *Last Chance to Advance Beyond Human*, dated Jan. 1994 with edits made Jan. 1997. Full text available online at: http://www.heavensgate.com/misc/lastchnc.htm.)

> Two thousand years ago, the Kingdom Level Above Human appointed an Older Member to send a Representative (His "Son"), along with some of their beginning students, to incarnate on this garden. (These students had brief periods of association with and guidance from Members of the Kingdom Level Above Human during the early generations of this civilization.) While on Earth as an "away team" with their "Captain," they were to work on their overcoming of humanness and tell the civilization they were visiting how the *true* Kingdom of God can be entered. The humans under

the control of the adversarial space races killed the "Captain" and His crew, because of the "blasphemous" position they held, and quickly turned the teachings of the "Captain" (the Older Member's "Son") into watered-down *Country Club* religion—obscuring the remnants of the Truth....

> These space alien adversaries, for the most part, are about to be "recycled" as this human civilization is "spaded." They know that "rumor has it" that their days are numbered. They refuse to believe it and are desperate to recruit souls from the human kingdom into *their* "heavenly kingdom." There are many "counterfeit" heavens, and each "heaven" is at this time collecting "names in their book," forcing a stand of allegiance, polarizing each individual's commitment to his chosen "God."

> . . . When this present "away team" leaves (which will be very soon), the Truth will go with them. You cannot *preserve* the Truth in your religions. It is present only as long as a *Truth bearer* (Older Member from the *true* Kingdom of God) is present....

> Humans of this civilization have periodically been given laws by the Next Level to upgrade their behavior. For example, the laws given to Moses were elementary "commandments" designed to make order and to raise the standards of a very "young" (primitive, barbaric) society. Then some 2000 years later, the Level Above Human, through Jesus' teachings, brought major updates (far more demanding): the greatest commandment is to *"Love the Lord thy God with **all** thy heart, with **all** thy soul, and with **all** thy mind"* (Matthew 22:37)—*"If anyone comes to Me and does not hate his father and mother and his wife and children and brothers and sisters—and even his own life also—he*

cannot be My disciple" (Luke 14:26). Those wanting to go with Him had to *do* as He did. His teachings clearly spelled out the requirements (the actual *formula*) for making the literal and difficult transition from the human kingdom into the Kingdom Level Above Human.

◆ **STUDY AND DISCUSSION QUESTIONS**

1. What examples can you think of in which insider and outsider perspectives of a religious group are extremely different from each other? What are the main causes of these opposing perspectives?

2. Using examples of specific groups discussed, apply the different definitional schemas described in the section on "Historical Development." What are the strengths and weaknesses you find with each schema?

3. If you wanted to get a full understanding of any religious group, what steps would you have to take, and what sources would you need to consult? What kinds of sources do you think would be the least valuable for learning about an NRM?

4. How many different cultural and ideological influences can you identify in the Heaven's Gate text excerpt? What kind of audience do you think this text would appeal to?

◆ **KEY TERMS**

affiliation

apostate

brainwashing

charism

charismatic leader

cult

disaffiliation

new religious movement (NRM)

routinization

sect

◆ **FOR FURTHER READING**

BOOKS

Daschke, Derek, and W. Michael Ashcraft, eds. *New Religious Movements: A Documentary Reader*. New York: New York University Press, 2005.

Dawson, Lorne L. *Comprehending Cults: The Sociology of New Religious Movements*. 2nd ed. New York: Oxford University Press, 2006.

———, ed. *Cults and New Religious Movements: A Reader*. Malden, MA: Blackwell, 2003.

Jenkins, Philip. *Mystics and Messiahs: Cults and New Religions in American History*. New York: Oxford University Press, 2001.

Lewis, James R., ed. *Violence and New Religious Movements*. New York: Oxford University Press, 2011.

Pereira, Ronan Alves, and Hideaki Motsuoka, eds. *Japanese Religions in and beyond the Japanese Diaspora*. Berkeley: University of California Press, 2007.

Wessinger, Catherine. *How the Millennium Comes Violently: From Jonestown to Heaven's Gate*. 2000. Full text available online at http://www.loyno.edu/~wessing/book.htm.

◆ **SUGGESTED WEBSITES**

CESNUR: Center for Studies on New Religions, http://www.cesnur.org.

New Religious Movements, managed by Gene Thursby, http://www.religiousworlds.com/newreligions.html.

Skepsis: Online Texts about Cults and New Religions, http://www.skepsis.nl/onlinetexts.html.

Religious Tolerance: Cults and NRMs, http://www.religioustolerance.org/cultmenu.htm.

World Religions and Spirituality Project/VCU, http://www.has.vcu.edu/wrs/index.html.

GLOSSARY

Note regarding cross-referencing: bold-faced terms in glossary definitions (below) indicate that those words also appear as glossary terms of their own.

Abbasids: A dynasty of **caliphs** (132–668 AH/ 750–1258 CE) that took its name from its original founder, Abu Abbas. The center of its power was Iran. Abu Abbas founded the capital city of Baghdad on the Euphrates in 183 AH/ 803 CE.

Aeon: In the ancient philosophy of Gnosticism, the aeons were godlike beings with everlasting power that came from the Supreme Being. The Supreme Being used the aeons to create action in the universe.

Affiliation: The process by which a person joins a religion.

Affinal relations: Social relations defined by marriage, the crux of reciprocity among indigenous cultures throughout the world.

Agape: In Greek Christian communities, an agape was a meal for people in need of help and was given as a sign of love and goodwill. This Greek word meant "the tenderness that comes from God."

Aggadah: (Also Haggadah, "narrative"). The non-legal aspects of Judaism that include theology, ethics, stories, and parables. One of the two main elements of the rabbinic tradition of Judaism, the other being **Halakhah**.

Agiary: Name for the fire temple among **Parsis**.

Ahimsa: "Absence of the desire to kill." This doctrine of nonviolence inspires an absolute respect toward all living creatures. It first appeared about the sixth century BCE in Hinduism and was adopted by Buddhism and Jainism.

Ahreman: Middle Persian name of **Angra Mainyu**.

Ahura Mazdā: the "Wise Lord." The supreme deity in Zoroastrianism.

Ai You Chadeng: "Love with distinction." Confucianism emphasizes love with distinction. Love for one's family members should be different from love for other human beings; love for virtuous people should be different from love for vicious people; and love for human beings should be different from love for nonhuman beings.

Ajiva: "Nonlife monad"; matter.

Al-Hallaj: Born in Iran in 858 CE, he meditated on the Qur'an, interiorizing Islam and discovering the splendor and pure love of God. Stressing God's pact with man, al-Hallaj taught that man is the image of God and that, through love, God becomes present in the mystical man. His preaching began a movement that drew the attention of the political authorities of Baghdad. After nine years of imprisonment, he was tortured and executed on March 9, 922 CE. His body was then cast into the Tigris River from atop a minaret. His disciples were persecuted in the hope of destroying the **Sufi** movement, the form of Muslim mysticism that obtains its names from *suf*, "wool," the white woolen habit that Muslim mystics adopted from Christian monks.

Allah: The one God, lord of all creation, the proper name of God. In pre-Islamic Arabia, the word referred to God the creator among the other gods. The Qur'an affirms Allah as the one God. There are ninety-nine names of God in the Qur'an.

Amaterasu-O-Mi-kami: Heavenly-shining-deity. The central female deity of Japan, who is associated with the sun and plays a central part in important mythic cycles and ritual traditions.

Ame-no-minaka-nushi: The **kami** who, according to early Japanese mythology, ruled the universe and stood separate above all others.

Aməša Spəntas: Seven "holy immortals" in the Zoroastrian pantheon.

Amitabha: Known in Japan as Amida, he is a Buddha, serving as a symbol of the purity of the soul and of spiritual awakening, a representative of life after death, and as such fervently venerated in China, Japan, and Southeast Asia. Amitabha is especially revered in pietist monasteries, whose monks stress the need for a devout life nourished by religious sentiments. An entire literature about paradise or Amitabha's land of domicile has developed within this Buddhism of devotion (amidism).

Anabaptists: Members of the Radical Reformation movement who believed that **baptism** should be a mature testimony of faith, appropriate for adults rather than infants, and who wished to separate the church from the state.

Ananda: "Beatitude." The name of one of the **Buddha's** cousins, his disciple and the guide of the community after his death. As "the first listener to the word," he played a fundamental role in the council of Rajagrha and has been credited with the compilation of the first Buddhist **sutra**.

Anatman: "Absence of the self." This is the way Buddhism expresses the doctrine of the nonexistence of a personality, of a "self." The individual exists as a complex of psychic phenomena but not as a personal being.

Angra Mainyu: The "destructive spirit." The leader of the demons in the Zoroastrian pantheon.

Animism: The widespread belief among indigenous peoples that the material world in which we live is totally occupied and enlivened by spirits, which can be helpful or harmful to humans and which may be seen in their human or animal form by the shamans.

Antimony: Orthodox theology and liturgy often utilize antimony. It poses two contradictory affirmations and says that they are both true, in a difference-identity. Thus God is one and three, Christ is truly God and truly a man, and glory and the cross are inseparable.

Anti-Semitism: Prejudice and hostility against Jewish people and Judaism.

Apapaatai: Spirit-people of the Arawak-speaking Wauja of the Xingu River basin in Brazil, who can either be friends to humans and help them cure sickness or can be harmful in provoking sickness.

Apocalypse: The imminent destruction of the world.

Apologists: Apologists were Greek and Latin writers who defended the Christian faith from insults and persecutions from the pagans during the second and third centuries. The apologists wrote about the spiritual beliefs of Christians as well as their feelings about and engagements with the ancient world's traditions and culture.

Apophatism: With respect to God, there must be no assertion, image, quality, or symbol that could be a limitation. God is always beyond, even beyond the concept of God. God cannot be described in human terms.

Apostate: A former member of a religion who has a negative view of that religion and a bad relationship with its members and leaders. An apostate often speaks publicly against his or her former religion, and the religion often considers the former member to have gone astray from truthful teachings.

Apostolic tradition: In the second century, the Christian church opposed the philosophy of **Gnosticism**. Gnostics understood Christian doctrines or beliefs quite differently. The church, in conflict with the Gnostic priest Marcion, developed the canon, which was the official list of books in the New Testament. The church established that this list contained the whole and truthful Christian faith, also known as the apostolic tradition. The church, especially according to the writers Irenaeus and Tertullian, also established that this was the faith upon which the whole church agreed. The apostolic tradition according to Clement of Alexandria forms the rule of religious faith.

Aranyaka: "Of the forest." The name given to a group of "forest texts," written by Vedic hermits, probably at the end of the **brahmana** period.

Arhat: "Worthy, saintly, respectable." Epithet of the **Buddha**, but also of the saint who has completed the Path of Liberation in this life and has therefore reached **nirvana** and will not be reborn again.

Arian, Arianism: A religious belief first preached by the priest Arius, in 320 CE. Arius taught that Jesus Christ, the Son, was lower than God the Father in rank, power, and glory, and therefore cast doubts on the divinity of Christ. Arius asserted that the Father alone is eternal, and while the Son is the foremost and most excellent among all creatures, he was only an instrument in the hands of the Father during creation. His theory was judged to be heretical by the Council of Nicaea in 325 CE. His followers, however, continued to teach his doctrine, and it was only the Council of Constantinople in 381 CE that decided the matter by fully establishing the doctrine of the Trinity: one God or divine nature in three divine persons.

Ark: In this book, the term refers to the cabinet where the **Torah** scrolls are kept in the synagogue. It is the most sacred place in the synagogue. The term applies also to the ark of the covenant and to the ark in which Noah, his family, and the ancestors of all living beings took refuge during the universal flood.

Aryasatya: "Noble truth." The **Catvary aryasatyani** are the four noble truths about suffering, the origin of suffering, the surcease of suffering, on the path that leads to the end of suffering, as they were preached by the **Buddha** in his sermon in Benares.

Aša: The concept of "truth" and "order" in Zoroastrianism.

Ašāvan: In Zoroastrianism, an *ašāvan* is a "sustainer of the truth."

Asceticism: This word refers to exercise, interior fight—through spiritual fasting, celibacy, and keeping vigils (**nepsis**), for example—undertaken to reach a state of grace.

Ashkenazi: A Jew whose family originated in central or eastern Europe. Named after Ashkenaz (Gen. 10:3).

Ashoka: Third emperor (272–236 BCE) of the Maurya dynasty of Magadha. A convert to Buddhism and founder of a great empire, Ashoka was tolerant and preoccupied with the well-being of his subjects. He wrote numerous edicts that were carved in stone and on columns to make the Buddhist **dharma** the basis of human and social ethics.

Ātar: "Fire." As a proper noun, Ātar is the name of the Zoroastrian divinity (*yazata*) of fire. Zoroastrians venerate and perform sacrifices to fire, which since ancient times has been regarded as the visible expression of Ātar. In exchange for regular sacrificial offerings, Ātar is thought to protect and provide support and sustenance for the faithful.

Ātaš Bahrām: Highest grade of fire in a Zoroastrian fire temple.

Atashkadeh: Name for the fire temple among Iranian Zoroastrians.

Ātaš-zōhr: "Offering to fire." This is a fundamental ritual in Zoroastrianism.

Athos: Mount Athos, also known as the "Holy Mountain," is a long peninsula located in northern Greece. Its hills and mountains reach two thousand meters. Since the tenth to the twelfth centuries, it has been a federation of twenty sovereign monasteries, of all nationalities (there are also other less important communities and hermitages). When visiting Mount Athos, one discovers with amazement the beauty of nature, architecture, and frescoes, as well as the intensity of constant prayer, both liturgical and personal. All women are barred from Mount Athos, except for the Mother of God. For this reason, it is known as the "Garden of the Virgin." Today there are almost two thousand monks living there, many of whom are young and culturally sophisticated. A recent church reform consolidated and developed community monasticism, to the detriment of "idiorhythmic" **monasticism** (that is, a way of life in which each monk follows "his own rhythm").

Atman: The name given to the eternal principle that gives life to the individual; "the self," "the personal soul," the substratum of the subconscious. Many Hindu texts expound the Brahmanic ideas about the *atman*, the principle of life, the central power of man, the immortal spiritual principle. Buddhism opposed this doctrine.

Australian aboriginal dreamtime: Belief among Australian Aboriginal peoples that the world is real only because it has been dreamed into being by the ancestral Totemic spirit beings. Dreamtime was a "time before time," and dreaming was the foundation of an individual's or group's spiritual beliefs.

Autocephalous churches: Orthodoxy is composed of independent self-governed national churches, each of which elects its own primate—that is, "its own head." Autocephalous churches are interdependent of one another. They must be recognized by others and, most importantly, by the ecumenical patriarchate of Constantinople.

Avesta: The central corpus of Zoroastrian sacred literature.

Baptism: The word *baptism* comes from a Latin term meaning "immersion," or dipping into water. From the earliest centuries, new believers were plunged completely into running water. This baptism was a symbol of the death and resurrection of Jesus Christ. After baptism, believers then began a new regenerated life as children of God.

Baptism-Chrismation: These two **sacraments**, administered together through one rite, constitute the Christian initiation that permits an individual to take Communion. The **baptism** is a death-resurrection with Christ. The chrismation (anointing with oil) is a personal **Pentecost**.

Benedict of Nursia: Founder of the Benedictine Order. He was born at Nursia, Italy, around 480 and, after becoming a hermit and a monk within the community of Subiaco, founded the abbey of Monte Cassino, in 529. There he composed the *Regula*, which became the rule followed by most monasteries during and after the Middle Ages. He died at Monte Cassino in 547.

Bhagavad Gita: "The song of the Lord." A poem that comprises the sixth book of the Mahabharata. This text becomes the foundation of devotional Hinduism and consists of a dialogue between **Krishna** and his faithful follower Arjuna, and emphasizes devotion as the path of salvation. The poem inspired Mohandas (Mahatma) Gandhi.

Bhagavan or bhagavat: "Blessed." One of the epithets of the **Buddha**.

Bhakti: From Ibhaj, "to share with others." A religious philosophy that establishes ties of love and devotion between gods and their devoted followers, who serve them with love. Known in India since the beginning of the Common Era, *bhakti* has been responsible for great changes in both religious thought and practice and has made popular the worship of **Krishna**, intensified the cult of Vishnu, and has influenced Buddhism. It has also greatly influenced Indian art.

Bhikshu (also Bhikkhu): A Buddhist monk, a bonze; bhikshuni (Bhikkuni): Buddhist nun.

Bodhi: From *budh*, "to awaken." The awakening of the supreme consciousness that allows one to see within oneself the sequence of all one's previous existences and to recognize the cause of suffering and rebirth. Thanks to the *bodhi*, the **Buddha** discovered the chain of causes and effects and this awakening liberated him from the cycle of rebirth.

Bodhisattva: An awakened individual who has renounced Buddhahood to help others achieve the **Bodhi**. This renunciation out of pure compassion is a doctrine that began five centuries after the beginning of Buddhism. It has become one of the pillars of religious Buddhism.

Bogomils, Bogomilism: A Balkan variation of the heresy of the **Cathars**, which was based on the two concepts of good and evil and which drew its inspiration from Paulicianism, a Near Eastern Manichaean movement. Hounded out of Bulgaria, where it was spreading, Bogomilism filtered into Bosnia, Dalmatia, Slovenia, and, finally Serbia. Byzantium continuously harassed the Bogomils until they finally disappeared, around the 1400s.

Brahman: In its neuter form, the word refers to a ritual formula, then Vedic wisdom, and the knowledge of the Brahmin, the Hindu priest. In its masculine form, the **Brahmin** is one of the ministers of the Vedic sacrifice; it also refers to the priest, the spiritual master of society, in which case the plural is **Brahmins**, the members of the highest caste of Vedic society. **Brahman** with a capital *B* refers to the Absolute, the Universal, the Pure Energy, which becomes **Brahma** when it is invoked as a personal god.

Brahmana: "Belonging to the brahmins." In its neuter form, the word refers to a number of texts that make up Vedic revelation. These prose texts were written between 800 and 600 BCE and describe the celebration of sacrifices (ceremonies, myths, legends).

Brainwashing: Intensive thought reform and mind control, believed to be used to get people to convert to and remain faithful to alternative forms of religion. The existence of brainwashing has been heavily debated by scholars, with varying conclusions drawn in different times and places.

Buddha: The Awakened One who has discovered the true knowledge and consciousness of the real state of all creatures and things by means of the opening of his mind. Siddhartha Gautama, also called Shakyamuni, "the Sage of the Shakya," was the first Awakened One. He discovered the four sacred truths and has therefore become a guide for all humanity. In the course of time, Buddhism turned to other **Buddhas**, in addition to the historical one, who were figures of the essence of **Buddha**.

Burning Bush: The angel of God appeared to Moses on Mount Horeb, in the form of a bush that was burning without being consumed or destroyed. This is a symbol with multiple meanings in Judaism and Christianity.

Cakra: "Wheel." A Sanskrit word, an Indian symbol of fullness, which in Buddhism symbolizes the fullness of the law (**dharma**) but also the cycle of rebirth and the impermanence of creatures and of things—that is, their essentially transitory character—since the wheel touches the ground only for a brief moment as it moves forward.

Caliph: The "successor" of the one sent by God. The caliph's mission is to continue the political action of the Prophet, the original prophetic mission having been concluded. The role of the caliphate has changed profoundly over the centuries.

Cathars, Catharism: A dualistic **heresy** of the twelfth and thirteenth centuries, extremely widespread in France (Albigenses) and the Balkans. Rooted in **Manichaean** and **Gnostic** beliefs, it was probably imported from the East by the Crusaders. The Cathar movement believed in two powers ruling over sky and earth, good and evil. The evil god is the creator of matter, while the good god is the creator of the spirit and of light. Moreover, Cathars practiced a most austere morality that forbade sex and the consumption of meat; they believed in a **baptism** of the Spirit that led the perfect ones along the path of salvation; and they disregarded the church and the **sacraments**. Catharism affected all of Europe.

Cemetery, coemeterium: *Cemetery* is from the Greek word meaning "place where one sleeps." For both Jews and Christians, the word meant "the burying of the dead." To them, the idea of sleeping was connected to belief in the resurrection (or rebirth) of the dead as a reawakening. Also, the word *deposition* meant "a temporary putting down."

Charism: Special powers or qualities that are believed to have been given to a person from God.

Charismatic leader: A leader who is recognized by followers as having special, God-given abilities that set him or her apart from other people.

Christian Humanism: Christian Humanism started with Pico della Mirandola (d. 1494), Marisilio Ficino (d. 1499), and Nicholas of Cusa (d. 1464), who had escorted the orthodox delegation during the Council of Florence in 1439. Christian Humanism developed in the sixteenth century under professors of the *studia humanitatis*, who yearned for a return to the Bible, Christian antiquity, and the Greek and Latin classics but who were also conscious of the dangers of a return to paganism. Important examples are Thomas More (d. 1535), Erasmus (d. 1536), and Lefévre d'Étaples (d. 1536). Their teachings characterize that century and were instrumental in a renewal of Catholicism.

Circumcision: This ritual, called *bris*, is a Jewish religious ceremony during which a mohel cuts and removes the foreskin of the penis of an eight-day old male in order to observe the brit milah, "covenant of circumcision," first practiced by Abraham as part of the covenantal relationship between the Jewish people and God (Gen. 17:10-14).

Cistercians: Benedictine monks adhering to the reform of Cîteaux initiated by Bernard of Clairvaux. His reform upheld the rigorous observance of the Benedictine rule, the ideal of complete retirement from the world to dedicate oneself to contemplation of God, and observance of total poverty. The golden age of this order was reached in the twelfth and thirteenth centuries, when the number of abbeys rose from 343 in 1153 to 694 in 1300. This order spread throughout Europe and is held in high regard by the church.

Clan: A social group that comprises a number of families (decided by maternal or paternal descent). Religious traditions may be enacted and transmitted through clan structures where they are vibrant. Clans serve to pass on Islamic tradition.

Coenobitism, Coenobite: Coenobitism comes from the Greek word meaning "those who live in a community." In Egypt, following the example of Anthony (250–356 CE), some Christians became known as "anchorites." They wanted to seek a holy life in the quiet of the desert. In 320 CE, Pachomius organized a community in Thebes, and from there coenobitism spread both West and East. A similar movement, the monasticism of Egypt, established a way of life that inspired Saint **Benedict** when he organized his community.

Commemorate: To remember an event or a person in a ceremony.

Congregation: A community of lay people, vowed religious persons, or priests, who share beliefs and "gather together" to live accordingly. In Roman Catholicism, a congregation can also refer to one of the Vatican organs responsible for the running of an administrative department (for example, the Congregation for

Eastern Churches). More generally, the term "congregation" can refer to a group of Christians who regularly gather together to worship.

Consanguineal kin: All kinspeople related to each other by blood connections. Peoples vary on how far they wish to stretch the limits of who may or may not be not recognized as blood kin.

Conservative Judaism: Modern movement that holds that changes in traditional Jewish life are acceptable and inevitable in modern times but for whom the history and traditions of Judaism remain very important. Conservative Jews try to conserve as much tradition as possible but believe changes may be made to ensure the vitality of Judaism for all people.

Contemplation: Devotional meditation on spiritual matters.

Cosmogony: The beginning, or primordial times, when all of creation came into being.

Cosmology: The universe as it has been envisioned and is understood by religious specialists, taught to new generations of adults, often visible through landmarks in the sacred geography where indigenous peoples dwell.

Council: A group of bishops that gathered to discuss and decide upon church problems and questions was called a council. An "ecumenical council" brought together bishops from the whole church. Smaller, more local councils were held by the church as early as the second century CE. The first ecumenical council was held at Nicaea in 325 CE. The term "council" as used in this volume also applies to an assembly of bishops that specifies the rules of faith and the organization of the Church. It makes decisions unanimously, but the Council's authority and decisions have to be "welcomed" by the community of the faithful. There are local, regional, and universal Councils. It is important to distinguish between Councils convened for special events having to do with matters of spiritual nature, and those convened regularly for administrative purposes (for example, those convened once or twice a year in a metropolitan see).

Covenant: Agreement or treaty between two parties; the promise between God and the Jewish people on which the Jewish people base their religious life and observance.

Crusades: Military expeditions by Western Christianity in an attempt to reconquer Jerusalem after its taking by Muslims in 1009 and the devastation of the Holy Sepulcher. The Crusades drew support from three factors: the great popularity of pilgrimages to Jerusalem, the demographic expansion in the Western world, and the emergent Christian orders of knighthood. During the Council of Clermont (1095), Pope Urban II launched a campaign for Christians to brandish the cross in support of the appeal of Byzantine Emperor Alexios Komnenos. There were eight Crusades.

Cult: Technically, a small community of religious believers; in popular thought, however, the terms often refers to a religious group that many people consider illegitimate.

Daijo-sai: The Great Thanksgiving and First-fruits Ceremony celebrated following the enthronement of a new emperor in Japan.

Dao (Tao): Literally means "way" in the strict sense of "road" but also in the figurative sense of "method," "doctrine," and "rule of conduct." Dao refers also to the power, both magical and religious, that kings and magicians use to make heaven, earth, and humans communicate with one another. From the philosophical point of view, Dao underlies the order of nature, the order of the cosmos; but the word *Dao* also designates a specific philosophy, since each philosophical school has its Dao. In the outlook of religious Daoism, *Dao* is the ultimate reality that lies beyond all appearances and concepts.

Dao de jing (Tao te ching): Title of the work known as "The Way and the Power of the Way" (*jing* or *ching* means "book"), written in five thousand characters on two scrolls. This is the fundamental text of Daoism. It consists of eighty-one chapters in the form of parallel verses and short poems, whose meanings are sometimes difficult to puzzle out, frequently based on oppositions. One of the essential notions is that of "non-striving" (**Wu Wei**). Authorship of the *Dao de jing* is traditionally attributed to **Lao-zi**, even though scholars see the hands of several writers at work on the text from the fourth to the third centuries BCE. The Dao de jing is used widely in various schools of Daoism, Confucianism, Chinese legalism, and Chinese folk practice.

Deism: A natural religiosity based on the idea of a Supreme Being who does not exercise any influence on human behavior.

Dēnkard: "Acts of the Religion." A ninth- to tenth-century-CE Middle Persian (Pahlavi) encyclopedic work that deals with numerous customs and doctrine of the Zoroastrian religion (*dēn*). It was composed in a Persian environment that had already become Islamicized, and thus many of the books in this work are regarded as Zoroastrian apologetics or rational responses to Muslim critiques of Zoroastrian theology and practice.

Denomination: A group of religious congregations that share a common faith, name, and administration.

Depravity: The human condition of moral corruption or sin.

Devotio Moderna: A spiritual movement of the fourteenth and fifteenth centuries that enjoyed great popularity in Flanders and the Rhine Valley. It originated among the groups of Brethren of the Common Life inspired by John of Ruysbroeck and Thomas of Kempen (or à Kempis) of the Congregation of the Canons Regular of St. Augustine. This devotion sought to foster attachment to the person of Christ, his passion, and the Holy **Eucharist**. In this regard, the classical text was *The Imitation of Christ* of Thomas à Kempis. Erasmus and Nicholas of Cusa were disciples of the Brethren of the Common Life of Deventer.

Dharma: "The law." Buddhist doctrine or teaching, one of the Three Jewels of Buddhism, together with the **Buddha** and the community (**samgha**). These three treasures constitute three "refuges." The dharma consists of the laws to which all living beings and things, all phenomena, and all ideas must submit. Dharma also refers to the cosmic and social order that keeps the universe in existence. Immutably fixed, this order is supported by a synthesis of rules and natural phenomena. The behavior of individuals conditions the proper functioning of the universe and their normal life in the dharma. As part of the sacred realm, the dharma is looked after by the **Brahmins**.

Dhatu: "Foundation layer." That which is placed or established, according to Ayurveda Dhatu, consists of the fundamental elements of sensory consciousness, that is, those six (or seven) organs, objects, and corresponding awarenesses of conscious sensation. They are also, then, the material elements that are sensed: earth, water, fire, and wind; and include as well the three worlds of desire (**karma**), of the forms (**rupa**), and of the non-forms (**arupa**).

Diaspora: This word (from a Greek agricultural term meaning "to spread seed,") taken from the spread of the Jewish community throughout Jewish history, also designates the modern dispersal of members of the Orthodox faith and other religious communities. How to organize the diaspora is a problem that remains a challenge to many religious communities, from Judaism and the Orthodox Church to Tibetan Buddhists.

Digambara: "Sky-clad"; Jain sect whose male renouncers are naked.

Disaffiliation: The process by which a person separates from a religion.

Disestablishment: The act of depriving a church of official government support.

Dogma: A principle, belief, or idea that is authoritative and set forth as true for a community or particular group. The term derives from the Greek *dokeo*, meaning "to suppose, to imagine."

Dogon Kanaga masks: These masks represent the first human beings and are worn during the Dama dancing ceremonies. The Dogon believe that the Dama dance creates a bridge into the supernatural world without which the dead cannot cross over into peace.

Donatism: Donatism was a schism of the North African Christian church that resulted from the persecution of 303–305 CE. It was thought some bishops and priests had betrayed the church by giving holy writings to persecutors. The argument between Donatists and Catholics was about the personality of the church: How should the church interact, as a group, with the world and its institutions? Donatism was gone completely by the time of the introduction of Islam.

Dongtian: "Heavenly grottoes." Holy places in the form of mythical mountain caves, connected to one another via underground passages, where heaven becomes present and accessible. Dongtian are the womb of the earth, where the principles of life and holy Scripture are kept hidden. The caverns are illuminated from within by their own light or by light rays that descend from heaven through special passages.

Drəgvant: In Zoroastrianism, a *drəgvant* is a "sustainer of the Lie."

Druǰ: The concept of "lie" or "disorder" in Zoroastrianism.

Druze: A people who inhabit the mountain chains of Lebanon and the Anti-Lebanon, the Damascus region, and the Jabal Hawran massif in southwestern Syria. They are descendants from a dissenting sect of the Fatimid Muslims of Egypt, founded in the early eleventh century CE.

Duhkha: "Suffering." A Buddhist concept of suffering that constitutes the first of the four

noble truths. It is the lot of all beings who are tied to the cycle of rebirth (**samsara**). It is evil in the form of corporal and mental pain, evil in the form of oppression, and evil that derives from impermanence.

Easter: The "feast of feasts," that of the resurrection, when Christians commemorate that "Christ was resurrected from the dead, through death He defeated death, to those who are in tombs (that is, all men), He gave life."

Ecumenical: First meaning, "universal, the inhabited earth." From this meaning comes the expressions "ecumenical empire," "ecumenical council," and "ecumenical Patriarchate." In modern times, this word designates the effort of Christians to regain their unity. The Orthodox churches are, not without great difficulties, part of the Ecumenical Council of Churches, which brings together Protestants, Anglicans, and Orthodox.

Elkesaism: Elkesaism was the faith followed by some Jewish-Christian Baptists who believed they could purify themselves and be spiritually saved by two special ceremonies. First, the believer's body was washed with a daily **baptism** in water; and second, the believer's food was also made holy, purified, by water. This belief first came from Jewish ritual laws and became very popular. This practice occurred all across the Middle East in the second and third centuries. The philosopher Mani lived in an Elkesaite community for twenty years.

Empires: **Orthodoxy** has mostly existed in multinational empires, whether they were inspired by **Orthodoxy** (Byzantine Empire, Russian Empire), tolerated it (Arab Empire,

Ottoman Empire), or fought against it (Communist Empire).

Encratism: Encratism was a spiritual discipline that was not trusted by the early church. It renounced all goods created by God, forbade eating meat, and rejected sex and marriage. The fathers of the Christian church were against these teachings. They worried Encratism could be confused with another spiritual discipline, monasticism, that was helpful to the church. The early church leaders also thought Encratism threatened the state of peace in the Christian world.

Enculturation of the Gospel: A new theological concept, coined by Pope John Paul II in his encyclical *Slavorum Apostoli* (1985): "the embodiment of the Gospel within indigenous cultures and the integration of these same cultures in the life of the church." Enculturation begins with the proclamation of the gospel, which, together with the people who accept it, enjoys a primary role. The encounter of culture with gospel leads to a creative response by human beings.

Engishiki: "Procedures of the Engi Era." A tenth-century collection of regulations for governmental administration in Japan, including ceremonies, gathered in fifty books.

Enryaku-ji: A Shinto deity who was an incarnation of Shakyamuni **Buddha**.

Episcopacy: A system of church government in which bishops (from Greek, *episcopoi*, meaning "supervisors"), are the chief officers.

Eschatology: Views of the end of time, whether these views be about the time that begins with the death of a specific individual or with the demise of the cosmos itself.

Eucharist: *Eucharist* comes from the Greek word meaning "thanksgiving." This ceremony of breaking bread at the table and dividing it among the guests is linked to the Jewish Passover meal as well as to the **Hellenistic** philosophical meal, the Symposium. For early Christians, the Eucharist became the sign of their unity, a commemoration of Jesus' Last Supper with his disciples, when he ate bread and drank wine with them before his death. The Eucharist has been ever since a symbol of their coming together with Jesus Christ, just as he had promised during the Last Supper. The Eucharist is also known as "the breaking of the bread" and has always been the most special ceremony in Christianity.

Excommunicate: To exclude someone from membership in the church.

Fa-lu: A brief meditation aimed at purifying the hearts and minds of the devotees by emptying all irrelevant images and disturbing thoughts.

Fathers of the Church: These are the major witnesses of faith—speaking theologically—who lived during the first millennium, particularly during the fourth century. If occasionally a saint, such as Maximus the Confessor during the seventh century, was merely a simple monk, most of the Church Fathers were bishops commenting on Scripture to their people, often explaining **liturgies**, deepening faith through their writings, defending against the political and military powers the independence of the church, and developing ample social services for the benefit of the poor.

Fatima: The daughter of Muhammad and Khadija and the bride of Ali, the fourth **caliph**. She is especially admired by the **Shiites**, who call her al-Zahra, "the resplendent one."

Febronianism: An ecclesiological concept embraced by the Luxembourg theologian Nicolas von Hontheim (1701–1790), who served as auxiliary bishop of Trier. In 1763, under the pseudonym Febronius (from which Febronianism is derived), he published a treatise on the rights of national bishops. He upheld an all-powerful episcopate that refuted the primacy of the pope over the council and appealed to lay princes to assume direction over religious matters in their countries.

Fen-Deng: A Daoist ritual during which one lights three candles, each one with special significance.

Festival of Light: Celebrates the first full moon of the New Year with a procession of lanterns, floats, dances, and poems.

Fidelity (*xin*): Keeping one's word is one of the five constant virtues of Confucianism. Faithfulness to one's promises is a fundamental condition of society.

Filial piety (*xiao*): In Confucianism, family love is regarded as the root of humanity (*ren*), while humanity is the extension of family love.

Fiqh: The science of Islamic law. *Fiqh* refers to the juridical decisions inferred from the Qur'an or the **Sunna**, with the consensus of the Muslim community.

Five Scriptures (*Wujing*): One of the two groups of Confucian classics (with the other being the **Four Books**), referring to the *Book of Rites*, the *Book of Poetry*, the *Book of Changes*, the *Book of Documents*, and the *Spring and Autumn Annals*.

Four Books (*sishu*): Four Confucian texts canonized by Zhu Xi (1130–1200): the *Analects*, the *Mencius*, the *Great Learning*, and the *Doctrine of the Mean*. Later, they became basic texts for civil examinations.

Four Sprouts (*sishu*): Four beginnings. Mencius believes that every human being is born with the beginnings of four cardinal moral virtues: the feeling of commiseration as the beginning of **humanity (*ren*)**, the feeling of shame and dislike as the beginning of **rightness (*yi*)**, the feeling of deference and compliance as the beginning of **propriety (*li*)**, and the feeling of right and wrong as the beginning of wisdom.

Fravaši: In Zoroastrianism this is the "pre-soul" of an individual that preexists a person's current lifetime but also will survive after death, making it somewhat synonymous with the Christian notion of "soul."

Fukko Shinto: Revival Shinto. A movement that arose in the eighteenth century seeking to restore and reconstruct ancient Japanese native religious practices as they were imagined to exist prior to the introduction of foreign creeds like Buddhism and Confucianism.

Gallicanism: A doctrine diffused in France between the fifteenth and nineteenth centuries that asserted a certain autonomy of the French church in its relations with Rome, and a number of rights by French kings in matters of ecclesiastical administration. In 1438, the Pragmatic Sanction of Bourges invested the king of

France with rights over church nominations. The conciliar decrees of Trent remained unrecognized under French law, which considered them a violation of Gallican rights. Gallicanism was finally addressed by the Vatican Council I through its precepts regarding the pope's teaching office.

Ganadhara: Mahavira's closest disciples.

Gāthās: The sacred "hymns" of **Zarathuštra**.

Geshojo: A Shinto term (borrowed from Buddhism) meaning "outer purity," which is accomplished ritually, usually through purification of the body by washing.

Gētīg: (also *gētīy*) A Middle Persian philosophical-theological term used to describe the corporal and visible elements of worldly existence.

Gnosticism: A philosophy that, at one time, included several different schools of philosophy and religious groups. There are three main ideas to Gnosticism: The belief that humans possess an awareness, a gnosis, that, through the work of God, bestowed intelligence; a framework of oppositions, such as a view that the evil, material world is opposed to the bright, spiritual one; and the idea that a yawning, unending emptiness, the cosmos, was caused by a "crisis in the divine," a sort of trouble in paradise. This crisis caused a godlike being, an **Aeon**, to fall from the primordial universe, the **Pleroma**.

Gopura: Towers with a rectangular base that, from the eleventh century, were built in southern India above the entrance to the walled area of a temple. Built with a varying number of floors, each tower progressively narrows as it rises. Each floor is decorated with hundreds of statues of gods and saints.

Goshintai: "Divine bodies." In Shinto the term refers to the physical images or objects on which **kami** descend and with which specific **kami** become identified.

Grace: Divine love, sanctity, and power granted by God.

Great Western Schism (1378–1417): Following the return of the popes from Avignon to Rome in 1378, the cardinals elected two popes, Urban VI and Clement VII, both of whom were supported by different monarchs. Even the religious orders and dioceses were divided. The cardinals then elected Alexander V, who was in turn substituted within a year by John XXIII (a so-called antipope). At Constance, a council deposed John XXIII and in 1417 elected Pope Martin V, thereby ending the thirty-nine-year-old schism.

Gregory Palamas: This monk, a fourteenth-century theologian and bishop of Thessaloniki, specialized in the mental prayer practice known as Hesychasm, "prayer of the heart." In order to hold the reality of "deification," Gregory used the image of light to distinguish between God's *inaccessible*, invisible essence and his visible energies which, like visible light, allow for human participation. This was not a dichotomy but rather what Gregory called an antimony, because "all of God is inaccessible and all of God is participable," which means "capable of being shared with humans."

Guarani theory of souls: The soul consists of two parts: the "animal" soul (*atsygua*) that is the source of passions, desires, fears, excesses; and the "true" soul (*ayvukwe*), which is the "name" soul bestowed by the elder shaman/priests in trance on the newborn. The latter is considered the "true essence, the beautiful name" of the person.

Gurdwara: Sacred space of the Sikhs.

Guru Granth: Sacred Scripture of the Sikhs; center of Sikh rites and ceremonies.

Hadaka Matsuri: An elaborate Shinto festival performed in the heart of every winter in the city of Konomiya to purge men and communities of physical and moral weaknesses.

Hadith: The traditions that report the deeds and words of Muhammad and, for Shiites, even those of the **Imam**. Various collections of these deeds and words were compiled in the early centuries of Islam.

Haiden: Hall of worship; a building in a Shinto shrine complex, used as an oratory for prayer and worship.

Hajj: The pilgrimage to Mecca, one of the five duties (pillars) of Islam. The great pilgrimage must be carried out during the prescribed month, while the lesser pilgrimage (**umra**) can be performed at any time. The institution of the pilgrimage was initiated by the Prophet.

Halakhah: All of the Jewish law, in the broad sense of religious norms, observances, and communal practice, from Scripture to recent rulings by rabbis. Halakhah is rooted in God's revealed will.

Haram: "Forbidden, sacred." Those places, things, and beings whose free use has been forbidden by divine command are separated from others and are called haram. These are the places rendered holy by the divine presence, as well as private property and certain foods. Sacred haram concerns divine presence, while forbidden haram concerns divine commands. The meaning of the word *haram* therefore remains ambivalent.

Hasidism: A pious movement founded by wandering popular preachers, especially Israel ben Eliexer Baal Shem Tov, in the late eighteenth century in eastern Europe. It emphasizes that one should find joy and union with God in everyday life. A spiritual leader called a *zaddik* usually leads the Hasidic community.

Hatsumiyamairi: Ceremony of the first visit, when a child is brought to a Shinto shrine by parents or relatives under the special protection of **kami**.

Heart/mind (*xin*): In Confucianism, a faculty of both intellectual cognition and moral sensibility.

Heaven (*tian*): During Shang and Zhou periods, regarded as the supreme deity. Confucius uses the term in both this religious sense and its naturalist sense to refer to natural phenomena. In Neo-Confucianism, *tian* is regarded as the origin of the universe and source of morality. In contemporary new Confucianism, it refers to the moral sources immanent in every one of us.

Hellenism: Term describing the culture and ideas found in the Roman Empire between Alexander the Great (fourth century BCE) and the Emperor Constantine (fourth century CE). During this time, the Greek-influenced culture of the Romans mixed with the culture of the conquered people of the area, resulting in a new culture that was a blending of many types of ideas, religions, and art.

Heresy: The term applied to ideas or beliefs that run contrary to the authoritatively defined religious teachings in a community. In history the term has especially been applied to describe versions of Christian thought and practice that appear error-ridden. Heretics may think and live separated from the rest of the Orthodox Christian community.

Hijra: "Detachment." On July 16, 622 CE, Muhammad left Mecca and his fellow refugees (muhajirun) for Medina. This date marks start of the Hijran lunar calendar, in which the year is composed of twelve months with twenty-eight days each. The hijra marks the start of the Muslim era.

Human nature (*xing*): A central Confucian idea. Neo-Confucians further develop the idea of Mencius that human nature is good, linking human nature and the human heart/mind (*xin*) to the fundamental principle of the universe (*li*).

Humanism: An intellectual movement dating to the Renaissance that emphasized the study of human culture, especially the liberal arts, and the study of the texts and arts that lie at the heart of classical cultures.

Humanity (*ren*): The most important Confucian virtue. Sometimes regarded as the leading virtue and sometimes regarded as the comprehensive virtue. It is the distinguishing mark of being human; its central meaning is human love; and its two parts in Chinese character means two persons.

Iconoclast (from a Greek word meaning "image-destroyer"): Supporter of iconoclasm, a religious movement in the Byzantine Empire that in the eighth and ninth centuries denied the holiness of sacred images and prohibited the use of such images. Iconoclasm was condemned by the second **Council** of Nicaea, in 787.

Iconostasis: From a Greek word meaning "stand for image." A partition with tiers of icons and three doors (the central one is called "royal door") separating the *bema* (the "sanctuary" where the altar is located and where only the priests are allowed for the celebration of the **liturgy**) from the nave (where the faithful stay) in Orthodox churches. The rows of icons display, from top to bottom, the history of salvation: the patriarchs, the prophets, the church with the *Deesis* (a representation of Christ the Judge flanked by the intercessory figures of the Mother of God at his right and John the Baptist at his left).

Ideology: The science of ideas, especially those of the eighteenth century. Today the term is used especially to denote any abstract theory about powers that undergird reality, such as positivist or Marxist ideologies. The term "ideological systems" refers to philosophical systems that analyze the meaning of life.

Idolatry: Idolatry is a belief in idols and the worship of idols. The early Christians opposed all groups that worshiped false idols. It was considered to be an error and a sin. The ban on worshipping idols prevented Christians who had converted from **paganism** from returning to the temples and participating in their old religion.

Ijma: The consensus of the community, one of the sources of Islamic law, whose authority is derived from the **hadith** of the Prophet: "My community does not agree on an error."

Ikk Oan Kar: "One Being Is." Sikh expression for the one Divine.

Imam: "The guide," who stands before the believers in the mosque, leads the prayer service, and also guides the community in other aspects of life. In **Shiism**, the imam is the spiritual successor of the Prophet, the equivalent of the **caliph** in **Sunnism**.

Imi: Shinto term for abstinence and the avoidance of polluting behavior during mourning or periods that require ritual purity.

Impartial love (*jian li*): A central Mohist idea that emphasizes equal love for all, in sharp contrast with the Confucian idea of love with distinction.

Indulgence: Lifting the punishment due for a sin after it has been forgiven in the sacrament of confession.

Inerrantism: Belief that what is written in the Bible contains no errors and is literally true.

Infallibility: The capacity to state the truths of faith without error.

Inferior person (*xioaren*): In Confucianism, a morally petty person in contrast to the **superior person (*junzi*)**.

Initiation rites: Initiation rites often take place in a religious ceremony. They symbolize a passage from one state of life to another and could also be thought of as an entry or training period. Initiation includes two things: physically entering a new community and accepting new religious values to lead a better life or to achieve a goal. Most religions use initiation rites to symbolize entry into a holy world. For early Christians, the passage to new life was effected first through **baptism** and then through admission to the **Eucharist**, two closely linked ritual moments that often included calling on the Spirit and placing oil on the forehead. Invoking the Spirit and anointing with oil date back to the Old Testament and continue today in the Christian ceremony of confirmation.

Inquisition: The thirteenth-century Inquisition was an investigative body for the maintenance of public order, with rules guaranteeing a fair hearing for the accused. It was adopted around 1230 to inquire into cases of matters of faith, in view of the threats posed by the Cathars and the Waldenses. By 1231, the Inquisition had evolved into a special tribunal for the judging of heretical crimes in Germany and Italy and, by 1233, also in France. After 1252, the Inquisition assumed the power of inflicting torture on those accused of heresy, prior to their being handed over to the secular tribunal. The Spanish Inquisition goes back to 1478 and was established on the initiative of the Spanish monarchs against Jewish and Muslim minorities.

Interrelationality: A term used to describe the rapport between human beings and other-than-human beings who populate the world and with whom native peoples interact. These interactions range from harmonious conviviality to permanent conflict.

Ise jingu: The Shinto Grand Shrine in the town of Ise, Japan, dedicated to the sun goddess Amaterasu-omikami and commonly regarded as the most ancient shrine in Japan.

Islam: "Abandoning oneself to God, submission to God," an act that corresponds to belonging to the Prophet's community, manifested in the cultural and social acts of this religion. Islam is both a religion and worldwide community (ummah).

Islamism: The contemporary phenomenon and movements associated with Islamic militancy that began in the nineteenth century to create an umma on earth to represent divine unity with particular legal, political, cultural, and military dimensions. The movement gave birth to various revolutionary **sects**.

Izanagi: Mythical figure in Shinto. The male-who-invites. Co-creator, with **Izanami**, of Japan.

Izanami: The female-who-invites. Shinto co-creator, with **Izanagi**, of Japan.

Janamsakhis: Narratives about the birth and life of the first Sikh guru.

Jansenism: Theological movement (from the late sixteenth to the eighteenth century) concerned with the opposition between free will and grace. Drawing from a pessimistic philosophy and emphasizing the profound corruptive influence of sin on the human being, Jansenists upheld a rigorous moral code while emphasizing the act of faith. They differed from Protestants in their Eucharistic and Marian devotions. The controversy between Jansenists and the Jesuits was particularly bitter.

Jiao Festival: A renewal festival, generally celebrated around the time of the winter solstice.

Jihad: "Struggle, effort, tension." The duty of the individual and community to serve Islam with one's full effort. The major jihad, or the jihad of bodies, is an action of war to defend or spread the religion. The minor jihad, or the jihad of souls, is the forgiving of offenses, conversion by means of persuasion, and one's personal effort to remain faithful to the message of the Qur'an.

Jina: "Conqueror." Title conferred on the twenty-four liberated teachers in each cycle of time in Jainism.

Jingu: Grand Shrines of Shinto of which there are three in Japan: Ise, Izumo, and Atsuta.

Jinja: Shinto shrines found throughout Japan.

Jiva: "Life monad"; soul or self.

Jnana: Transcendent knowledge and awareness of the ultimate reality. In Buddhism, it is the knowledge about the holy truths, beings, and objects, as well as the overcoming of passion.

Josephism: Term used to denote the enlightened despotism of the Austrian emperor Joseph II (1765–1790), who gathered all churches under his supervision in order to control, administer, and reform them, disregarding all rights of the papacy. He was pitilessly opposed to monasteries and religious orders, considering them useless.

Judeo-Christianity: A term that aims to describe the mutual influence of the Christian life with the Jewish life. Judaism had a strong influence on early Christianity. It gave Christianity certain biblical texts, patterns of interpreting them, symbols, practices, beliefs such as angels, and religious writings that tried to explain the beginning and future of humankind.

Judeo-Hellenism: Judeo-Hellenism is a blending of the Jewish life with Greek culture. This took place especially in Alexandria, Egypt. Philo of Alexandria was a great supporter of this combination.

Justification: To be made right with God; to be freed from the guilt and penalties attached to sin.

Kaaba: The holy shrine of Islam situated at Mecca, rebuilt at the time of Muhammad, a place of symbolic and spiritual reference for all Muslim shrines worldwide, the cosmic pole in the direction of which all Muslims turn during their prayers.

Kaguraden: Hall of sacred dance found in Shinto shrines.

Kamakura period: The period in Japanese history from the twelfth to the fourteenth century.

Kami: Powerful beings, worshiped in Shinto, who are linked with the very first forces that shaped the world, when Japan and its people were being formed. The kami are active in special ways, places, moments, objects, or natural phenomena, and are believed to possess a mysterious power or spirit. Kami are present everywhere, in nature and in people.

Kamidana: In Japanese homes, a center of symbols honoring the **kami**. A shelf where sacred objects are kept and daily prayers are said, devoted to **kami** who protect the family.

Kami-no-michi: The way of the **kami**. Name that refers to Shinto practices and beliefs.

Kannushi: Shinto priest who looks after a shrine and conducts ceremonies there, especially rites of purification.

Karahprashad: Warm and sweet sacred dish shared by the congregation in the presence of the Sikh holy book.

Karma: That which provides the basis of the ritual act, its value, and its action. It is an invisible and invincible force that penetrates the soul and starts it on the cycle of rebirth. The doctrine of karma, which affirms the need of rebirth in order to reap the fruits that had not "matured" in the present life, has become universally accepted in India. Karma therefore refers to the "law of actions," which says that each action produces its effects on the cumulative spiritual totality of each living being and on his or her cosmic future. Each action possesses in itself a moral value, which can be good, bad, or neutral.

Kashrut: Rules in Judaism concerning which foods may or may not be eaten and how foods should be prepared.

Kerygma: The *kerygma* is the message announced in the gospel and proclaimed by the entire early-Christian community. This message was simply, "salvation through Jesus Christ." The *kerygma* includes the preaching of both the apostles and their disciples.

Kevala-jnana: "Knowledge isolated [from karmic obstruction]"; omniscient knowledge.

Kevalin: "One who has achieved absolute isolation"; one who is omniscient.

Kinensai: Shinto prayer for success of the new crop cycle.

Kingdom: "Of God," or, out of respect for the divine name, "of heaven." The experience of God's presence, a kingdom Christians hold is already here, but not yet fully realized. God is glimpsed in the ritual mysteries and in mystical experiences, as well as in beauty and love. But God will manifest himself fully in the kingdom to come, at the time of the ultimate transfiguration of the universe.

Kojiki: "Records of Ancient Matters" dating back to 712 CE, written in Chinese characters; the earliest Japanese written account and the source book of Japanese mythology.

Kokoro: Japanese term meaning "heart or mind"; the fundamental and interior nature of a person.

Kokugaku: School of national learning whose foremost task was to study ancient Japanese literature by means of scrutinizing the exact meaning of ancient words. It sought to highlight Japanese tradition freed from foreign ideas and thoughts.

Krishna: A Hindu deity whose name means the "black" god, or the "dark" lord, and who is the eighth *avatara* of the god Vishnu. Krishna has become very popular throughout India. His worship seems to stem from Mathura (Uttar Pradesh), a city that is described as the seat of wisdom and knowledge. Krishna is the god who destroys evil, inspires knowledge, and engenders loving devotion. The schools of late Visnuism (also called Vaishnavism) consider Krishna as the plenary reincarnation of the Supreme Being. The dialogue between the god Krishna and the warrior prince Arjuna on the field of battle is recorded in a 700-verse poem titled the **Bhagavad Gita**—"the song of the blessed one."

Kulturkampf ("Cultural Struggle"): The battle (1871–1878) waged by Chancellor Bismarck against German Catholics to stamp out church influence over internal politics. It included the suppression of the Jesuits, the promulgation of the "May Laws" (which established state supervision over the education of the future priests), the control of ecclesiastical jurisdiction, and compulsory civil marriage. The term is also used politically to denote any organized opposition against the church's influence over the civil and social life of the state.

Kuni no Tokodachi no Mikoto: A **kami** present at the foundation of the universe, in the Shinto view. That is, a founding deity in Japan.

Kusti: Sacred rope received at a Zoroastrian initiation ceremony.

Kyoha: Shinto organizations at the level of **sects**.

Laicism: Deriving from the Latin term *laicus*, "layman," the term signifies a modern tendency to oppose any overlapping, or indeed any relationship, between the spiritual and the temporal realms. In certain countries, laicism expresses itself as a form of anticlericalism with de-Christianizing tendencies. This was, for example, the case in Germany between 1870 and 1900 with the **Kulturkampf** and in France with the oppression of religious houses and monastic orders in 1880. For Catholics, the term *laicism* can also mean the legitimate distinction of powers between church and state, based on mutual respect and tolerance. The Second Vatican Council produced clear statements on such a relationship.

Lama: Buddhist religious leader of Tibet, Nepal, Sikkim, and Bhutan. The title "lama" is theoretically reserved for the superiors of monasteries but is actually given to all monks. The Dalai Lama is the supreme head of Lamaism; until 1950 he lived in Lhasa in Tibet.

Langar: A Sikh term for a community meal.

Lao-zi (Lao-tzu): A Chinese sage living in the fifth century BCE, during a period called the epoch of the Warring Kingdoms. His name would have been Li, the archivist in the Zhou court, who left home because of the moral decadence of that kingdom. Tradition attributes to him the **Dao de jing** (The Book of the Way), the fundamental book of Daoism. Legend has it that Lao-zi was born at the age of twenty-four, after having passed all that time meditating in his mother's womb. He is said to have died at 160 or 200 years of age, in keeping with the meaning of his name, Lao-zi ("Old One"). Under the name Loazhun, Daoism reveres him as a divine figure.

Lectern: A stand that holds the Bible when it is read during religious services.

Lingbao: "Sacred treasure." A group of Daoist writings dating to the fourth century CE. These texts focus on public liturgical practices performed on behalf of the living and the dead. The Daoism of Lingbao links individual spirituality to community practices (contrast with the Daoism of **Shangqing**).

Liturgy: In a broad sense, services and prayers. In a more specific Christian sense, the celebration of the **Eucharist**, which commemorates the Last Supper of Jesus, when he ate the **Passover** meal with his disciples before his death.

Lubavitch Hasidism: Also known as Habad or Chabad, Lubavitch is a branch of mystical Hasidism that is based in Brooklyn, New York, though originally from Belarus via Latvia and Poland. The Lubavitchers preserve traditional piety and hold that divinity is present throughout the universe. They integrate modern techniques into the bounds of Jewish law, under the direction of the rebbe.

Lunar New Year Festival: A celebration of the Chinese New Year according to the lunar calendar, in the most auspicious way with certain rituals and customary practices signifying the meaning of renewal.

Lustration Festival: *Qing-Ming*. Beginning the third day of the third lunar month in the Chinese calendar, the festivities culminate on the 105th day after the winter solstice (April 4 or 5), thus joining the lunar calendar to the solar cycle. The Lustration Festival—also called the Spring Festival or the Pure and Bright Festival—is a prolonged purifying rite of spring, which links the life of the living to the commemoration of the dead and the ancestors: their tombs are cleaned; offerings are made; ancestral villages are visited.

Magisterial tradition: The official authoritative teaching of the church throughout history.

Magokoro: A true and pure heart. This is the Shinto ideal.

Mahavrata: "Great vow"; refers to the vows adopted by all Jain renouncers.

Makoto: Truthfulness; the willingness to live life in accordance with the powers that surpass human understanding.

Man: In Sikhism, "heart or mind." There is no distinction between the two in Punjabi language.

Man kita bhau: In Sikhism, this term means "to nurture love."

Mania: In Sikhism, "keeping in mind."

Manichaeism: Manichaeism is a type of Gnostic belief founded by the philosopher Mani (216–277 CE). He believed that there were two basic yet different principles at the very origin of things: light and dark. This belief became central to a worldview affecting all knowledge and all life. Manichaeism became an organized church with its own Scriptures, priestly hierarchy, traditions, and missionaries, called "the elected ones."

Manthra: Sacred utterance (of the divinity **Ahura Mazdā**) in Zoroastrianism.

Marcionism: Marcion was a priest born in Sinope (in Pontus, part of Asia Minor). He went to Rome to preach and began his own church in 144 CE. He thought the God of the Old Testament was a mean and cruel god, and he refused to believe that this God could be the father of Jesus Christ. Instead, Marcion's believed that God created matter and the world. Marcion rewrote the New Testament, except for Paul's letters, to suit his needs. He influenced the philosopher Mani, who used Marcion's beliefs to develop his own Gnostic beliefs. This philosophy of **Gnosticism** included two opposing yet equal forces: good versus bad, light versus dark.

Marga: "Path"; astangamarga: "Eight paths of perfection." This is the fourth noble truth of Buddhism, the eightfold path by means of which a disciple reaches **nirvana**. Buddhism is a middle way that furnishes morality and wisdom by maintaining a balance between **ascetic** rigor and ecstatic **mysticism**.

Mass: Term used by Roman Catholics to refer to the sacramental commemoration of the Last Supper of the Lord Jesus; the liturgy of the **Eucharist**.

Matsuri: Festivals.

Mennonites: Members of an Anabaptist sect named after Menno Simons (1496–1561), a former Roman Catholic priest from Friesland in the Netherlands.

Mēnōg (also *mēnōy*): A Middle Persian philosophical-theological term used to describe the conceptual, immaterial, and thought elements of existence in the Zoroastrian tradition.

Methodists: Members of the evangelical Protestant church formed on the principles set out by John Wesley and his brother Charles Wesley.

Midrash: Rabbinical writings that are interpretations of the Bible. They help people understand the stories, prophecies, and other parts of the Bible. Midrash can also mean the particular way the rabbis study the Bible in order to correctly interpret it.

Miko: Women who are dedicated to the service of the **kami** in Shinto. They are specially prepared for ritual roles. Also called kamiko.

Mikoshi: A portable shrine used in festive processions. These shrines may be large, special litters made of black lacquered wood with gilded bronze or gold fixtures secured to a platform with two long poles carried by teams of devotees.

Minhag: Customs of the Jewish community. These can be as important as the **Halakhah**, and sometimes can even be preferred over it.

Minister: Person appointed to perform religious functions for the church.

Minyan: The group of at least ten men that is required to form a community for worship in a Jewish synagogue.

Minzoku Shinto: Shinto folk practices, including for example the charms in one's car or home for protection.

Mishnah: The oral law as written down by the rabbis. It includes rules for worship and everyday life and is divided into six parts. It was first written down and organized at the beginning of the third century CE.

Misogi: An act of ritual purification in Shinto, performed at a river or seashore for the purpose of cleansing pollution from the body.

Mitarasi: Basin found in Shinto shrines for purification.

Mitzvot: Commandments, duties, responsibilities, or good deeds that Jews must fulfill after they have undergone their bar mitzvah ceremony.

Modernist Crisis, Modernism: A reform movement (at the end of the nineteenth and beginning of the twentieth century) that aimed at divesting Catholicism of those traditional elements deemed as obsolete and replacing them with a way of thinking and of living compatible with the modern world. In his encyclical letter *Pascendi* (1907), Pope Pius X condemned doctrinal errors resulting from the unorthodox tenets of this widespread movement.

Moksha: "Release"; liberation from the cycle of rebirth according to Hinduism and Jainism. Moksha refers to the final liberation from the cycle of rebirth through union with the **Brahman**. It represents salvation for the Hindu.

Monasticism: In the second century CE, the word *monachos* meant "unique, loved by God in a special way." In the fourth century CE, some unmarried people in Egypt and Syria came together to pray. Some of them chose to live alone. Others, known as **Coenobites**, lived in communities. The church saw that these communities were living a special type of Christian life. In the East, the **Coenobites** helped poor people, worked hard, and took on the religious duties of priests and bishops. In the West, monasticism took on more ceremonial and preaching duties.

Moravians: Members of the Moravian Brethren, founded by Count Zinzendorf in Germany in 1722.

Musubi: A deep and mysterious power that is associated, in Shinto belief, with creation and the harmony undergirding the natural world.

Mysteries: The mysteries were cults, or secret groups of worshipers and beliefs in Greek antiquity. The name *mysteries* is from a Greek phrase that means "keeping your mouth shut." Some mysteries began in Greek culture, while others came from Eastern cultures. The mysteries became very popular and spread first to Rome and then to the entire Roman-Hellenistic world. The mysteries were more acceptable than Christianity to the rulers because the celebrations, representations, and ideas of the mysteries were similar to those of the official religion of the empire. The mysteries also taught people about their own spiritual future.

Mystical: An experience of spiritual realities and divine powers not readily available to ordinary sensation.

Mysticism: Special and extraordinary religious experiences that are by definition difficult to describe because they are nothing like the everyday experiences most people have. Mystics often receive knowledge that people cannot receive in normal study or experience.

Naishojo: A Shinto term referring to purification of heart and mind.

Naorai: Festival meal in Shinto.

Navjote: Name of the initiation ceremony among the **Parsis**.

Nepsis: Vigil, vigilance. Night prayer. In a broad sense, it refers to "keeping watch or paying attention" to Christ who comes through people and things.

New Religious Movement (NRM): A term chosen by scholars to refer to religious groups that are outside of the social mainstream. Some groups are called NRMs even though they are not particularly "new" and are unlikely to ever become "movements."

Nihon Shoki: "Chronicles of Japan," dating to 797 CE, written in Chinese characters, and important to Shinto.

Niinamesai: Thanksgiving for harvest. An important annual Shinto rite in Japan, celebrated in the eleventh month, when an offering of the newly harvested rice is made to the **kami** of heaven and earth.

Nirvana: "Extinction." The point of no return of the **samsara**; liberation from the cycle of rebirth with the achieving of absolute beatitude, perfect happiness, and unalterable joy. The **parinirvana** is the complete extinction that takes place with the death of an **arhat** or a **Buddha** who has reached the fullness of happiness.

Norito: A category of Shinto prayers. Sacred words and prayers expressed in elegant ancient Japanese and addressed to the **kami** in Shinto worship.

Observance: Following the law, obeying the will of God by participating in a ceremony or ritual, or fulfilling the obligations of Judaism in other ways.

Oharae: Exorcism; expulsion of what is unclean, usually in a Shinto ceremony or ritual gesture.

Ohrmazd: Middle Persian name of Ahura Mazdā.

O-mamori: Amulet. An object (often a small placard, emblem, or card in a talismanic case) obtained from Shinto shrines or from temples for protection from evil and misfortune.

Omnipotence: The unlimited power and authority that belong to God alone.

Orthodox Judaism: Modern movement that was founded as a reaction to Reform Judaism. Orthodox Jews believe that Jews must follow the law completely, and they believe that the **Torah** and law are God-given.

Orthodoxy: Refers to correct doctrine, correct celebration, and correct action (the latter sometimes called *orthopraxy*).

Ottoman: The Ottoman Empire was founded by Osman the Turk and lasted from 1299 to 1922. Following the conquest of Asia Minor, eastern Europe, and North Africa, it began its decline in the eighteenth century. After the First World War (1914–1918), only Ottoman Turkey remained.

Pagan, paganism: The word *paganus* originally meant "a man from the countryside." In the fourth century CE, Christians used the word to describe a belief in false gods and its connected ceremonies, practices, and customs. The label of paganism was also used to criticize the people who shared these beliefs and took part in the ceremonies.

Pancanamaskara: "Five Homages" mantra in which Jains express their homage to revered renouncers.

Papa: Harmful **karma**.

Parsi: An Indian Zoroastrian.

Passover (Pesach): On this feast, the Jewish people remember their liberation from captivity in Egypt by celebrating with a **seder**, a ritual dinner.

Patriarch: Title given to the bishop who heads an **autocephalous** ("with its own head, or leader") church. The patriarch is always seated "in his synod."

Pentateuch: The first five books of the Hebrew Bible: Genesis, Exodus, Leviticus, Numbers, and Deuteronomy. The Pentateuch as we know it was composed after the destruction of the temple in 586 BCE. It begins with God's creation of the world and traces the history of his holy people, Israel, up until the **covenant** God established with them through Moses on Mount Sinai.

Pentecost: The seventh Sunday after Easter, when the Holy Spirit descended upon the disciples of Jesus in the form of tongues of fire.

Persecutions: Persecutions in this volume refer to acts of violence against religious individuals and communities. Christians were persecuted by their enemies, for instance. The first such acts occurred in Jerusalem, then in Rome. The persecutors had many different reasons: They wanted to stop the spread of Christianity and suspected Christians of committing secret crimes and black magic; they accused the Christians of wickedness and being against the protecting gods of the Roman Empire; they were angry that the Christians would not believe in the gods of Rome or in the holiness of the emperor himself. Many religious communities across the world and throughout time have suffered persecution on account of their distinctive beliefs and practices.

Persian Rivayats: Letters about practical matters of the Zoroastrian religion written by Zoroastrian priests in Iran for the newly established **Parsis** in India.

Perspectivism: Specifically in ethnology, a theory that all types of beings share in the same culture (celebrating dance festivals, obeying rules of marriage, animals are the "ancestors" of humans). Perspectivism also holds that indigenous perceptions of the world are based on multiplicity—each "species" (or "people") has a different "body," hence their perceptions of the world likewise differ: a human does not "see" a jaguar's action the same way that the jaguar understands what it is doing. The differences in perception are due to the perceptual and emotional faculties of each, which modifies the interpretations of similar situations.

Philokalia: Translated literally, this means "love of beauty." It is an anthology of mystical theological texts. The Greek *Philokalia*, initially translated into **Slavonic** and then Russian, was published in Venice in 1782. In modern times, in Romania, Father Dumitru Staniloae edited an immense *Philokalia* with commentaries on current events.

Pinjrapole: Animal hospital.

Pleroma: In the ancient philosophy of Gnosticism, the pleroma is the universe "on high," which is full of life, harmony, and light. It is the opposite of the lower world, which is full of greed, confusion, sadness, and violence. Pleroma, which is fullness itself, is also the opposite of the Gnostic idea of the cosmos, which is a form of unending emptiness and void.

Preksha Dhyana: "Concentration of perception." A systematic form of Jain modern yoga found in the **Shvetambara** Terapanth sect.

Polity: The form of government of a nation, church, or organization.

Popol Vuh: The "Book of Counsel" of the K'iche Maya, written in the early years of Spanish colonialism, by a K'iche scribe/priest who wished to preserve the stories of creation. The "Chichicastenango manuscript" was left on the doorstep of the cathedral at the capital of El Quiche province. Neglected for centuries in a library, the manuscript was finally translated into Spanish and other languages and has become one of the best-known sources on early K'iche religious traditions.

Positivism: The teachings of Auguste Comte (1798–1857), upholding positivist science as the sole valid philosophy. This doctrine drew its inspiration from the Enlightenment, which aimed to free humanity's intellect from religious illusions and to lead it back to the reality of experience. Before Comte, David Hume had criticized all religious beliefs. Now that the development of human sciences has slowed considerably, positivism has placed in perspective among the exact sciences, which offer critiques of it.

Prajna: Wisdom, intelligence, faculty of understanding and comprehending.

Preksha Dhyana: "Concentration of perception"; a systematic form of Jain modern **yoga** introduced by the Shvetambara Terapanth.

Prelature: A church office or government bureau run by a high-ranking member of the clergy.

Presbytery: Government of a church by elders chosen to represent their **congregations**.

Principle (li): Primarily a term used in Neo-Confucianism referred to as the "Learning of Principle." For Neo-Confucians *Li* is both the ultimate reality of the universe and the fundamental principle of morality.

Propagation of the Faith, Congregation for: In 1622, Pope Gregory XV instituted the Congregation *De Propaganda Fide* to spread Christianity in distant lands. With the aim of distancing itself from colonialism, the church encouraged the formation of an indigenous clergy, established a seminary in Rome to train priests from around the world, and a publishing house for the publication of catechisms in different languages. It thus embarked on a program of **enculturation of the gospel**.

Prophetism: Leadership by the "wise men and women" of a native people: religious savants, seers, and counselors of their people in times of crisis. They foresee another condition, different from the present one, which they proclaim is flawed, contaminated, imperfect, and morally "bad."

Propriety (li): Rituals or ritual propriety. One of the four Confucian virtues, it also refers to rules of propriety governing human actions. In contrast to coercive laws, rules of propriety aim at cultivating human virtues.

Proselyte: The name *proselyte* was given to pagans who had converted to Judaism. This name comes from a Greek word meaning "stranger," which is based on the Hebrew word *gur*.

Puja: A public or private Hindu or Jain prayer and sacrifice. It includes a system of rites (and occasionally chants) that vary according to different regions and times.

Punya: Beneficial karma; merit.

Purgatory: A condition of the souls of those who have died in a state of grace in which they are purged of the effects of sins committed during their life.

Purusha: "Male," "man." Masculine spirit, global spirit of humanity, human unit that derives from the **Veda**. Cosmic man who gave birth to the universe during a sacrifice celebrated by the gods.

Qi (Ch'i): "Moist breath," in Chinese. Qi is the energy, the vital force, that animates all creatures. The concept of breath gives rise to the meaning "vital spirit" or "vital power." Qi fills all forms of reality and the differences among them is due to the different conditions of qi (such as density, transparency, fluidity) and the different ways that qi is shaped into patterns by li, the basic ordering principles of existence.

Qibla: The direction toward which one prays; that is, towards the Kaaba in Mecca. In the mosque, this direction is indicated by the **mihrab**, a shallow alcove in the wall. It is the qibla that makes the mosque a cultic place dedicated to God, a holy place.

Quakers: Members of the Religious Society of Friends, founded by the English Dissenter George Fox (1624–1691).

Quietism: A spiritual movement formed in reaction to the ascetic expressions to which the Counter-Reformation had attributed too much importance. This "charismatic" movement that encouraged "quiet prayer" gave rise to heated debates in Italy and France. The Roman Catholic Church was suspicious of this religious practice of the heart and its "mysticism of pure love," which considered as useless all human efforts in prayer and Christian life. Its condemnation in 1685 cast a shadow over Christian **asceticism**.

Rabbi: An ordained teacher who is the spiritual leader of his community and studies and interprets the **Torah**.

Ramadan: The Muslim month of fasting fixed by the Qur'an and by the **Hadith**. It is a month for recollection and the slowing down of activity. Through the twenty-eight-day fast, observed from sunrise to sunset, the community realizes its unity and its mission, making each adult conscious of being a Muslim.

Reconstructionism: Modern Jewish movement founded by Mordecai Kaplan which understands Judaism as a religious civilization changing and evolving through history but always remaining committed to the continuation of the Jewish people and their values.

Redemption: Salvation from the sinfulness of the human condition.

Reform of Gregory VII (d. 1805): Archdeacon of Rome, elected pope in 1073, Hildebrand of Soana took the name of Gregory VII and dedicated himself to the reform of the church, insisting on compulsory priestly celibacy and the independence of papal power. He instituted permanent ambassadors for the Holy See and resisted the German emperor Henry IV. He implemented a great reform within the church, thanks to the Cluniac and Cistercian revivals and to a reformed episcopate.

Reform Judaism: Modern movement, grown out of the European Enlightenment, that tries to adjust Judaism to the present-day world. Reform Jews focus more on the moral and ethical aspects of Judaism and less on the strict observance of all the rules of the **Halakhah**.

Refrigerium: This word is often found on early Christian graves. It refers to the heavenly rest, eternal peace, and everlasting happiness enjoyed by the dead. The meaning of *refrigerium* later changed to refer to the meals held during funerals or on their anniversaries. **Pagans** often celebrated the anniversary of a funeral. The pagans then started to build tombs, large underground graves that were also used for funeral ceremonies.

Religious specialists (shamans, priests, savants, karai, "big men," seers): Specialists acquire access to the spirit worlds and to divinities through training and practice over many years and can help or harm the community. Whereas shamans, for instance, who use techniques of ecstasy to send their souls out of their bodies at will, are generally sought for their healing services, they can also exercise their special powers for the opposite function of harming an enemy, in which case they are seen as sorcerers. And whereas the "priestly" specialists possess knowledge necessary for the reproduction and protection of society as a whole, the shamans and sorcerers are engaged in a never-ending struggle for knowledge and power.

Remission of sins: In Christian thinking, remission of sins is a gift from Christ, which is a gift provided by an outpouring of his re-creating and loving Spirit. Remission of sins was a power extended to the apostles and the people who succeeded them so they could wipe away sins, a divine power mentioned in the Gospels (Matt. 18:18; John 20:22-23).

Rightness (*yi*): Confucius often contrasts *yi* with material benefit: while **superior persons** are concerned about moral rightness, **inferior persons** are concerned about material benefit. Mencius, regarding it as one of the four cardinal virtues, claims that moral rightness is the straight way to becoming human.

Risi: "Sages." Poets and soothsayers of the Vedic era who, according to tradition, composed the hymns of the **Rig Veda** ("knowledge of hymns"). This collection of 1,017 hymns and the oldest Vedic book were generated by the nomadic Indo-European tribes who arrived in India. The *risi* received the Vedic hymns as revelations from the gods. These hymns and chants invoke and celebrate the gods.

Rita: "Natural order of things." Owing to this order, which is looked after by the god Varuna, and to the inner forces, life is conserved. Every

act contrary to rita constitutes a ritual crime that demands expiation.

Rosh Hashanah: "Head of the Year," in Hebrew. The Jewish New Year, which occurs in the autumn, being the first of the High Holy Days (Yamim Norai'im, "Days of Awe"). Rosh Hashanah is celebrated on the first two days of the Jewish month of Tishrei by sounding the Shofar, a ram's horn trumpet, in a special sequence of sounds and by praying to God as the crowned King who judges the universe and all humanity.

Routinization: The process by which a religious leader's personal charism becomes identified with the office of the leader rather than the specific person who holds the office. This process most often, but not always, happens after the death of a founding leader.

Ru ("Confucian"): Although *ru* now normally refers to the school founded by Confucius, there were people of *ru* even before Confucius.

Sacrament: A sacrament is a Christian ceremony, described by the Greek word *mysterion* and the Latin word *sacramentum*, often rooted in earlier Jewish practice. Christians and Jews, however, did not agree that Jesus Christ, a Jew from Nazareth, on whose actions the Christian sacraments are modeled, was the savior who came to bring salvation to his followers through the good news announced and good works practiced by the church.

Sage (*sheng*): A sage is a person of moral perfection. In the Confucian tradition, although it is believed that everyone can become a sage, only Yao, Shun, Yu, Tang, King Wen, King

Wu, Duke of Zhou, and Confucius have been regarded as sages.

Sakaki: A kind of tree. Its branches are used in purification ceremonies in Shinto.

Sallekhana/Samthara: Ritual voluntary fast unto death in Jainism.

Samadhi: A state of meditation in which the consciousness of the meditator is completely absorbed into the object being contemplated. Through severe discipline and mental concentration one's psychic being, while remaining perfectly stable, is led to complete unification with one's chosen subject. According to Japanese Zen thinking, one can reach Samadhi without preparation following a psychic or psychological trauma.

Samgha: The community of Buddhists, particularly those ordained as monks and nuns. The term also refers, especially in early Buddhism, to monks, nuns, laymen, and laywomen; namely, all those who faithfully treasure the three "jewels" of Buddhist practice: Buddha, Dharma, and Samgha.

Samsara: "Continuous flow"; cycle of rebirth that conditions all living beings according to their karma, or retribution of actions. The only way of breaking out of this cycle of transmigration is to achieve **moksha**, or **nirvana**.

Sangat: Sikh congregation.

Santideva: A Buddhist philosopher of the seventh century who came from Saurastra, in India. He wrote a religious epic poem, a collection of teachings, and a collection of **sutras**.

Saošyant: Variously translated as "one who will be strong," "one who brings benefit," "future world savior," among other things. In the *Farvadīn Yašt*, the *saošyant* Astvatərəta (literally, "he who has **aša** in his bones" or "he through whom **aša** becomes embodied") is said to be the last *saošyant* and the final truly successful venerator of *haoma*, defeater of the Lie and of all enemies of Iran, and savior of Zoroastrianism.

Sat Santokh Vicar: These are the Sikh virtues of truth, contentment, and reflection.

Sat Sri Akal: Sikh greeting; "Truth is the Timeless One."

Satya: "Reality, truth." In particular, in Hinduism, the four holy truths of suffering, the origin of suffering, the surcease of suffering, and the path that leads to the end of suffering.

Satyagraha: "Fortitude of truth." It is the spirit of the followers of **ahimsa**, nonviolence. Mahatma Gandhi used the term and developed the theory to launch his movement to obtain independence for India.

Schism: *Schism* is a Latin Christian word from the third century, meaning a disagreement that causes one community to split into two warring groups. Schism is similar to **heresy**. Heresy is a division of religious ideas within the church; schism is a division of the people that are the church.

Scholar-official (*shi*): In the Shang dynasty, Western Zhou tradition, and spring and autumn periods, the lowest noble classes. Later, *shi* refers to the literati of the ruling class, and Confucius himself is a *shi*.

Sect: A religious group that occupies a middle social space between a culture's dominant religions and its most marginalized religions; it can also refer to a group that has broken away from a larger religious tradition.

Secularization: This ambiguous and multifaceted term describes varying degrees of passage from a religious to a lay state, such as the transfer of an ecclesiastical right to a lay owner; the demotion of a consecrated person to a lay state; the withdrawal of society from religious practice; the total disenchantment of religious sentiment in the world; and the removal of religious influence from civil life and state education, even to the point where complete desacralization is reached, where all religious concerns are ignored.

Seder: The meal at the heart of the Jewish celebration of **Passover**. The meal is highly ritualized and follows a prescribed order of storytelling and prayer, in conjunction with traditional foods that honor Jewish history.

Seijin no Hi: A day when young people, usually in their twentieth year, visit a Shinto shrine to mark their transition into adulthood.

Seljuks: The name of a ruling house of Turkish sultans in Asia, five dynasties of which have great importance in Islamic history. The "great Seljuks" took Baghdad, where they saved **Sunnite** Islam. The Christian crusaders fought with the Seljuks in Asia Minor and Syria.

Sephardim: Jews whose families originated in Portugal or Spain (called Sepharad as mentioned in Obad. 20).

Seva: Voluntary, selfless service in Sikhism.

Shāhnāma: National epic of Iran composed by the Persian poet Ferdowsi (ca. 1010 CE).

Shangqing: "High purity." Group of Daoist texts from the fourth century CE, issued by a sect that favored trance states in their religious experience. Texts "revealed" in trances were set down through automatic writing and were considered as dictated to the mediums by the immortals or gods. Spiritual exercises consist of reciting these sacred texts and visualizing the scenes and spirits depicted in them. The Daoism of Shangqing is a way of meditation and personal spiritual realization (to compare and contrast with the Daoism of **Lingbao**).

Sharia: "The way." It is the path prescribed for believers by Allah to obtain salvation. This law, based on the Qur'an and the **Sunna**, is made up of all the commands of Allah relative to human actions. It includes cultic, ritual, political, and juridical duties. Both a divine and a human law, it is the model for every generation of Muslims.

Shichigosan: The Japanese Shinto ritual performed on the fifteenth of November for children of ages three (*san*), five (*go*), and seven (*shichi*).

Shiism: In Arabic *shi'at'Ali* means "the faction of Ali." The term refers to fidelity to Ali, who was designated by Muhammad as his legitimate successor. In a battle between the legitimists and other factions, Ali emerged victorious and became the fourth caliph. The Shiite **caliph** is the expression of the impeccability of the **imam**, recipient of his mission from all eternity and seen as the legitimate successor of the Prophet. This legitimacy claims to be the foundation for Islamic **orthodoxy**. Shiism has experienced great internal divisions. Shiites form the majority of Islamic populations in Iran, Iraq, Pakistan, and Afghanistan.

Shikinen Sengu: Solemn Shinto rituals in which the **Ise grand shrine** is rebuilt and the deity **Amaterasu-O-Mi-kami** is transferred to her new residence every twenty years.

Shingon: A school of esoteric Buddhism in which special experiences are reserved for the initiated.

Shin-otoko: "Divine man." In the Konomiya Hadaka festival, a man chosen by lot to play the principle ritual role and purified through weeks of fasting and ritual isolation.

Shin tao: The way of the gods (Shinto, in Japanese). This term appeared in the eighth century after Buddhism and writing were introduced to Japan from abroad.

Shiva: The Jewish customary seven-day mourning period after a death. During this time, the bereaved stay home to receive visitors.

Shraddha: "Faithful love and reverence." A Vedic form of consecration, especially performed for one's deceased ancestors. The name is sometimes applied the offerings made by a **Brahmin**.

Shugendo: The religious life associated in Japan with the sacredness of mountains.

Shvetambara: "White-clad"; Jain sect whose renouncers wear white robes.

Sikh: Disciple or student, from Sanskrit *shishya*, Pali *sekha*.

Simenawa: Large ceremonial rope strung alongside the entrance gate of Shinto shrines.

Six arts (*liu yi*): The six subjects in ancient Chinese education: rituals, music, archery, charioteering, writing, and mathematics.

Skandhas: "Aggregates." The five groups of phenomena that together make up the "person."

Slavonic: The language created for the Slavs by the Greek brothers Cyril and Methodius in the ninth century, still used liturgically in the Russian Church.

Social Catholicism: A nineteenth-century movement that originated among working-class poor in the wake of the Industrial Revolution and the economic liberalism generated by the French Revolution. Priests and laypersons mobilized to help the working classes. In France, Frederick Ozanam (d. 1853) founded the Society of St. Vincent de Paul; in Germany Adolf Kolping (d. 1865) and William von Ketteler (1877) pioneered social legislation and established networks of cooperative worker societies. Albert de Mun (d. 1914) and René de la Tour du Pin (d. 1924) set up Catholic worker circles; Léon Harmel (d. 1924) was the forerunner of social charitable patronage. In Italy, Giovanni Bosco (d. 1888), Guiseppe Tovini (d. 1897), and Giuseppe Toniolo (d. 1918) upheld the social involvement of Catholics. In regard to Social Catholicism, the encyclical letter of Pope Leo XIII *Rerum Novarum* (1891) proved to be both a culmination of what had developed as well as a new starting point for what was to come.

Soma: A potion used in Vedic times in the celebration of sacrifices. This intoxicating drink was made from the plant of the same name and was considered holy and able to confer immortality.

Starets (plural startsy): "Elder" in Russian; "geronda" in Greek. Every person, man or woman, no matter his or her place in the hierarchy, who receives, after a long **asceticism** of deprivation, the spiritual gift of "discernment of spirits" or "cardiognosis" (reading of the heart)—that is, the spiritual gift of recognizing the "other" as a revelation.

Stupa: Buddhist monument originally associated with a burial mound. It consists of a tower, generally in the shape of a bell, which holds the relics of the historical **Buddha**, a saint, or one who has reached Buddhahood.

Sudreh: Sacred shirt received at a Zoroastrian initiation ceremony.

Sun Dance (for example, among the Crow, Lakota, Shoshone, Kiowa, Northern Plains, Paiute tribes): Dance of power, one of the seven sacred ceremonies for the Lakota people; it is a self-sacrificing ritual, in which participants undergo food deprivation and exhaustion from continuous dancing toward a central pole, an axis mundi that links the different levels in the cosmos, in order to receive the powers and the blessings of the sun deity.

Sunia: In Sikhism, "hearing."

Sunna: The attachment to ancestral traditions. This pre-Islamic concept was adopted by the Muslim world, beginning in Medina, where it referred to the actions, deeds, and words of the Prophet. From the early days of Islam, all deeds practiced by the Prophet were considered Sunna. The Sunna has a very precise place in Muslim life: together with the Qur'an, the central religious text of Islam, the Sunna constitutes the tradition of the Prophet.

Sunnism: A current of thought in Islam according to which the agreement of the community on the person of the **caliph** (agreement, in fact, on the first four caliphs after the death of the prophet Muhammad) guarantees the law. This branch of Islam, which is the larger of the two major branches of Islam, began in the **Umayyad** Empire. Sunnis have remained faithful to tradition in communities that unite in a spirit of moderation, manifesting the tolerance and inclusion that often marks a large group of believers. The **Seljuk** and **Ottoman** Turks, like the Muslim Berbers, have supported the idea of a majority Sunni Islam, in contrast to one based on the **Shiite** branch.

Superior person (*junzi*): Literally meaning "son of the king." In Confucianism, the term refers to persons with superior moral qualities.

Susano-o: Shinto storm deity who is the brother of **Amaterasu**, the sun goddess.

Sutra: "Thread." A Buddhist text built around a sermon or sayings of the Buddha or one of his disciples. Jainism uses the term to refer to certain sermons of the Mahavira contained in the Jain Agamas. Hindu sutras are literary works centered on condensed aphorisms designed to be memorized.

Sutrapitaka: "Basket of sutra." A part of the ancient Buddhist canon containing the Buddha's sermons, sayings, and texts connected with them.

Swami or svami: A title of respect given to Hindu philosophers and religious teachers who are considered masters.

Synod: A church council or assembly.

Taiji: The Great Ultimate Principle that lies at the origin of all created things and unites the cosmic forces of **yin and yang**. Taiji also expresses the essence of virtue and perfection.

Taiping: "Great peace" or "great purity." A doctrine expressed especially in the Taipingjing (Book of Great Peace) from the second century CE. The doctrine of Taiping announces the arrival of a new era, an age of new harmony among all realities in the world, signaled by social revolts and powerful sectarian organizations. The Daoism of the Great Peace emphasizes collective expressions.

Talmud: Literally, "learning." Talmud is a compilation of commentaries on the **Mishnah**. It is an authoritative source of Jewish tradition and deals with both **Halakhah** and **Aggadah**.

Tao, Taoism: One of the most ancient accounts of the genesis of human beings and their place in the universe, in addition to being one of the most refined forms of spirituality of humankind. Its principal text is the *Tao Te Ching (Dao de Jing*, (The Book of the Way and of Virtue), also called the **Lao-zi**, a collection of aphorisms and poems constituting a brief treatise of natural **mysticism**.

Tetrarchy: Tetrarchy was a system of government with four people sharing control of the Roman Empire. These four were known as emperors, and each controlled a different part of the Roman land. Diocletian ruled from 284 to 305 CE, Galerius ruled from 305 to 311 CE, Maximian ruled from 284 to 293 CE, and Constantius Chlorus ruled from 305 to 306 CE.

The Jesus Prayer: "Lord Jesus Christ, Son of God, have mercy on me, a sinner." This prayer, often recited continuously, has enjoyed special use in the Eastern Orthodox church and has drawn commentary throughout the history of eastern Christianity, from St. Paul's "unceasing prayer" to Gregory of Palamas's theology of this formula in the fourteenth century.

Tirthankara: "Maker of the ford"; epithet of the twenty-four liberated teachers per time cycle in Jainism. See also **Jina**.

Torah: Refers to both the Hebrew Bible (especially the first five books) and all the teaching that constitutes the Jewish tradition, including methods of inquiry about them. Since the teaching and interpretation that make up part of the Torah are always being added to, the Torah is not just the story of what happened to a group of people thousands of years ago. The Torah remains revelatory to new generations of Jews through time.

Torii: A stately gateway, usually made of red cedar wood painted in bright red, to Shinto shrines with a double-lintel overhead. It marks the entrance to the shrine space.

Tribe: A group of clans that share a common language and territory.

Tsutsushimi: Shinto term describing the devout precision, self-control, and modesty evident in ritual.

Ujigami: A Shinto deity associated with a group of related kin, who in former times resided in the same village. An ujigami was a divine, life-giving ancestor who founded the clan.

Ujiko: The kin group to which the Japanese family belonged.

Umayyads: A dynasty founded by Mu'awiyah in 661, at the end of the reign of the four caliphs. The Umayyads reigned in Damascus from 661 to 744 and in Cordoba in Spain from 756 to 1027.

Umma: The Muslim community in its religious and political unity. The Prophet saw his umma as a unity and as the point of reference for all humanity. The community must generate people who believe in God and who live together according to his ideals.

Ummat an-nabi: The community of the Prophet, made up of all those who wish to live Islam, who profess the Islamic faith, who pray in the direction of Mecca, and who read and meditate upon the Qur'an. The *ummat an-nabi* is the Islamic institution for all the world.

Uniatism: In 1596, in Poland-Lithuania, in 1700 in Hungary, and in 1714 in the Middle East, the Catholic Church annexed ("united," from the Roman perspective) many Orthodox regions, allowing them to maintain their rites while Romanizing their theology. After World War II, in Eastern Europe, Stalin destroyed these communities. They were reconstructed after 1989, not without tensions with the Orthodox communities in these areas.

Upanishads: Philosophical texts, also known as Vedanta, because they form the final, commentarial portion of the Vedic revelations. The Upanishads disclose the nature of the Absolute, the essence of the **Veda** (revealed knowledge), and show the way toward liberation from the cycle of rebirth. Beginning as oral traditions, the oldest Upanishads date back probably to the sixth or fifth centuries BCE. The Upanishads announce salvation through realizing the oneness of the **atman** with the **brahman**. According to the Upanishads, such salvation is achieved through mystical knowledge.

Vandals: Germanic tribes who inhabited the region between the Vistula and the Oder in the third century CE. In 407, they crossed the Rhine and plundered Gaul, reaching Spain in 409, which they controlled by 425. North Africa followed by 429. They looted and destroyed the cities in their paths. Establishing themselves as masters of all North Africa and the Mediterranean Sea, they ravaged all along its coasts. As **Arians**, they persecuted Catholics. In 430 CE, they seized Hippo, the chief town in Numidia, and conquered Rome in 455 CE. These new lands made the Vandal Empire very large. They were subdued by Emperor Justinian I in 533–534. The Vandals never rose to power again, but they destroyed Christianity in North Africa.

Varna: "Class." The word refers to a social function, a statute, and one's relationship to the **Vedas**. Vedic society was ideally divided into four *varnas*: the **Brahmins**, men dedicated to the sacred; the **Kshatriya,** the warriors who defended society; the **Vaishya**, who were farmers, livestock breeders, and tradesmen, and had the duty to feed society; and the **Shudra (Dalits),** a group composed of non-Aryans who had no access to the Vedas.

Veda: "Knowledge." This is the knowledge of the revelation transmitted through the most ancient sacred texts. Hindus speak of **sanatana dharma**, "the eternal law," which has been given to man and which is immutable. The term "Veda" also refers to sacred texts. **Rig Veda** consists of a collection of hymns; the **Sama Veda**, contains chants and melodies indispensable for the cult, and the **Yajur Veda**, collects sacrificial rites and consists of the ritual of celebration. The **Atharva Veda** brings together magic and gnosis, which is a Greek word meaning "knowledge," that is a form of wisdom allowing for salvation.

Vinayapitaka: "Basket of discipline." A part of the Buddhist canon containing the teachings regarding monastic organization, life, and discipline.

Virtue (*de*): In Confucianism, *de* refers to one's moral character and moral virtues. Confucius claims that cultivation of such moral virtues as humanity, rightness, filial love, loyalty, putting oneself in others' shoes, deference, and brotherly love are vital for an ideal person.

Waheguru: "Wonderful guru"; common Sikh exclamation.

Waldensians, Waldenses: Toward 1170, a rich merchant from Lyons named Valdus founded a religious movement that proclaimed the need for evangelical poverty, vernacular translations of the gospel, and the abolition of the cult of saints and relics. Harassed by the **Inquisition**, the Waldenses sought refuge in the Alpine valleys, embraced Protestantism, and then migrated into the Italian Alps. The Waldenses constitute the most numerous branch of Protestantism in Italy.

World Tree of Life: The image found in many indigenous sacred stories of an original tree that bore all the species of non-cultivated foods that sustain humanity.

Wu Wei: "Non-action" or "non-striving." Essential to The Book of the Way and the Power of the Way, wu wei suggests an attitude of prudence and respect for the autonomy of all other things. Through non-action, the Daoist does nothing other than to conform to the **Dao**, which according to the **Dao de jing**, is always without action but nevertheless brings about everything.

Wu Xing: "Five phases," which take their name from the five material elements: (1) water, (2) fire, (3) wood, (4) metal, and (5) earth. The five phases represent categories of thought and serve as key ordering concepts in the worldview of traditional Chinese philosophy.

Yajé (*ayahuasca, Banisteriopsis caapi*): A sacred drink of the Tukano Indians that produces visions. The psychoactive Dimethyltryptamine has been identified as the principal agent, inducing visions that receive differing interpretations among cultures where it is connected with religious rituals.

Yakudoshi: An unlucky year or period of time in one's life, when misfortune could enter in the form of illness, poor crops, or bad luck. Shinto rituals are organized to ward off harm and usher in health and good fortune.

Yasna: "Sacrificial worship." The *Yasna* is also the name of the Zoroastrian texts recited during religious rituals; this portion of the *Avesta* contains the *Gāthās*.

Yin and Yang: The primary meaning of yin and yang refers to shade and light (as in the shade and light cast onto opposite sides of the same mountain). But the two terms have come to describe the two opposing and complementary aspects of the **Dao**, the natural order. The yin indicates the shady, feminine, cold, passive, the moon, and that which lies low. The yang represents the light, masculine, hot, active, the sun, and that which is on high. Thus the use of the terms of *yin* and *yang* aptly suit the dualism of Chinese thought, a dualism in which the two aspects are not antagonistic toward each other. Indeed, yin and yang are complementary to each other and must be understood in their mutual relationship.

Yoga: From *yug*, "to tie, to yoke together." A complex of philosophical systems and physical techniques that teach the means of liberating the spirit restrained by the body. Yoga demands physical, spiritual, and moral training, as well as breathing techniques, concentration, and meditation. The various techniques are ultimately aimed at unifying the human spirit with the Universal Principle.

Yom Kippur: The Day of Atonement. On this day, Jewish people ask God's forgiveness for whatever wrongs they have done during the year.

Yomi-no-kuni: The Japanese phrase for land of the dead.

Yü: The mythical emperor who founded the Xia dynasty. Yü is the engineer-hero who controlled the waters of the great world-flood and oversaw the construction of the first irrigation works. Yü organized the Chinese world by arranging the five great mountains at the cardinal points and center of the earth. He assumed animal form and limped as a result of his titanic labors.

Yuruparí tradition: The worldviews of Tukanoan- and Arawakan-speaking peoples of the border of Colombia, Brazil, and Venezuela. They attribute great importance to the "Child of the Sun," who taught the rites of initiation to humanity, whose body became the sacred flutes and trumpets used today, and who is considered the source of all sickness in the world.

Zarathuštra: The prophet of Zoroastrianism, putative composer of the *Gāthās*, recipient of **Ahura Mazdā**'s *manthras*.

Zhengming: "Rectification of Names." First developed by Confucius, it takes as its basis the principle that for every action there must be a word that describes that action. Rectification of Names aims to make name and reality correspond to one another, particularly as regards names of roles that are central to vital relationships: king, minister, father, and son. Xunzi, emphasizing the correspondence between name and reality, sees **zhengming** as a way to avoid the confusion of one name with another name, of name with reality, and of reality with a name.

Zhuang-zi (Chuang-tzu): Philosopher of the fourth century BCE and, along with **Lao-zi**, the principle teacher of Daoism. Zhuang-zi is the author of the book known by his name, the Zhuang-zi. That book (in thirty-three chapters) expresses his thought through brief, entertaining accounts and conversations involving Chinese sages or through poetic fables. Zhuang-zi makes a plea for spiritual freedom that leads to liberation from thoughtless social convention and the limits of the mind.

Zionism: Movement dedicated to the creation of a homeland for the Jewish people. Throughout their life in the **Diaspora**, Jewish people hoped and prayed for a return to the land of Israel. In the late nineteenth century, Theodor Herzl began the modern Zionist Movement in order to promote the political establishment of an independent Jewish nation.

Zoroastrianism: Zoroastrianism was for centuries the dominant religion of ancient Persia. After the Arabs' conquest of Persia (present-day Iran), some Zoroastrians fled the region (such as the **Parsis**, who emigrated to India), and some converted to the religion of the Arabs, Islam, and a small minority remained in Persia. Zoroastrianism is named after its founder, Zoroaster, as he is often known in the West (or Zarathuštra, which is his Persian name).

CREDITS

Figs. 2.2, 2.3, 2.4, 2.5, 2.6, 2.7, 2.8, 2.9, 2.10, 2.11, 2.12, 2.14, 3.1, 3.4, 3.6, 3.7, 3.9, 3.10, 3.11, 3.13, 3.14, 3.15, 3.16, 3.17, 6.1, 6.2, 6.3, 6.4, 6.5, 6.6, 6.7, 6.8, 6.9, 8.1, 8.2, 8.4, 8.6, 8.7, 8.8, 8.9, 8.10, 8.11, 9.1, 9.2, 9.3, 9.4, 9.5, 9.7, 9.8, 9.9, 9.11, 9.12, 9.13, 9.14, 9.15, 10.1, 10.2, 10.3, 10.4, 10.5, 10.6, 10.7, 10.8, 10.9, 10.10, 10.11, 10.12, 10.13, 10.14, 11.1, 11.2, 11.3, 11.4, 11.5, 11.6, 11.7, 11.8, 11.9, 11.10, 11.11, 11.12, 11.13, 11.14, 12.1, 12.2, 12.3, 12.4, 12.5, 12.6, 12.7, 12.8, 12.9, 12.10, 12.11, 12.12, 12.13, 13.1, 13.2, 13.3, 13.4, 13.6, 13.7, 13.8, 13.9, 14.1, 14.2, 14.3, 14.4, 14.7, 14.8, 14.9, 14.10, 14.11, 14.12, 14.13, 14.14, 14.15: Courtesy of Jaca Book.

Figs. Intro. 3, Intro. 5, Intro. 7, Intro. 11, Intro. 12, Intro. 14, Intro. 15, Intro. 17, Intro. 19, 1.9, 1.10, 1.11, 1.13, 1.15, 1.16, 1.17, 1.18, 1.19, 1.20, Chap. 2 opener, 2.20, Chap. 4 opener, 4.3, 5.3, 5.6, 5.8, 5.11, Chap. 6 opener, Chap. 7 opener, 7.1, 7.3, 7.5, 7.6, 7.7, 7.12, Chap. 8 opener, 8.5, 8.12, Chap. 9 opener, 9.10, Chap. 10 opener, Chap. 11 opener, Chap. 12 opener, Chap. 13 opener, 13.5, Chap. 14 opener, Chap. 15 opener, 15.1, 15.4, 15.6, 15.7, Chap. 16 opener, 16.5, 16.7, 16.10, 16.12, 16.13: Public domain.

Figs. Intro. 9, 2.13, 2.15, 2.16, 3.2, 3.3, 3.8, 3.12, 6.10, 6.11, 8.13, 14.5, 15.2, 15.3, 15.8, 15.9, 15.10, 15.11, 15.12: Used here courtesy of Creative Commons GNU Free Documentation License.

Figs. Intro. 8, Intro. 18, 1.1, 1.5, 5.10, 5.12, 5.13, 5.14, 5.16, 15.5, 16.1, 16.6, 16.9: Used here under Creative Commons Share Alike License 2.0 Generic License.

Figs. Intro. 2, 1.2, 1.3, 8.3, 16.3: Used here under Creative Commons Share Alike License 2.5.

INDEX